SLEEPY PRINCESS IN THE DEMON CASTLE

12

Story & Art by

KAGIJI KUMANOMATA

NIGHTS

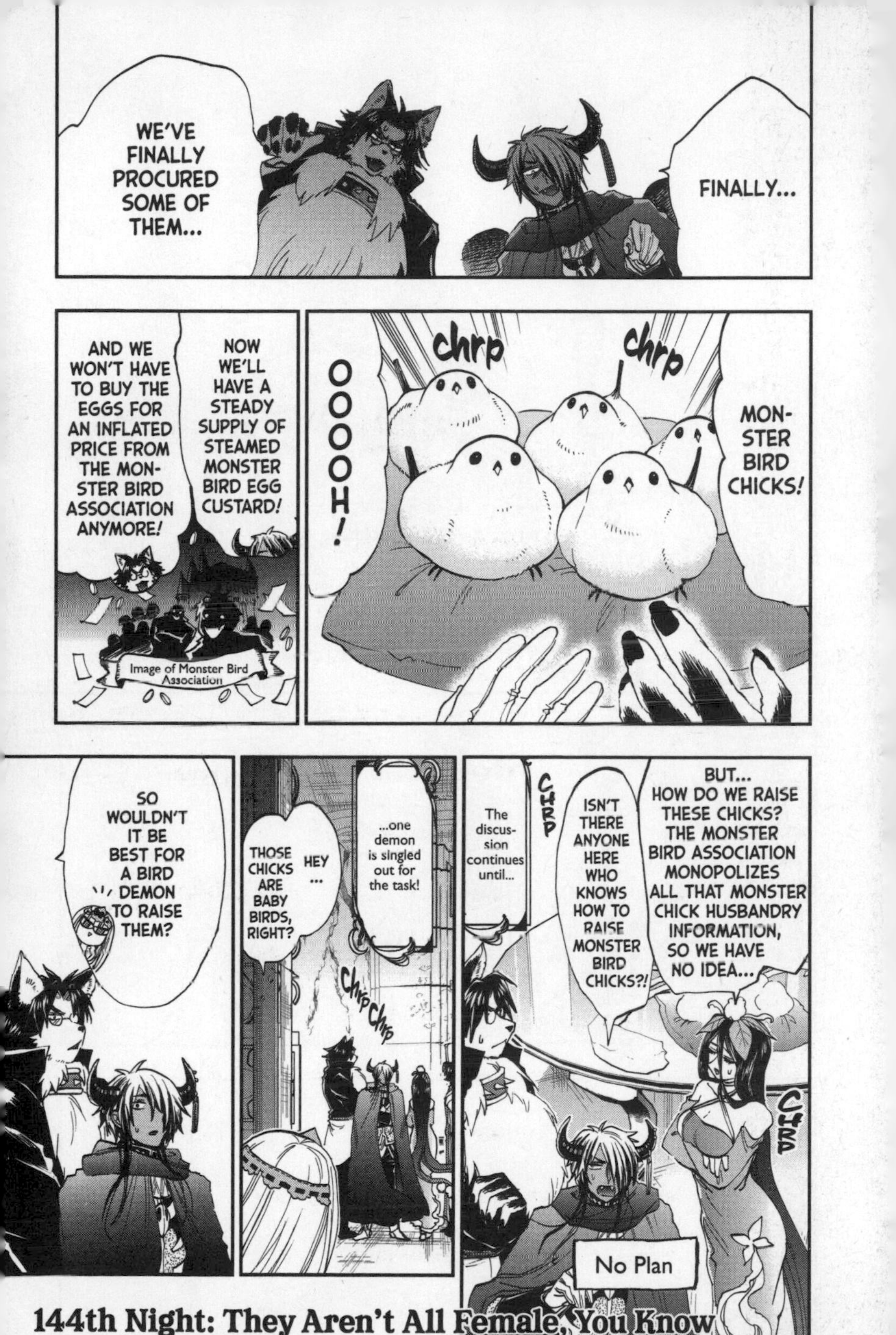
FINALLY...
WE'VE FINALLY PROCURED SOME OF THEM...
MON-STER BIRD CHICKS!
chrp
chrp
OOOOOH!
NOW WE'LL HAVE A STEADY SUPPLY OF STEAMED MONSTER BIRD EGG CUSTARD!
AND WE WON'T HAVE TO BUY THE EGGS FOR AN INFLATED PRICE FROM THE MON-STER BIRD ASSOCIATION ANYMORE!
Image of Monster Bird Association
BUT... HOW DO WE RAISE THESE CHICKS? THE MONSTER BIRD ASSOCIATION MONOPOLIZES ALL THAT MONSTER CHICK HUSBANDRY INFORMATION, SO WE HAVE NO IDEA...
ISN'T THERE ANYONE HERE WHO KNOWS HOW TO RAISE MONSTER BIRD CHICKS?!
CHRP
CHRP
The discus-sion continues until...
No Plan
...one demon is singled out for the task!
HEY...
THOSE CHICKS ARE BABY BIRDS, RIGHT?
Chirp Chirp
SO WOULDN'T IT BE BEST FOR A BIRD DEMON TO RAISE THEM?

144th Night: They Aren't All Female, You Know

144th Night: They Aren't All Female, You Know

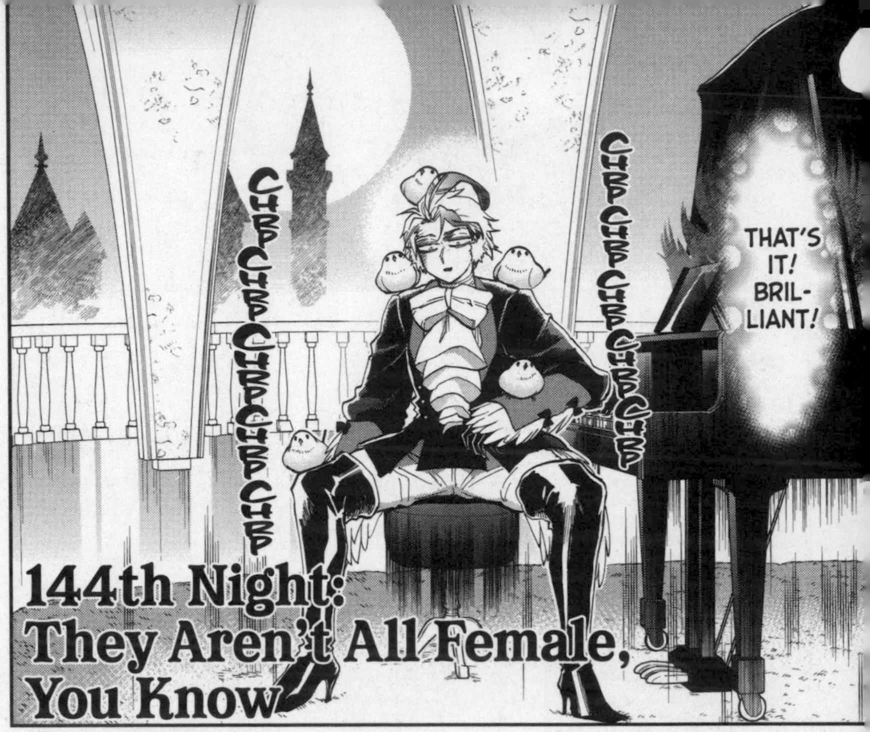
THAT'S IT! BRIL-LIANT!
CHRP CHRP CHRP CHRP CHRP CHRP
CHRP CHRP CHRP CHRP CHRP CHRP
144th Night: They Aren't All Female, You Know

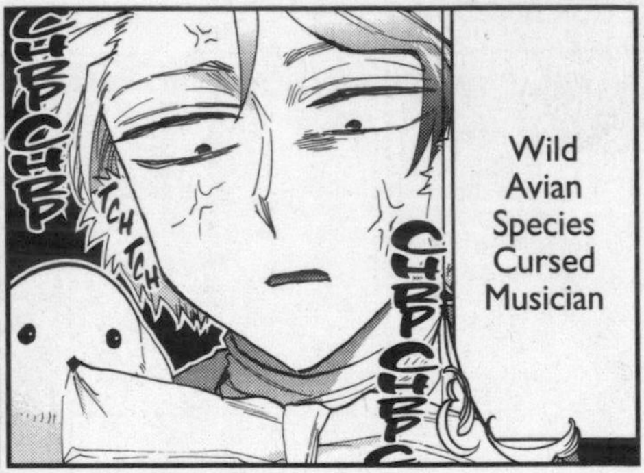
Wild Avian Species Cursed Musician
CHRP CHRP CHRP
TCH TCH
CHRP CHRP CHRP

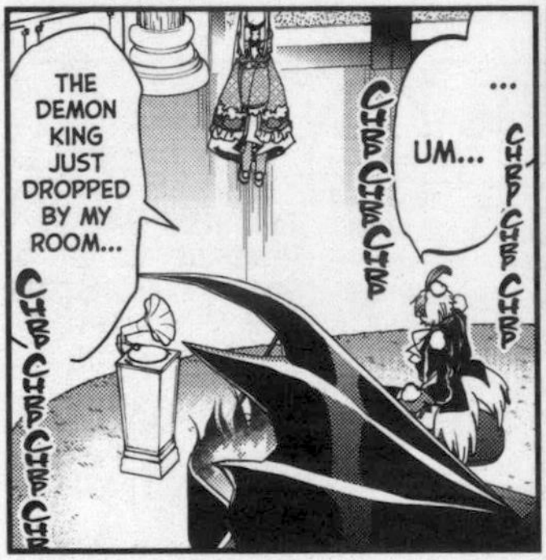
...
UM...
CHRP CHRP CHRP
CHRP CHRP CHRP
THE DEMON KING JUST DROPPED BY MY ROOM...
CHRP CHRP CHRP CHRP

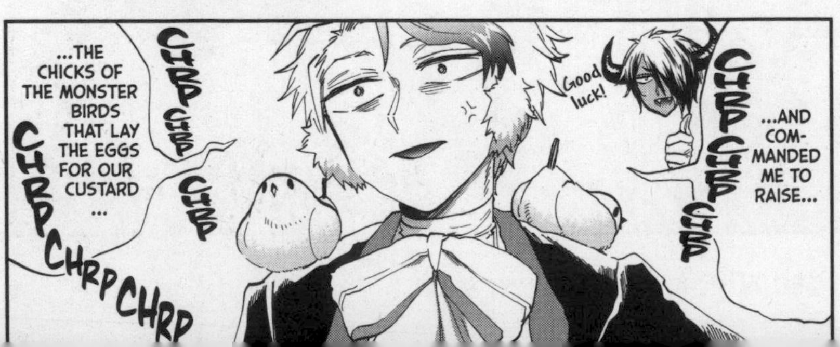
...AND COM-MANDED ME TO RAISE...
CHRP CHRP CHRP CHRP
Good luck!
CHRP CHRP
...THE CHICKS OF THE MONSTER BIRDS THAT LAY THE EGGS FOR OUR CUSTARD ...
CHRP
CHRP CHRP CHRP

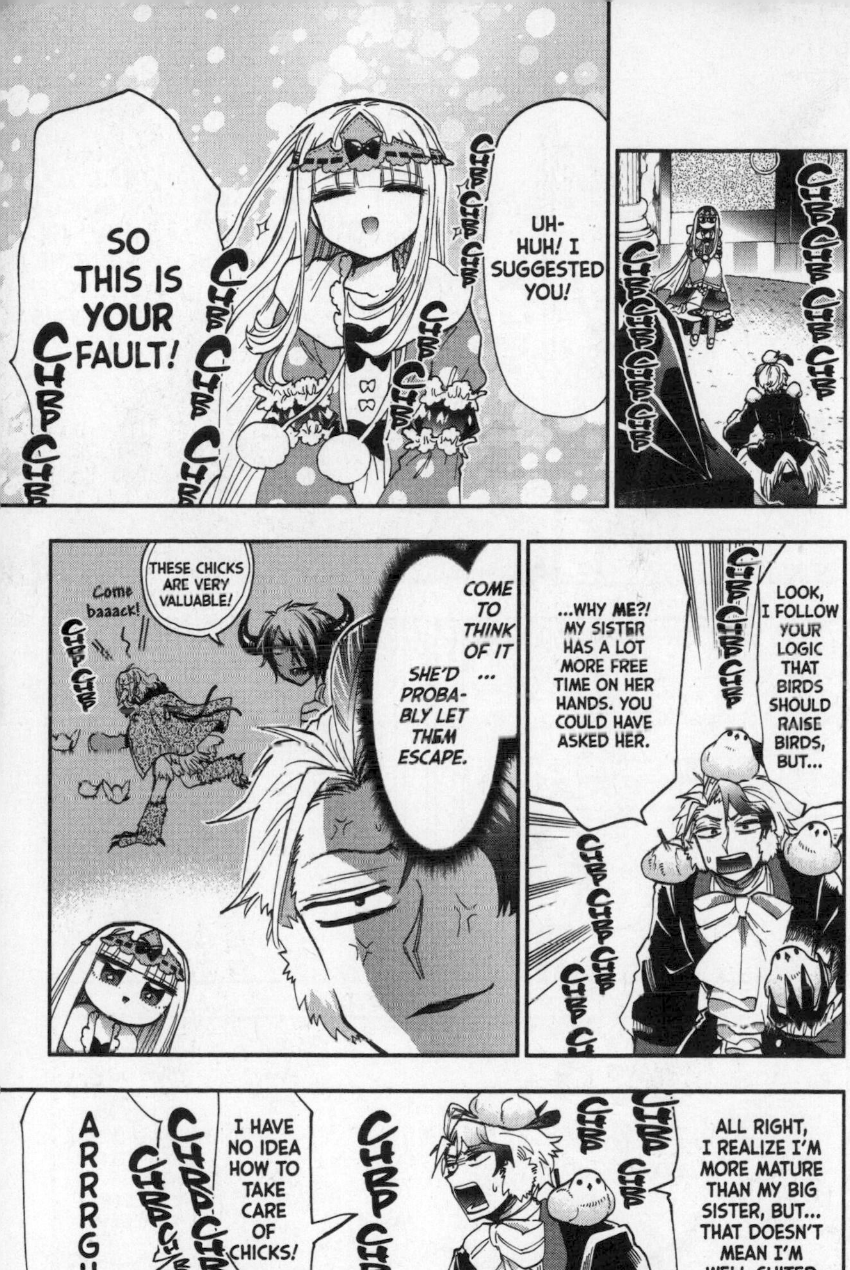
CHIRP CHIRP CHIRP CHIRP
CHIRP CHIRP CHIRP CHIRP
CHIRP CHIRP CHIRP
UH-HUH! I SUGGESTED YOU!
SO THIS IS YOUR FAULT!
CHIRP CHIRP
CHIRP CHIRP CHIRP
LOOK, I FOLLOW YOUR LOGIC THAT BIRDS SHOULD RAISE BIRDS, BUT...
CHIRP CHIRP CHIRP
...WHY ME?! MY SISTER HAS A LOT MORE FREE TIME ON HER HANDS. YOU COULD HAVE ASKED HER.
CHIRP CHIRP CHIRP CHIRP
COME TO THINK OF IT...
SHE'D PROBABLY LET THEM ESCAPE.
THESE CHICKS ARE VERY VALUABLE!
Come baaack!
CHIRP CHIRP
ALL RIGHT, I REALIZE I'M MORE MATURE THAN MY BIG SISTER, BUT... THAT DOESN'T MEAN I'M WELL SUITED FOR THE JOB!
CHIRP CHIRP CHIRP
CHIRP CHIRP
I HAVE NO IDEA HOW TO TAKE CARE OF CHICKS!
CHIRP CHIRP CHIRP CHIRP
ARRRGH!

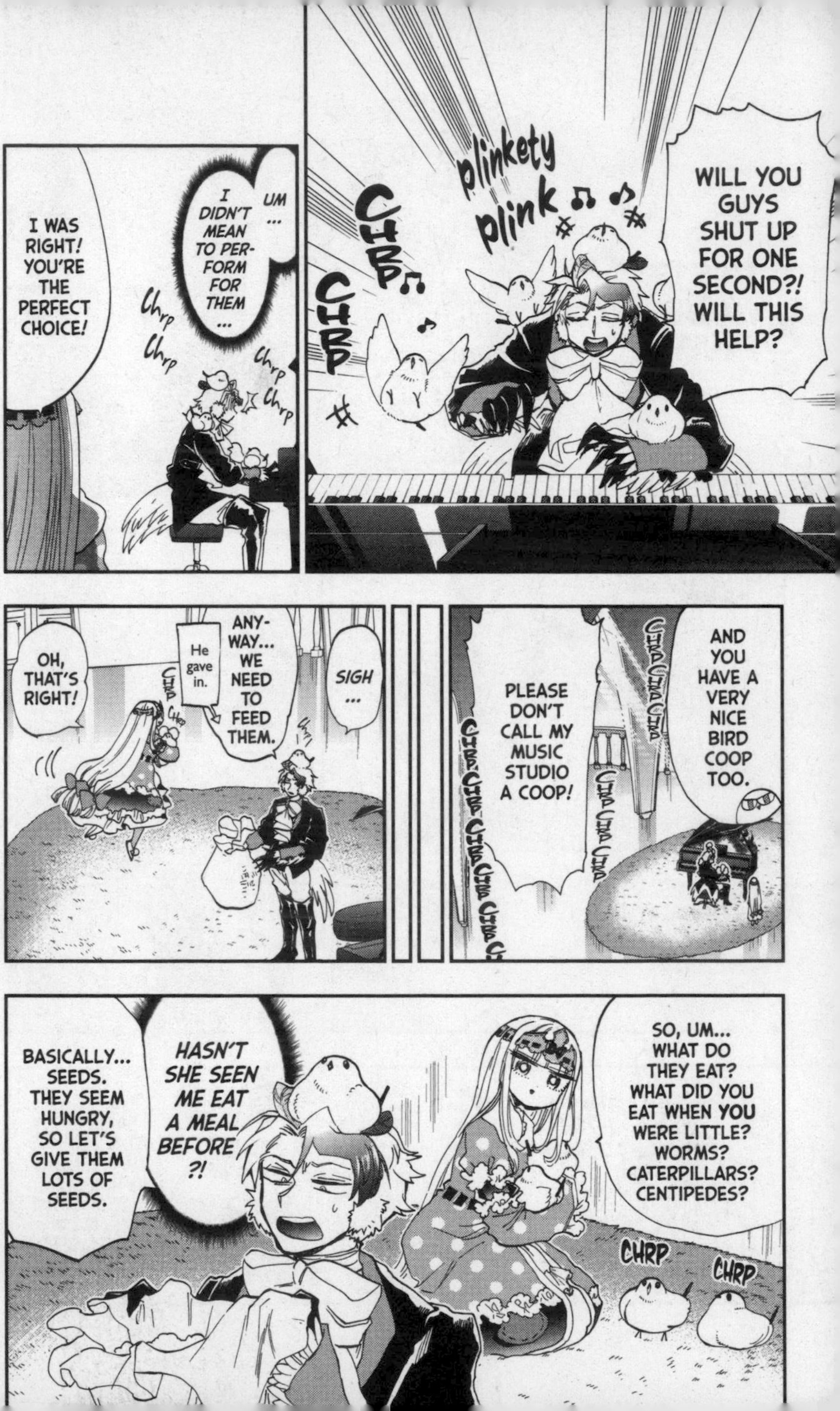

WILL YOU GUYS SHUT UP FOR ONE SECOND?! WILL THIS HELP?
plinkety plink
CHRP
CHRP
UM...
I DIDN'T MEAN TO PERFORM FOR THEM...
Chrp Chrp
Chrp Chrp
I WAS RIGHT! YOU'RE THE PERFECT CHOICE!
AND YOU HAVE A VERY NICE BIRD COOP TOO.
PLEASE DON'T CALL MY MUSIC STUDIO A COOP!
SIGH...
ANYWAY... WE NEED TO FEED THEM.
He gave in.
OH, THAT'S RIGHT!
SO, UM... WHAT DO THEY EAT? WHAT DID YOU EAT WHEN YOU WERE LITTLE? WORMS? CATERPILLARS? CENTIPEDES?
HASN'T SHE SEEN ME EAT A MEAL BEFORE?!
BASICALLY... SEEDS. THEY SEEM HUNGRY, SO LET'S GIVE THEM LOTS OF SEEDS.
CHRP
CHRP

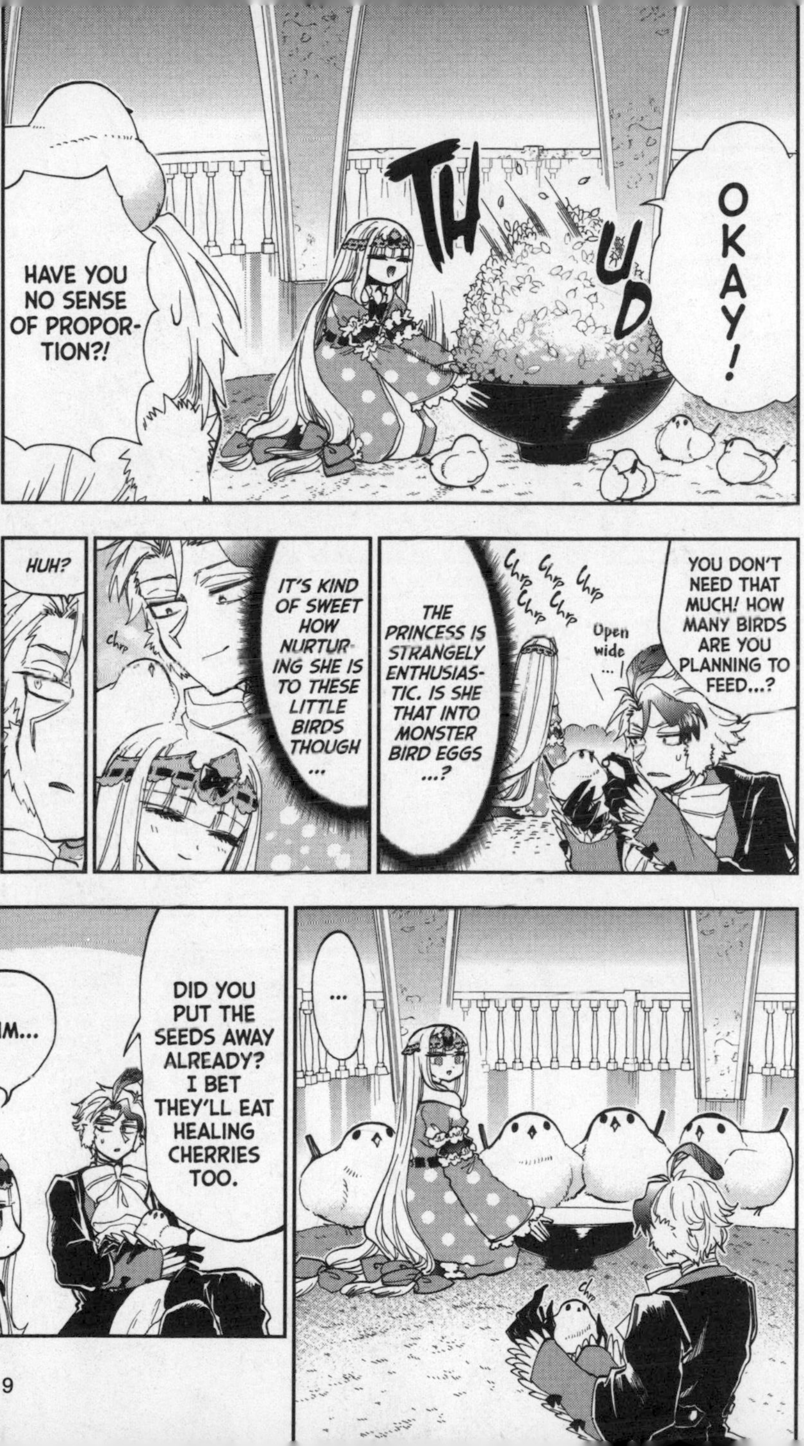
OKAY!
THUD
HAVE YOU NO SENSE OF PROPORTION?!
YOU DON'T NEED THAT MUCH! HOW MANY BIRDS ARE YOU PLANNING TO FEED...?
Chrp Chrp Chrp Chrp Chrp
Open wide...!
THE PRINCESS IS STRANGELY ENTHUSIASTIC. IS SHE THAT INTO MONSTER BIRD EGGS...?
IT'S KIND OF SWEET HOW NURTURING SHE IS TO THESE LITTLE BIRDS THOUGH...
Chrp
HUH?
...
Chrp
DID YOU PUT THE SEEDS AWAY ALREADY? I BET THEY'LL EAT HEALING CHERRIES TOO.
HM...

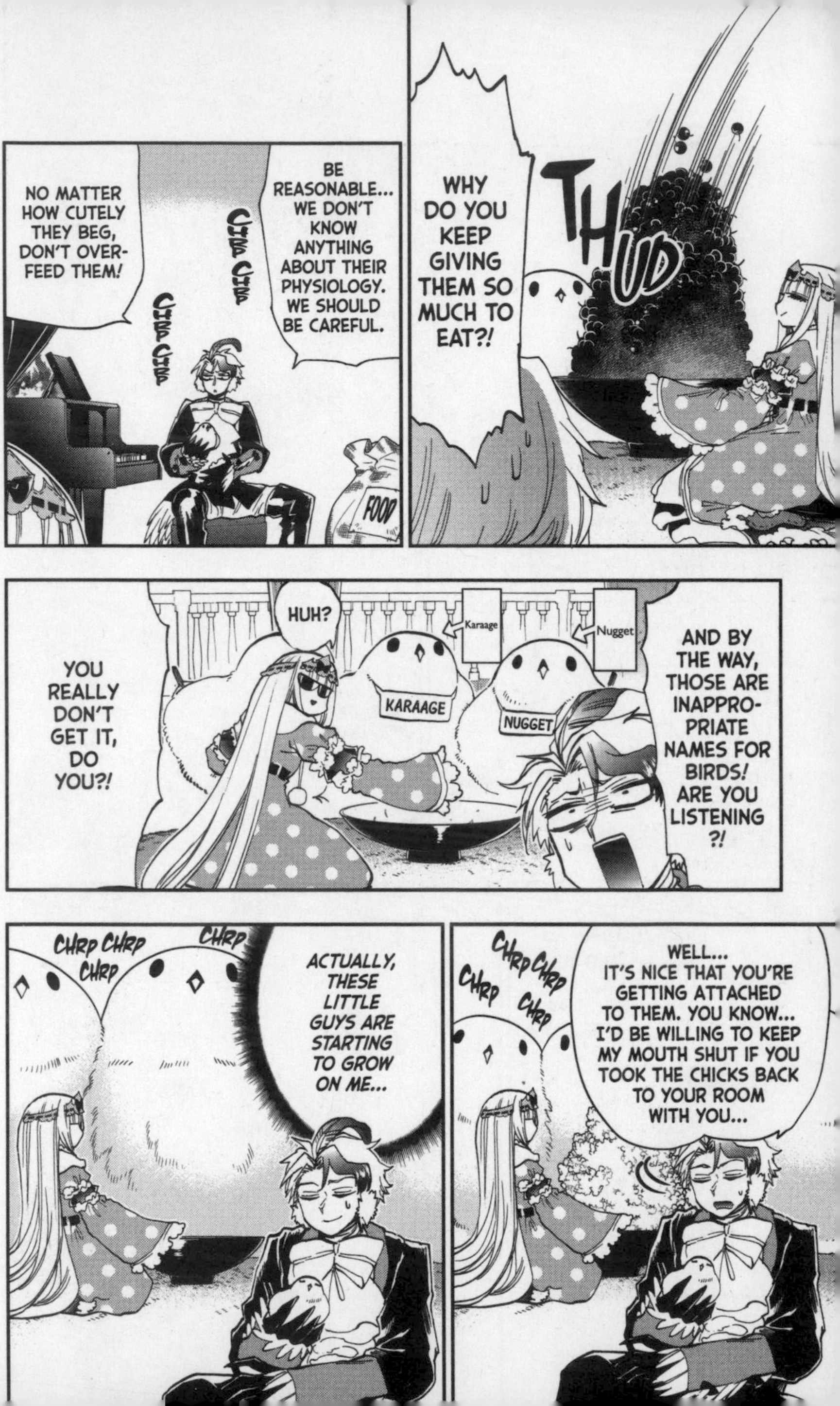
WHY DO YOU KEEP GIVING THEM SO MUCH TO EAT?!
THUD
BE REASONABLE... WE DON'T KNOW ANYTHING ABOUT THEIR PHYSIOLOGY. WE SHOULD BE CAREFUL.
CHRP CHRP
NO MATTER HOW CUTELY THEY BEG, DON'T OVER-FEED THEM!
CHRP CHRP
FOOD
AND BY THE WAY, THOSE ARE INAPPRO-PRIATE NAMES FOR BIRDS! ARE YOU LISTENING ?!
Nugget
NUGGET
Karaage
KARAAGE
HUH?
YOU REALLY DON'T GET IT, DO YOU?!
WELL... IT'S NICE THAT YOU'RE GETTING ATTACHED TO THEM. YOU KNOW... I'D BE WILLING TO KEEP MY MOUTH SHUT IF YOU TOOK THE CHICKS BACK TO YOUR ROOM WITH YOU...
CHRP CHRP
CHRP
CHRP
ACTUALLY, THESE LITTLE GUYS ARE STARTING TO GROW ON ME...
CHRP
CHRP CHRP
CHRP

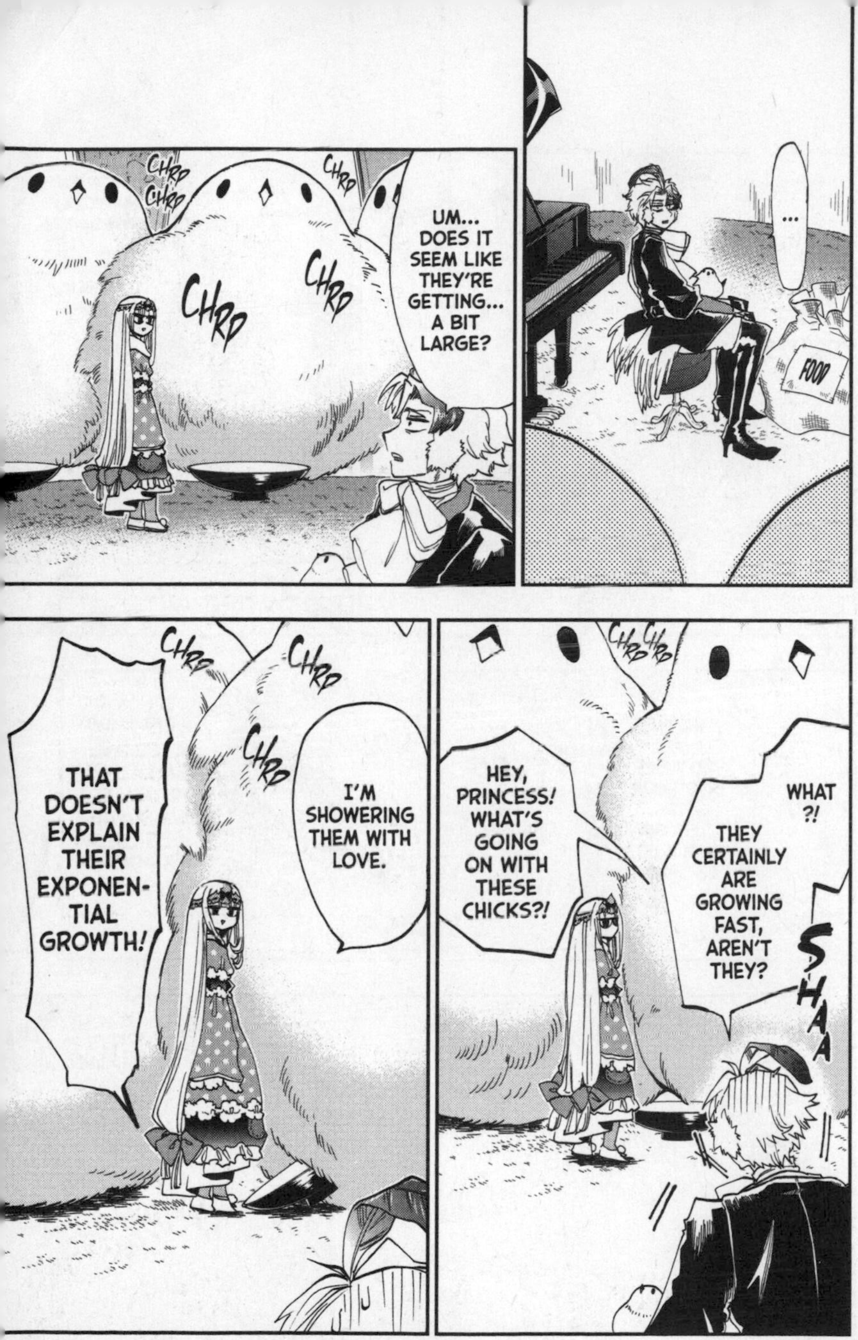
...
CHRP CHRP
CHRP
CHRP
CHRP
UM... DOES IT SEEM LIKE THEY'RE GETTING... A BIT LARGE?
CHRP CHRP
WHAT ?!
THEY CERTAINLY ARE GROWING FAST, AREN'T THEY?
SHAA
HEY, PRINCESS! WHAT'S GOING ON WITH THESE CHICKS?!
CHRP
CHRP
CHRP
I'M SHOWERING THEM WITH LOVE.
THAT DOESN'T EXPLAIN THEIR EXPONEN-TIAL GROWTH!

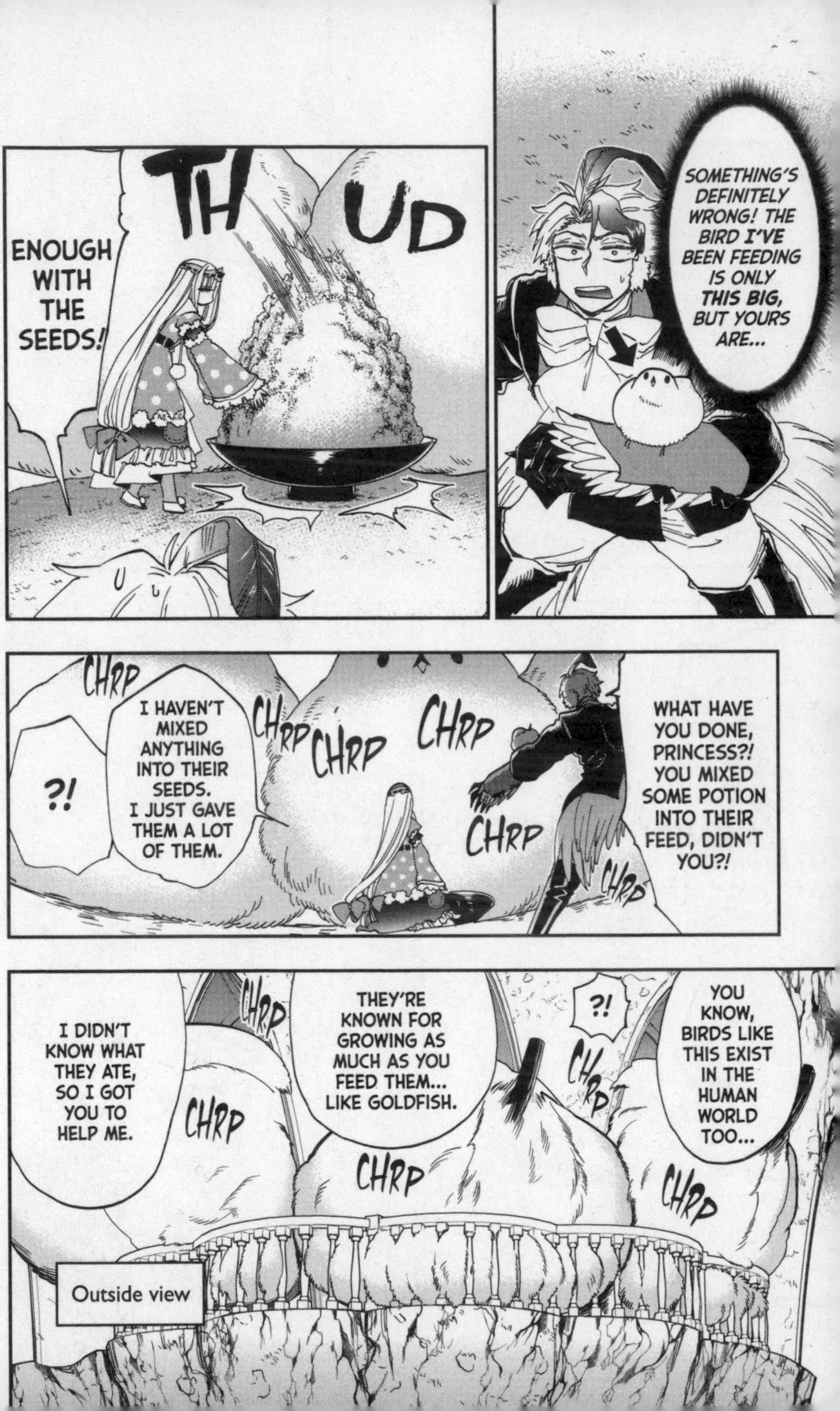
SOMETHING'S DEFINITELY WRONG! THE BIRD I'VE BEEN FEEDING IS ONLY THIS BIG, BUT YOURS ARE...
THUD
ENOUGH WITH THE SEEDS!
WHAT HAVE YOU DONE, PRINCESS?! YOU MIXED SOME POTION INTO THEIR FEED, DIDN'T YOU?!
CHRP
CHRP
CHRP
CHRP
CHRP
I HAVEN'T MIXED ANYTHING INTO THEIR SEEDS. I JUST GAVE THEM A LOT OF THEM.
CHRP
?!
YOU KNOW, BIRDS LIKE THIS EXIST IN THE HUMAN WORLD TOO...
?!
CHRP
CHRP
THEY'RE KNOWN FOR GROWING AS MUCH AS YOU FEED THEM... LIKE GOLDFISH.
CHRP
CHRP
CHRP
I DIDN'T KNOW WHAT THEY ATE, SO I GOT YOU TO HELP ME.
Outside view

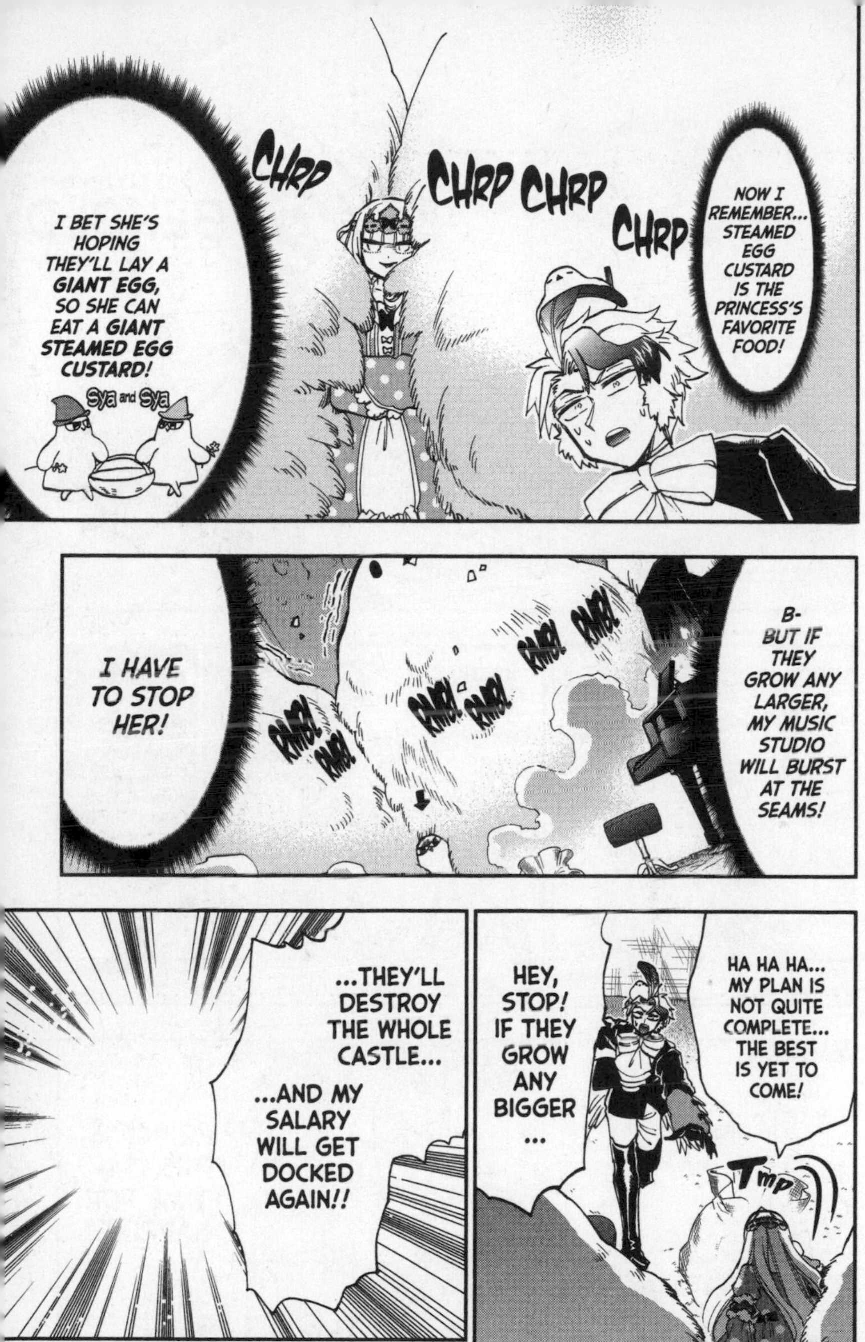
NOW I REMEMBER... STEAMED EGG CUSTARD IS THE PRINCESS'S FAVORITE FOOD!
CHRP CHRP CHRP CHRP
I BET SHE'S HOPING THEY'LL LAY A GIANT EGG, SO SHE CAN EAT A GIANT STEAMED EGG CUSTARD!
Sya and Sya
B-BUT IF THEY GROW ANY LARGER, MY MUSIC STUDIO WILL BURST AT THE SEAMS!
RMBL RMBL RMBL RMBL RMBL RMBL
I HAVE TO STOP HER!
HA HA HA... MY PLAN IS NOT QUITE COMPLETE... THE BEST IS YET TO COME!
HEY, STOP! IF THEY GROW ANY BIGGER ...
Tmp
...THEY'LL DESTROY THE WHOLE CASTLE...
...AND MY SALARY WILL GET DOCKED AGAIN!!

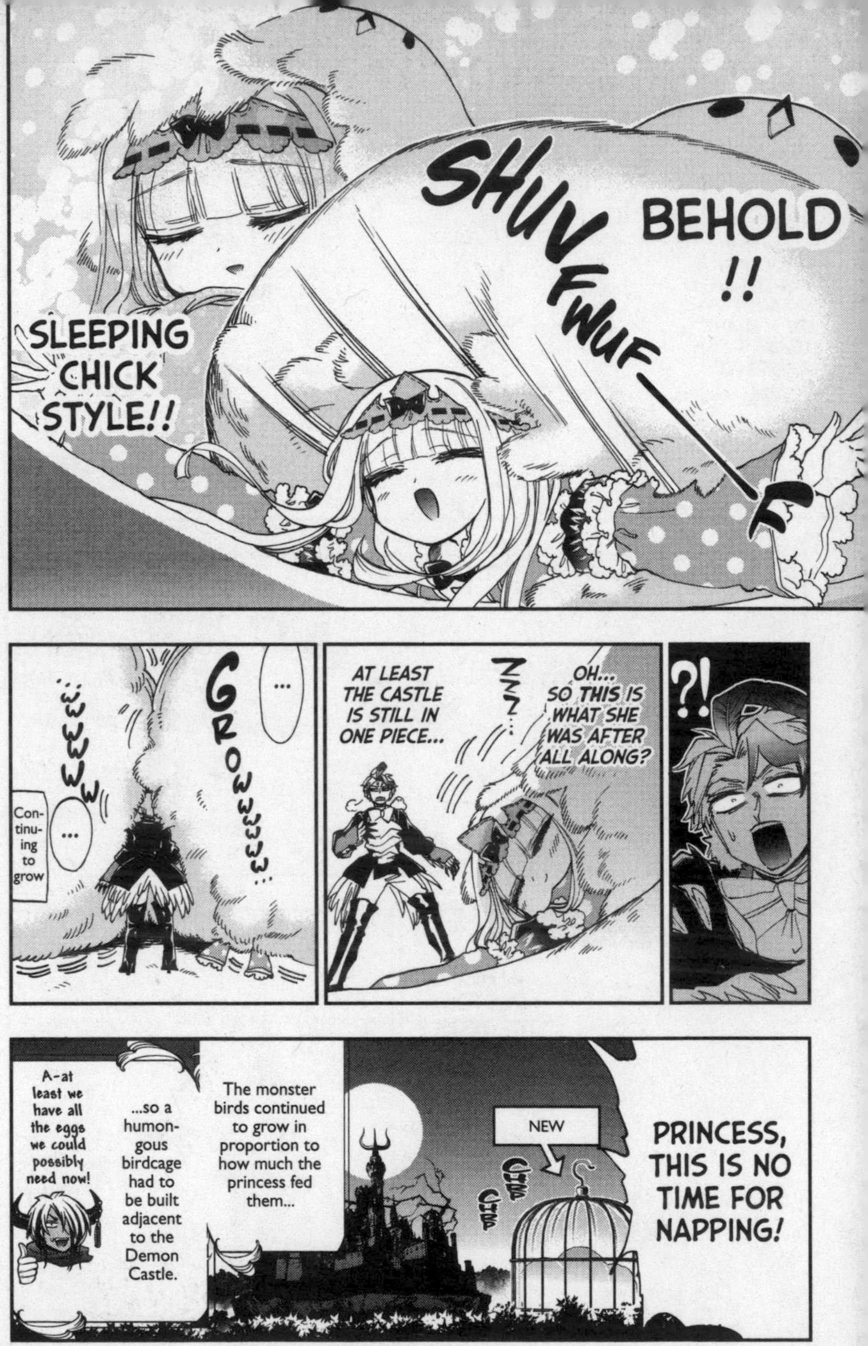
BEHOLD!!
SHUVFWUF
SLEEPING CHICK STYLE!!
?!
OH... SO THIS IS WHAT SHE WAS AFTER ALL ALONG?
ZZZ...
AT LEAST THE CASTLE IS STILL IN ONE PIECE...
...
GROWWWWWW..
...
..WWWWW
Continuing to grow
PRINCESS, THIS IS NO TIME FOR NAPPING!
NEW
The monster birds continued to grow in proportion to how much the princess fed them...
...so a humongous birdcage had to be built adjacent to the Demon Castle.
A-at least we have all the eggs we could possibly need now!

Monster Bird Chick

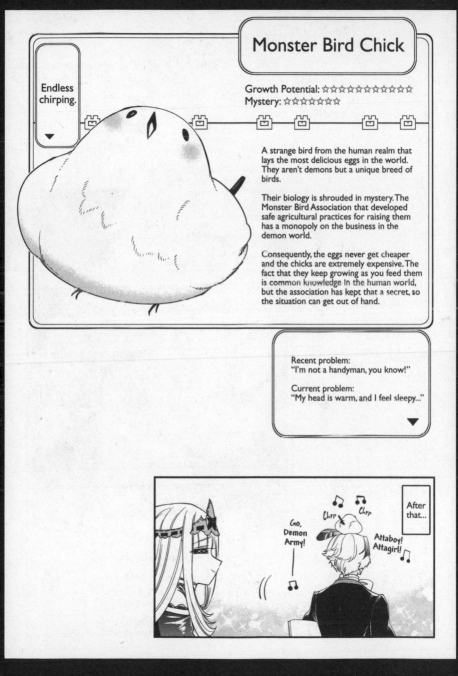

Growth Potential: ☆☆☆☆☆☆☆☆☆☆☆
Mystery: ☆☆☆☆☆☆☆

Endless chirping.

A strange bird from the human realm that lays the most delicious eggs in the world. They aren't demons but a unique breed of birds.

Their biology is shrouded in mystery. The Monster Bird Association that developed safe agricultural practices for raising them has a monopoly on the business in the demon world.

Consequently, the eggs never get cheaper and the chicks are extremely expensive. The fact that they keep growing as you feed them is common knowledge in the human world, but the association has kept that a secret, so the situation can get out of hand.

Recent problem:
"I'm not a handyman, you know!"

Current problem:
"My head is warm, and I feel sleepy..."

After that...
Attaboy! Attagirl!
Chrp
Chrp
Go, Demon Army!

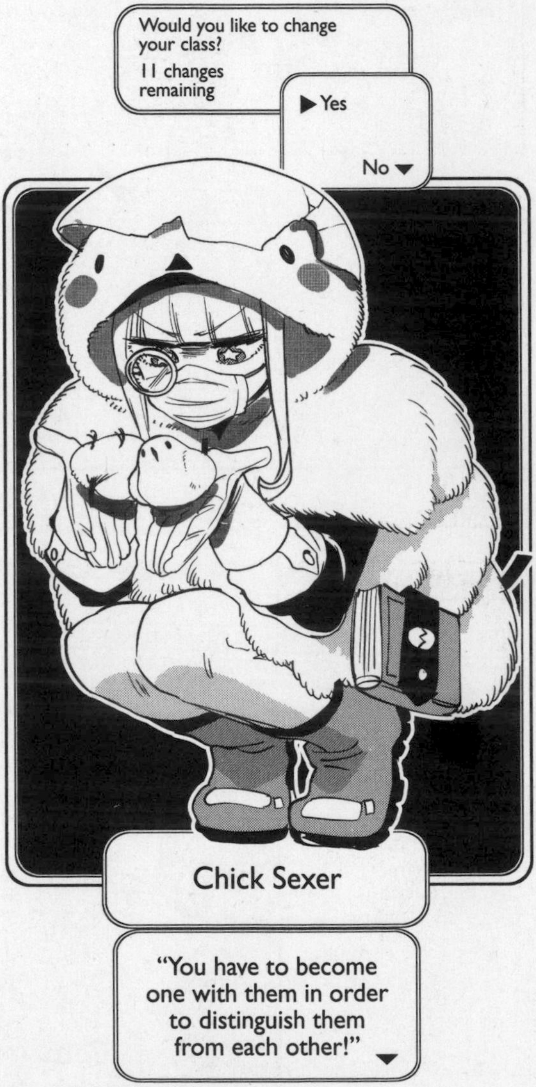
Would you like to change your class?
11 changes remaining
▶Yes
No
Chick Sexer
"You have to become one with them in order to distinguish them from each other!"

145th Night: House Hunting Is Fun☆

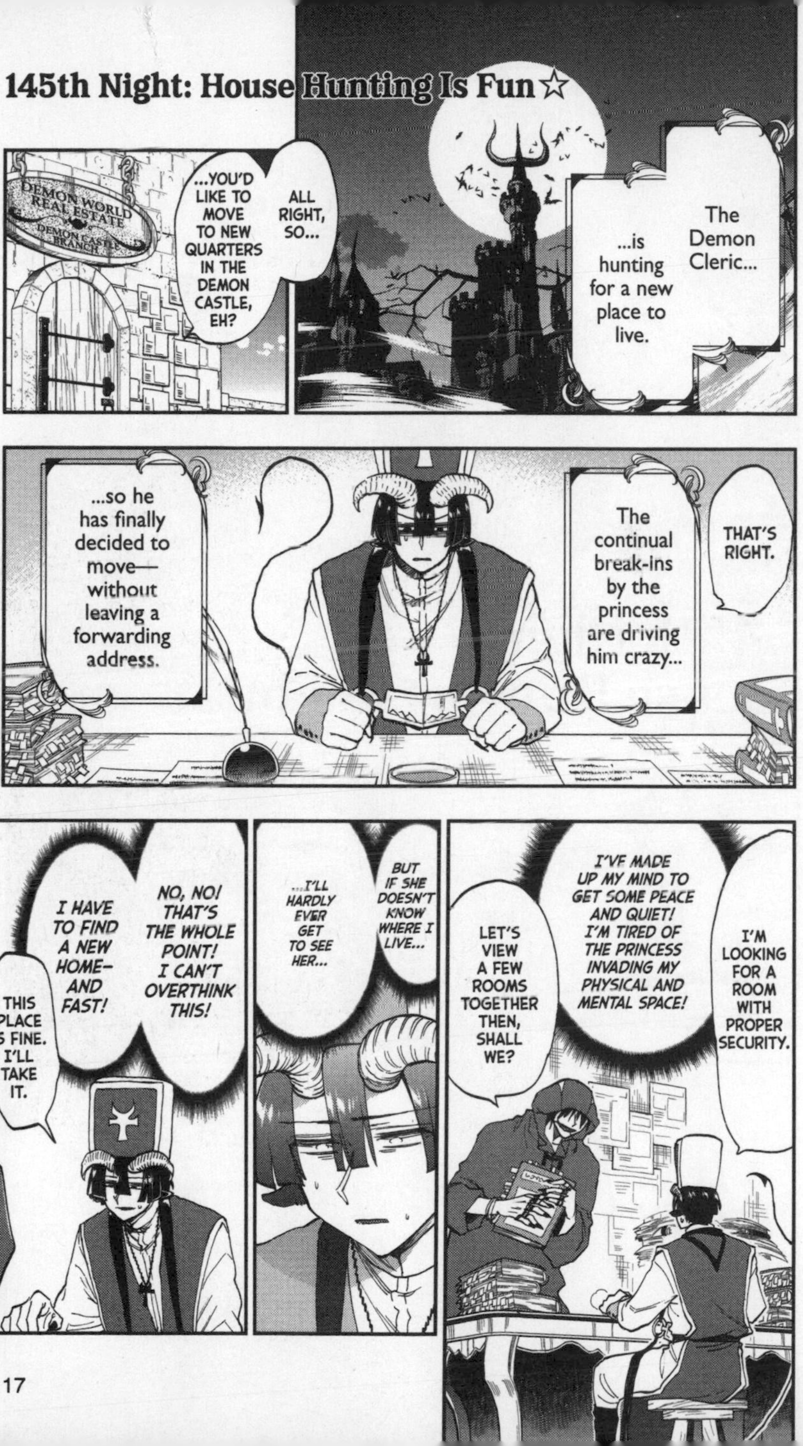

The Demon Cleric...
...is hunting for a new place to live.
DEMON WORLD REAL ESTATE DEMON CASTLE BRANCH
ALL RIGHT, SO...
...YOU'D LIKE TO MOVE TO NEW QUARTERS IN THE DEMON CASTLE, EH?
THAT'S RIGHT.
The continual break-ins by the princess are driving him crazy...
...so he has finally decided to move—without leaving a forwarding address.
I'M LOOKING FOR A ROOM WITH PROPER SECURITY.
I'VE MADE UP MY MIND TO GET SOME PEACE AND QUIET! I'M TIRED OF THE PRINCESS INVADING MY PHYSICAL AND MENTAL SPACE!
LET'S VIEW A FEW ROOMS TOGETHER THEN, SHALL WE?
BUT IF SHE DOESN'T KNOW WHERE I LIVE...
...I'LL HARDLY EVER GET TO SEE HER...
NO, NO! THAT'S THE WHOLE POINT! I CAN'T OVERTHINK THIS!
I HAVE TO FIND A NEW HOME—AND FAST!
THIS PLACE IS FINE. I'LL TAKE IT.

145th Night: House Hunting Is Fun☆

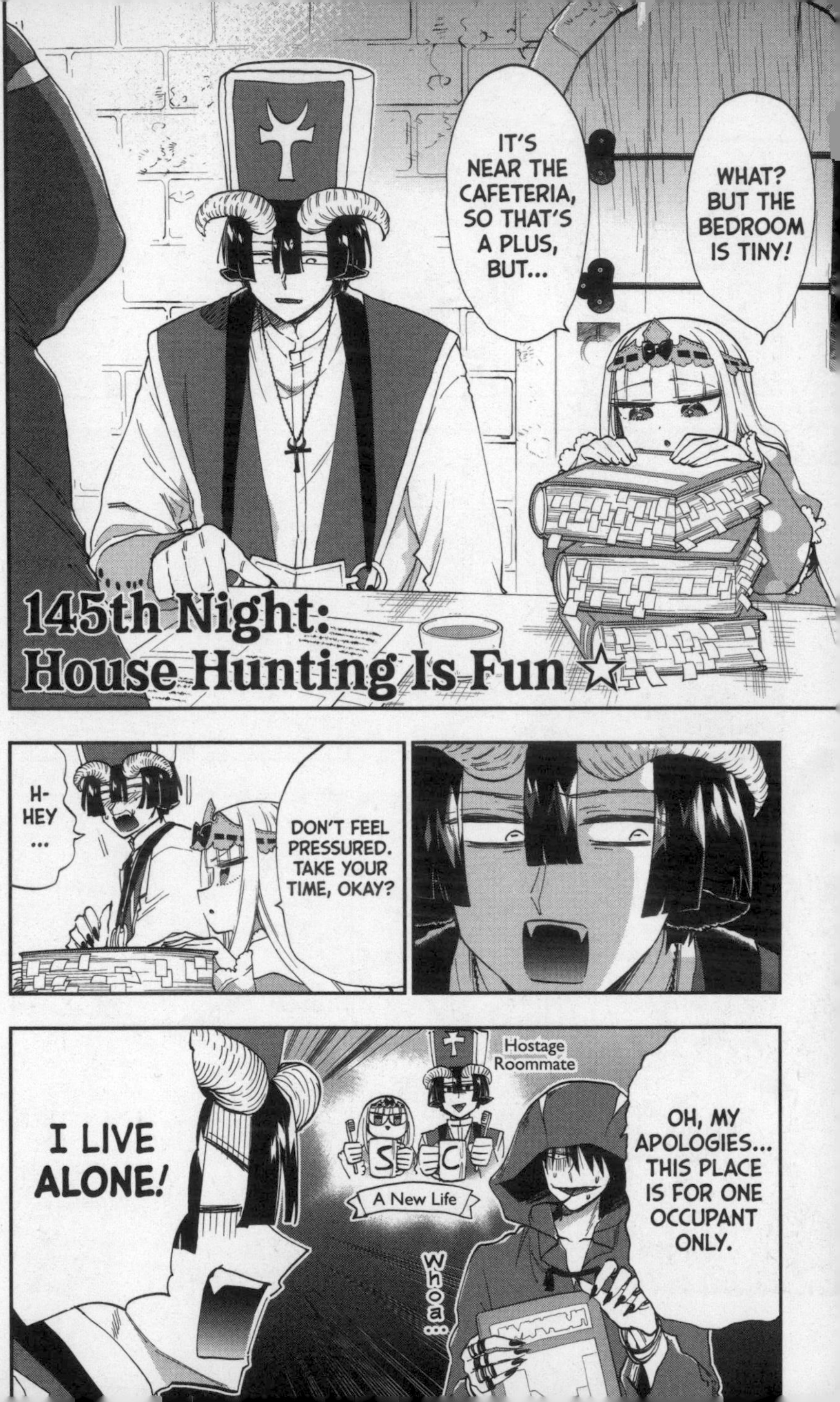
WHAT? BUT THE BEDROOM IS TINY!
IT'S NEAR THE CAFETERIA, SO THAT'S A PLUS, BUT...
DON'T FEEL PRESSURED. TAKE YOUR TIME, OKAY?
H-HEY ...
OH, MY APOLOGIES... THIS PLACE IS FOR ONE OCCUPANT ONLY.
Hostage Roommate
S
C
A New Life
Whoa...
I LIVE ALONE!

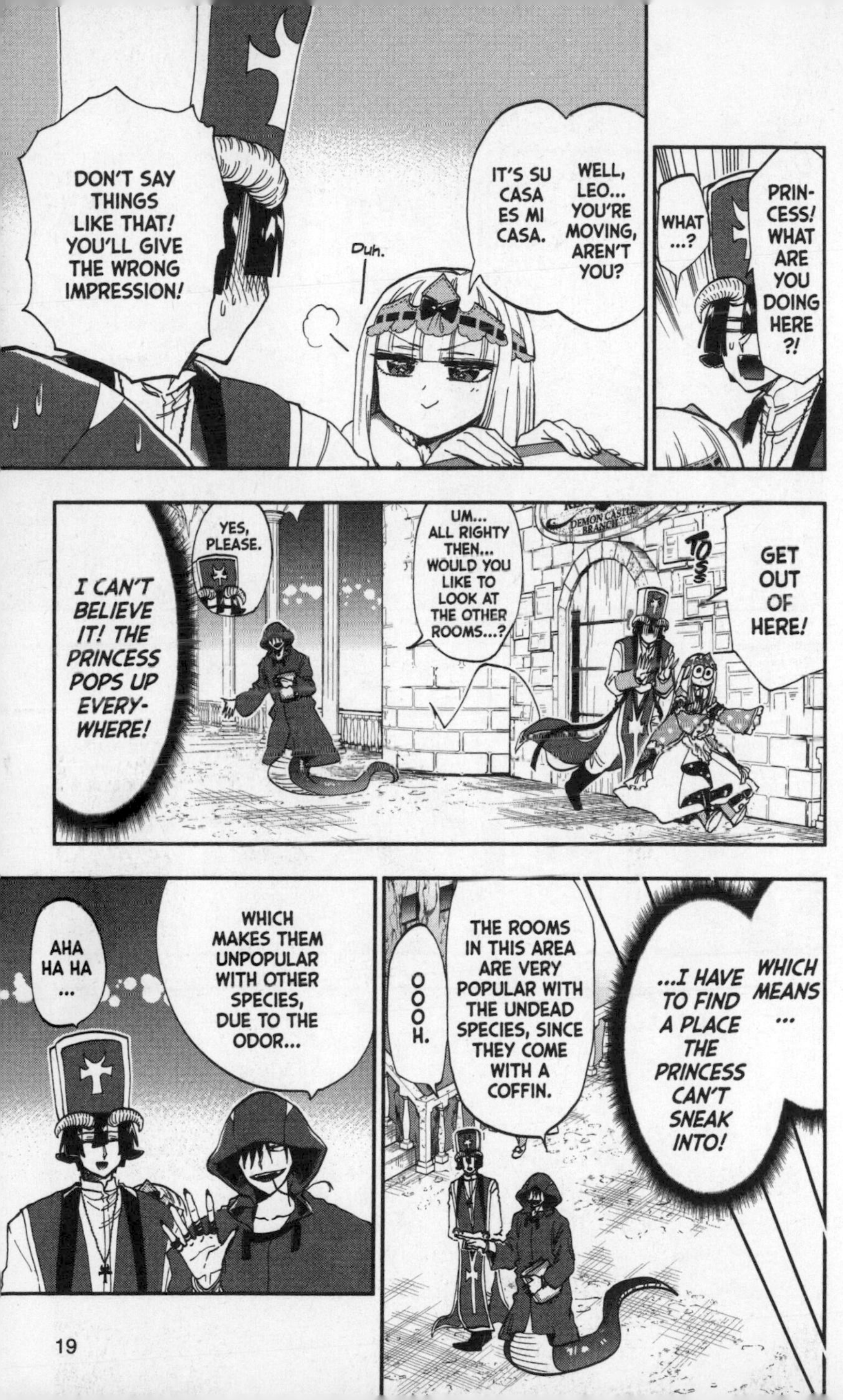

WHAT ...?
PRIN-CESS! WHAT ARE YOU DOING HERE?!
WELL, LEO... YOU'RE MOVING, AREN'T YOU?
IT'S SU CASA ES MI CASA.
Duh.
DON'T SAY THINGS LIKE THAT! YOU'LL GIVE THE WRONG IMPRESSION!
GET OUT OF HERE!
TOSS
DEMON CASTLE BRANCH
UM... ALL RIGHTY THEN... WOULD YOU LIKE TO LOOK AT THE OTHER ROOMS...?
YES, PLEASE.
I CAN'T BELIEVE IT! THE PRINCESS POPS UP EVERY-WHERE!
WHICH MEANS ...
...I HAVE TO FIND A PLACE THE PRINCESS CAN'T SNEAK INTO!
THE ROOMS IN THIS AREA ARE VERY POPULAR WITH THE UNDEAD SPECIES, SINCE THEY COME WITH A COFFIN.
OOOOH.
WHICH MAKES THEM UNPOPULAR WITH OTHER SPECIES, DUE TO THE ODOR...
AHA HA HA ...

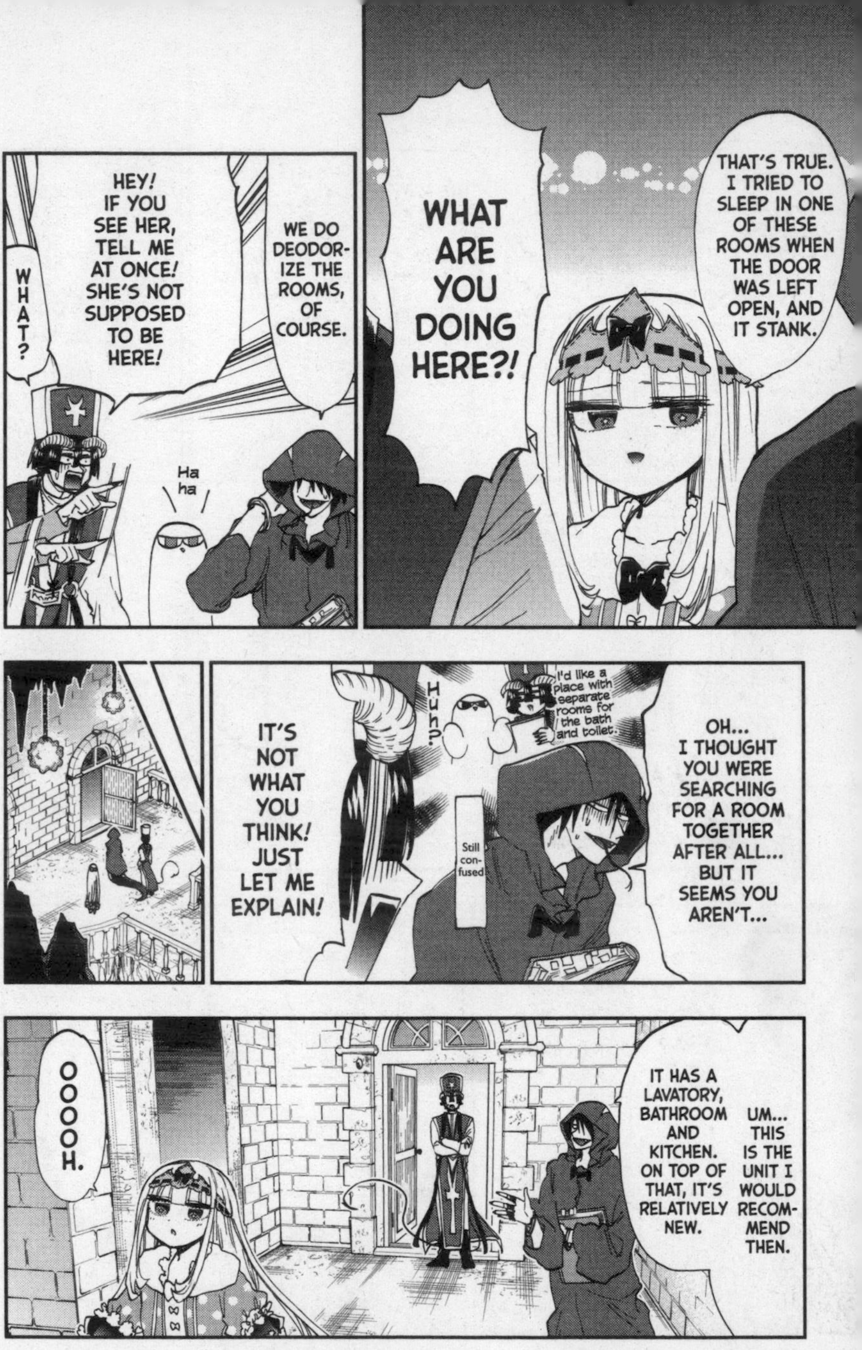
THAT'S TRUE. I TRIED TO SLEEP IN ONE OF THESE ROOMS WHEN THE DOOR WAS LEFT OPEN, AND IT STANK.
WHAT ARE YOU DOING HERE?!
WE DO DEODOR-IZE THE ROOMS, OF COURSE.
HEY! IF YOU SEE HER, TELL ME AT ONCE! SHE'S NOT SUPPOSED TO BE HERE!
WHAT?
Ha ha
OH... I THOUGHT YOU WERE SEARCHING FOR A ROOM TOGETHER AFTER ALL... BUT IT SEEMS YOU AREN'T...
I'd like a place with separate rooms for the bath and toilet.
Huh?
IT'S NOT WHAT YOU THINK! JUST LET ME EXPLAIN!
Still confused
UM... THIS IS THE UNIT I WOULD RECOMMEND THEN.
IT HAS A LAVATORY, BATHROOM AND KITCHEN. ON TOP OF THAT, IT'S RELATIVELY NEW.
OOOOH.

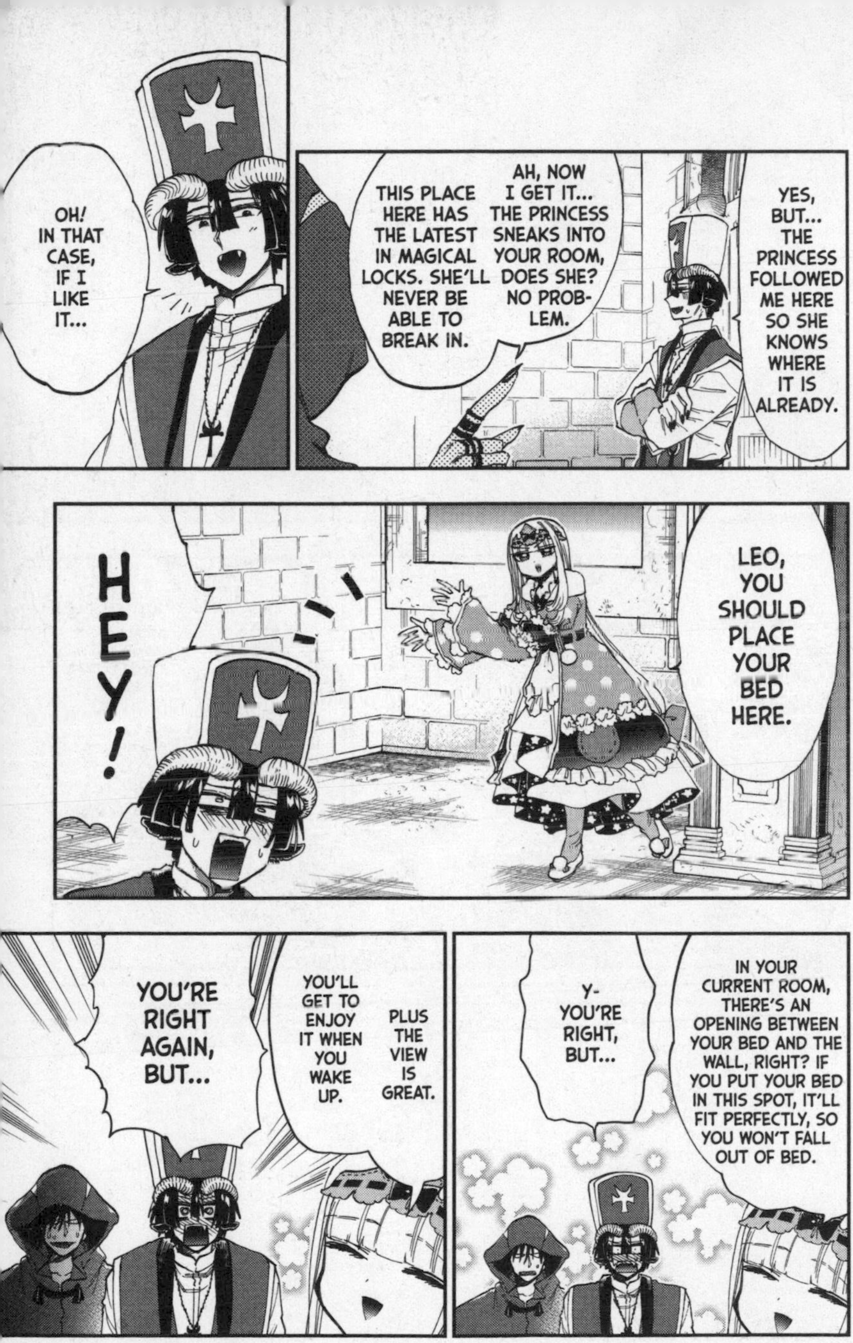
YES, BUT... THE PRINCESS FOLLOWED ME HERE SO SHE KNOWS WHERE IT IS ALREADY.
AH, NOW I GET IT... THE PRINCESS SNEAKS INTO YOUR ROOM, DOES SHE? NO PROB-LEM.
THIS PLACE HERE HAS THE LATEST IN MAGICAL LOCKS. SHE'LL NEVER BE ABLE TO BREAK IN.
OH! IN THAT CASE, IF I LIKE IT...
LEO, YOU SHOULD PLACE YOUR BED HERE.
HEY!
IN YOUR CURRENT ROOM, THERE'S AN OPENING BETWEEN YOUR BED AND THE WALL, RIGHT? IF YOU PUT YOUR BED IN THIS SPOT, IT'LL FIT PERFECTLY, SO YOU WON'T FALL OUT OF BED.
Y-YOU'RE RIGHT, BUT...
PLUS THE VIEW IS GREAT.
YOU'LL GET TO ENJOY IT WHEN YOU WAKE UP.
YOU'RE RIGHT AGAIN, BUT...

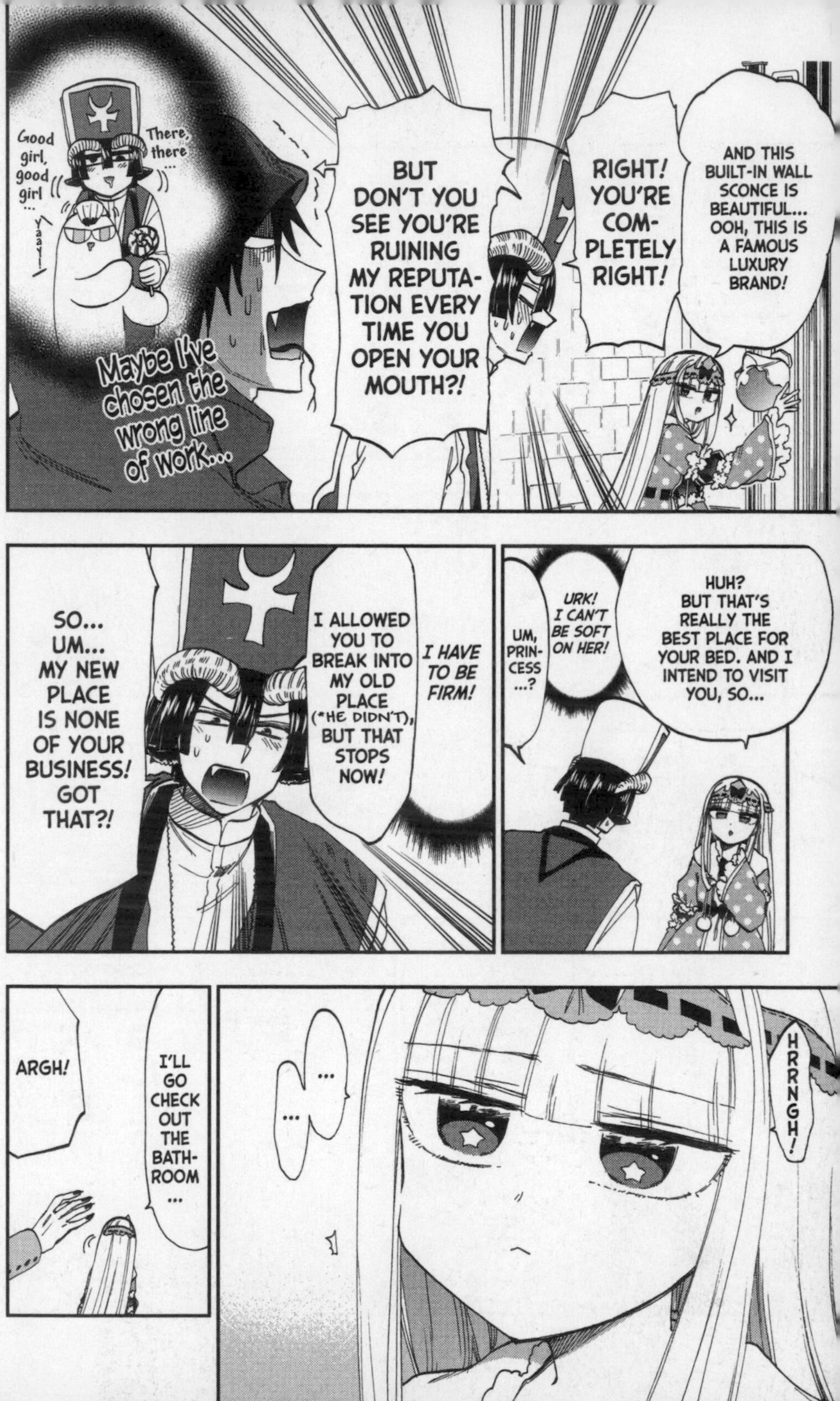
AND THIS BUILT-IN WALL SCONCE IS BEAUTIFUL... OOH, THIS IS A FAMOUS LUXURY BRAND!
RIGHT! YOU'RE COM-PLETELY RIGHT!
BUT DON'T YOU SEE YOU'RE RUINING MY REPUTA-TION EVERY TIME YOU OPEN YOUR MOUTH?!
There, there...
Good girl, good girl...
Yaay!
Maybe I've chosen the wrong line of work...
HUH? BUT THAT'S REALLY THE BEST PLACE FOR YOUR BED. AND I INTEND TO VISIT YOU, SO...
URK! I CAN'T BE SOFT ON HER!
UM, PRIN-CESS...?
I HAVE TO BE FIRM!
I ALLOWED YOU TO BREAK INTO MY OLD PLACE (*HE DIDN'T), BUT THAT STOPS NOW!
SO... UM... MY NEW PLACE IS NONE OF YOUR BUSINESS! GOT THAT?!
HRRNGH!
...
...
I'LL GO CHECK OUT THE BATH-ROOM...
ARGH!

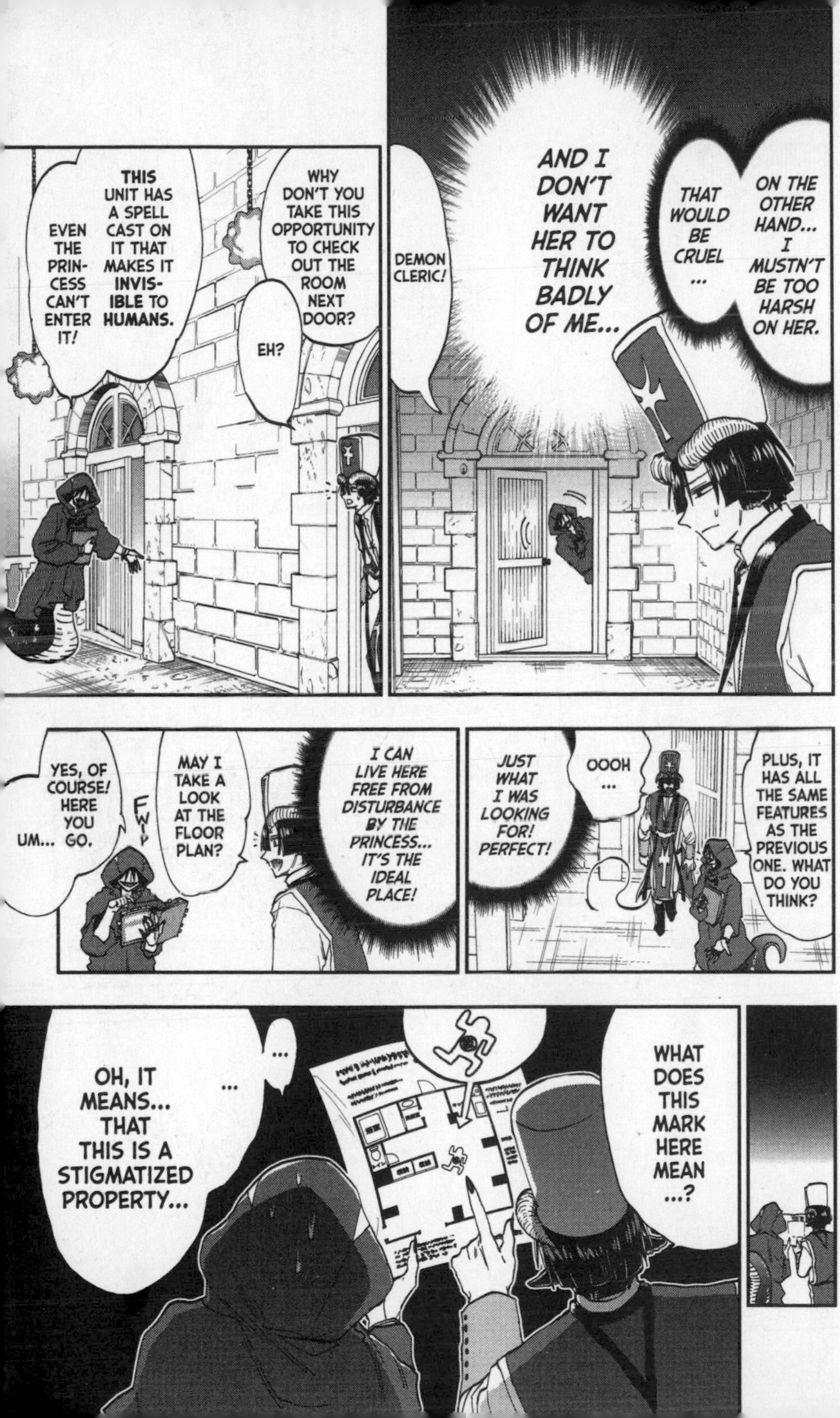
ON THE OTHER HAND... I MUSTN'T BE TOO HARSH ON HER.
THAT WOULD BE CRUEL ...
AND I DON'T WANT HER TO THINK BADLY OF ME...
DEMON CLERIC!
WHY DON'T YOU TAKE THIS OPPORTUNITY TO CHECK OUT THE ROOM NEXT DOOR?
EH?
THIS UNIT HAS A SPELL CAST ON IT THAT MAKES IT INVISIBLE TO HUMANS.
EVEN THE PRINCESS CAN'T ENTER IT!
PLUS, IT HAS ALL THE SAME FEATURES AS THE PREVIOUS ONE. WHAT DO YOU THINK?
OOOH ...
JUST WHAT I WAS LOOKING FOR! PERFECT!
I CAN LIVE HERE FREE FROM DISTURBANCE BY THE PRINCESS... IT'S THE IDEAL PLACE!
MAY I TAKE A LOOK AT THE FLOOR PLAN?
FWIP
YES, OF COURSE! HERE YOU GO.
UM...
WHAT DOES THIS MARK HERE MEAN ...?
...
...
OH, IT MEANS... THAT THIS IS A STIGMATIZED PROPERTY...

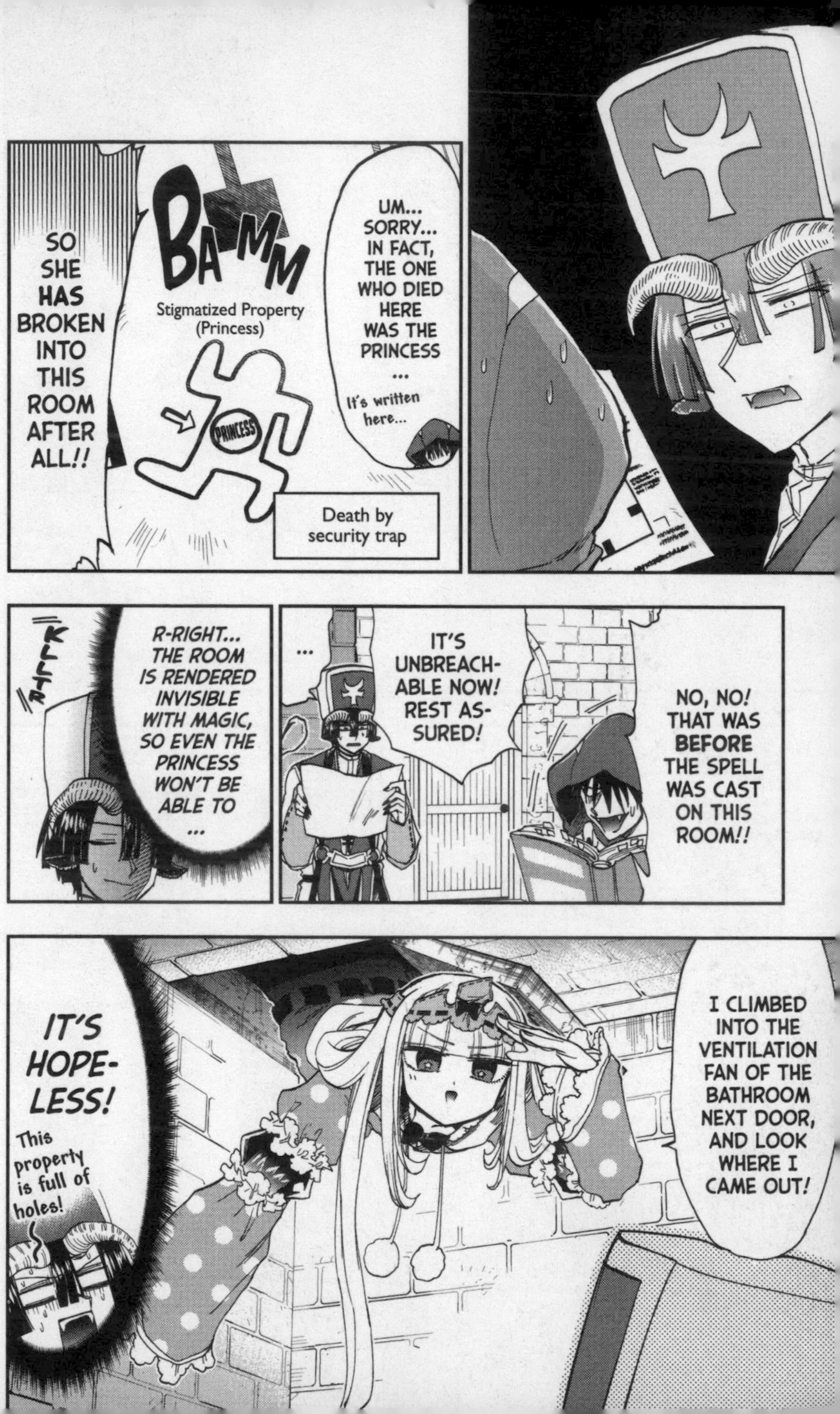
UM... SORRY... IN FACT, THE ONE WHO DIED HERE WAS THE PRINCESS ...
It's written here...
BAMM
Stigmatized Property (Princess)
PRINCESS
Death by security trap
SO SHE HAS BROKEN INTO THIS ROOM AFTER ALL!!
NO, NO! THAT WAS BEFORE THE SPELL WAS CAST ON THIS ROOM!!
IT'S UNBREACHABLE NOW! REST ASSURED!
...
R-RIGHT... THE ROOM IS RENDERED INVISIBLE WITH MAGIC, SO EVEN THE PRINCESS WON'T BE ABLE TO ...
I CLIMBED INTO THE VENTILATION FAN OF THE BATHROOM NEXT DOOR, AND LOOK WHERE I CAME OUT!
IT'S HOPE-LESS!
This property is full of holes!

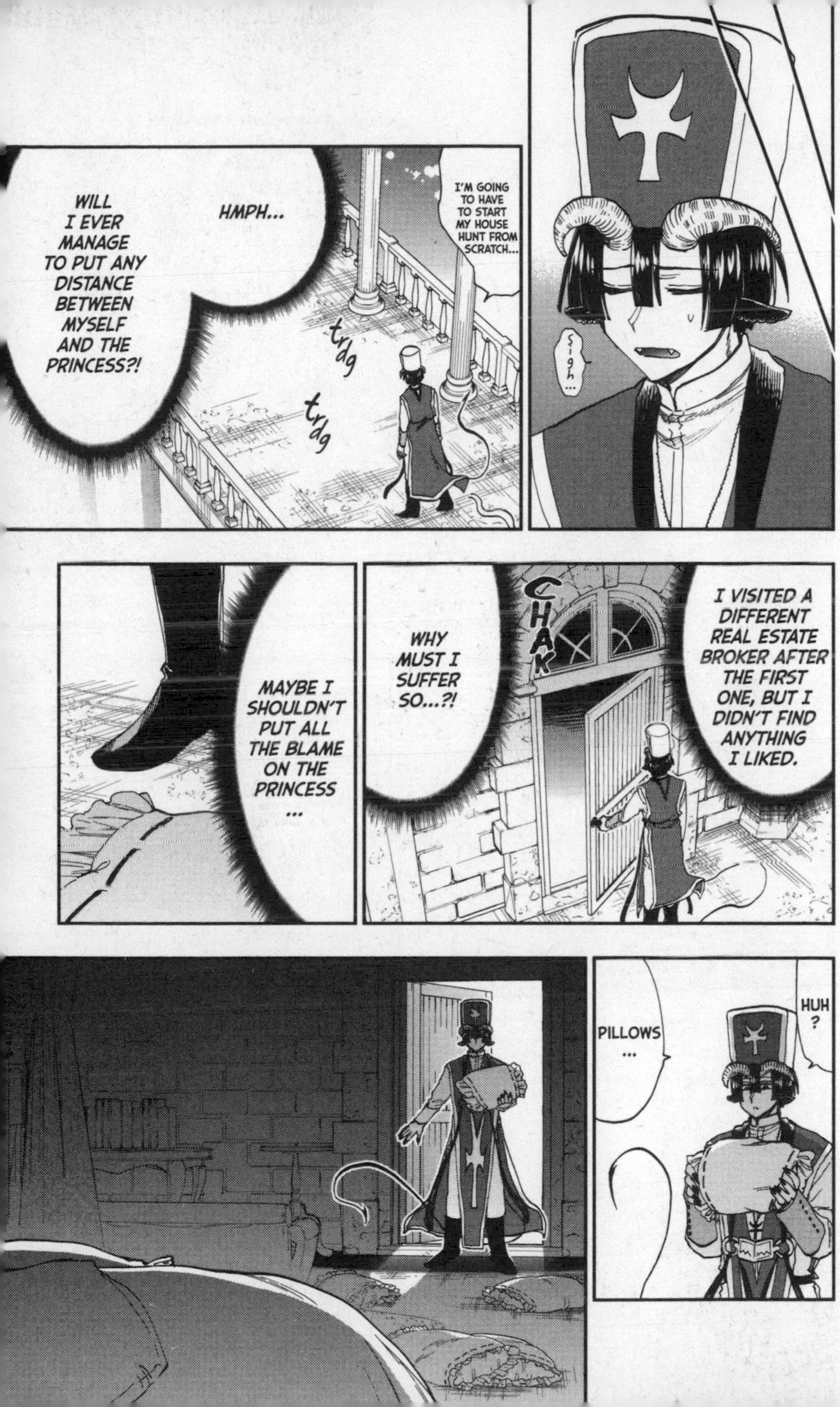
Sigh...
I'M GOING TO HAVE TO START MY HOUSE HUNT FROM SCRATCH...
HMPH...
trdg
trdg
WILL I EVER MANAGE TO PUT ANY DISTANCE BETWEEN MYSELF AND THE PRINCESS?!
I VISITED A DIFFERENT REAL ESTATE BROKER AFTER THE FIRST ONE, BUT I DIDN'T FIND ANYTHING I LIKED.
CHAK
WHY MUST I SUFFER SO...?!
MAYBE I SHOULDN'T PUT ALL THE BLAME ON THE PRINCESS...
HUH?
PILLOWS...

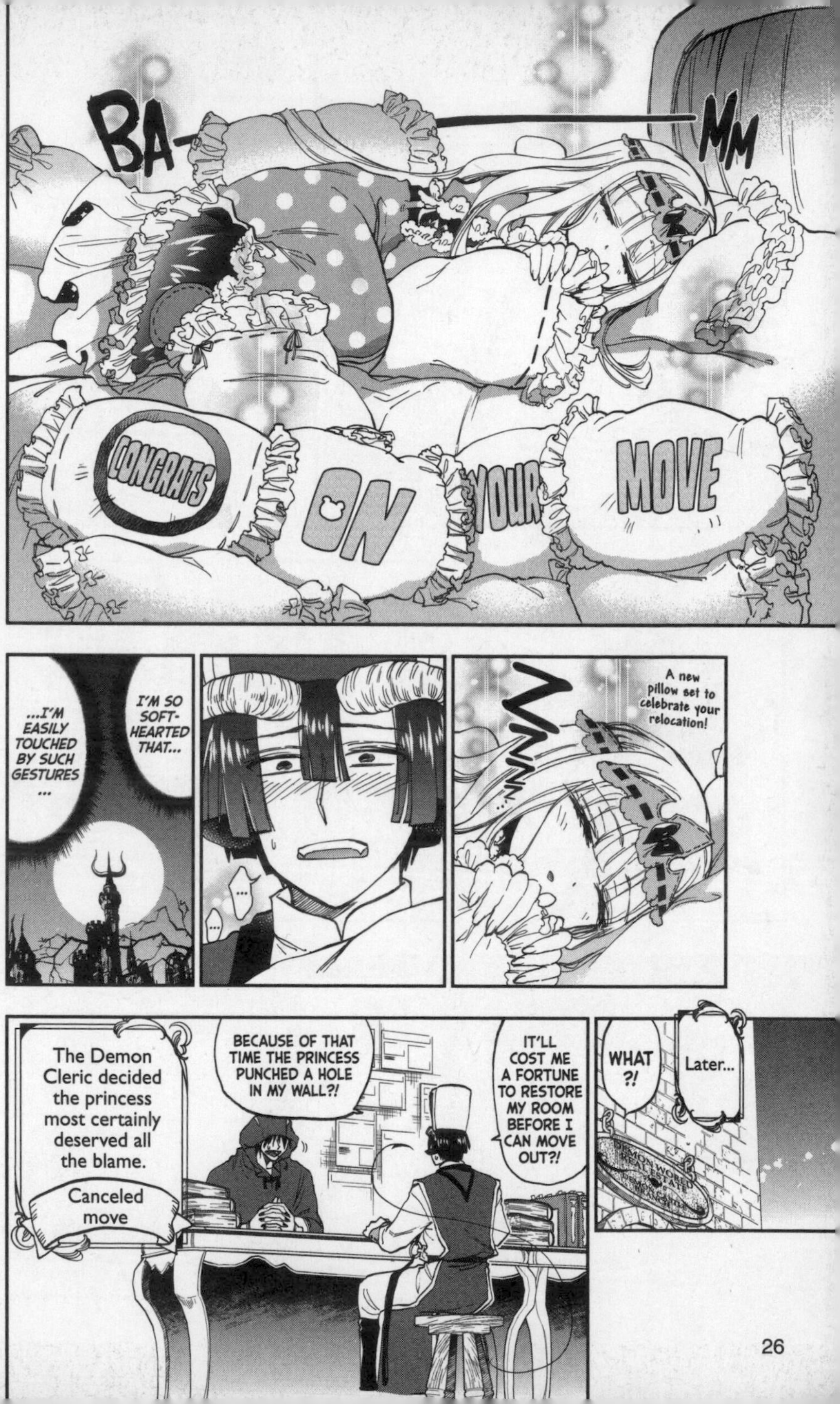
BA-MM
CONGRATS ON YOUR MOVE
A new pillow set to celebrate your relocation!
...
...
I'M SO SOFT-HEARTED THAT...
...I'M EASILY TOUCHED BY SUCH GESTURES...
Later...
WHAT?!
IT'LL COST ME A FORTUNE TO RESTORE MY ROOM BEFORE I CAN MOVE OUT?!
BECAUSE OF THAT TIME THE PRINCESS PUNCHED A HOLE IN MY WALL?!
The Demon Cleric decided the princess most certainly deserved all the blame.
Canceled move

Demon World Real Estate
Demon Castle Branch

If you lived at the Demon Castle, you'd be home now!

Deposit and Gratuity Fees: ☆☆☆☆☆☆☆☆☆
Stigmatization: ☆☆☆☆☆☆☆☆☆

DEMON WORLD REAL ESTATE
DEMON CASTLE BRANCH
Navigating Your Career Change

An outside agency that manages the large residential areas of the Demon Castle. The demons who work here are on temporary assignment and are dispatched from the Demon Castle.

The princess and the demons often damage the walls and furnishings in the room rentals, so the department has a hard time maintaining the facilities.

The cheapest rents are near the residences of the undead species. The rents near the cafeteria and the Mechanical Zone are the most expensive.

The upper floor is inhabited only by the Demon King and similar luminaries. This department isn't in charge of those residences.

Recent problem:
"I was stoked when I got hired at the Demon Castle, but this department has no battle duties..."

Current problem:
"Should I request a transfer to another department? Or should I quit entirely and find a new employer...?"

TOO MANY PROPERTIES HAVE BEEN STIGMATIZED BY THE PRINCESS!
HUH? WHAT ABOUT THIS MARK ...?
OH, THAT ONE'S DIFFERENT.
THAT MARKS THE DEATH OF A GHOST SHROUD.
DEATH
STILL THE PRIN-CESS'S FAULT ...

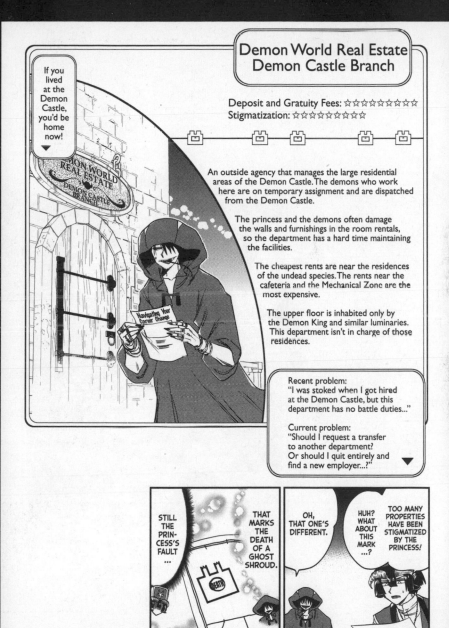

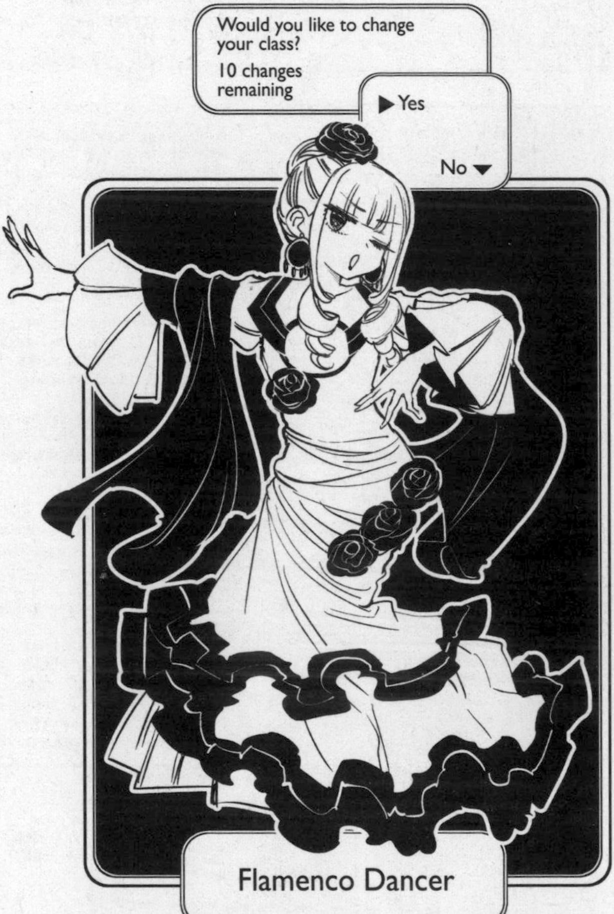
Would you like to change your class?
10 changes remaining
▶Yes
No
Flamenco Dancer
"Olé!!!"

146th Night: Buying People Off with Gifts Is Wrong

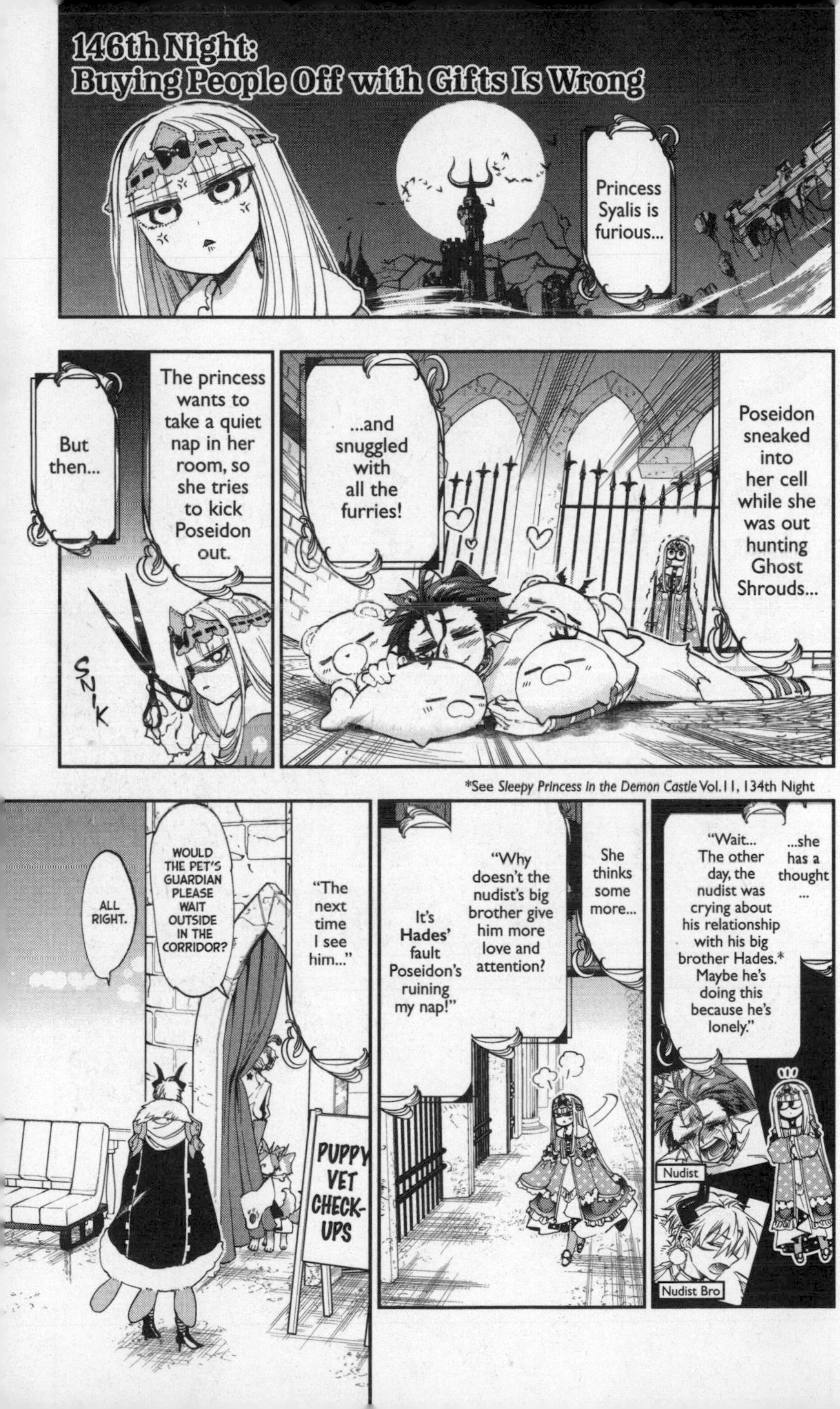
Princess Syalis is furious...
Poseidon sneaked into her cell while she was out hunting Ghost Shrouds...
...and snuggled with all the furries!
The princess wants to take a quiet nap in her room, so she tries to kick Poseidon out.
But then...
SNIK
...she has a thought...
"Wait... The other day, the nudist was crying about his relationship with his big brother Hades.* Maybe he's doing this because he's lonely."
Nudist
Nudist Bro
She thinks some more...
"Why doesn't the nudist's big brother give him more love and attention?
It's Hades' fault Poseidon's ruining my nap!"
"The next time I see him..."
WOULD THE PET'S GUARDIAN PLEASE WAIT OUTSIDE IN THE CORRIDOR?
ALL RIGHT.
PUPPY VET CHECK-UPS

*See *Sleepy Princess In the Demon Castle* Vol.11, 134th Night

146th Night: Buying People Off with Gifts Is Wrong

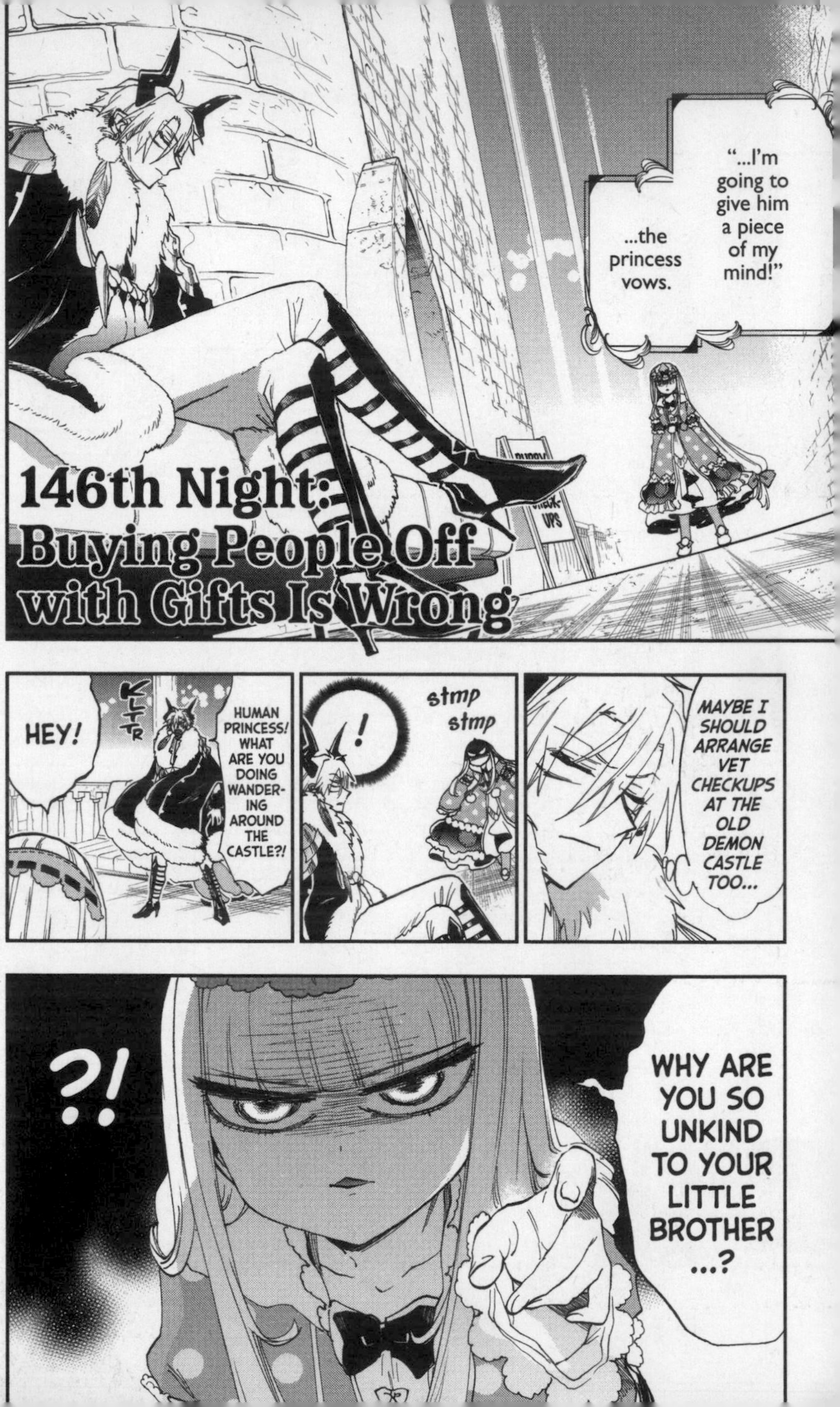

"...I'm going to give him a piece of my mind!"
...the princess vows.
MAYBE I SHOULD ARRANGE VET CHECKUPS AT THE OLD DEMON CASTLE TOO...
stmp stmp
!
HUMAN PRINCESS! WHAT ARE YOU DOING WANDER-ING AROUND THE CASTLE?!
KLTTR
HEY!
WHY ARE YOU SO UNKIND TO YOUR LITTLE BROTHER ...?
?!

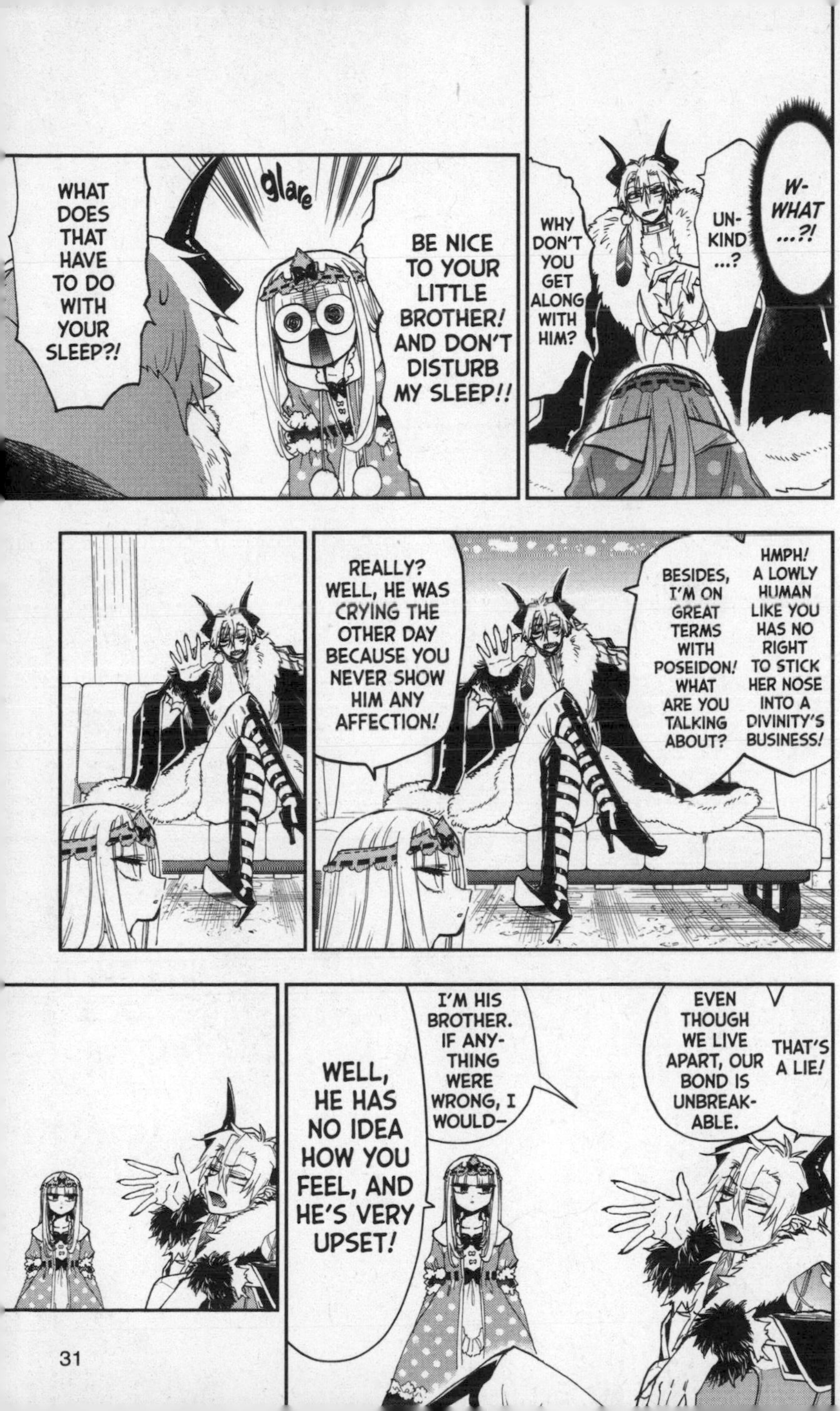
W-WHAT...?!
UN-KIND...?
WHY DON'T YOU GET ALONG WITH HIM?
glare
BE NICE TO YOUR LITTLE BROTHER! AND DON'T DISTURB MY SLEEP!!
WHAT DOES THAT HAVE TO DO WITH YOUR SLEEP?!
HMPH! A LOWLY HUMAN LIKE YOU HAS NO RIGHT TO STICK HER NOSE INTO A DIVINITY'S BUSINESS!
BESIDES, I'M ON GREAT TERMS WITH POSEIDON! WHAT ARE YOU TALKING ABOUT?
REALLY? WELL, HE WAS CRYING THE OTHER DAY BECAUSE YOU NEVER SHOW HIM ANY AFFECTION!
THAT'S A LIE!
EVEN THOUGH WE LIVE APART, OUR BOND IS UNBREAK-ABLE.
I'M HIS BROTHER. IF ANY-THING WERE WRONG, I WOULD–
WELL, HE HAS NO IDEA HOW YOU FEEL, AND HE'S VERY UPSET!

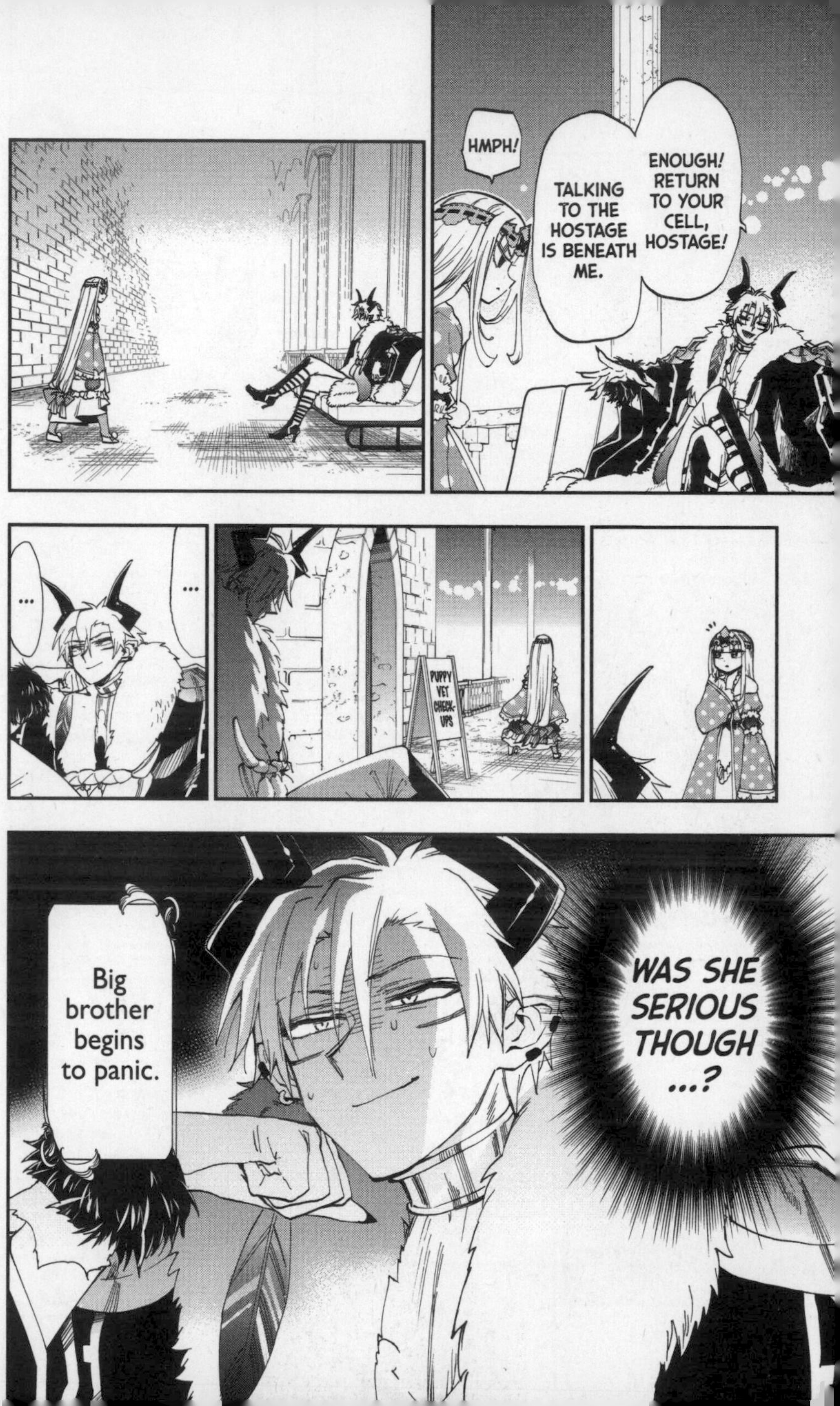
ENOUGH! RETURN TO YOUR CELL, HOSTAGE!
TALKING TO THE HOSTAGE IS BENEATH ME.
HMPH!
PUPPY VET CHECK-UPS
...
...
WAS SHE SERIOUS THOUGH ...?
Big brother begins to panic.

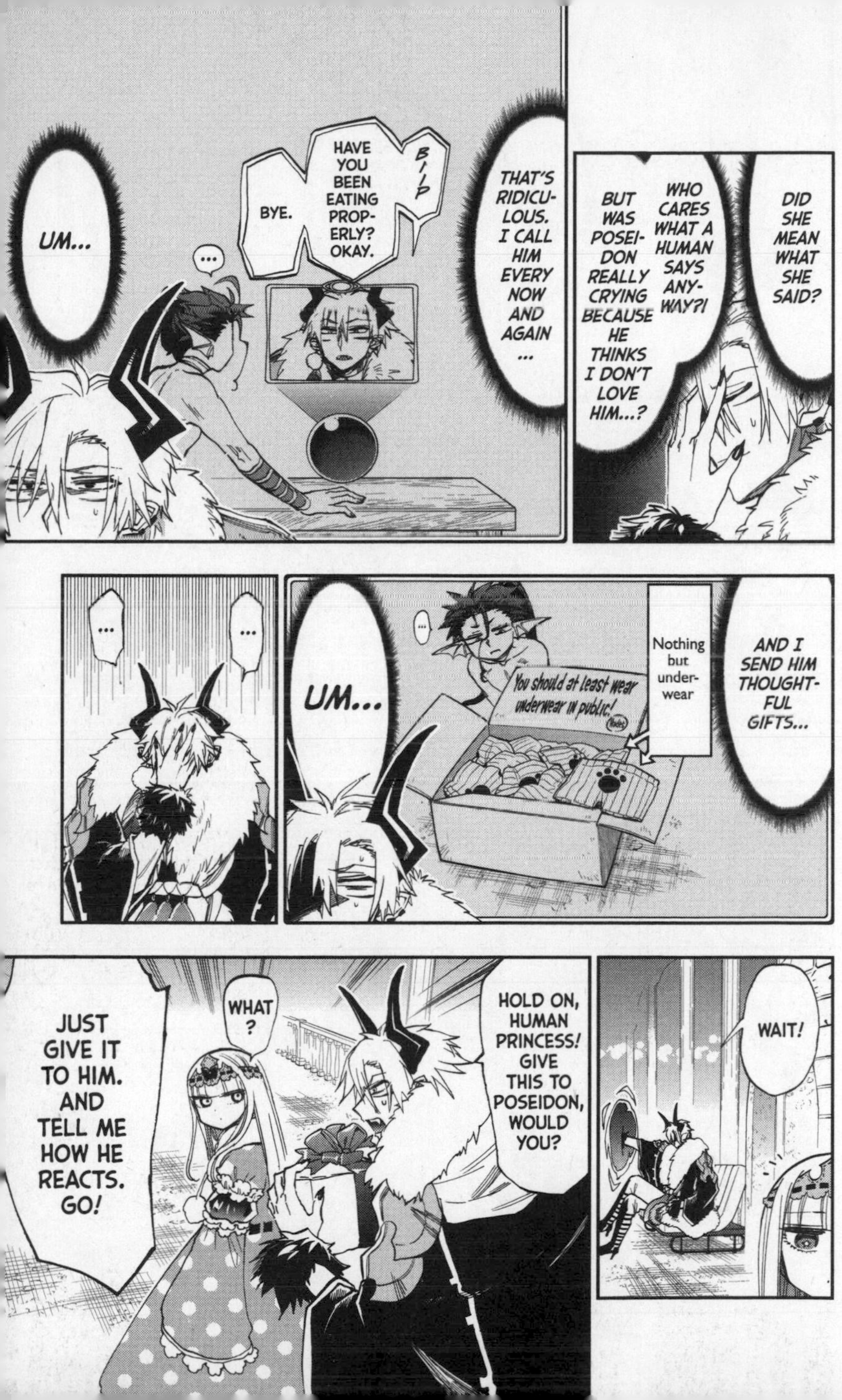
DID SHE MEAN WHAT SHE SAID?
WHO CARES WHAT A HUMAN SAYS ANYWAY?!
BUT WAS POSEIDON REALLY CRYING BECAUSE HE THINKS I DON'T LOVE HIM...?
THAT'S RIDICULOUS. I CALL HIM EVERY NOW AND AGAIN...
BIIP
HAVE YOU BEEN EATING PROPERLY? OKAY.
BYE.
...
UM...
AND I SEND HIM THOUGHTFUL GIFTS...
Nothing but underwear
You should at least wear underwear in public!
...
UM...
...
...
WAIT!
HOLD ON, HUMAN PRINCESS! GIVE THIS TO POSEIDON, WOULD YOU?
WHAT?
JUST GIVE IT TO HIM. AND TELL ME HOW HE REACTS. GO!

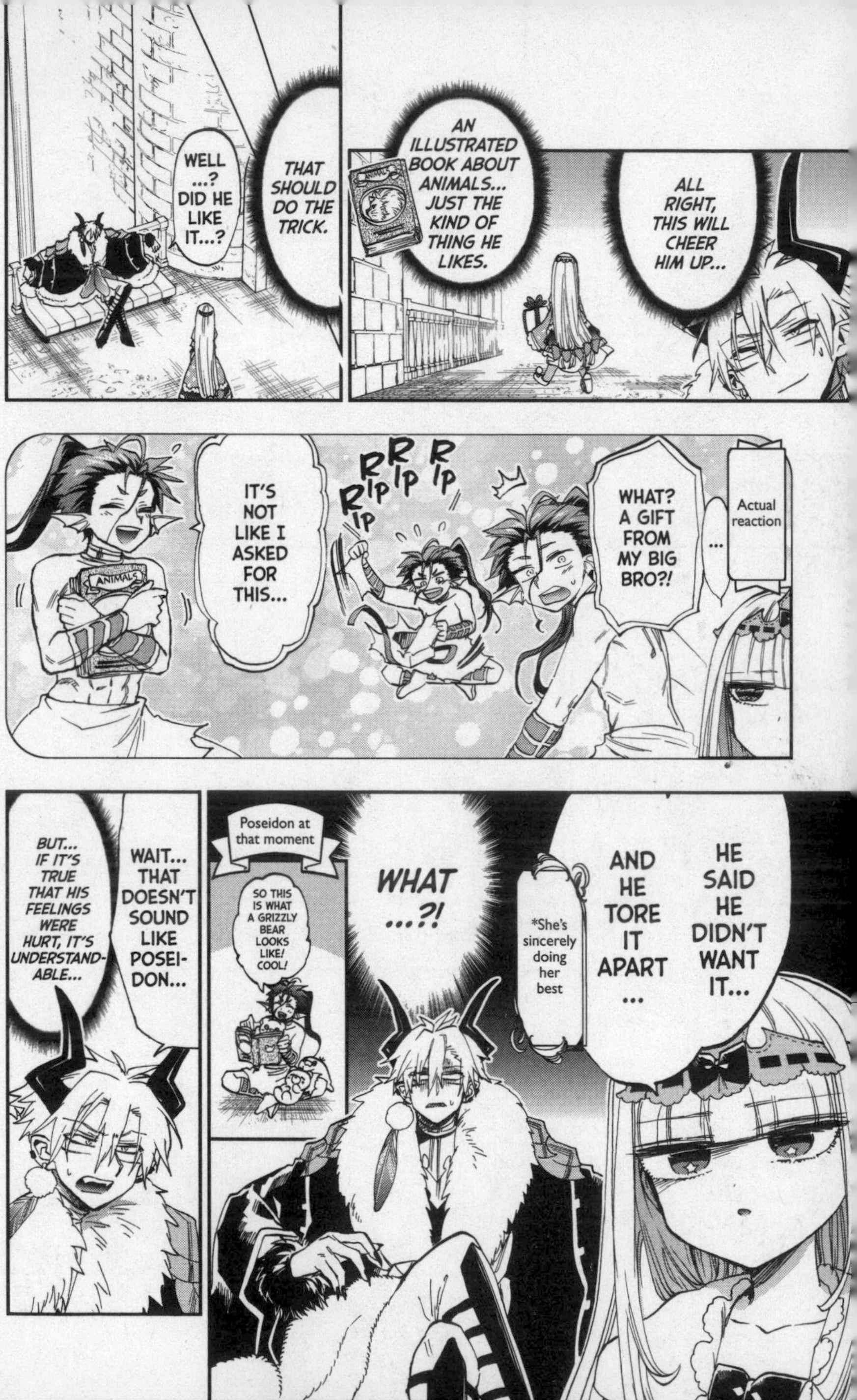
ALL RIGHT, THIS WILL CHEER HIM UP...
AN ILLUSTRATED BOOK ABOUT ANIMALS... JUST THE KIND OF THING HE LIKES.
ANIMALS
THAT SHOULD DO THE TRICK.
WELL ...? DID HE LIKE IT...?
Actual reaction
...
WHAT? A GIFT FROM MY BIG BRO?!
RIP RIP RIP RIP
IT'S NOT LIKE I ASKED FOR THIS...
ANIMALS
HE SAID HE DIDN'T WANT IT...
AND HE TORE IT APART ...
*She's sincerely doing her best
WHAT ...?!
Poseidon at that moment
SO THIS IS WHAT A GRIZZLY BEAR LOOKS LIKE! COOL!
WAIT... THAT DOESN'T SOUND LIKE POSEI-DON...
BUT... IF IT'S TRUE THAT HIS FEELINGS WERE HURT, IT'S UNDERSTAND-ABLE...

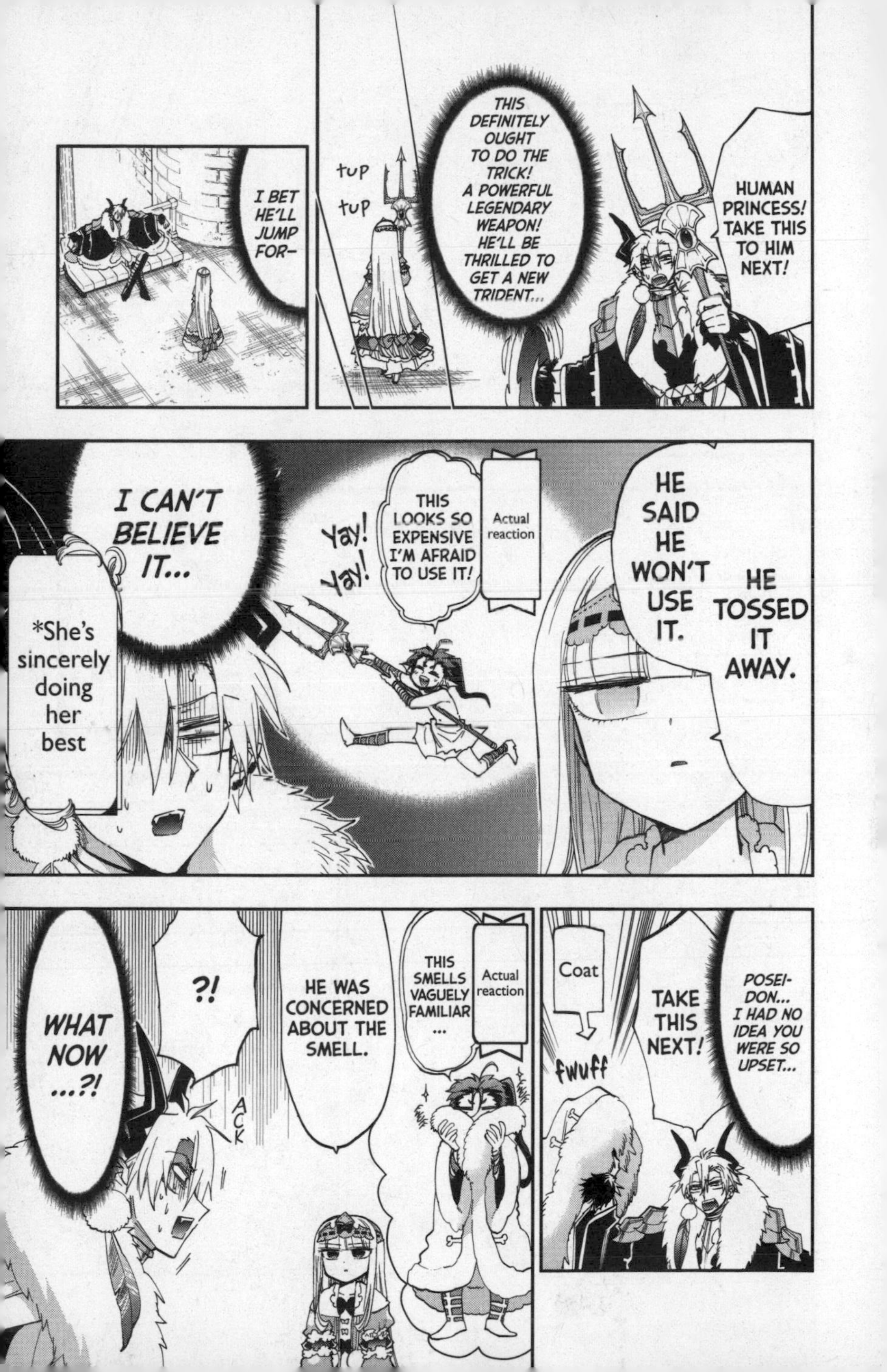
HUMAN PRINCESS! TAKE THIS TO HIM NEXT!
THIS DEFINITELY OUGHT TO DO THE TRICK! A POWERFUL LEGENDARY WEAPON! HE'LL BE THRILLED TO GET A NEW TRIDENT...
tup
tup
I BET HE'LL JUMP FOR–
HE SAID HE WON'T USE IT.
HE TOSSED IT AWAY.
Actual reaction
THIS LOOKS SO EXPENSIVE I'M AFRAID TO USE IT!
Yay!
Yay!
I CAN'T BELIEVE IT...
*She's sincerely doing her best
POSEIDON... I HAD NO IDEA YOU WERE SO UPSET...
TAKE THIS NEXT!
Coat
fwuff
Actual reaction
THIS SMELLS VAGUELY FAMILIAR ...
HE WAS CONCERNED ABOUT THE SMELL.
?!
ACK
WHAT NOW ...?!

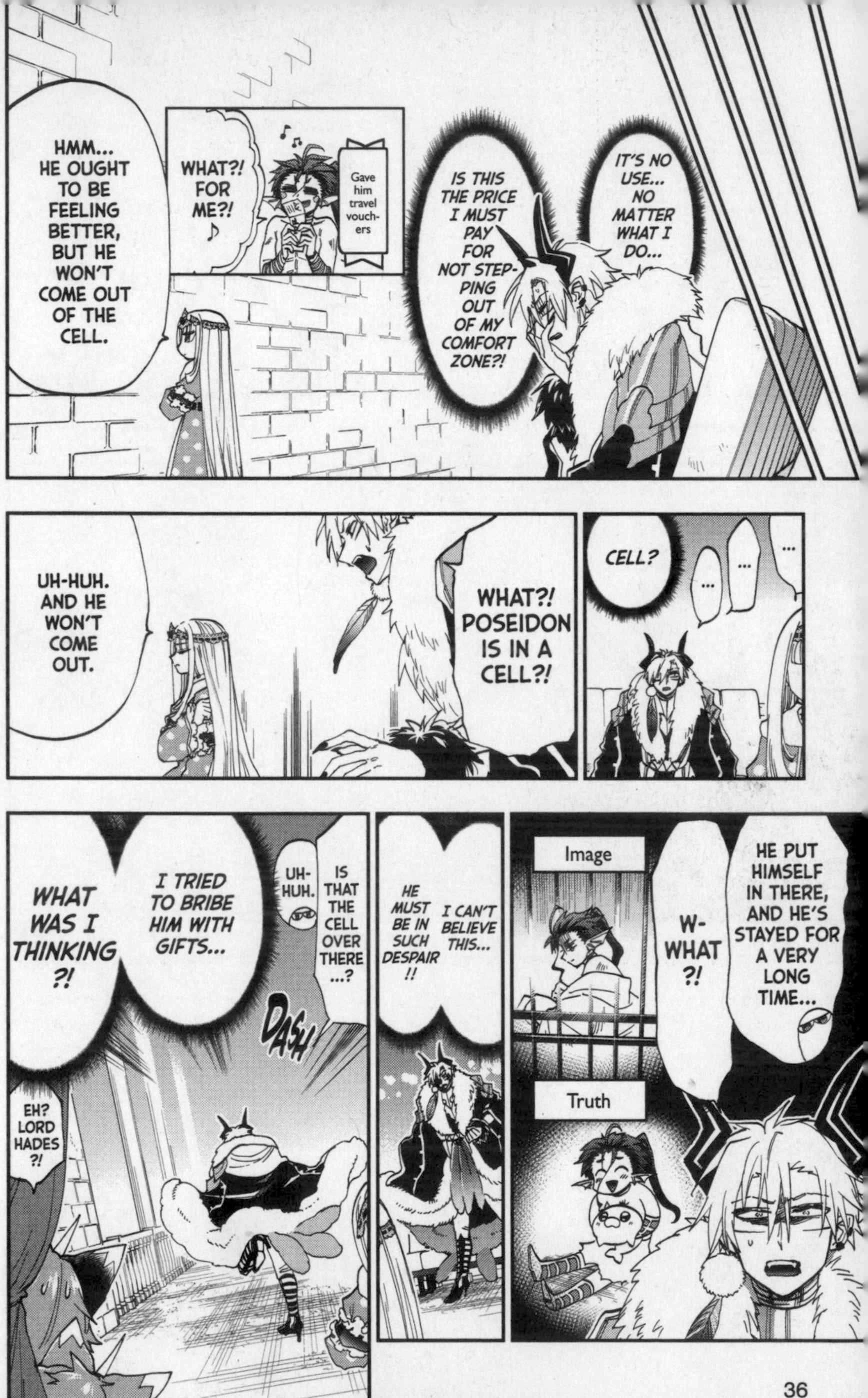
IT'S NO USE... NO MATTER WHAT I DO...
IS THIS THE PRICE I MUST PAY FOR NOT STEPPING OUT OF MY COMFORT ZONE?!
WHAT?! FOR ME?! ♪
Gave him travel vouchers
HMM... HE OUGHT TO BE FEELING BETTER, BUT HE WON'T COME OUT OF THE CELL.
...
...
...
CELL?
WHAT?! POSEIDON IS IN A CELL?!
UH-HUH. AND HE WON'T COME OUT.
HE PUT HIMSELF IN THERE, AND HE'S STAYED FOR A VERY LONG TIME...
W-WHAT?!
Image
Truth
I CAN'T BELIEVE THIS...
HE MUST BE IN SUCH DESPAIR!!
IS THAT THE CELL OVER THERE...?
UH-HUH.
I TRIED TO BRIBE HIM WITH GIFTS...
WHAT WAS I THINKING?!
DASH
EH? LORD HADES?!

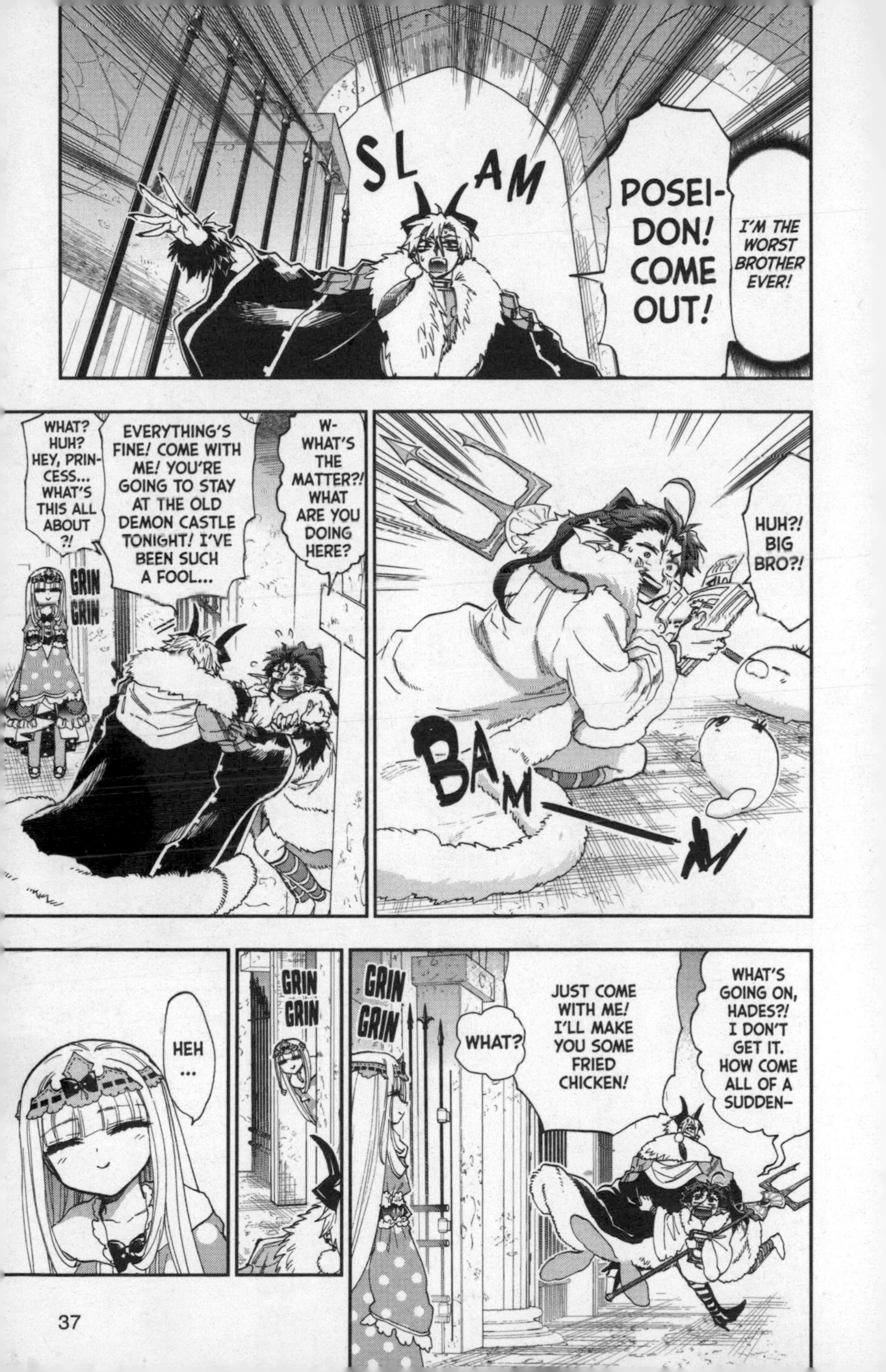
I'M THE WORST BROTHER EVER!
POSEI-DON! COME OUT!
SLAM
HUH?! BIG BRO?!
BAM
W-WHAT'S THE MATTER?! WHAT ARE YOU DOING HERE?
EVERYTHING'S FINE! COME WITH ME! YOU'RE GOING TO STAY AT THE OLD DEMON CASTLE TONIGHT! I'VE BEEN SUCH A FOOL...
WHAT? HUH? HEY, PRIN-CESS... WHAT'S THIS ALL ABOUT?!
GRIN GRIN
WHAT'S GOING ON, HADES?! I DON'T GET IT. HOW COME ALL OF A SUDDEN–
JUST COME WITH ME! I'LL MAKE YOU SOME FRIED CHICKEN!
WHAT?
GRIN GRIN
GRIN GRIN
HEH...

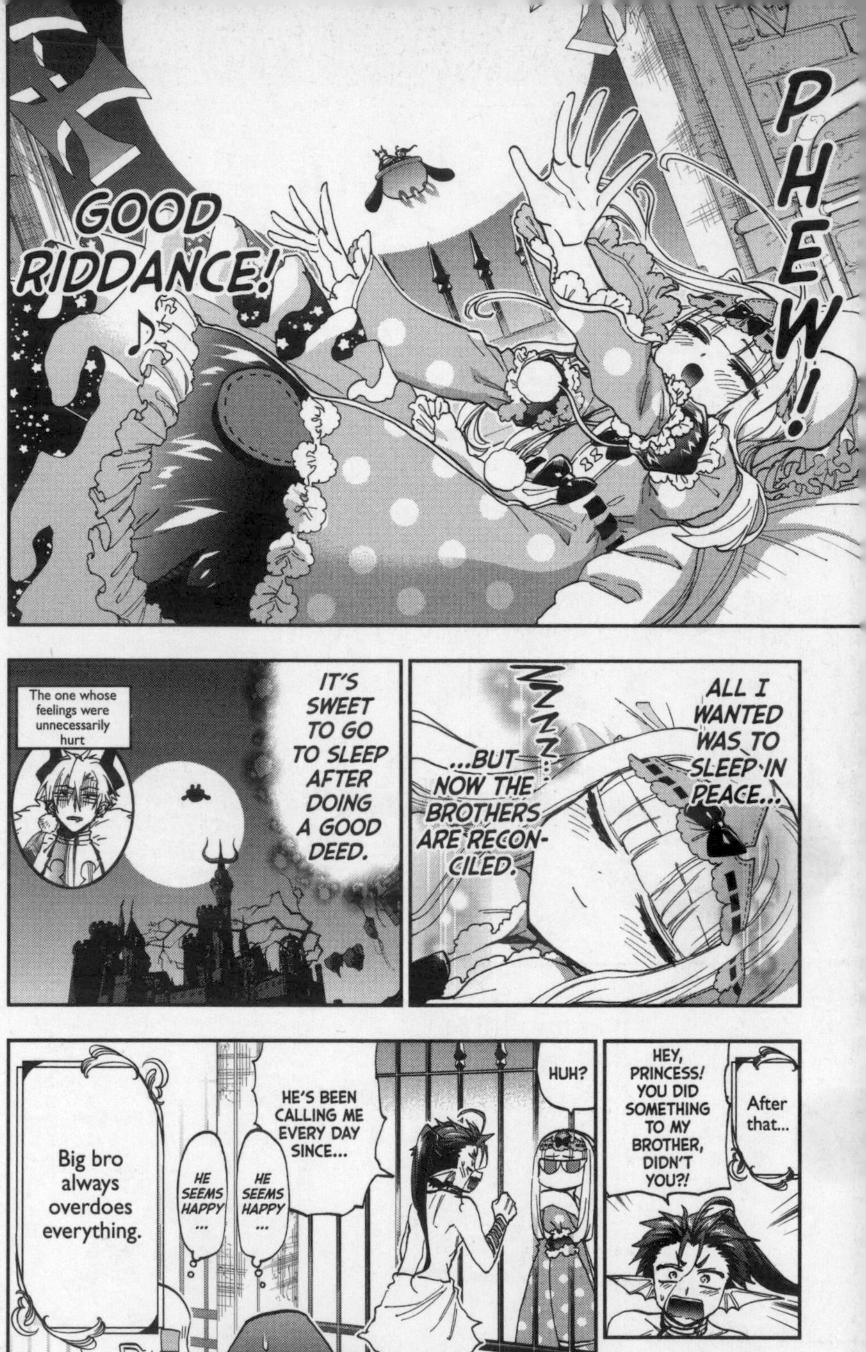
PHEW!
GOOD RIDDANCE!
ALL I WANTED WAS TO SLEEP IN PEACE...
ZZZZ...
...BUT NOW THE BROTHERS ARE RECONCILED.
IT'S SWEET TO GO TO SLEEP AFTER DOING A GOOD DEED.
The one whose feelings were unnecessarily hurt
After that...
HEY, PRINCESS! YOU DID SOMETHING TO MY BROTHER, DIDN'T YOU?!
HUH?
HE'S BEEN CALLING ME EVERY DAY SINCE...
HE SEEMS HAPPY...
HE SEEMS HAPPY...
Big bro always overdoes everything.

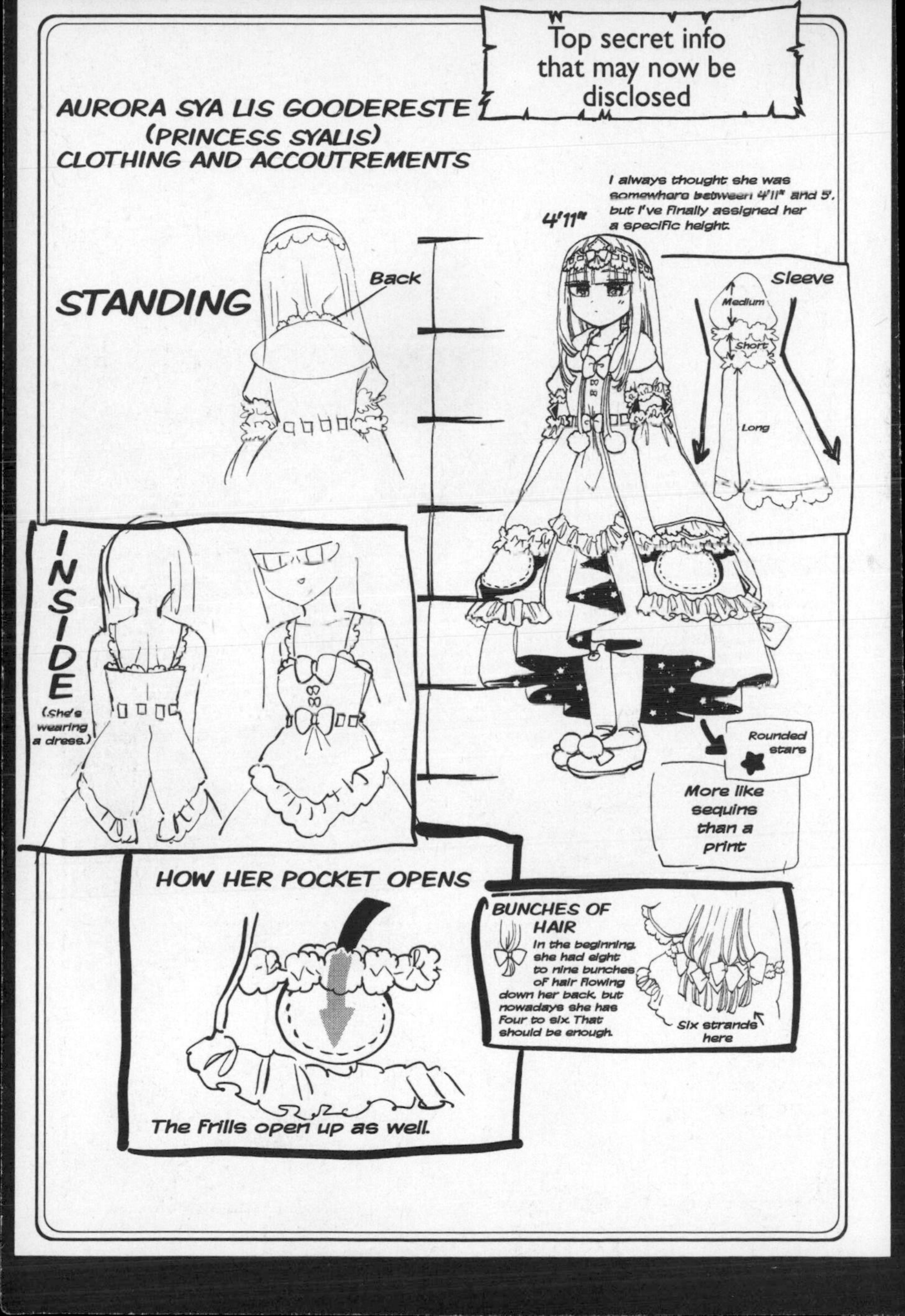
Top secret info that may now be disclosed
AURORA SYA LIS GOODERESTE (PRINCESS SYALIS) CLOTHING AND ACCOUTREMENTS
I always thought she was somewhere between 4'11" and 5', but I've finally assigned her a specific height.
4'11"
STANDING
Back
Sleeve
Medium
Short
Long
INSIDE
(She's wearing a dress.)
Rounded stars
More like sequins than a print
HOW HER POCKET OPENS
The Frills open up as well.
BUNCHES OF HAIR
In the beginning, she had eight to nine bunches of hair flowing down her back, but nowadays she has four to six. That should be enough.
Six strands here

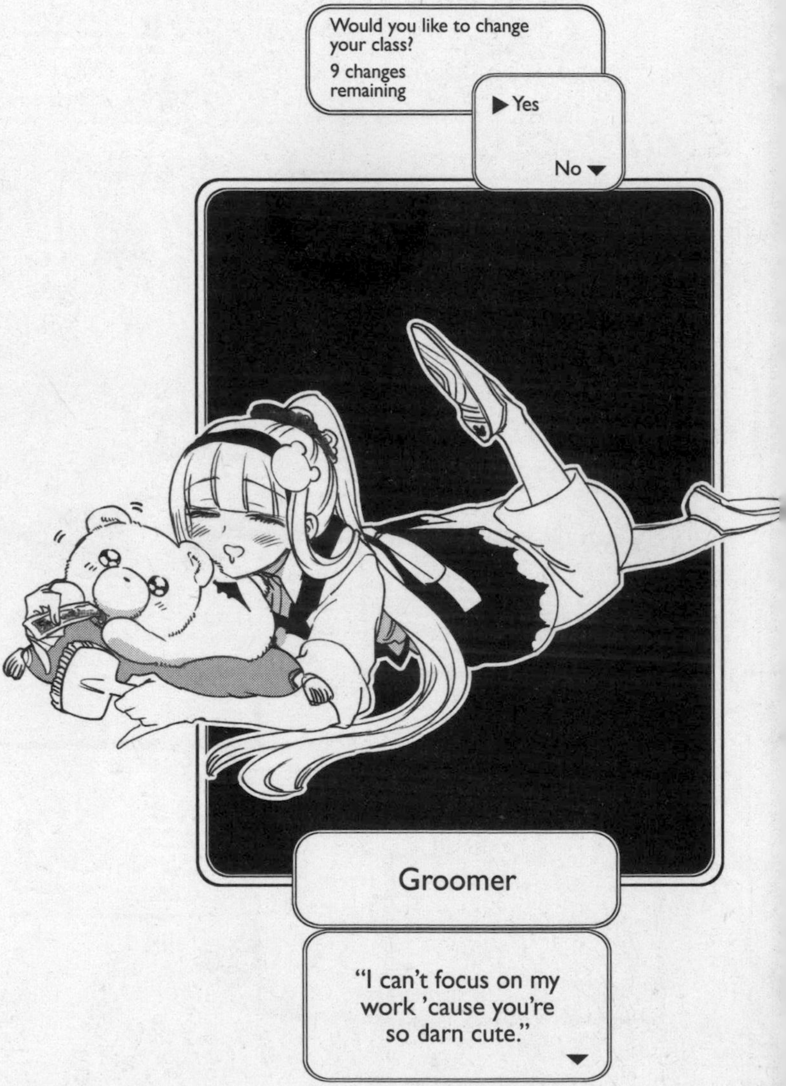
Would you like to change your class?
9 changes remaining
▶Yes
No
Groomer
"I can't focus on my work 'cause you're so darn cute."

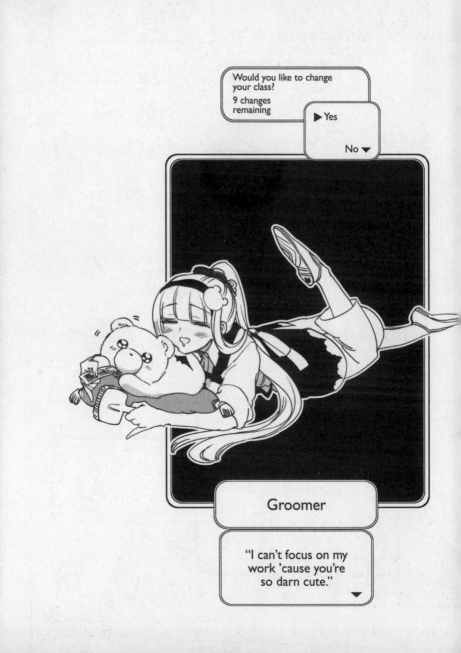

147th Night: Princess Sya Lis and the Chamber of Secrets

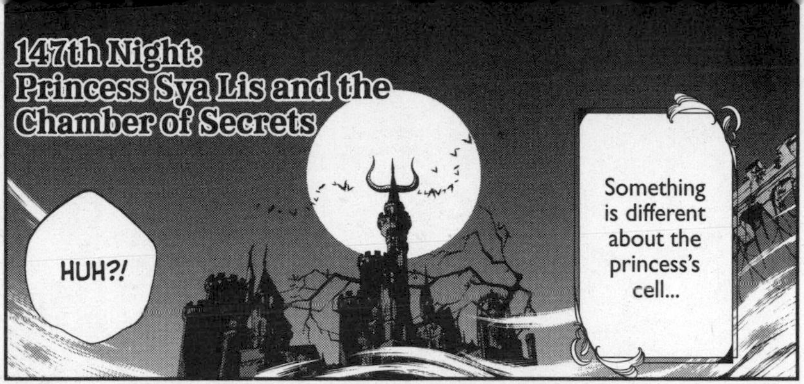
Something is different about the princess's cell...
HUH?!

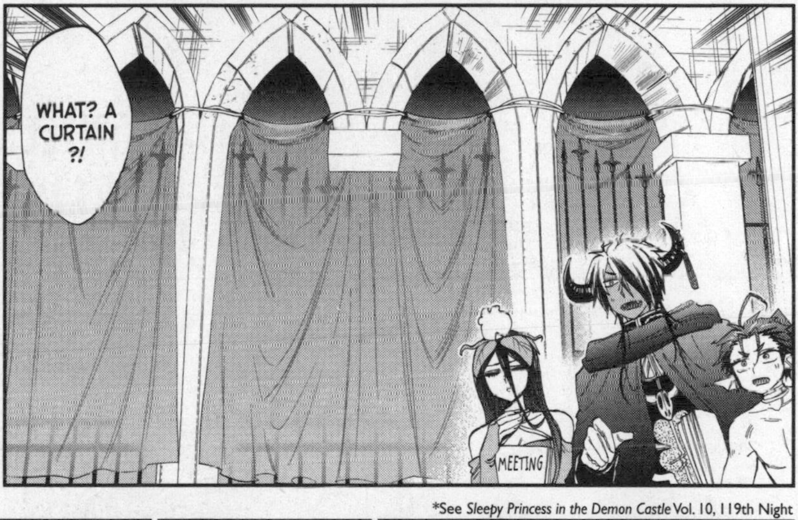
WHAT? A CURTAIN ?!
MEETING

*See *Sleepy Princess in the Demon Castle* Vol. 10, 119th Night

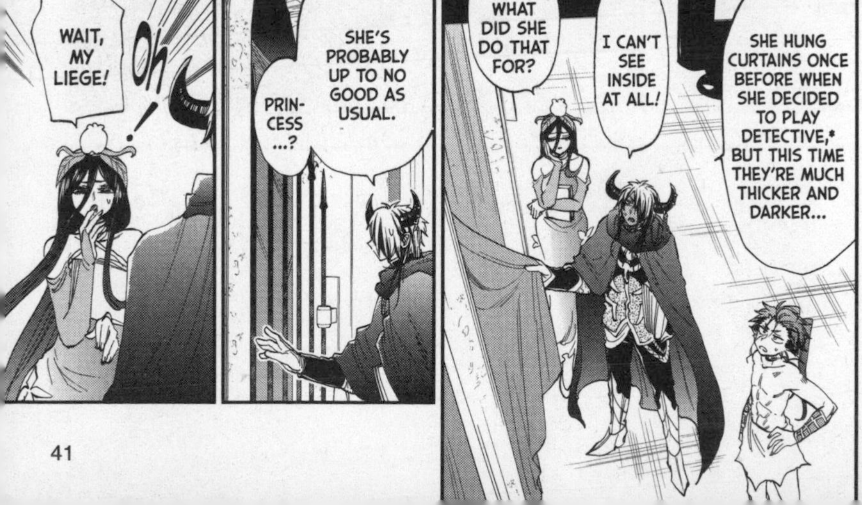
SHE HUNG CURTAINS ONCE BEFORE WHEN SHE DECIDED TO PLAY DETECTIVE,* BUT THIS TIME THEY'RE MUCH THICKER AND DARKER...
I CAN'T SEE INSIDE AT ALL!
WHAT DID SHE DO THAT FOR?
SHE'S PROBABLY UP TO NO GOOD AS USUAL.
PRIN-CESS ...?
Oh !
WAIT, MY LIEGE!

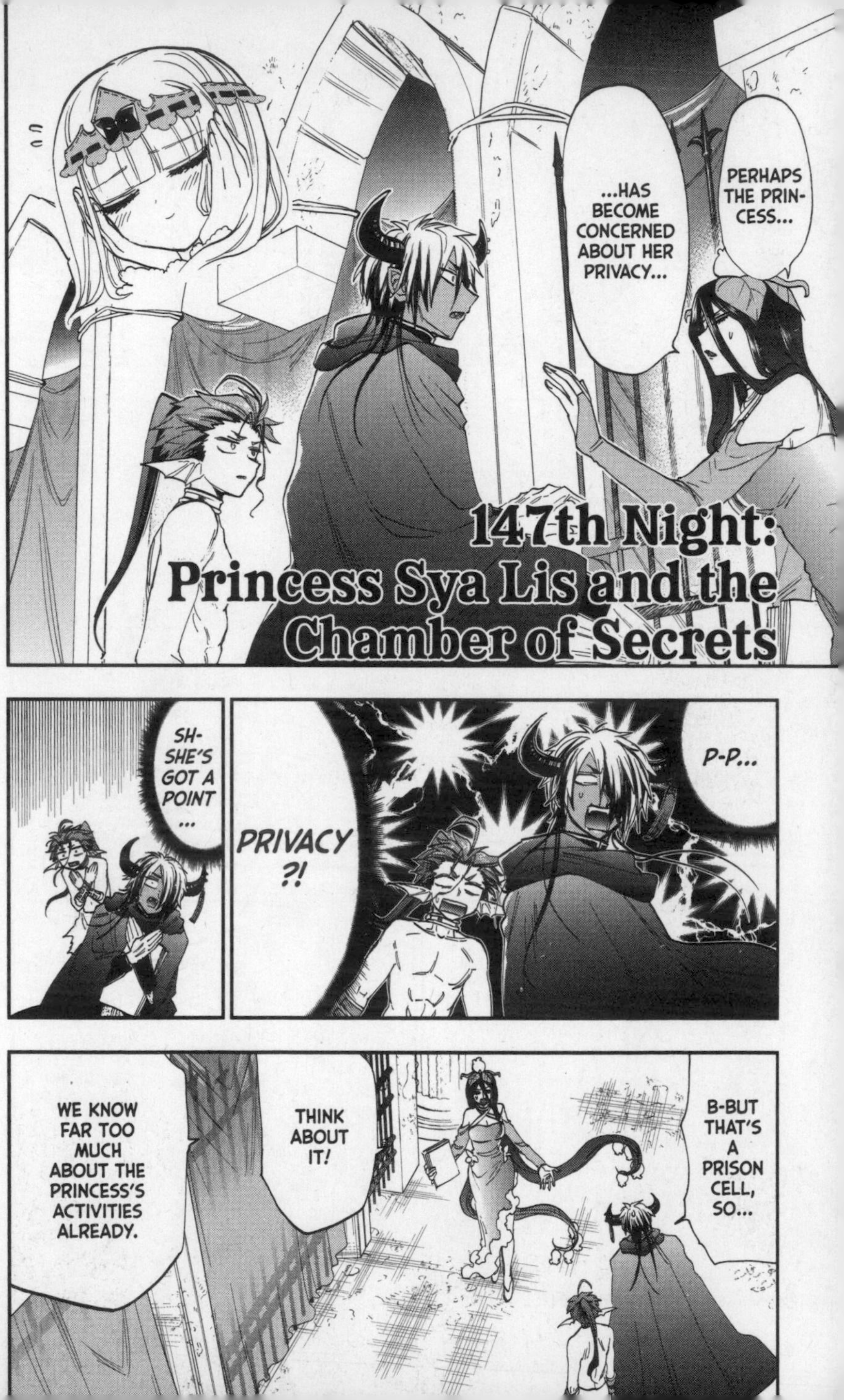
PERHAPS THE PRINCESS...
...HAS BECOME CONCERNED ABOUT HER PRIVACY...
147th Night: Princess Sya Lis and the Chamber of Secrets
P-P...
PRIVACY ?!
SH-SHE'S GOT A POINT ...
B-BUT THAT'S A PRISON CELL, SO...
THINK ABOUT IT!
WE KNOW FAR TOO MUCH ABOUT THE PRINCESS'S ACTIVITIES ALREADY.

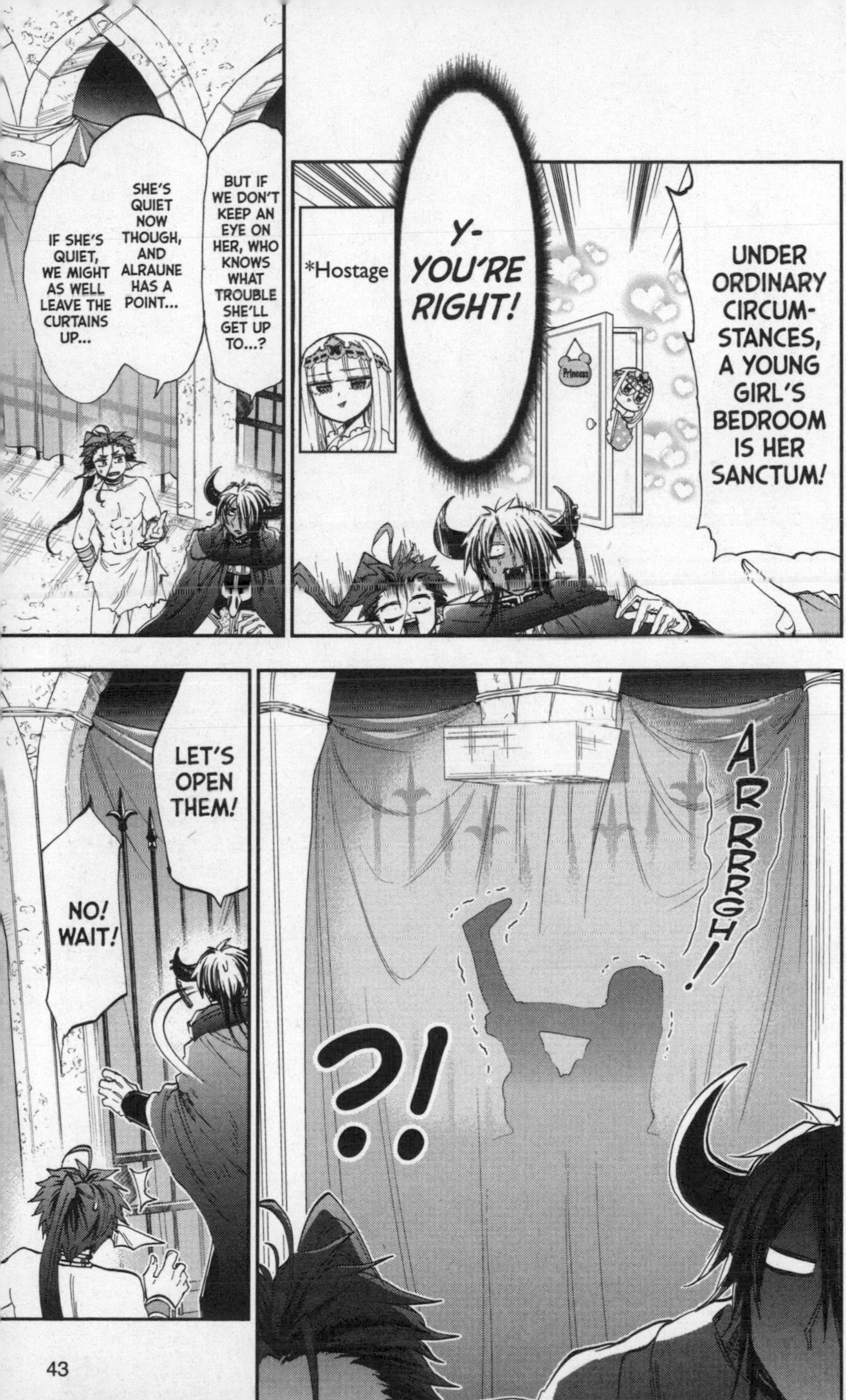

UNDER ORDINARY CIRCUMSTANCES, A YOUNG GIRL'S BEDROOM IS HER SANCTUM!
Y-YOU'RE RIGHT!
*Hostage
BUT IF WE DON'T KEEP AN EYE ON HER, WHO KNOWS WHAT TROUBLE SHE'LL GET UP TO...?
SHE'S QUIET NOW THOUGH, AND ALRAUNE HAS A POINT...
IF SHE'S QUIET, WE MIGHT AS WELL LEAVE THE CURTAINS UP...
ARRRRGH!
?!
LET'S OPEN THEM!
NO! WAIT!

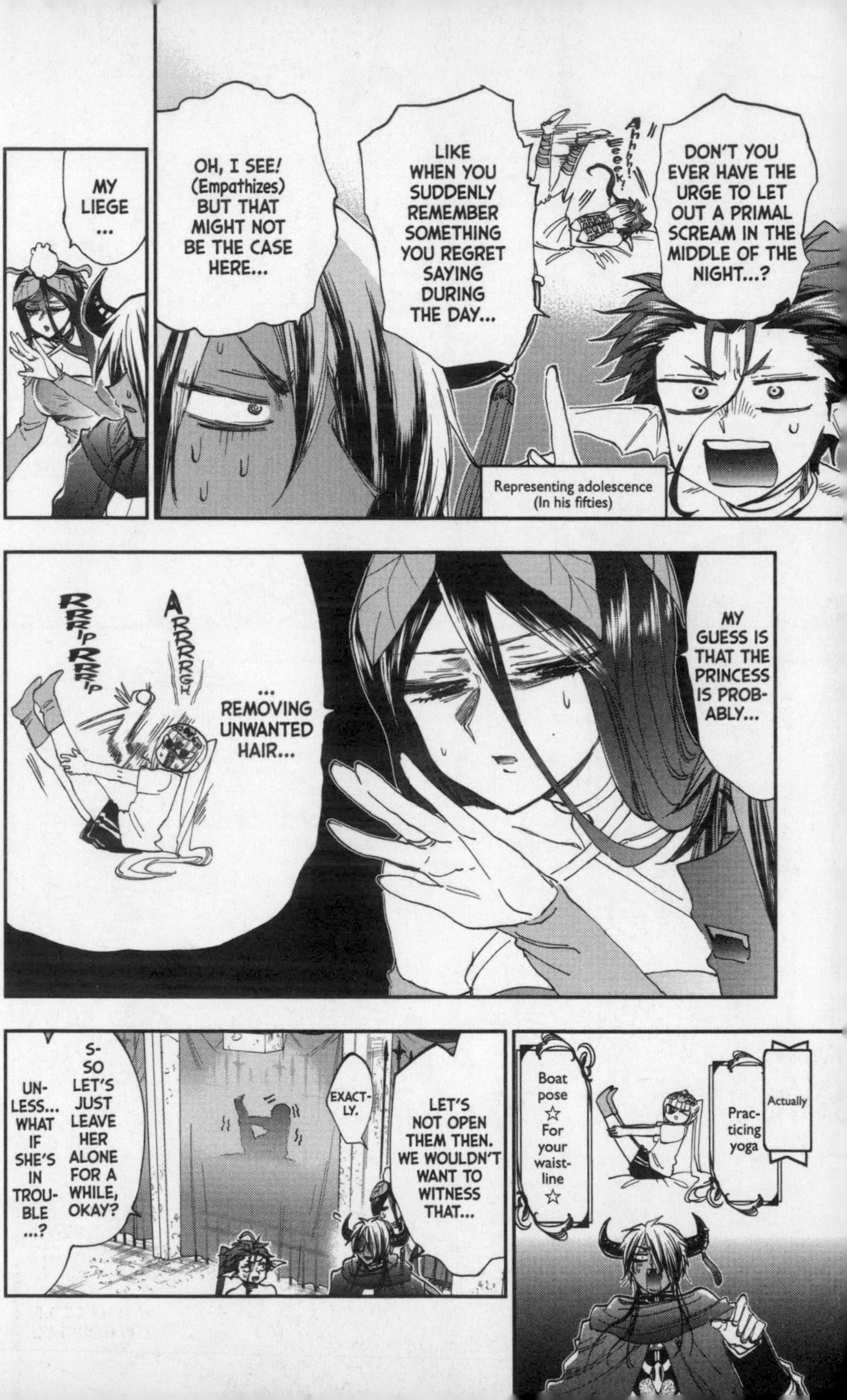
DON'T YOU EVER HAVE THE URGE TO LET OUT A PRIMAL SCREAM IN THE MIDDLE OF THE NIGHT...?
Ahhh!
Eeeek!
Representing adolescence (In his fifties)
LIKE WHEN YOU SUDDENLY REMEMBER SOMETHING YOU REGRET SAYING DURING THE DAY...
OH, I SEE! (Empathizes) BUT THAT MIGHT NOT BE THE CASE HERE...
MY LIEGE ...
MY GUESS IS THAT THE PRINCESS IS PROBABLY...
... REMOVING UNWANTED HAIR...
ARRRRGH
RRRIP RRRIP
Actually
Practicing yoga
Boat pose ☆ For your waistline ☆
LET'S NOT OPEN THEM THEN. WE WOULDN'T WANT TO WITNESS THAT...
EXACTLY.
S-SO LET'S JUST LEAVE HER ALONE FOR A WHILE, OKAY?
UNLESS... WHAT IF SHE'S IN TROUBLE...?

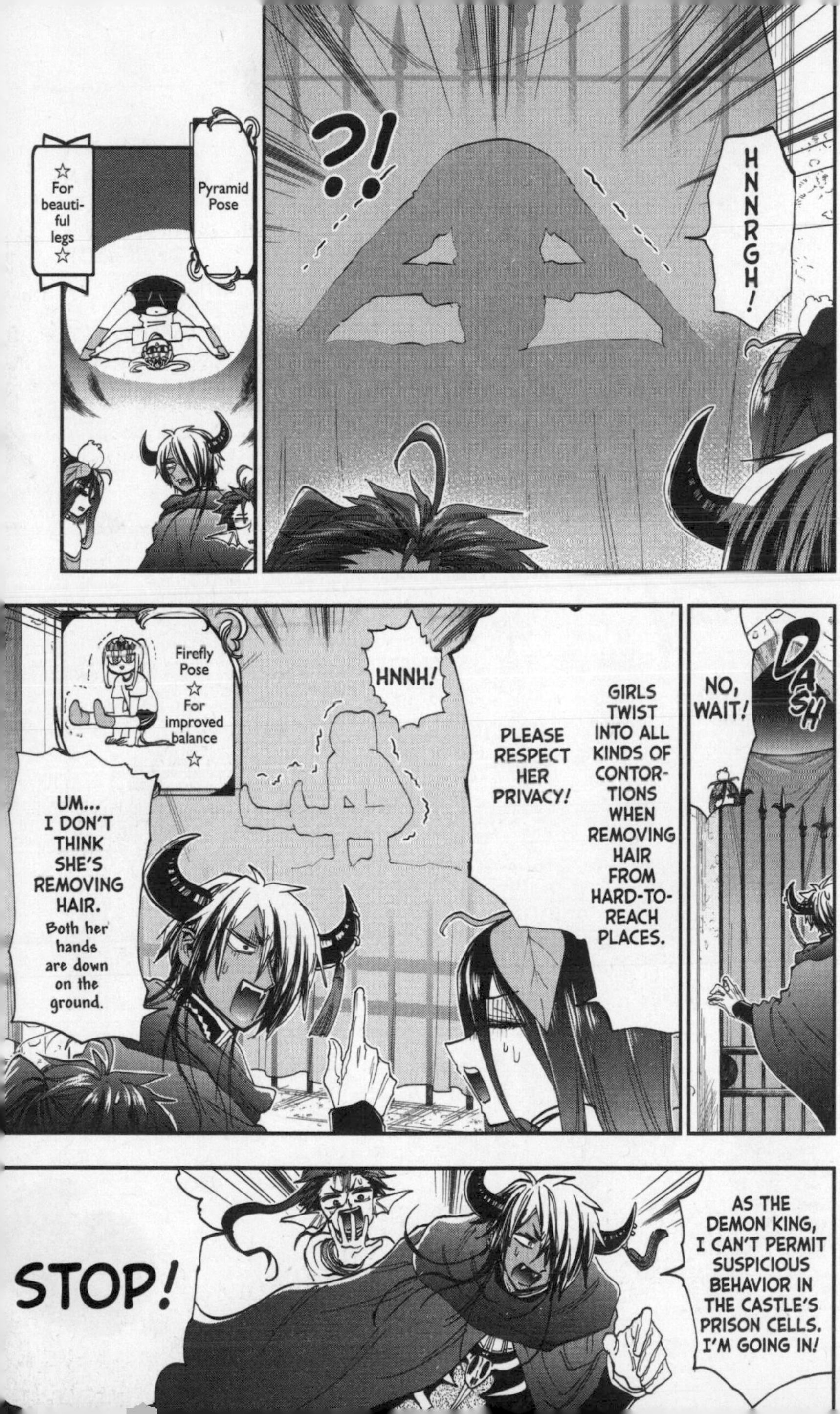
?!
HNNRGH!
Pyramid Pose
☆ For beautiful legs ☆
DASH
NO, WAIT!
GIRLS TWIST INTO ALL KINDS OF CONTORTIONS WHEN REMOVING HAIR FROM HARD-TO-REACH PLACES.
HNNH!
PLEASE RESPECT HER PRIVACY!
Firefly Pose ☆ For improved balance ☆
UM... I DON'T THINK SHE'S REMOVING HAIR.
Both her hands are down on the ground.
AS THE DEMON KING, I CAN'T PERMIT SUSPICIOUS BEHAVIOR IN THE CASTLE'S PRISON CELLS. I'M GOING IN!
STOP!

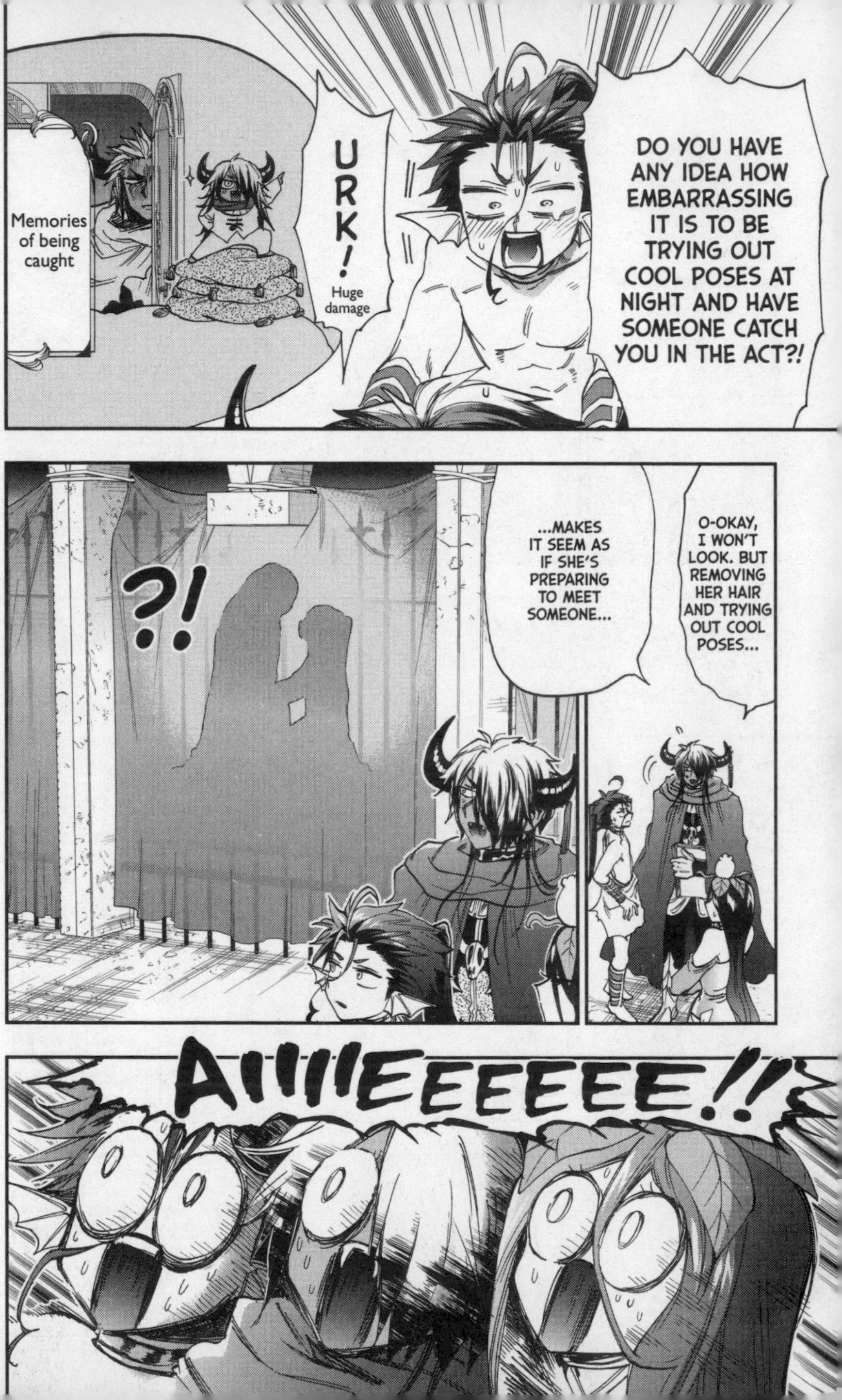
DO YOU HAVE ANY IDEA HOW EMBARRASSING IT IS TO BE TRYING OUT COOL POSES AT NIGHT AND HAVE SOMEONE CATCH YOU IN THE ACT?!
URK!
Huge damage
Memories of being caught
O-OKAY, I WON'T LOOK. BUT REMOVING HER HAIR AND TRYING OUT COOL POSES...
...MAKES IT SEEM AS IF SHE'S PREPARING TO MEET SOMEONE...
?!
AIIIEEEEEE!!

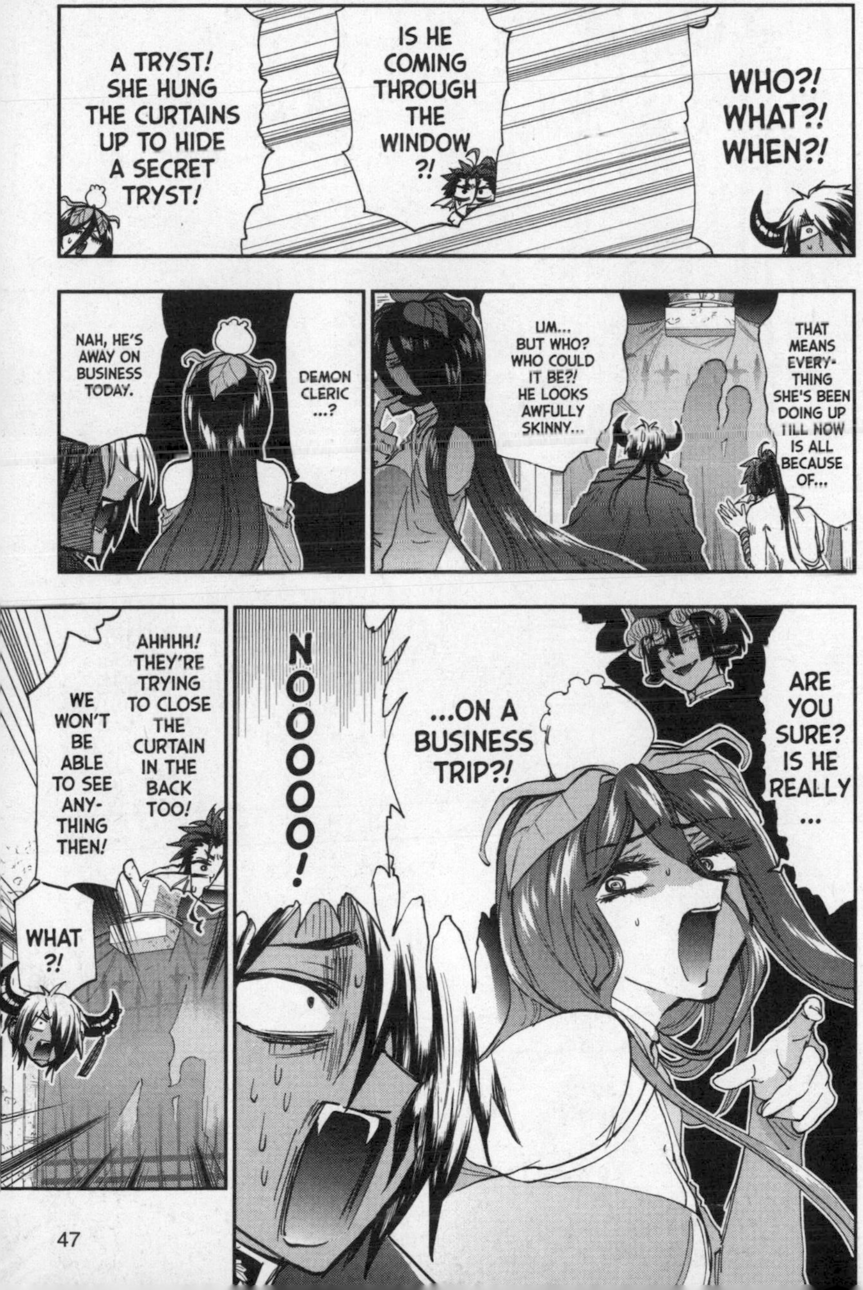
WHO?! WHAT?! WHEN?!
IS HE COMING THROUGH THE WINDOW?!
A TRYST! SHE HUNG THE CURTAINS UP TO HIDE A SECRET TRYST!
THAT MEANS EVERYTHING SHE'S BEEN DOING UP TILL NOW IS ALL BECAUSE OF...
UM... BUT WHO? WHO COULD IT BE?! HE LOOKS AWFULLY SKINNY...
DEMON CLERIC ...?
NAH, HE'S AWAY ON BUSINESS TODAY.
ARE YOU SURE? IS HE REALLY ...
...ON A BUSINESS TRIP?!
NOOOOO!
AHHHH! THEY'RE TRYING TO CLOSE THE CURTAIN IN THE BACK TOO!
WE WON'T BE ABLE TO SEE ANYTHING THEN!
WHAT?!

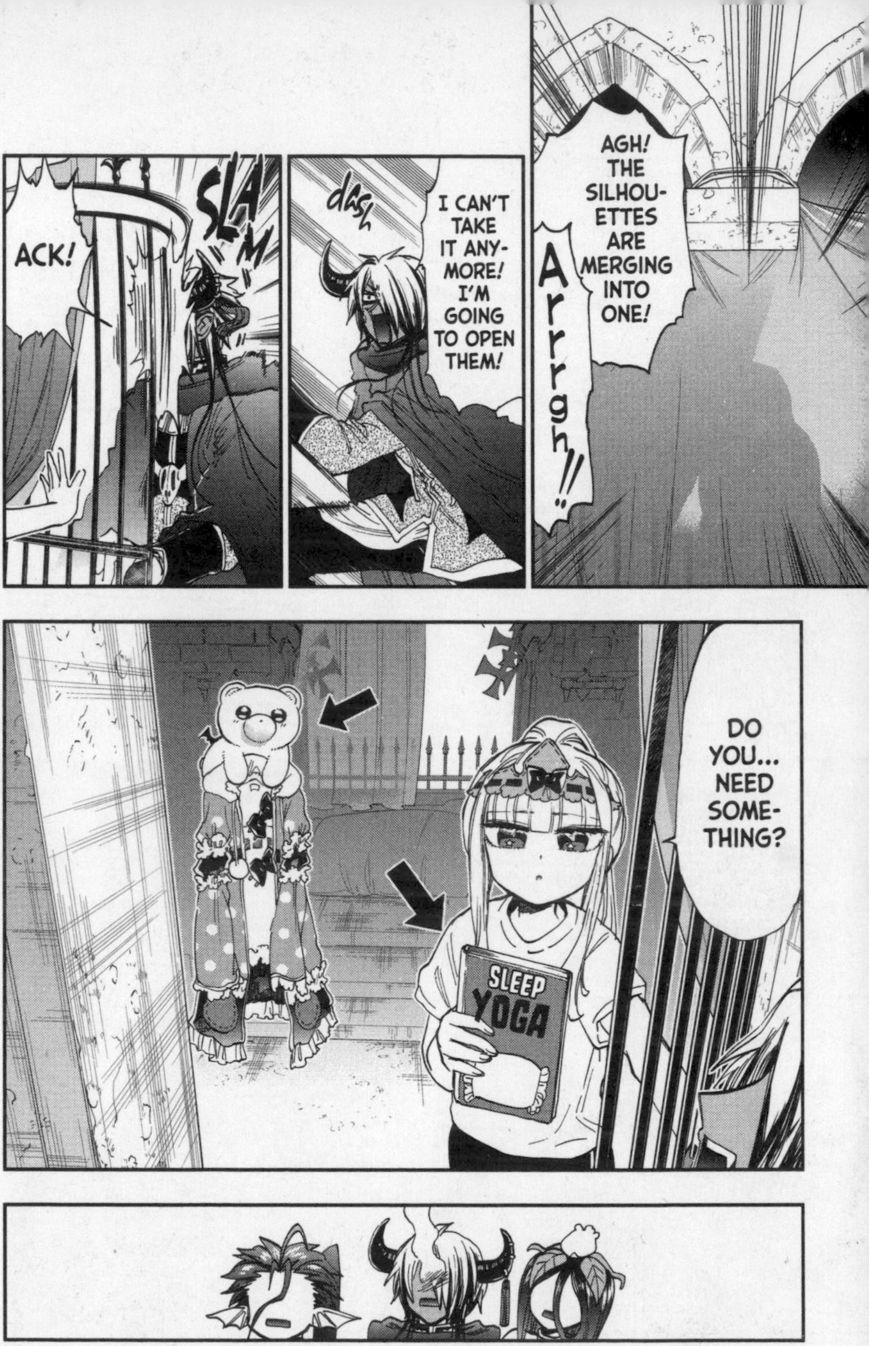
AGH! THE SILHOUETTES ARE MERGING INTO ONE!
Arrrgh!!
dash
I CAN'T TAKE IT ANYMORE! I'M GOING TO OPEN THEM!
SLAM
ACK!
DO YOU... NEED SOMETHING?
SLEEP YOGA

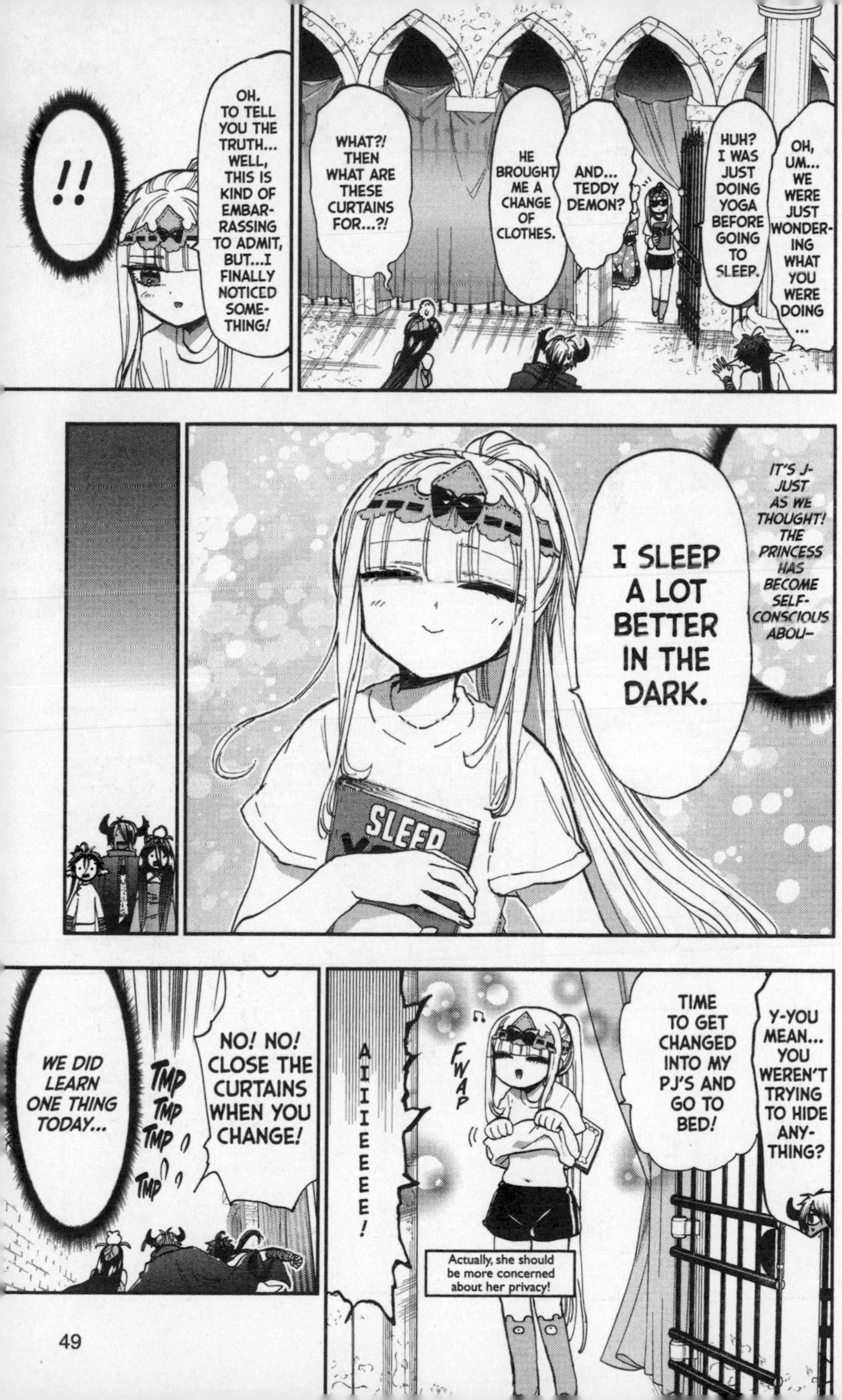

OH, UM... WE WERE JUST WONDERING WHAT YOU WERE DOING...
HUH? I WAS JUST DOING YOGA BEFORE GOING TO SLEEP.
AND... TEDDY DEMON?
HE BROUGHT ME A CHANGE OF CLOTHES.
WHAT?! THEN WHAT ARE THESE CURTAINS FOR...?!
OH. TO TELL YOU THE TRUTH... WELL, THIS IS KIND OF EMBARRASSING TO ADMIT, BUT...I FINALLY NOTICED SOMETHING!
!!
IT'S J-JUST AS WE THOUGHT! THE PRINCESS HAS BECOME SELF-CONSCIOUS ABOU-
I SLEEP A LOT BETTER IN THE DARK.
SLEEP
Y-YOU MEAN... YOU WEREN'T TRYING TO HIDE ANYTHING?
TIME TO GET CHANGED INTO MY PJ'S AND GO TO BED!
FWAP
AIIIEEEE!
Actually, she should be more concerned about her privacy!
NO! NO! CLOSE THE CURTAINS WHEN YOU CHANGE!
TMP TMP TMP TMP
WE DID LEARN ONE THING TODAY...

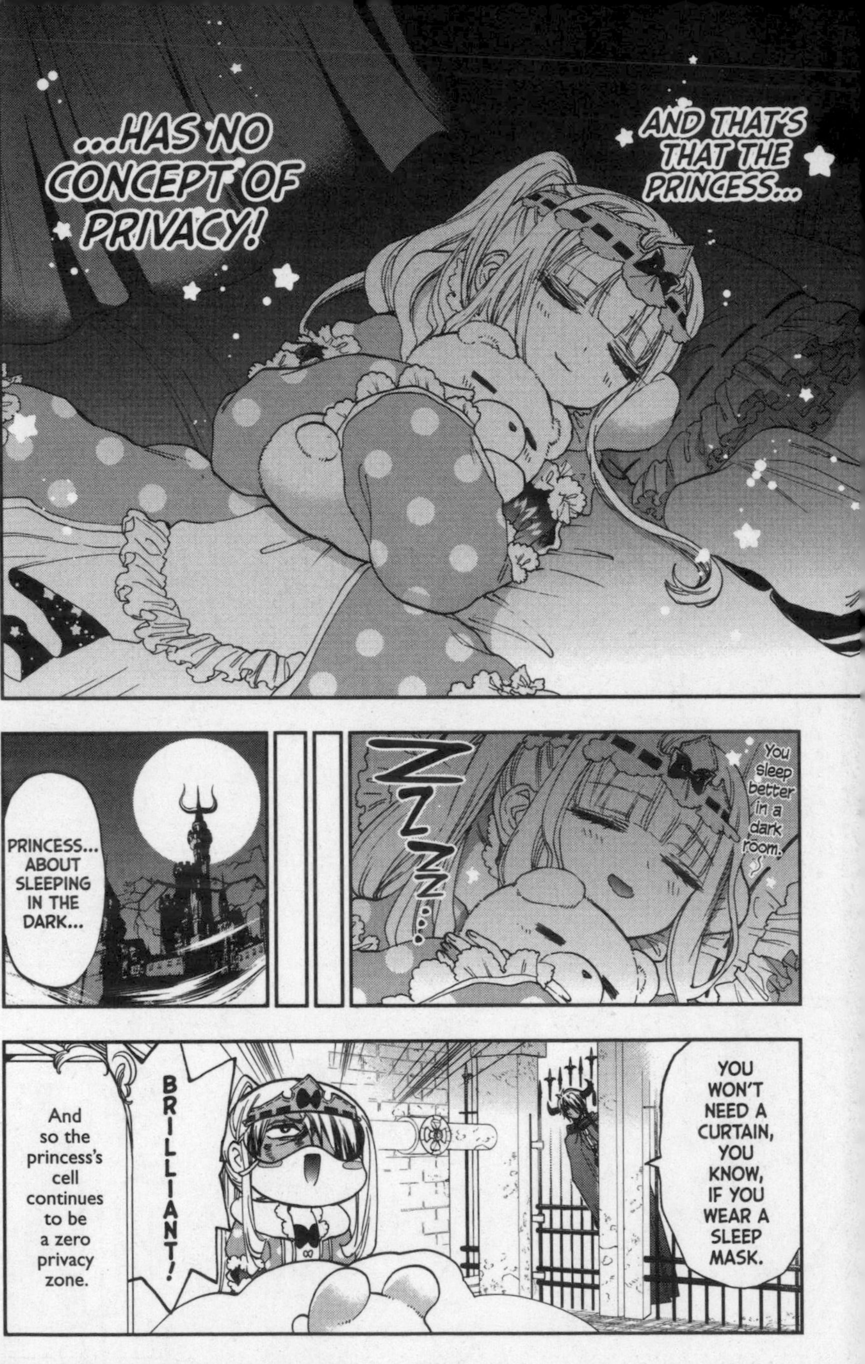
AND THAT'S THAT THE PRINCESS...
...HAS NO CONCEPT OF PRIVACY!
You sleep better in a dark room.
ZZZ...
PRINCESS... ABOUT SLEEPING IN THE DARK...
YOU WON'T NEED A CURTAIN, YOU KNOW, IF YOU WEAR A SLEEP MASK.
BRILLIANT!
And so the princess's cell continues to be a zero privacy zone.

Top secret info that may now be disclosed

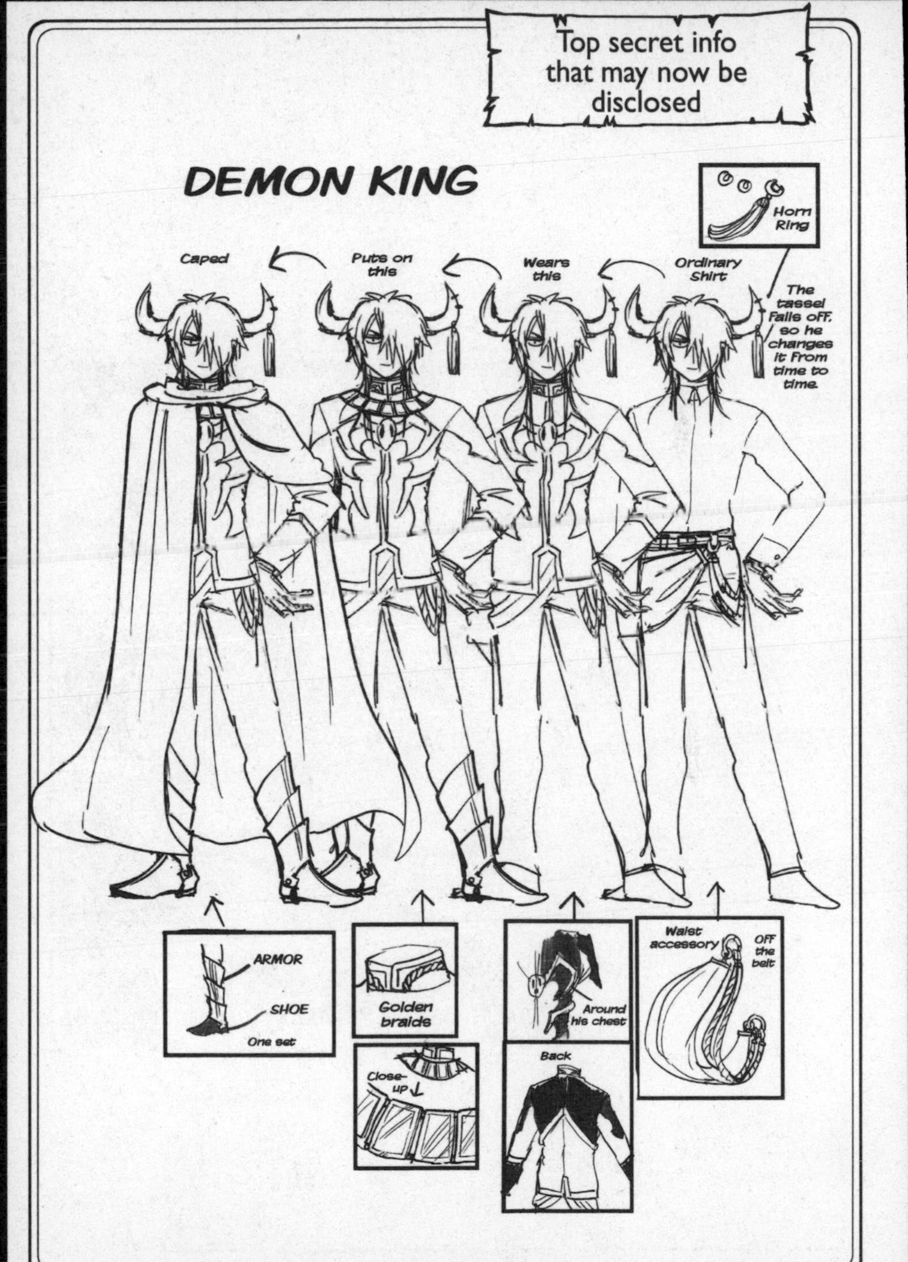
DEMON KING
Horn Ring
The tassel falls off, so he changes it from time to time.
Ordinary Shirt
Wears this
Puts on this
Caped
Waist accessory
Off the belt
Around his chest
Back
Golden braids
Close-up
ARMOR
SHOE
One set

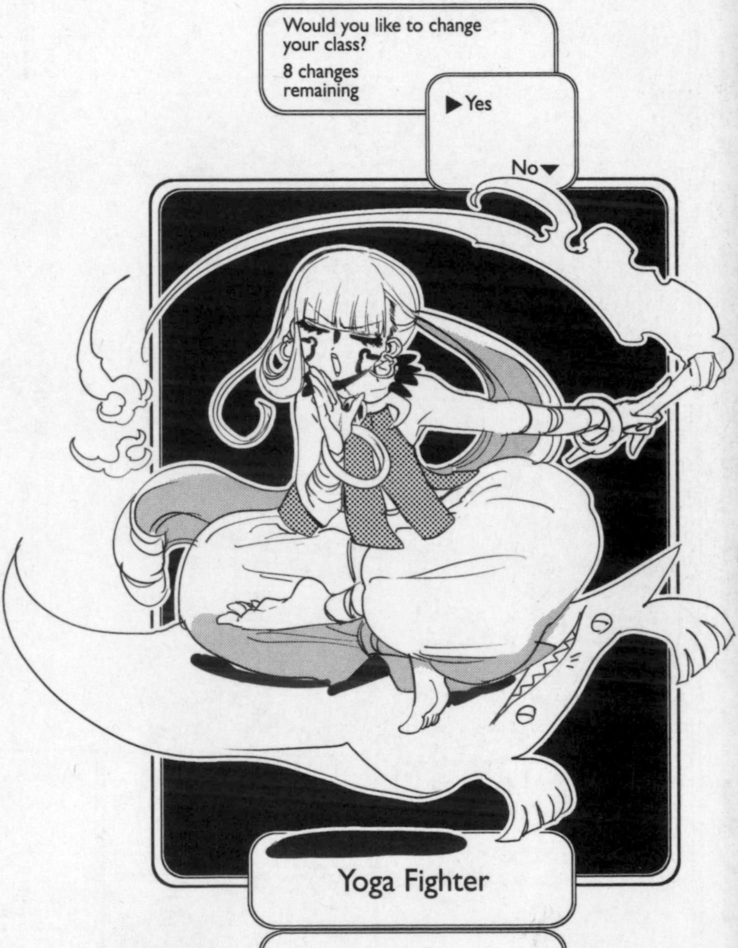
Would you like to change your class?
8 changes remaining
▶Yes
No▼
Yoga Fighter
"Yogaaaaa! (Battle Cry)"

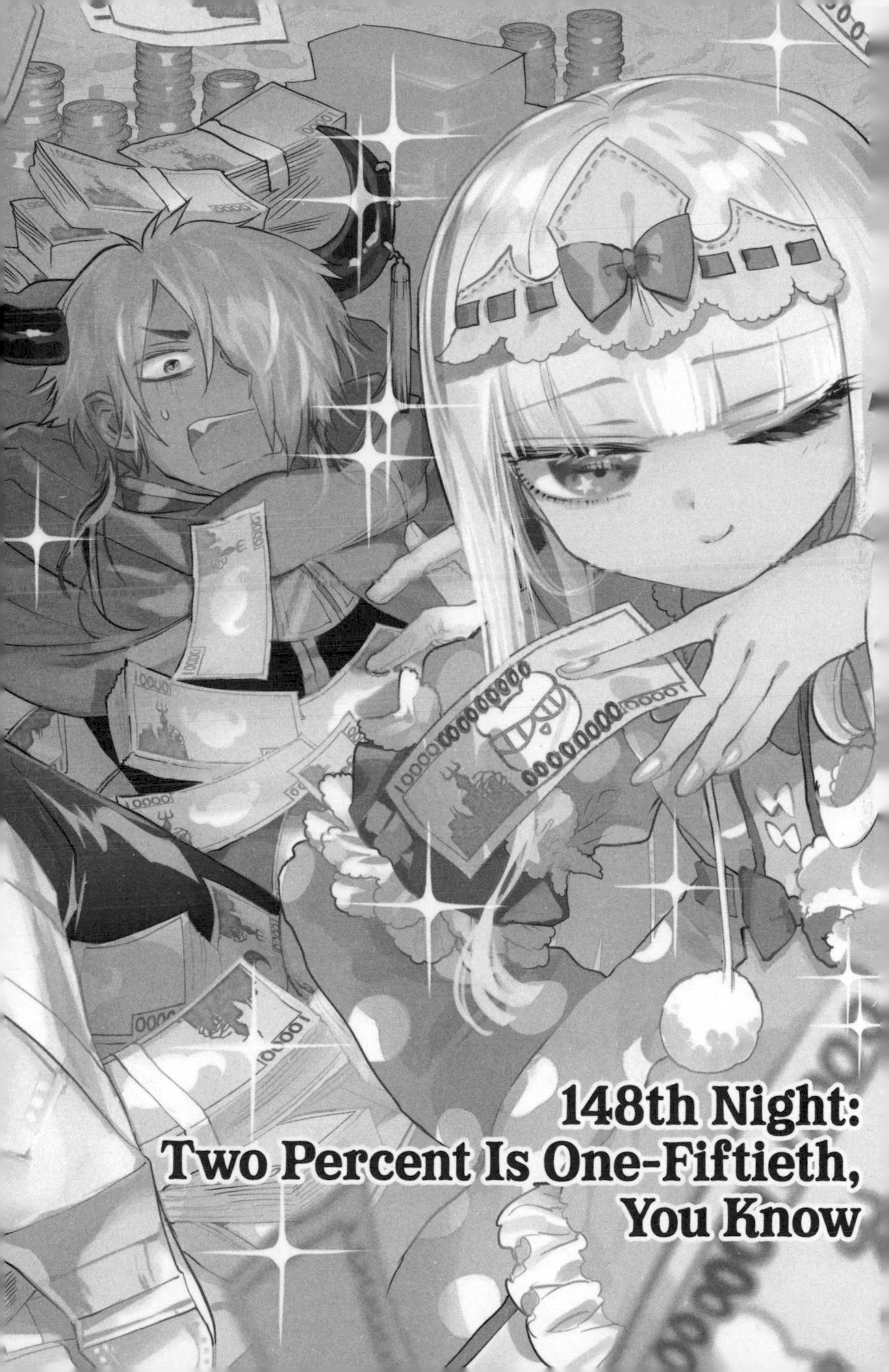
148th Night:
Two Percent Is One-Fiftieth,
You Know

SLEEPY PRINCESS
IN THE DEMON CASTLE

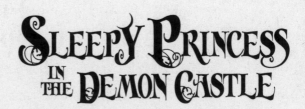

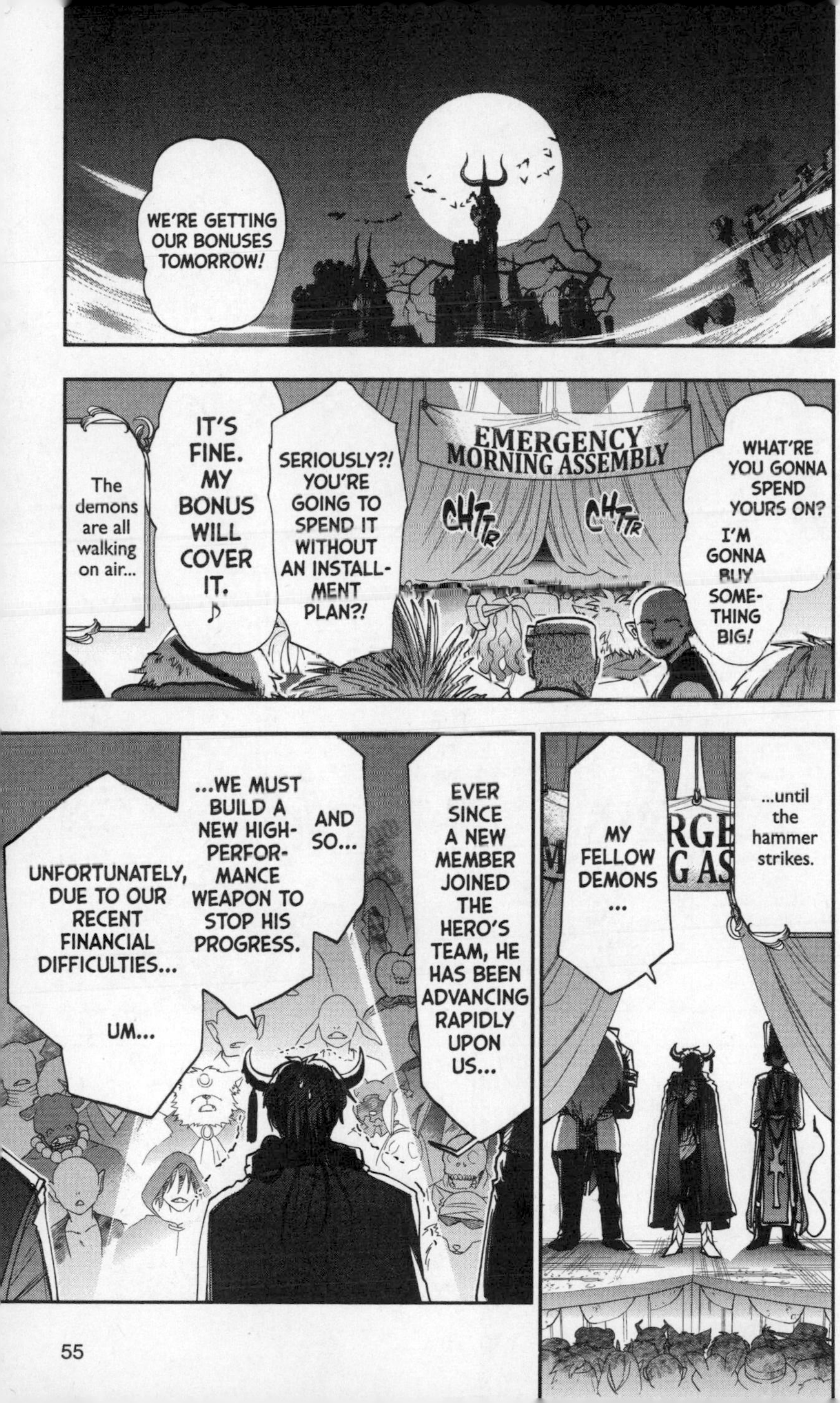
WE'RE GETTING OUR BONUSES TOMORROW!
EMERGENCY MORNING ASSEMBLY
WHAT'RE YOU GONNA SPEND YOURS ON?
I'M GONNA BUY SOME-THING BIG!
CHTTR
CHTTR
SERIOUSLY?! YOU'RE GOING TO SPEND IT WITHOUT AN INSTALL-MENT PLAN?!
IT'S FINE. MY BONUS WILL COVER IT. ♪
The demons are all walking on air...
...until the hammer strikes.
MY FELLOW DEMONS ...
EVER SINCE A NEW MEMBER JOINED THE HERO'S TEAM, HE HAS BEEN ADVANCING RAPIDLY UPON US...
AND SO...
...WE MUST BUILD A NEW HIGH-PERFOR-MANCE WEAPON TO STOP HIS PROGRESS.
UNFORTUNATELY, DUE TO OUR RECENT FINANCIAL DIFFICULTIES...
UM...

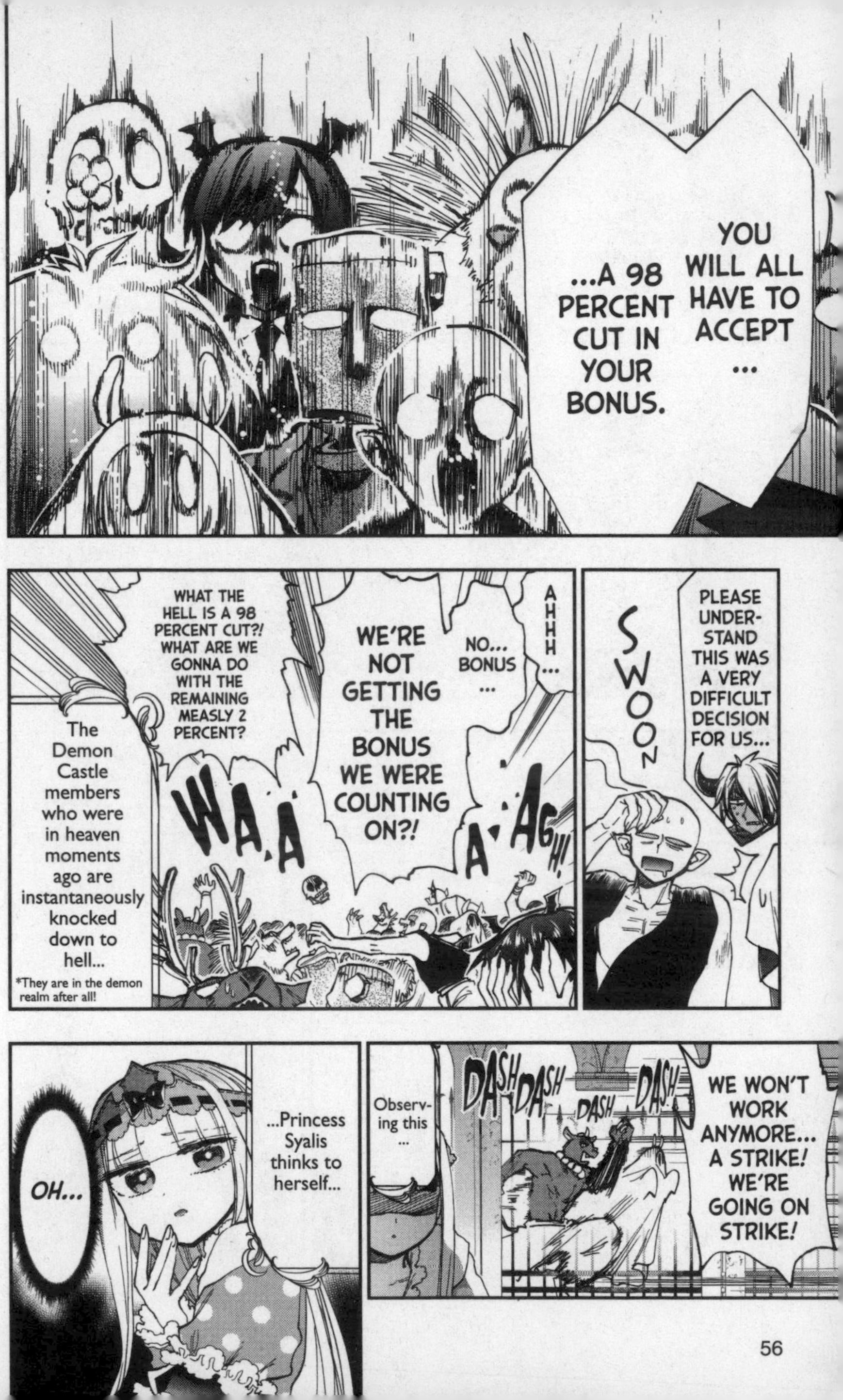
YOU WILL ALL HAVE TO ACCEPT...
...A 98 PERCENT CUT IN YOUR BONUS.
PLEASE UNDER-STAND THIS WAS A VERY DIFFICULT DECISION FOR US...
SWOOON
AHHH...
NO... BONUS...
WE'RE NOT GETTING THE BONUS WE WERE COUNTING ON?!
WHAT THE HELL IS A 98 PERCENT CUT?! WHAT ARE WE GONNA DO WITH THE REMAINING MEASLY 2 PERCENT?
AAGH!
WAA
The Demon Castle members who were in heaven moments ago are instantaneously knocked down to hell...
*They are in the demon realm after all!
WE WON'T WORK ANYMORE... A STRIKE! WE'RE GOING ON STRIKE!
DASH DASH DASH DASH
Observ-ing this...
...Princess Syalis thinks to herself...
OH...

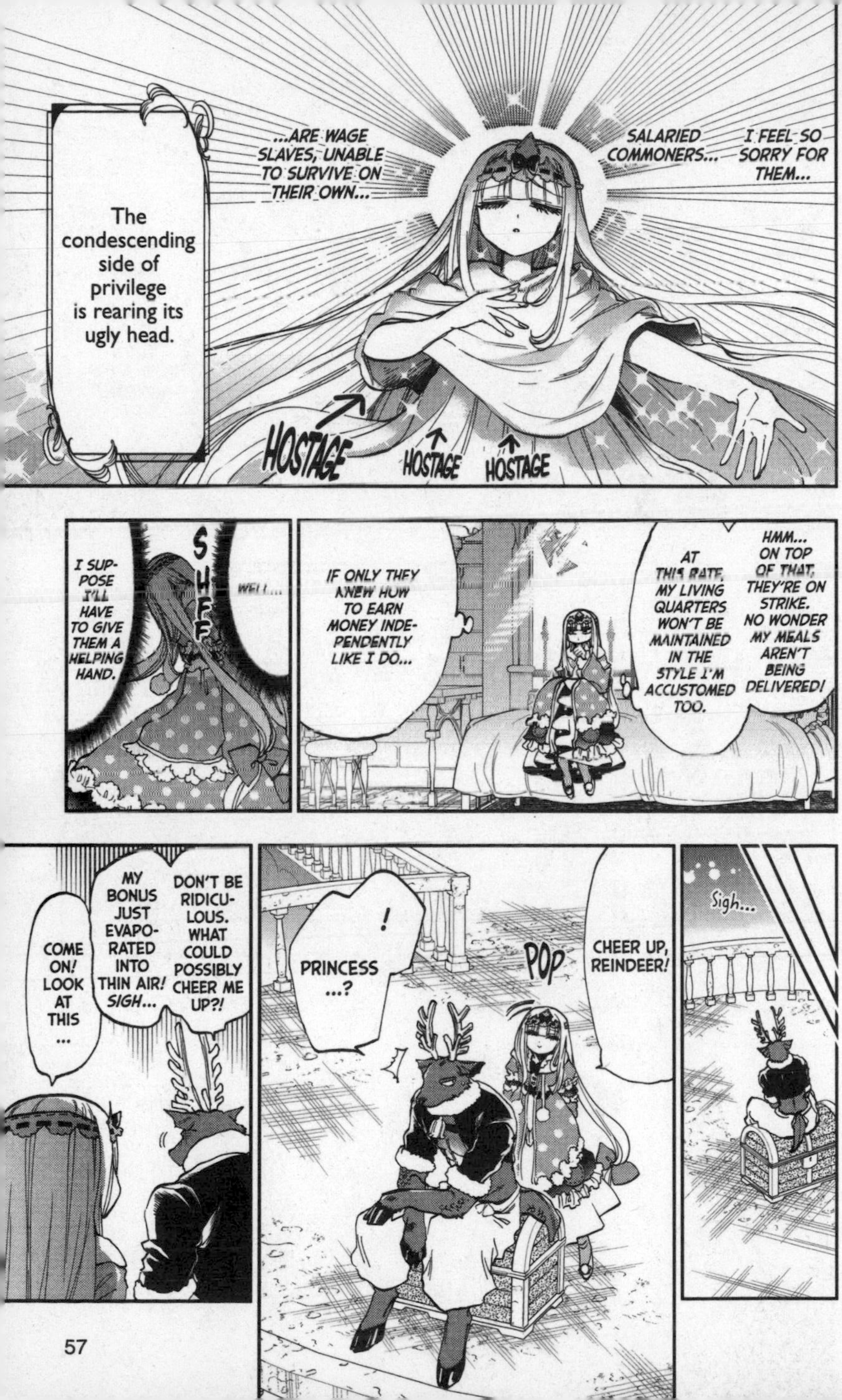
I FEEL SO SORRY FOR THEM...
SALARIED COMMONERS...
...ARE WAGE SLAVES, UNABLE TO SURVIVE ON THEIR OWN...
The condescending side of privilege is rearing its ugly head.
HOSTAGE
HOSTAGE
HOSTAGE
HMM... ON TOP OF THAT, THEY'RE ON STRIKE. NO WONDER MY MEALS AREN'T BEING DELIVERED!
AT THIS RATE, MY LIVING QUARTERS WON'T BE MAINTAINED IN THE STYLE I'M ACCUSTOMED TOO.
IF ONLY THEY KNEW HOW TO EARN MONEY INDE-PENDENTLY LIKE I DO...
WELL...
SHFF
I SUP-POSE I'LL HAVE TO GIVE THEM A HELPING HAND.
Sigh...
CHEER UP, REINDEER!
POP
!
PRINCESS ...?
DON'T BE RIDICU-LOUS. WHAT COULD POSSIBLY CHEER ME UP?!
MY BONUS JUST EVAPO-RATED INTO THIN AIR! SIGH...
COME ON! LOOK AT THIS ...

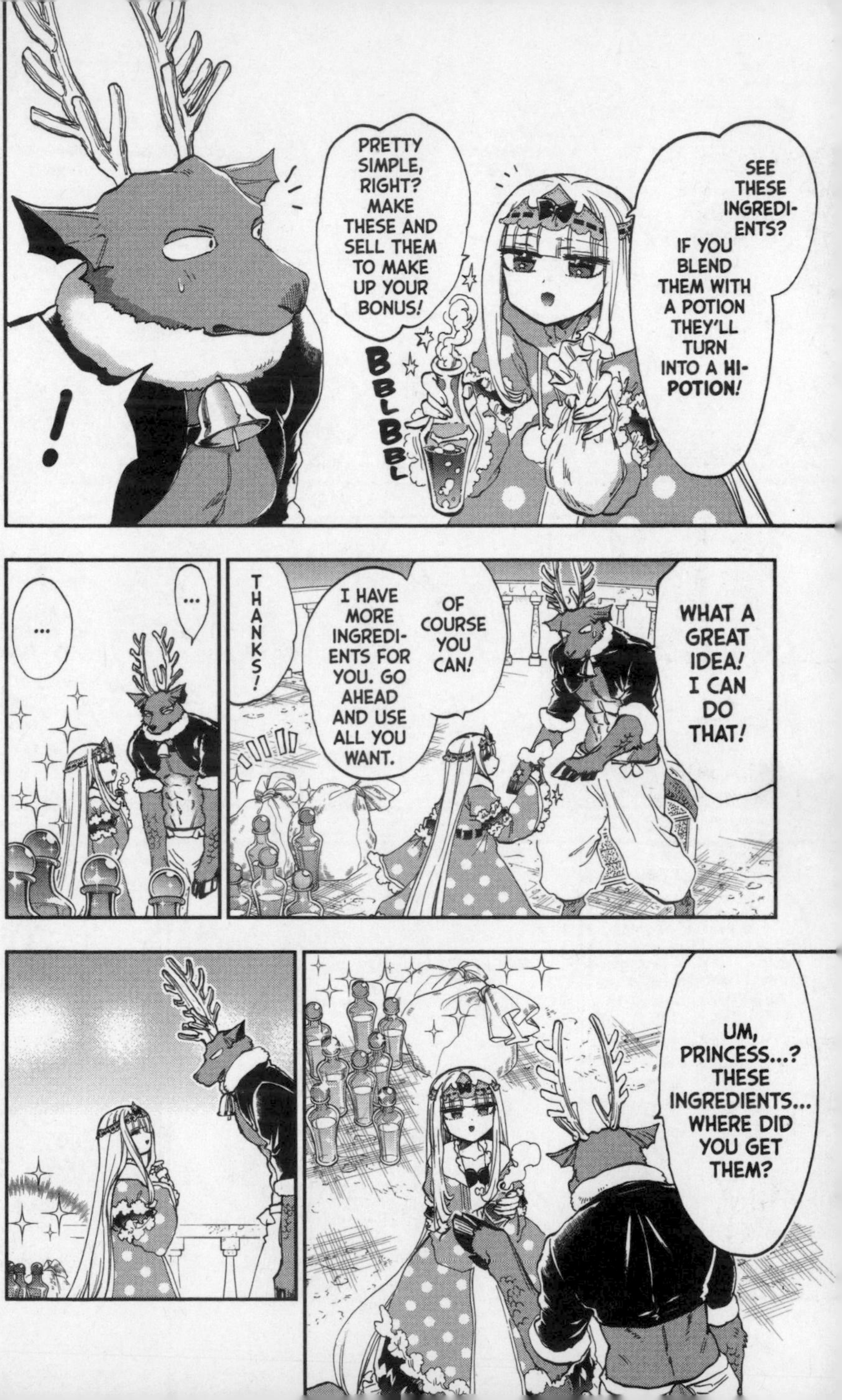
SEE THESE INGREDIENTS? IF YOU BLEND THEM WITH A POTION THEY'LL TURN INTO A HI-POTION!
PRETTY SIMPLE, RIGHT? MAKE THESE AND SELL THEM TO MAKE UP YOUR BONUS!
BBLBBBL
!
WHAT A GREAT IDEA! I CAN DO THAT!
OF COURSE YOU CAN!
I HAVE MORE INGREDIENTS FOR YOU. GO AHEAD AND USE ALL YOU WANT.
THANKS!
...
...
UM, PRINCESS...? THESE INGREDIENTS... WHERE DID YOU GET THEM?

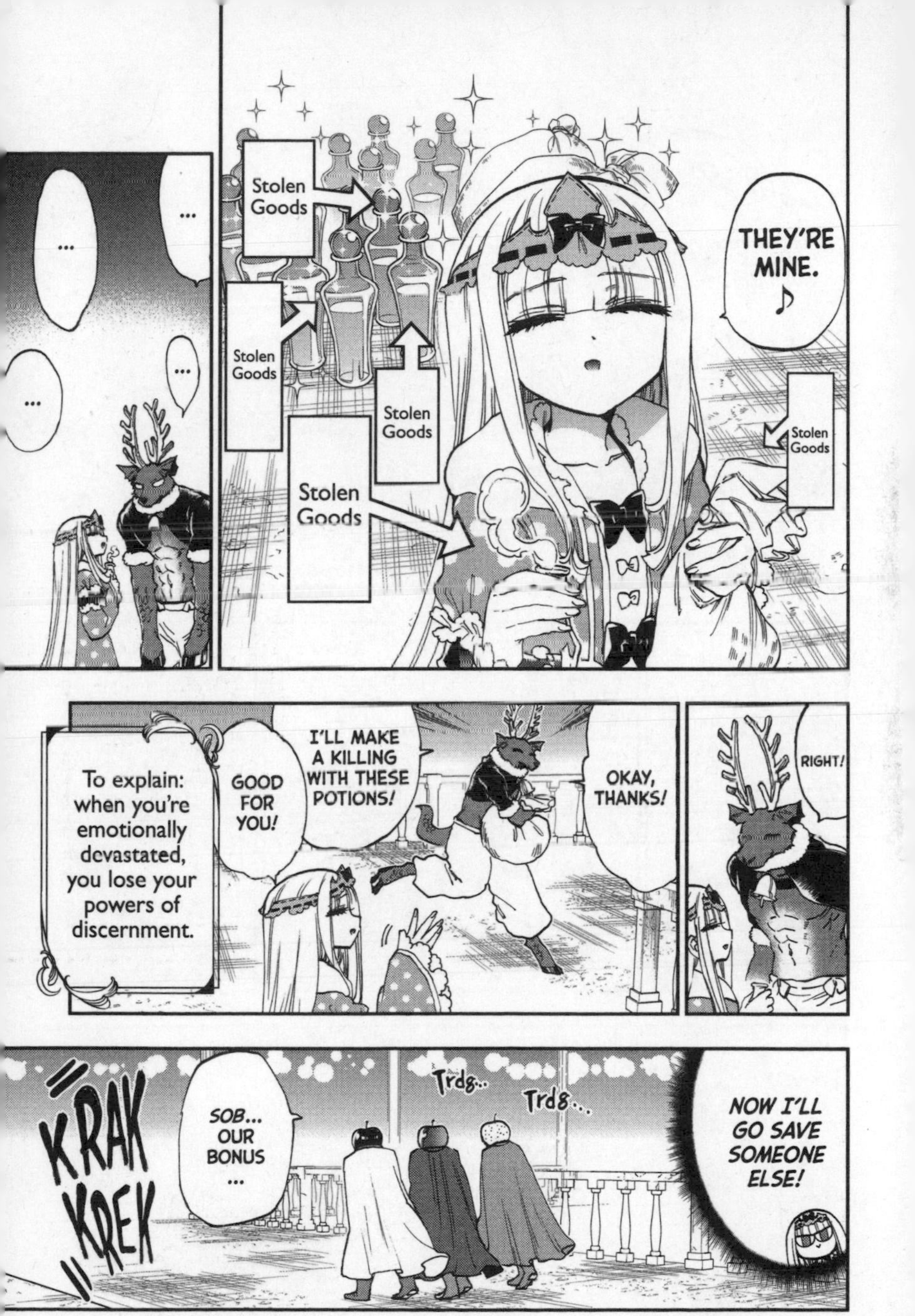
THEY'RE MINE. ♪
Stolen Goods
Stolen Goods
Stolen Goods
Stolen Goods
Stolen Goods
...
...
...
...
RIGHT!
OKAY, THANKS!
I'LL MAKE A KILLING WITH THESE POTIONS!
GOOD FOR YOU!
To explain: when you're emotionally devastated, you lose your powers of discernment.
NOW I'LL GO SAVE SOMEONE ELSE!
Trdg...
Trdg...
SOB... OUR BONUS...
KRAK KREK

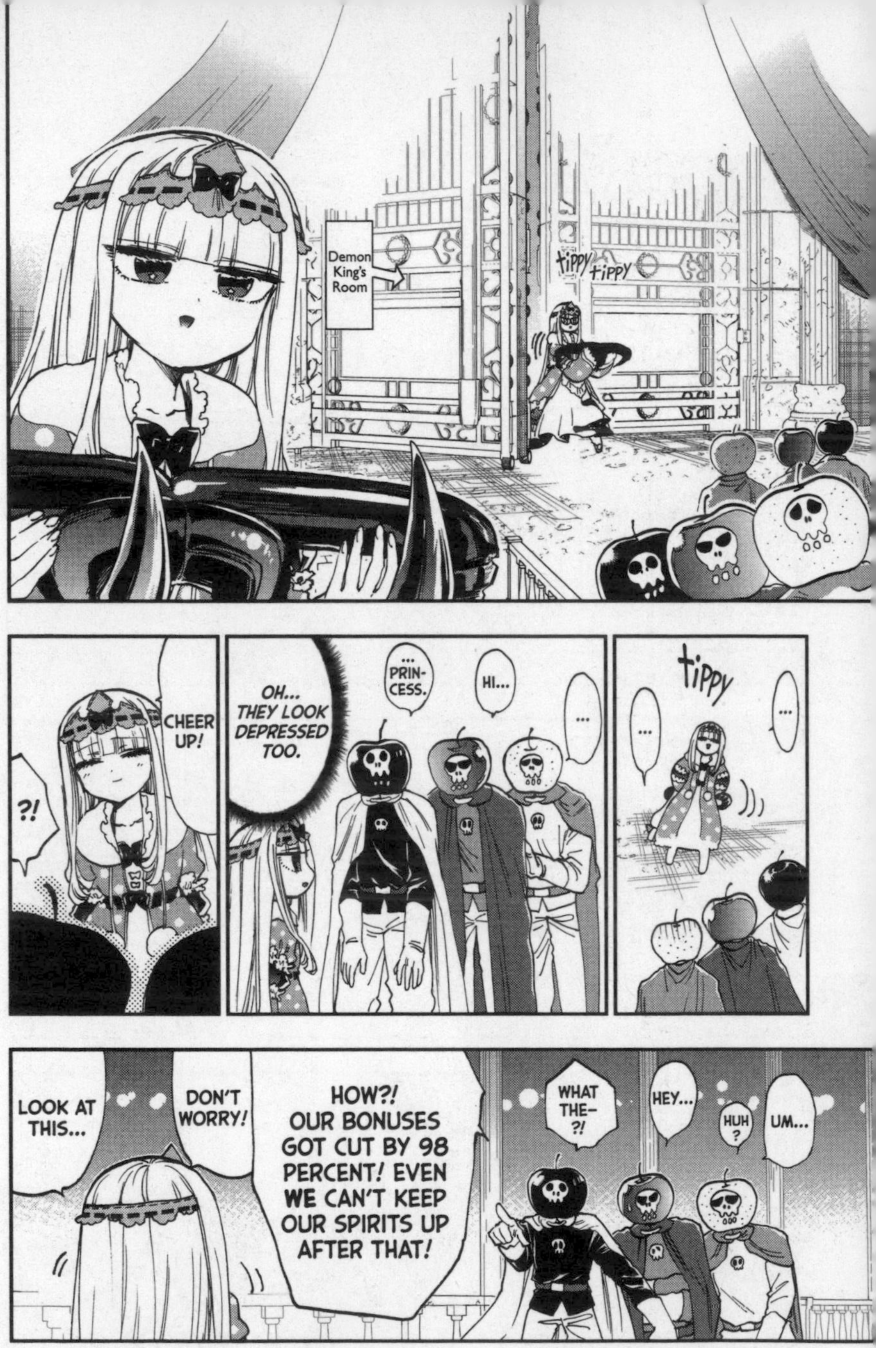
Demon King's Room
tippy tippy
tippy
...
...
...
HI...
... PRIN-CESS.
OH... THEY LOOK DEPRESSED TOO.
CHEER UP!
?!
UM...
HEY...
HUH?
WHAT THE—?!
HOW?! OUR BONUSES GOT CUT BY 98 PERCENT! EVEN WE CAN'T KEEP OUR SPIRITS UP AFTER THAT!
DON'T WORRY!
LOOK AT THIS...

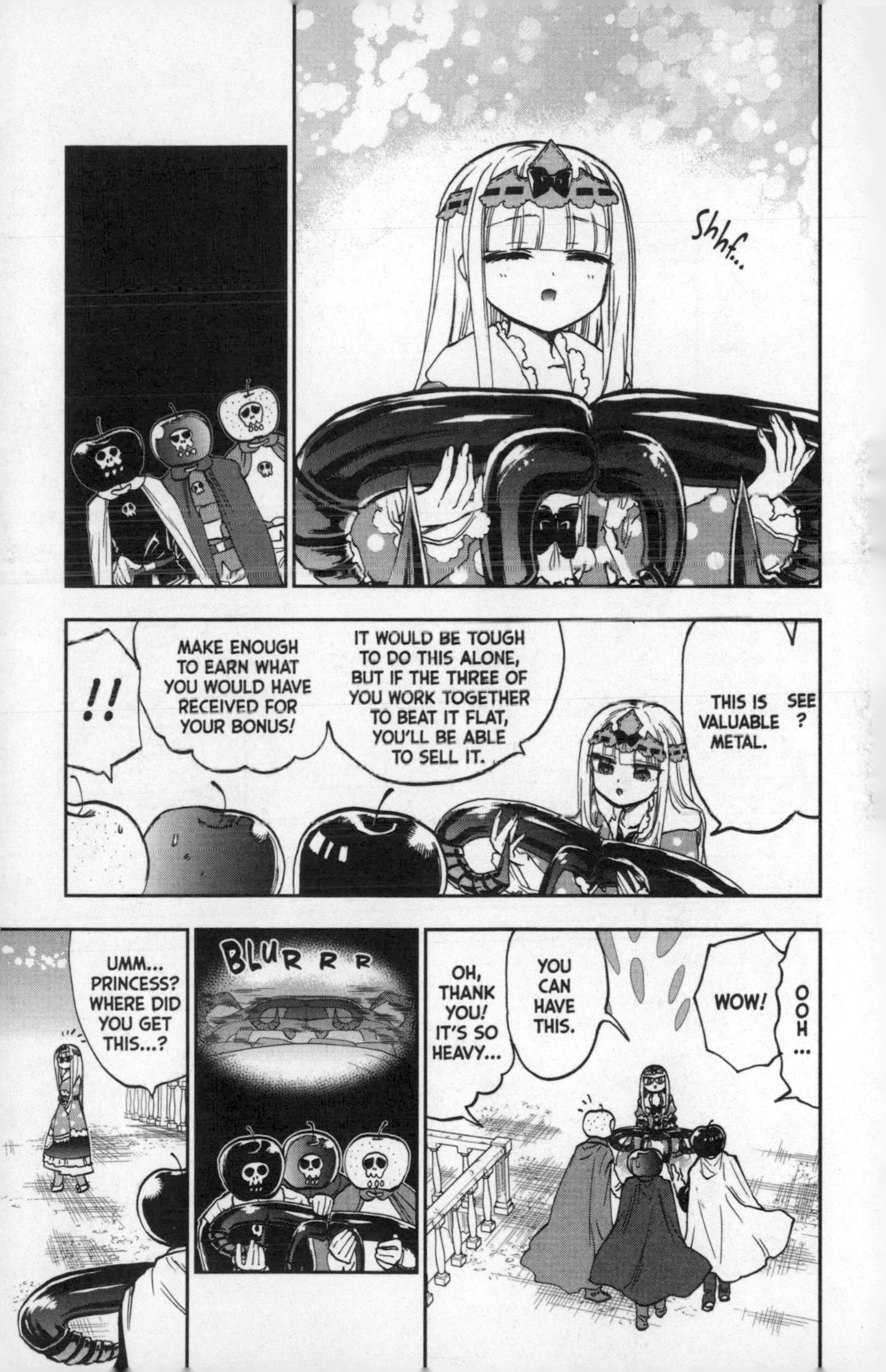
Shhf...
SEE? THIS IS VALUABLE METAL.
IT WOULD BE TOUGH TO DO THIS ALONE, BUT IF THE THREE OF YOU WORK TOGETHER TO BEAT IT FLAT, YOU'LL BE ABLE TO SELL IT.
MAKE ENOUGH TO EARN WHAT YOU WOULD HAVE RECEIVED FOR YOUR BONUS!
!!
OOOH...
WOW!
YOU CAN HAVE THIS.
OH, THANK YOU! IT'S SO HEAVY...
BLURRR
UMM... PRINCESS? WHERE DID YOU GET THIS...?

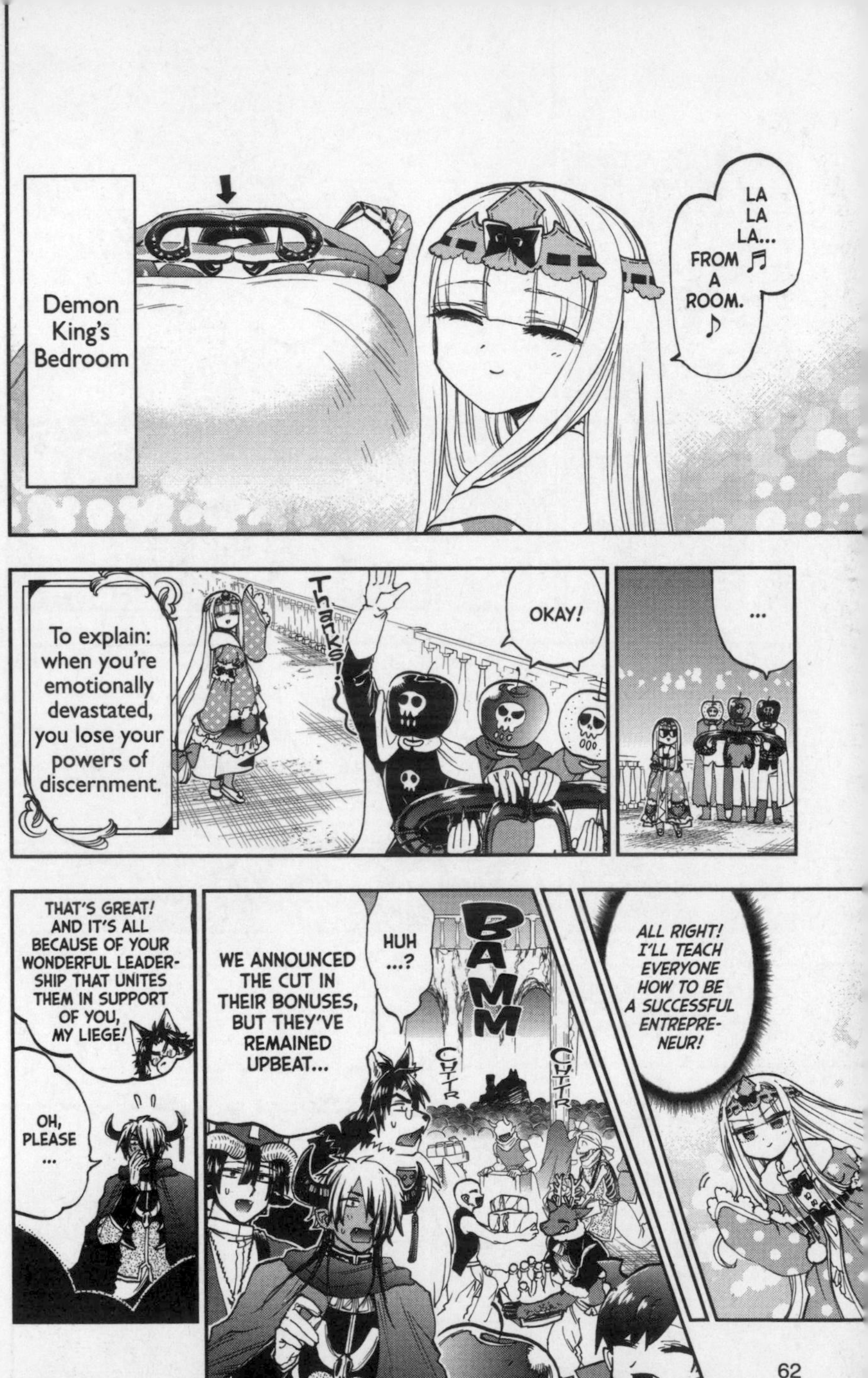
LA LA LA... FROM ♫ A ROOM. ♪
Demon King's Bedroom
...
OKAY!
Thanks!
To explain: when you're emotionally devastated, you lose your powers of discernment.
ALL RIGHT! I'LL TEACH EVERYONE HOW TO BE A SUCCESSFUL ENTREPRE-NEUR!
HUH ...?
BAMM
WE ANNOUNCED THE CUT IN THEIR BONUSES, BUT THEY'VE REMAINED UPBEAT...
CHTTR
CHTTR
THAT'S GREAT! AND IT'S ALL BECAUSE OF YOUR WONDERFUL LEADER-SHIP THAT UNITES THEM IN SUPPORT OF YOU, MY LIEGE!
OH, PLEASE ...

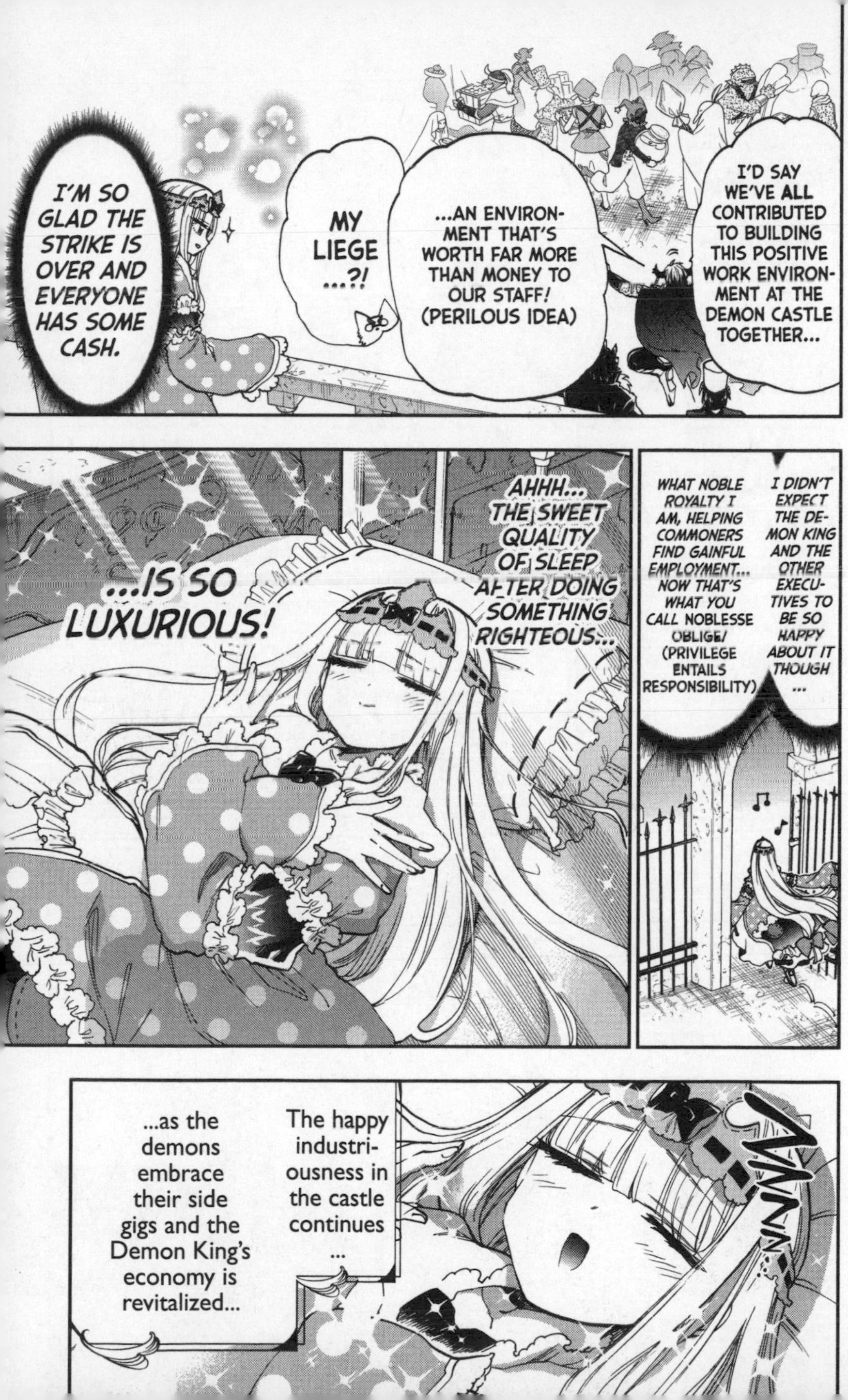
I'D SAY WE'VE ALL CONTRIBUTED TO BUILDING THIS POSITIVE WORK ENVIRONMENT AT THE DEMON CASTLE TOGETHER...
...AN ENVIRONMENT THAT'S WORTH FAR MORE THAN MONEY TO OUR STAFF! (PERILOUS IDEA)
MY LIEGE ...?!
I'M SO GLAD THE STRIKE IS OVER AND EVERYONE HAS SOME CASH.
I DIDN'T EXPECT THE DEMON KING AND THE OTHER EXECUTIVES TO BE SO HAPPY ABOUT IT THOUGH ...
WHAT NOBLE ROYALTY I AM, HELPING COMMONERS FIND GAINFUL EMPLOYMENT... NOW THAT'S WHAT YOU CALL NOBLESSE OBLIGE! (PRIVILEGE ENTAILS RESPONSIBILITY)
AHHH... THE SWEET QUALITY OF SLEEP AFTER DOING SOMETHING RIGHTEOUS...
...IS SO LUXURIOUS!
The happy industriousness in the castle continues ...
...as the demons embrace their side gigs and the Demon King's economy is revitalized...

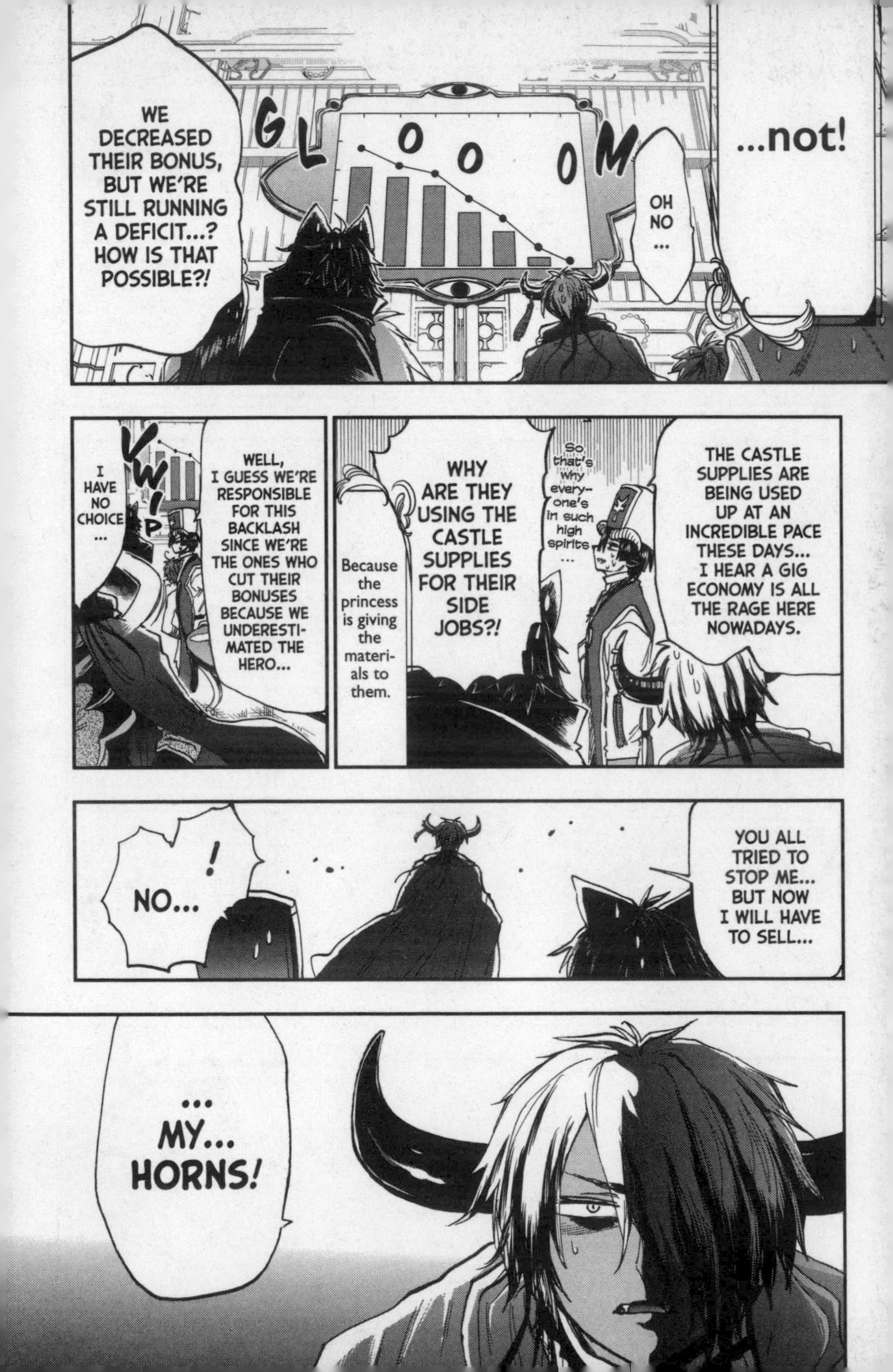
...not!
OH NO ...
GLOOOM
WE DECREASED THEIR BONUS, BUT WE'RE STILL RUNNING A DEFICIT...? HOW IS THAT POSSIBLE?!
THE CASTLE SUPPLIES ARE BEING USED UP AT AN INCREDIBLE PACE THESE DAYS... I HEAR A GIG ECONOMY IS ALL THE RAGE HERE NOWADAYS.
So that's why every-one's in such high spirits...
WHY ARE THEY USING THE CASTLE SUPPLIES FOR THEIR SIDE JOBS?!
Because the princess is giving the materi-als to them.
WELL, I GUESS WE'RE RESPONSIBLE FOR THIS BACKLASH SINCE WE'RE THE ONES WHO CUT THEIR BONUSES BECAUSE WE UNDERESTI-MATED THE HERO...
VWIP
I HAVE NO CHOICE ...
YOU ALL TRIED TO STOP ME... BUT NOW I WILL HAVE TO SELL...
!
NO...
... MY... HORNS!

Top secret info that may now be disclosed

ABOUT THE DEMON CLERIC

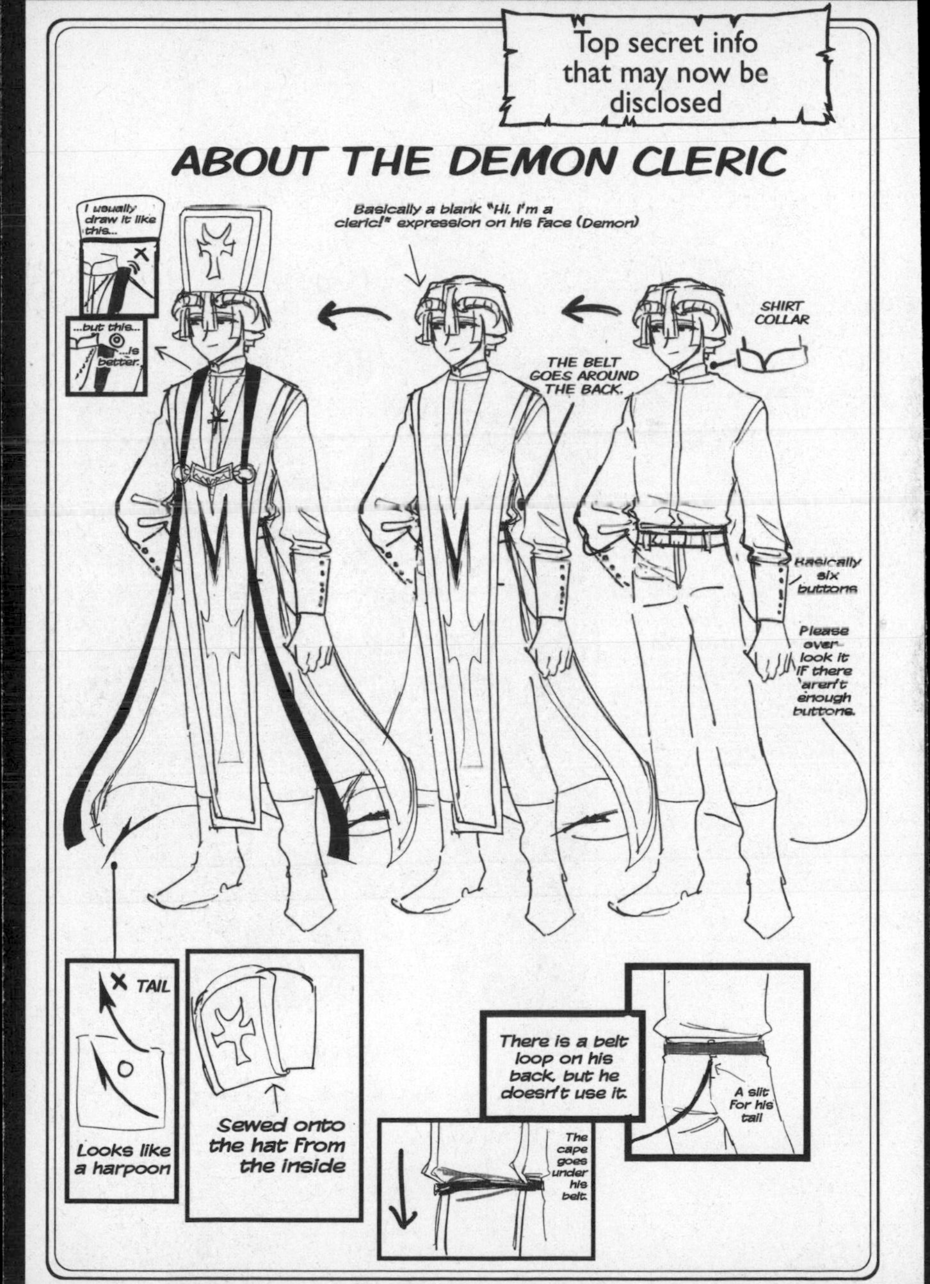
Basically a blank "Hi, I'm a cleric!" expression on his face (Demon)
I usually draw it like this...
...but this... ...is better.
SHIRT COLLAR
THE BELT GOES AROUND THE BACK.
Basically six buttons
Please overlook it if there aren't enough buttons.
TAIL
Looks like a harpoon
Sewed onto the hat from the inside
There is a belt loop on his back, but he doesn't use it.
A slit for his tail
The cape goes under his belt.

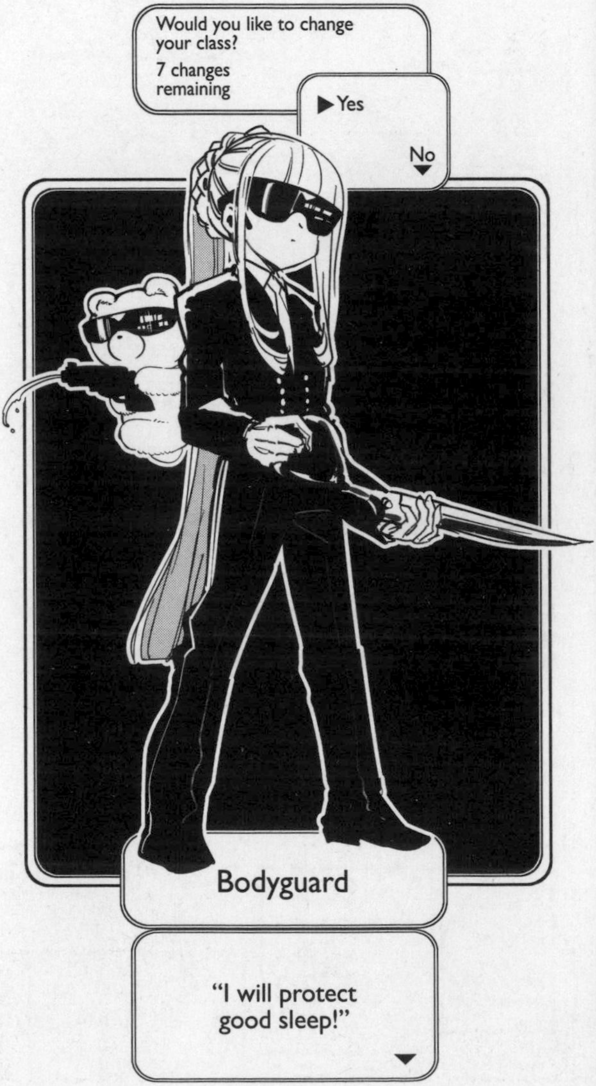
Would you like to change your class?
7 changes remaining
▶Yes
No
Bodyguard
"I will protect good sleep!"

149th Night: THE PRINCESSM@STER

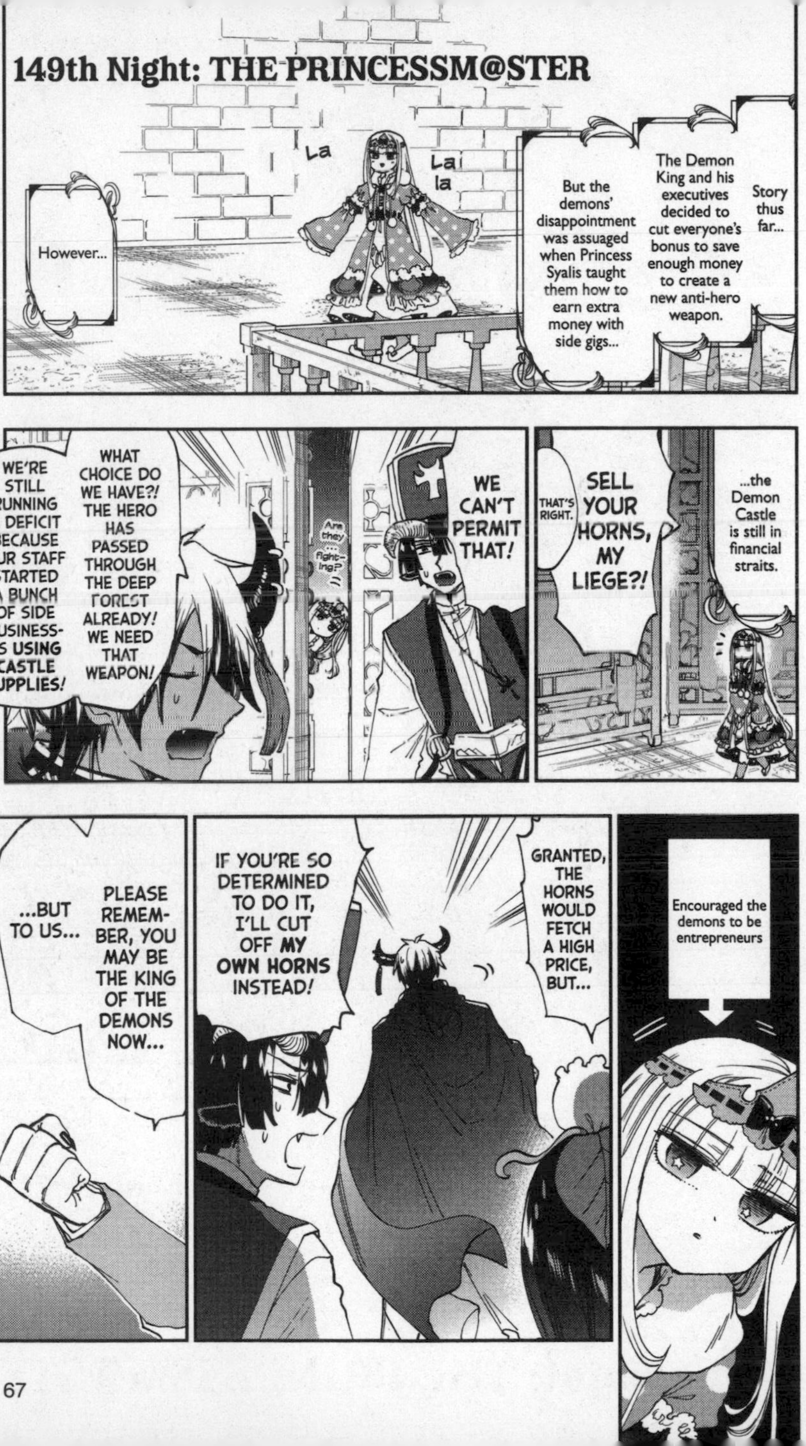
Story thus far...
The Demon King and his executives decided to cut everyone's bonus to save enough money to create a new anti-hero weapon.
But the demons' disappointment was assuaged when Princess Syalis taught them how to earn extra money with side gigs...
La
La la
However...
...the Demon Castle is still in financial straits.
SELL YOUR HORNS, MY LIEGE?!
THAT'S RIGHT.
WE CAN'T PERMIT THAT!
Are they ... fighting?
WHAT CHOICE DO WE HAVE?! THE HERO HAS PASSED THROUGH THE DEEP FOREST ALREADY! WE NEED THAT WEAPON!
WE'RE STILL RUNNING A DEFICIT BECAUSE OUR STAFF STARTED A BUNCH OF SIDE BUSINESSES USING CASTLE SUPPLIES!
Encouraged the demons to be entrepreneurs
GRANTED, THE HORNS WOULD FETCH A HIGH PRICE, BUT...
IF YOU'RE SO DETERMINED TO DO IT, I'LL CUT OFF MY OWN HORNS INSTEAD!
PLEASE REMEMBER, YOU MAY BE THE KING OF THE DEMONS NOW...
...BUT TO US...

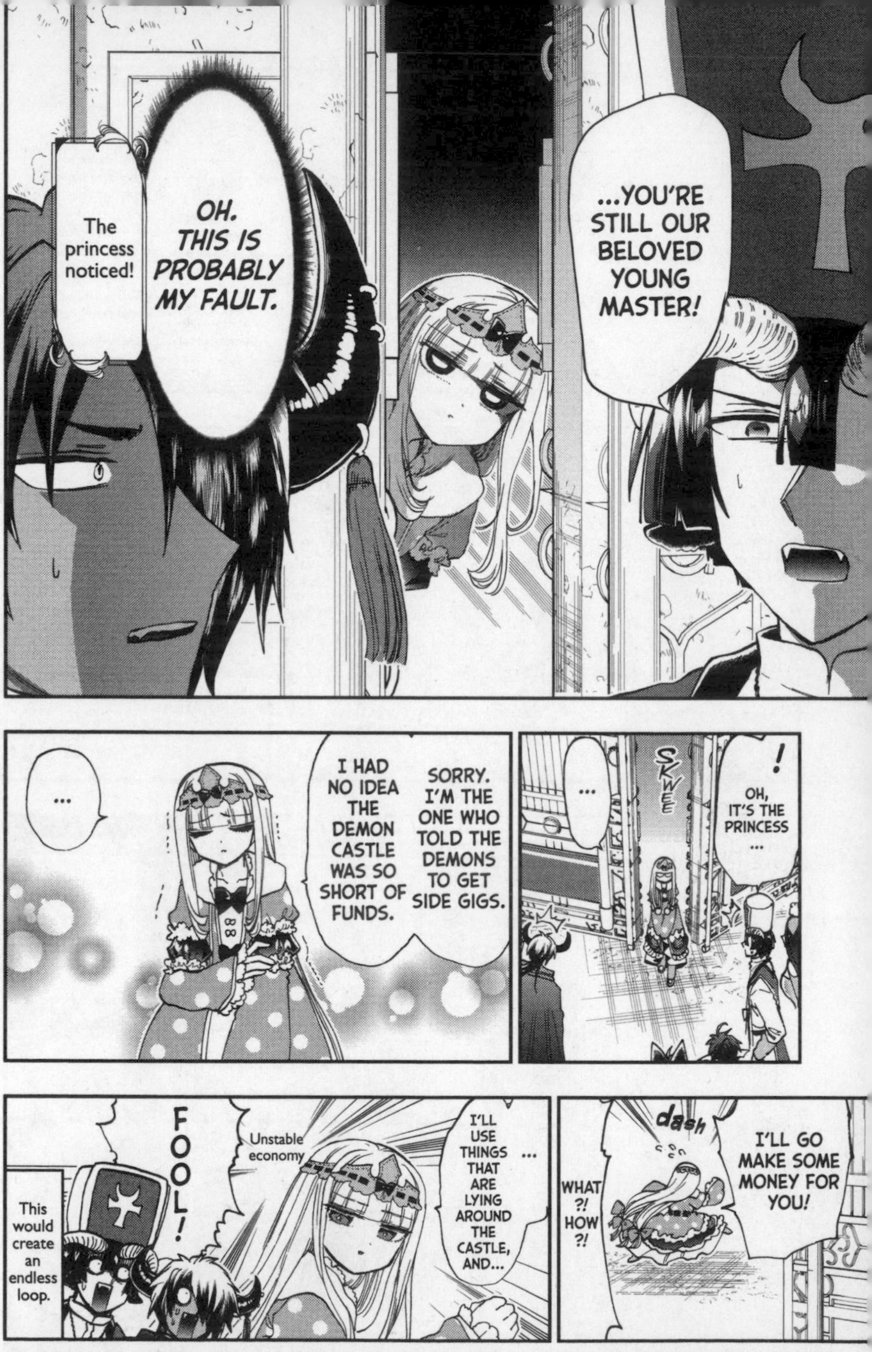
...YOU'RE STILL OUR BELOVED YOUNG MASTER!
OH. THIS IS PROBABLY MY FAULT.
The princess noticed!
!
OH, IT'S THE PRINCESS ...
SKWEE
...
SORRY. I'M THE ONE WHO TOLD THE DEMONS TO GET SIDE GIGS.
I HAD NO IDEA THE DEMON CASTLE WAS SO SHORT OF FUNDS.
...
I'LL GO MAKE SOME MONEY FOR YOU!
dash
WHAT?! HOW?!
...
I'LL USE THINGS THAT ARE LYING AROUND THE CASTLE, AND...
Unstable economy
FOOL!
This would create an endless loop.

149th Night: THE PRINCESSM@STER

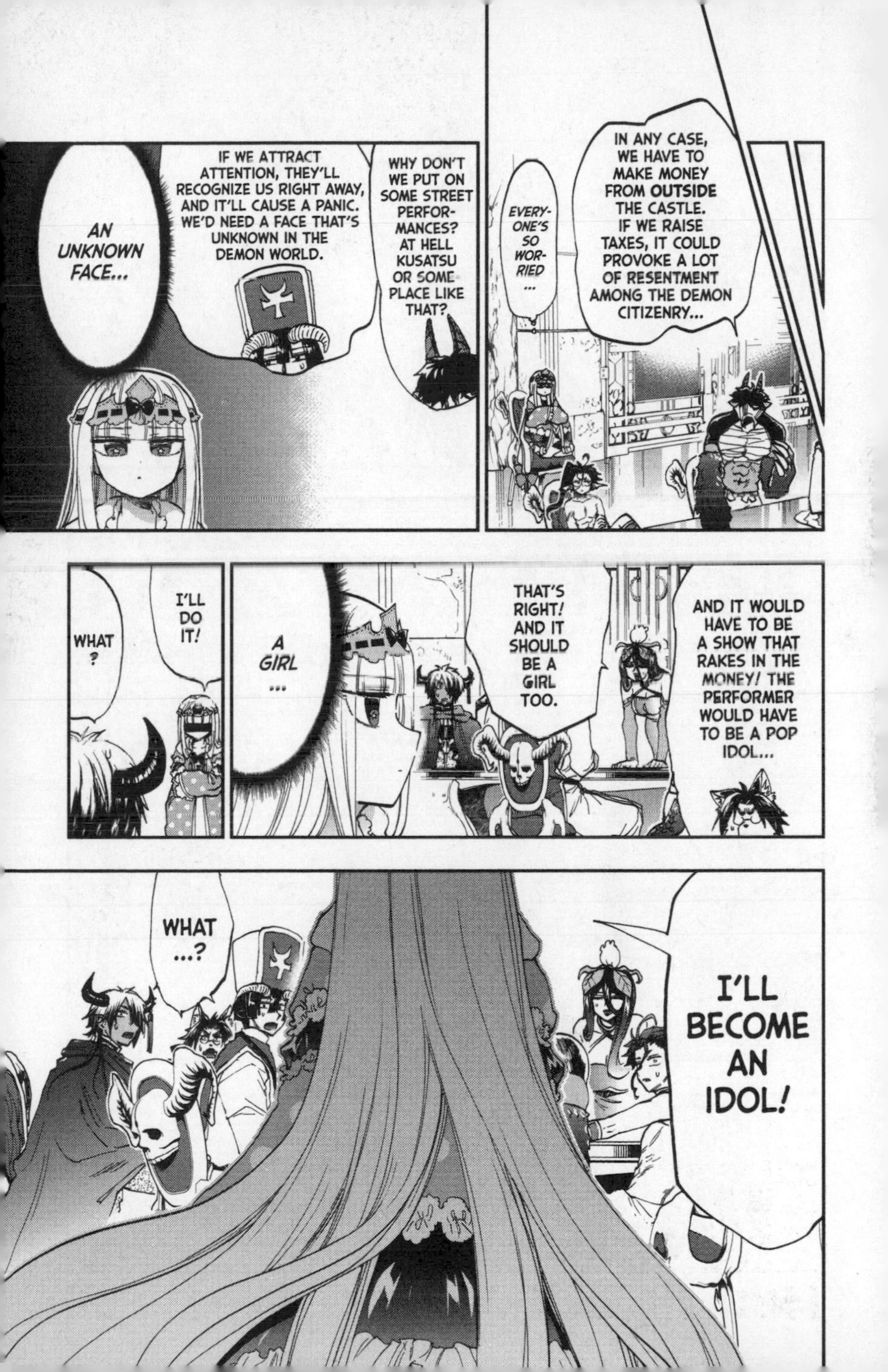

IN ANY CASE, WE HAVE TO MAKE MONEY FROM **OUTSIDE** THE CASTLE. IF WE RAISE TAXES, IT COULD PROVOKE A LOT OF RESENTMENT AMONG THE DEMON CITIZENRY...
EVERYONE'S SO WORRIED...
WHY DON'T WE PUT ON SOME STREET PERFORMANCES? AT HELL KUSATSU OR SOMEPLACE LIKE THAT?
IF WE ATTRACT ATTENTION, THEY'LL RECOGNIZE US RIGHT AWAY, AND IT'LL CAUSE A PANIC. WE'D NEED A FACE THAT'S UNKNOWN IN THE DEMON WORLD.
AN UNKNOWN FACE...
AND IT WOULD HAVE TO BE A SHOW THAT RAKES IN THE MONEY! THE PERFORMER WOULD HAVE TO BE A POP IDOL...
THAT'S RIGHT! AND IT SHOULD BE A GIRL TOO.
A GIRL...
I'LL DO IT!
WHAT?
I'LL BECOME AN IDOL!
WHAT...?

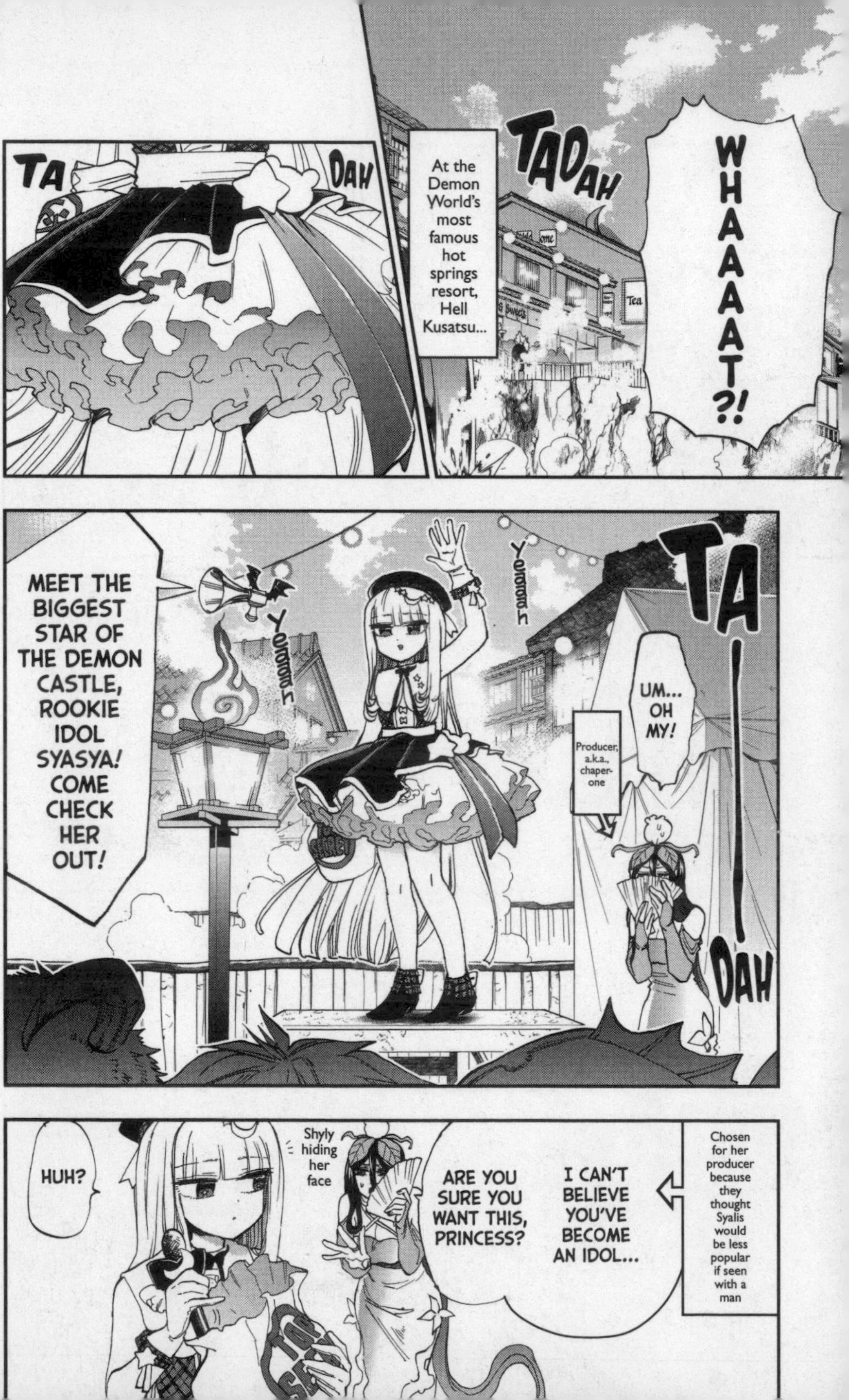
WHAAAAT?!
TADAH
At the Demon World's most famous hot springs resort, Hell Kusatsu...
Tea
TA DAH
TA—DAH
UM... OH MY!
Producer, a.k.a., chaper-one
MEET THE BIGGEST STAR OF THE DEMON CASTLE, ROOKIE IDOL SYASYA! COME CHECK HER OUT!
Chosen for her producer because they thought Syalis would be less popular if seen with a man
I CAN'T BELIEVE YOU'VE BECOME AN IDOL...
ARE YOU SURE YOU WANT THIS, PRINCESS?
Shyly hiding her face
HUH?

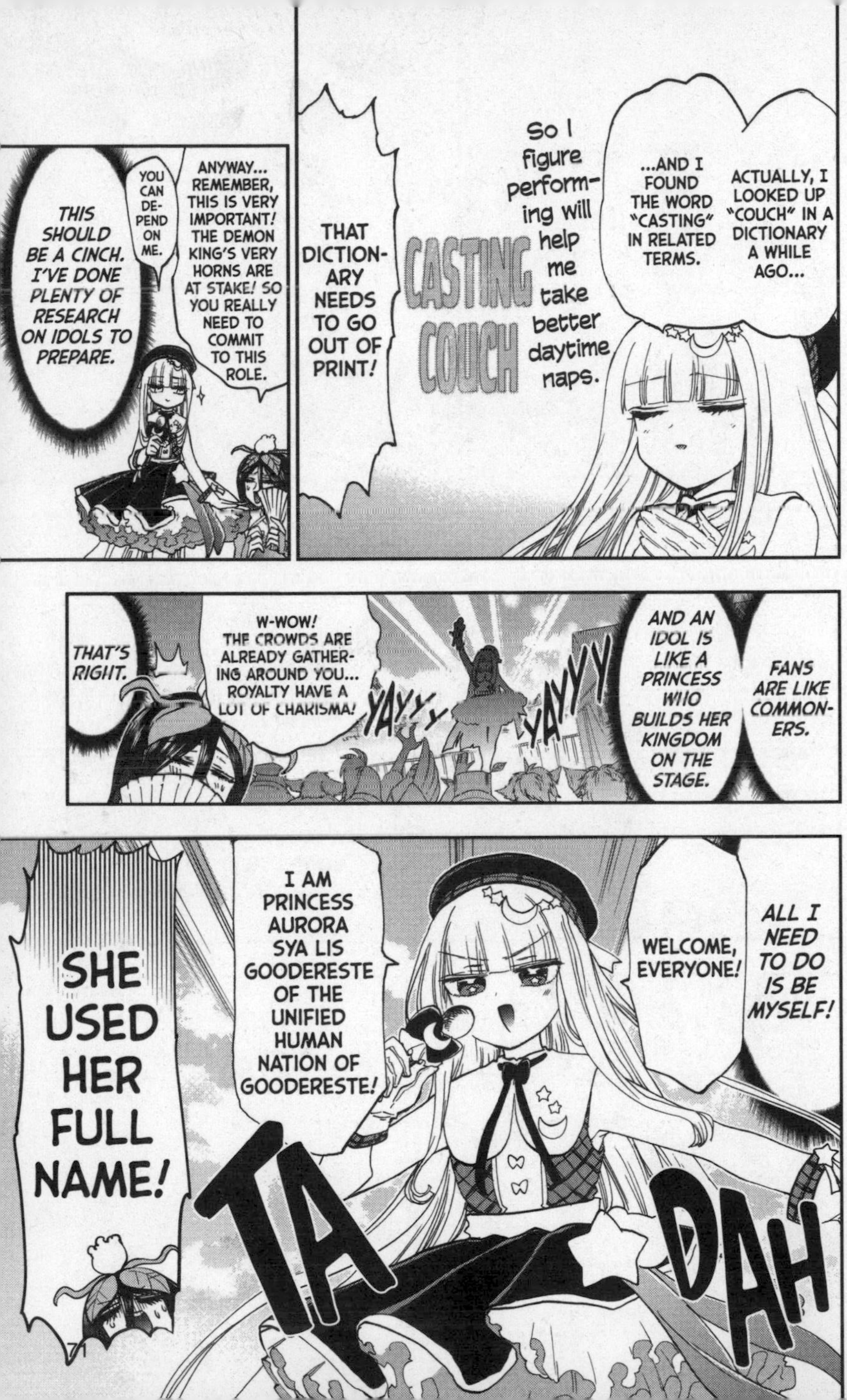

ACTUALLY, I LOOKED UP "COUCH" IN A DICTIONARY A WHILE AGO...
...AND I FOUND THE WORD "CASTING" IN RELATED TERMS.
So I figure performing will help me take better daytime naps.
CASTING COUCH
THAT DICTIONARY NEEDS TO GO OUT OF PRINT!
ANYWAY... REMEMBER, THIS IS VERY IMPORTANT! THE DEMON KING'S VERY HORNS ARE AT STAKE! SO YOU REALLY NEED TO COMMIT TO THIS ROLE.
YOU CAN DEPEND ON ME.
THIS SHOULD BE A CINCH. I'VE DONE PLENTY OF RESEARCH ON IDOLS TO PREPARE.
FANS ARE LIKE COMMONERS.
AND AN IDOL IS LIKE A PRINCESS WHO BUILDS HER KINGDOM ON THE STAGE.
YAYYY
YAYYY
W-WOW! THE CROWDS ARE ALREADY GATHERING AROUND YOU... ROYALTY HAVE A LOT OF CHARISMA!
THAT'S RIGHT.
ALL I NEED TO DO IS BE MYSELF!
WELCOME, EVERYONE!
I AM PRINCESS AURORA SYA LIS GOODERESTE OF THE UNIFIED HUMAN NATION OF GOODERESTE!
SHE USED HER FULL NAME!
TA DAH

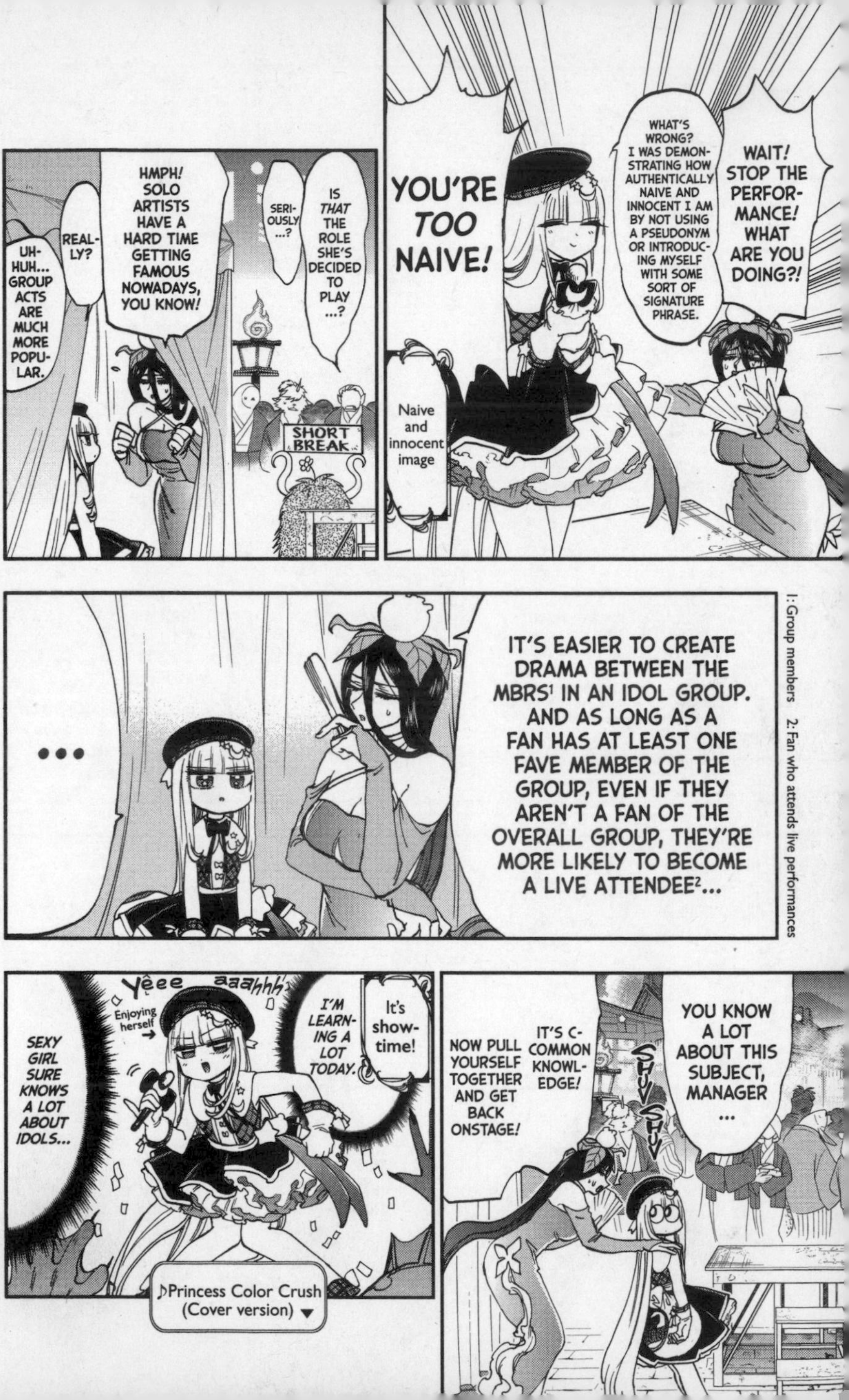
WAIT! STOP THE PERFORMANCE! WHAT ARE YOU DOING?!
WHAT'S WRONG? I WAS DEMONSTRATING HOW AUTHENTICALLY NAIVE AND INNOCENT I AM BY NOT USING A PSEUDONYM OR INTRODUCING MYSELF WITH SOME SORT OF SIGNATURE PHRASE.
YOU'RE TOO NAIVE!
Naive and innocent image
IS THAT THE ROLE SHE'S DECIDED TO PLAY ...?
SERIOUSLY ...?
HMPH! SOLO ARTISTS HAVE A HARD TIME GETTING FAMOUS NOWADAYS, YOU KNOW!
REALLY?
UH-HUH... GROUP ACTS ARE MUCH MORE POPULAR.
SHORT BREAK
IT'S EASIER TO CREATE DRAMA BETWEEN THE MBRS[1] IN AN IDOL GROUP. AND AS LONG AS A FAN HAS AT LEAST ONE FAVE MEMBER OF THE GROUP, EVEN IF THEY AREN'T A FAN OF THE OVERALL GROUP, THEY'RE MORE LIKELY TO BECOME A LIVE ATTENDEE[2]...
...
YOU KNOW A LOT ABOUT THIS SUBJECT, MANAGER ...
SHUV SHUV
IT'S C-COMMON KNOWLEDGE!
NOW PULL YOURSELF TOGETHER AND GET BACK ONSTAGE!
It's showtime!
I'M LEARNING A LOT TODAY.
Yêee aaahhh
Enjoying herself
SEXY GIRL SURE KNOWS A LOT ABOUT IDOLS...
♪Princess Color Crush (Cover version)

1: Group members 2: Fan who attends live performances

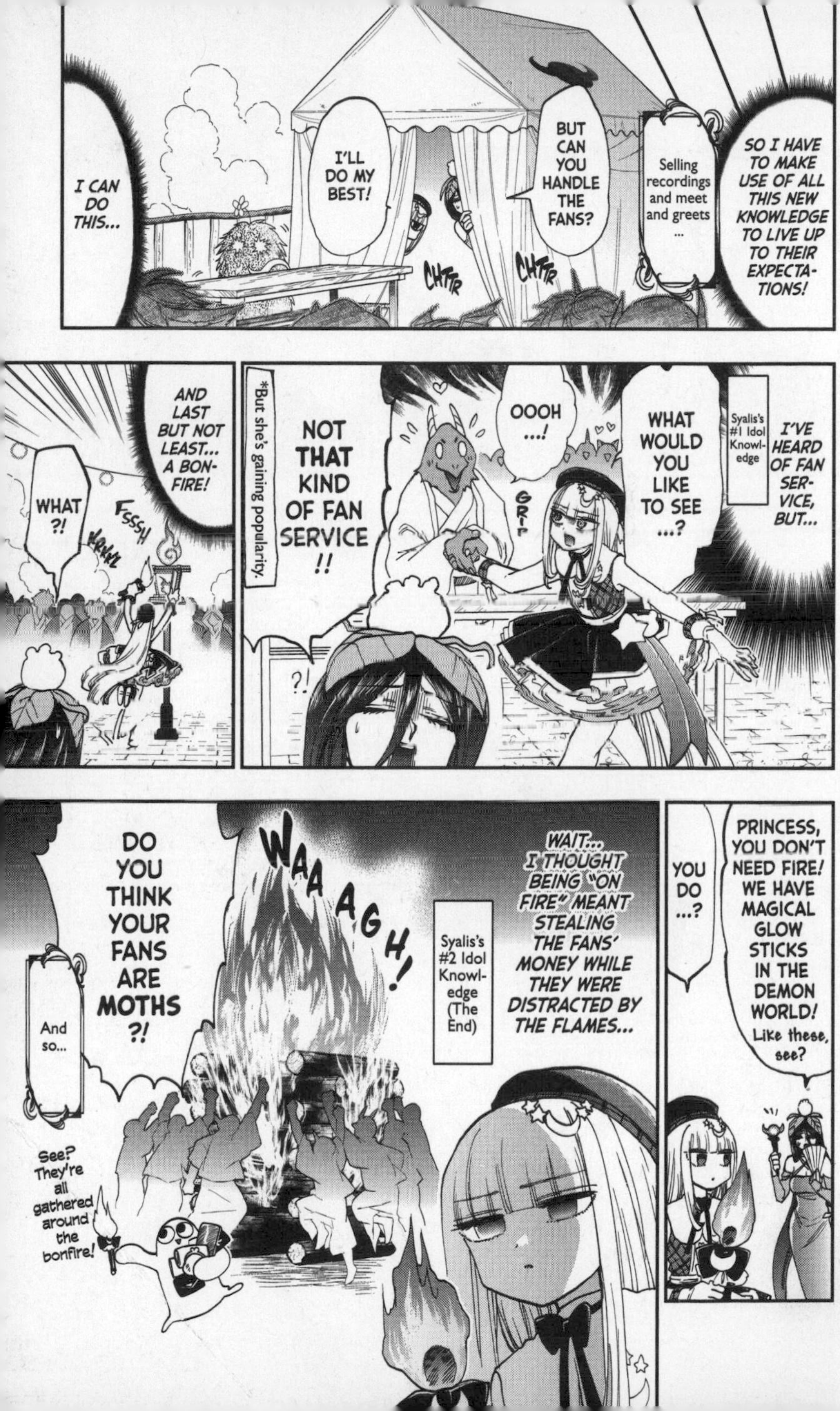
SO I HAVE TO MAKE USE OF ALL THIS NEW KNOWLEDGE TO LIVE UP TO THEIR EXPECTATIONS!
Selling recordings and meet and greets ...
BUT CAN YOU HANDLE THE FANS?
I'LL DO MY BEST!
CHTTR
CHTTR
I CAN DO THIS...
Syalis's #1 Idol Knowl-edge
I'VE HEARD OF FAN SER-VICE, BUT...
WHAT WOULD YOU LIKE TO SEE ...?
OOOH ...!
GRIP
NOT THAT KIND OF FAN SERVICE !!
*But she's gaining popularity.
?!
AND LAST BUT NOT LEAST... A BON-FIRE!
WHAT ?!
FSSSH
PRINCESS, YOU DON'T NEED FIRE! WE HAVE MAGICAL GLOW STICKS IN THE DEMON WORLD!
Like these, see?
YOU DO ...?
WAIT... I THOUGHT BEING "ON FIRE" MEANT STEALING THE FANS' MONEY WHILE THEY WERE DISTRACTED BY THE FLAMES...
Syalis's #2 Idol Knowl-edge (The End)
WAAAGH!
DO YOU THINK YOUR FANS ARE MOTHS ?!
And so...
See? They're all gathered around the bonfire!

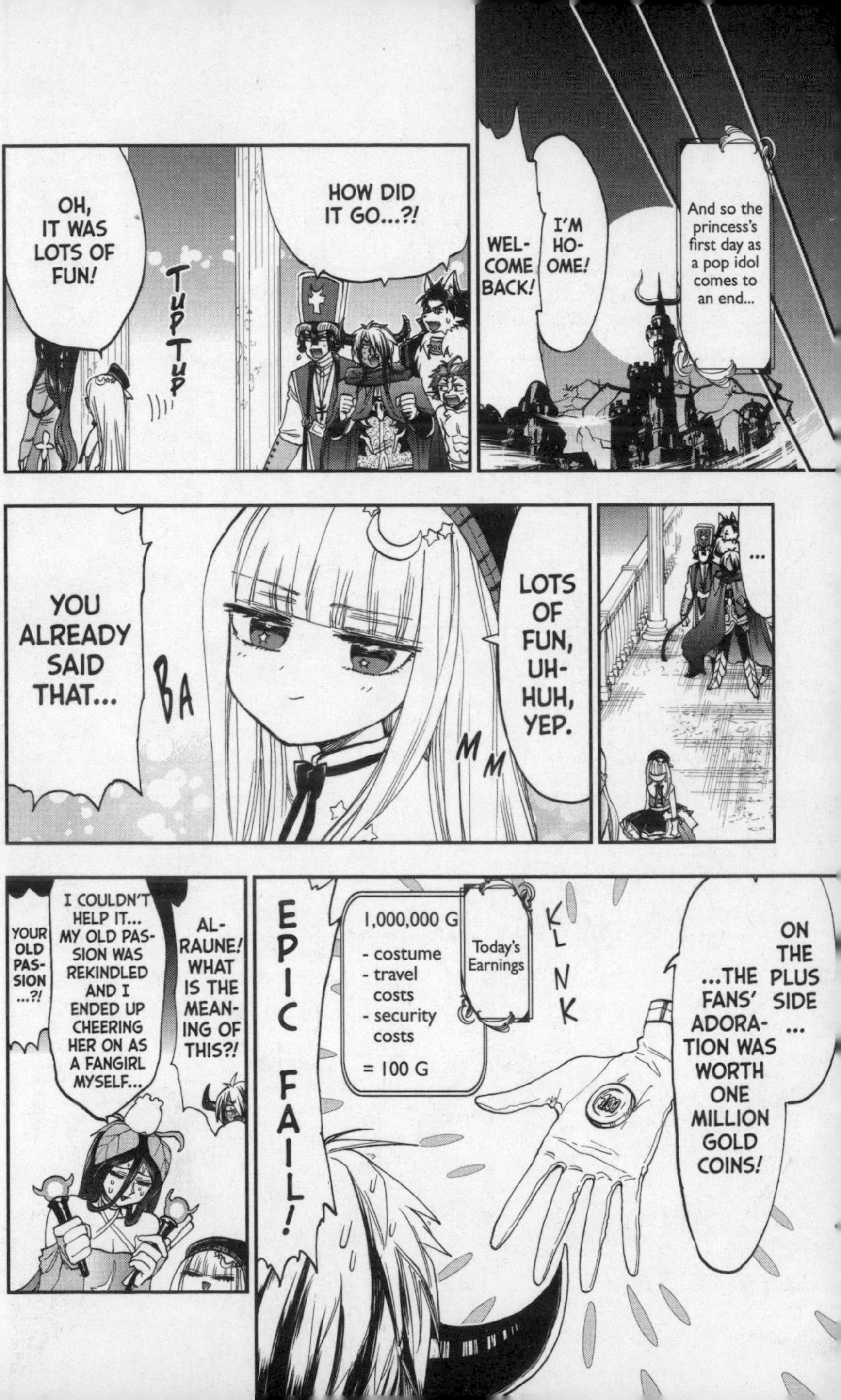
And so the princess's first day as a pop idol comes to an end...
I'M HO-OME!
WEL-COME BACK!
HOW DID IT GO...?!
TUP TUP
OH, IT WAS LOTS OF FUN!
...
LOTS OF FUN, UH-HUH, YEP.
MM
BA
YOU ALREADY SAID THAT...
ON THE PLUS SIDE...
...THE FANS' ADORATION WAS WORTH ONE MILLION GOLD COINS!
KLNK
Today's Earnings
1,000,000 G
- costume
- travel costs
- security costs
= 100 G
EPIC FAIL!
AL-RAUNE! WHAT IS THE MEAN-ING OF THIS?!
I COULDN'T HELP IT... MY OLD PAS-SION WAS REKINDLED AND I ENDED UP CHEERING HER ON AS A FANGIRL MYSELF...
YOUR OLD PAS-SION...?!

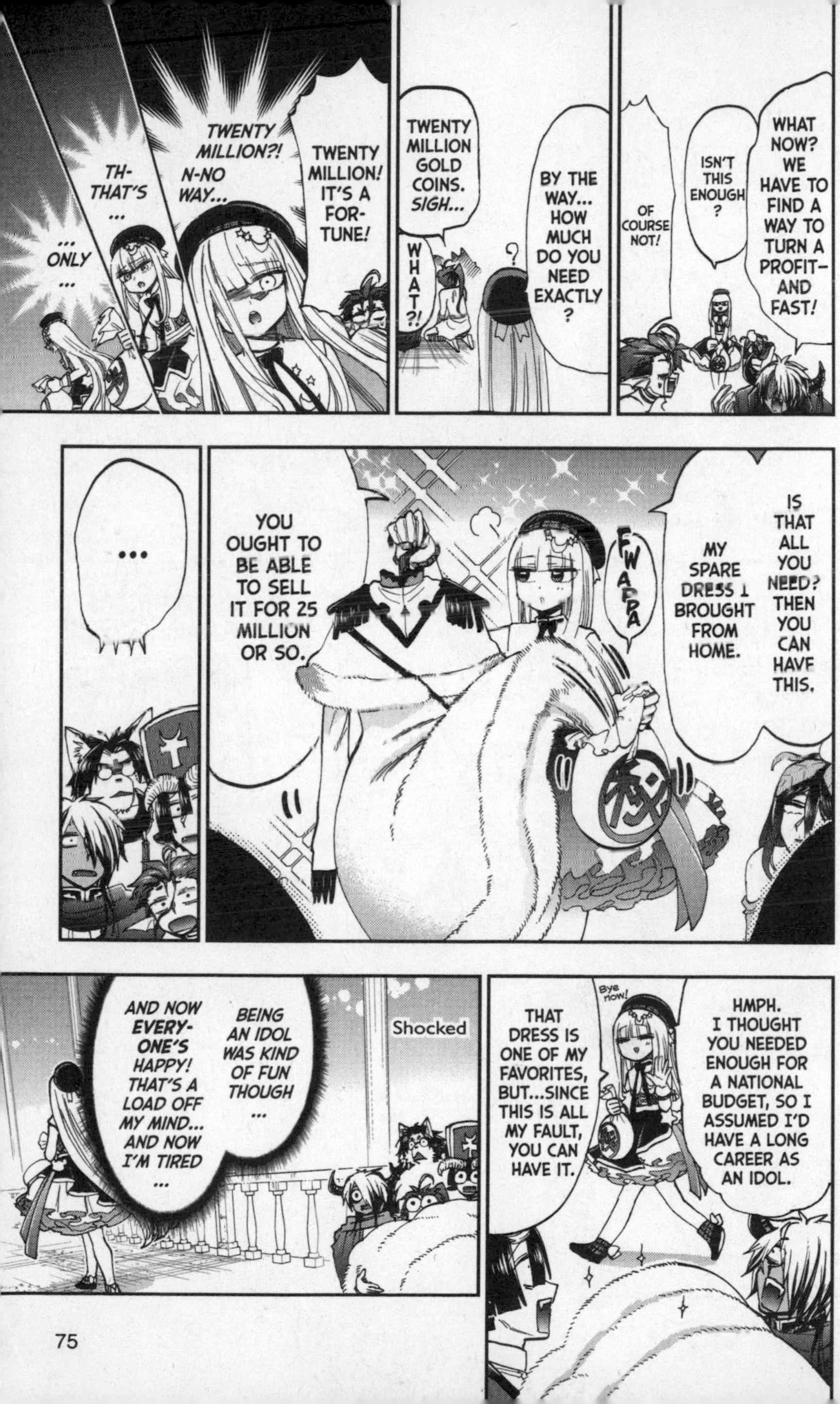
WHAT NOW? WE HAVE TO FIND A WAY TO TURN A PROFIT—AND FAST!
ISN'T THIS ENOUGH?
OF COURSE NOT!
BY THE WAY... HOW MUCH DO YOU NEED EXACTLY?
TWENTY MILLION GOLD COINS. SIGH...
WHAT?!
TWENTY MILLION! IT'S A FOR-TUNE!
TWENTY MILLION?!
N-NO WAY...
TH-THAT'S...
...ONLY...
IS THAT ALL YOU NEED? THEN YOU CAN HAVE THIS.
MY SPARE DRESS I BROUGHT FROM HOME.
FWAPPA
YOU OUGHT TO BE ABLE TO SELL IT FOR 25 MILLION OR SO.
...
HMPH. I THOUGHT YOU NEEDED ENOUGH FOR A NATIONAL BUDGET, SO I ASSUMED I'D HAVE A LONG CAREER AS AN IDOL.
Bye now!
THAT DRESS IS ONE OF MY FAVORITES, BUT...SINCE THIS IS ALL MY FAULT, YOU CAN HAVE IT.
Shocked
BEING AN IDOL WAS KIND OF FUN THOUGH...
AND NOW EVERY-ONE'S HAPPY! THAT'S A LOAD OFF MY MIND... AND NOW I'M TIRED...

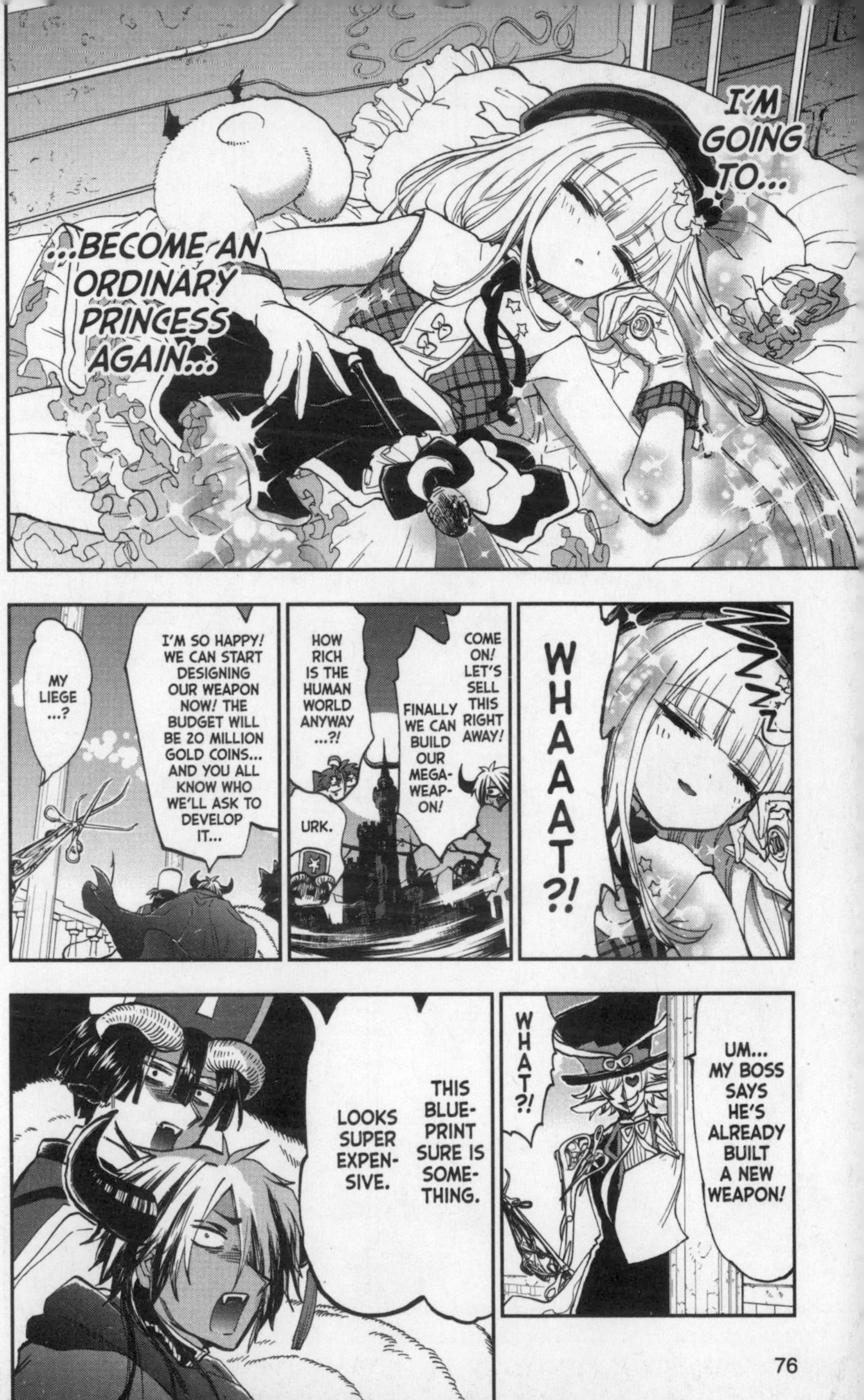
I'M GOING TO...
...BECOME AN ORDINARY PRINCESS AGAIN...
WHAAAAT?!
COME ON! LET'S SELL THIS RIGHT AWAY!
FINALLY WE CAN BUILD OUR MEGA-WEAPON!
HOW RICH IS THE HUMAN WORLD ANYWAY...?!
URK.
I'M SO HAPPY! WE CAN START DESIGNING OUR WEAPON NOW! THE BUDGET WILL BE 20 MILLION GOLD COINS... AND YOU ALL KNOW WHO WE'LL ASK TO DEVELOP IT...
MY LIEGE...?
UM... MY BOSS SAYS HE'S ALREADY BUILT A NEW WEAPON!
WHAT?!
THIS BLUEPRINT SURE IS SOMETHING.
LOOKS SUPER EXPENSIVE.

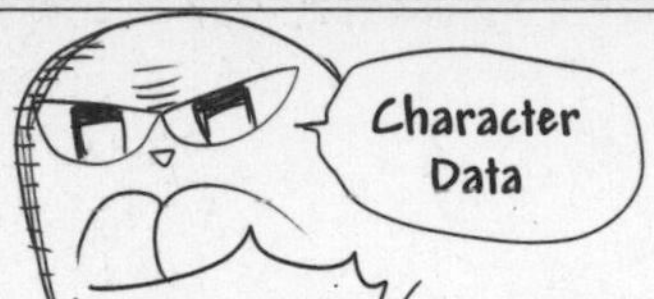
Character Data

Top secret info that may now be disclosed

BIRTHDAYS (According to the human world calendar)

Princess	December 22
Demon King	June 6 (6:06:06 a.m.)
Demon Cleric	November 11 (For the castle records. His memories are rather vague.)
Great Red Siberian	January 10 (The day the Demon King found him wandering the streets.)
Poseidon	July 20 (The date of his latest rebirth.)
Neo Alraune	April 4 (Originally sprouted as a lily of the valley.)
Fire Venom Dragon	December 1 (There is no record of his birth. This is his first day of employment at the Demon Castle.)
Quilladillo	September 15 (At Hell Kusatsu.)
Castle Grunt Goblin	May 5
Minotaur	July 27
Frankenzombie	October 11 (The day he woke up after being cobbled together.)
Bussy	December 23
Harpy	October 25
Cursed Musician	February 5
Hades	February 18 (The day of his latest rebirth.)
Hypnos	January 1 (For the castle records. There is no record of his birth.)
Cer, Ber, Rus	March 3 (The day Hades found them wandering the streets.)
Scissors Sorcerer	December 10 (The day he was created.)
Teddy Demon	Every day ♡
Eggplant Seal	Every day ♡

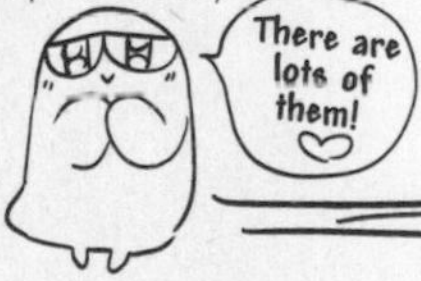
There are lots of them! ♡

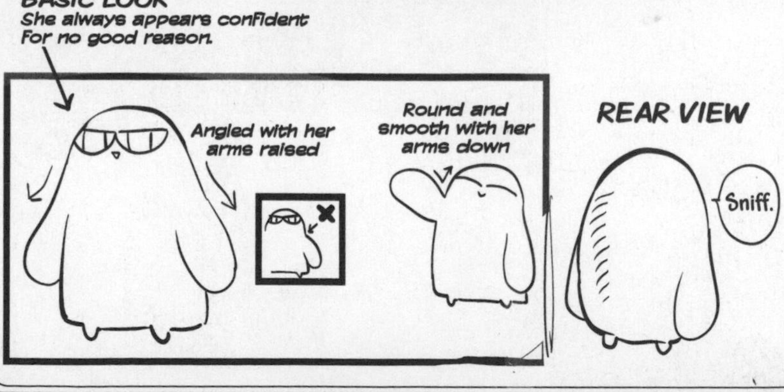
BASIC LOOK
She always appears confident for no good reason.
Angled with her arms raised
Round and smooth with her arms down
REAR VIEW
Sniff.

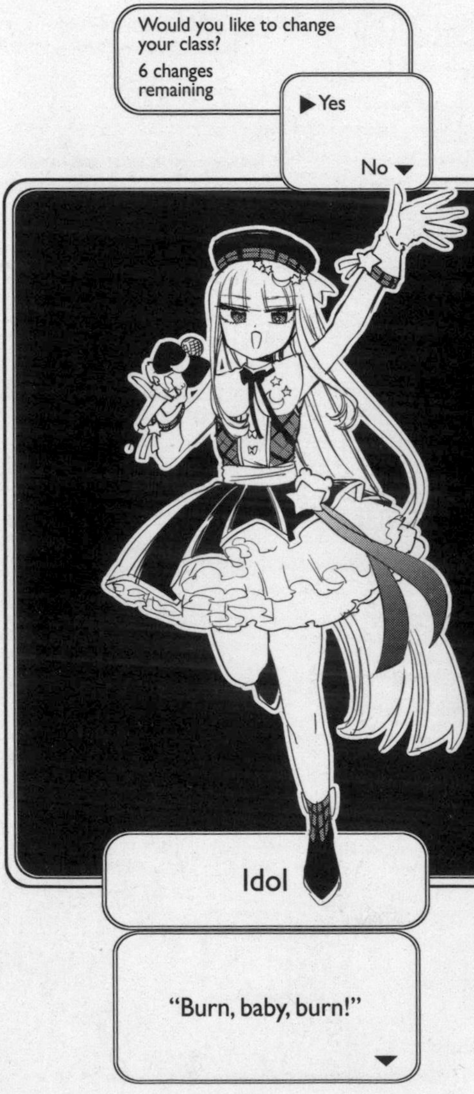
Would you like to change your class?
6 changes remaining
▶Yes
No
Idol
"Burn, baby, burn!"

150th Night: Well, It Is Modeled After You-Know-Who

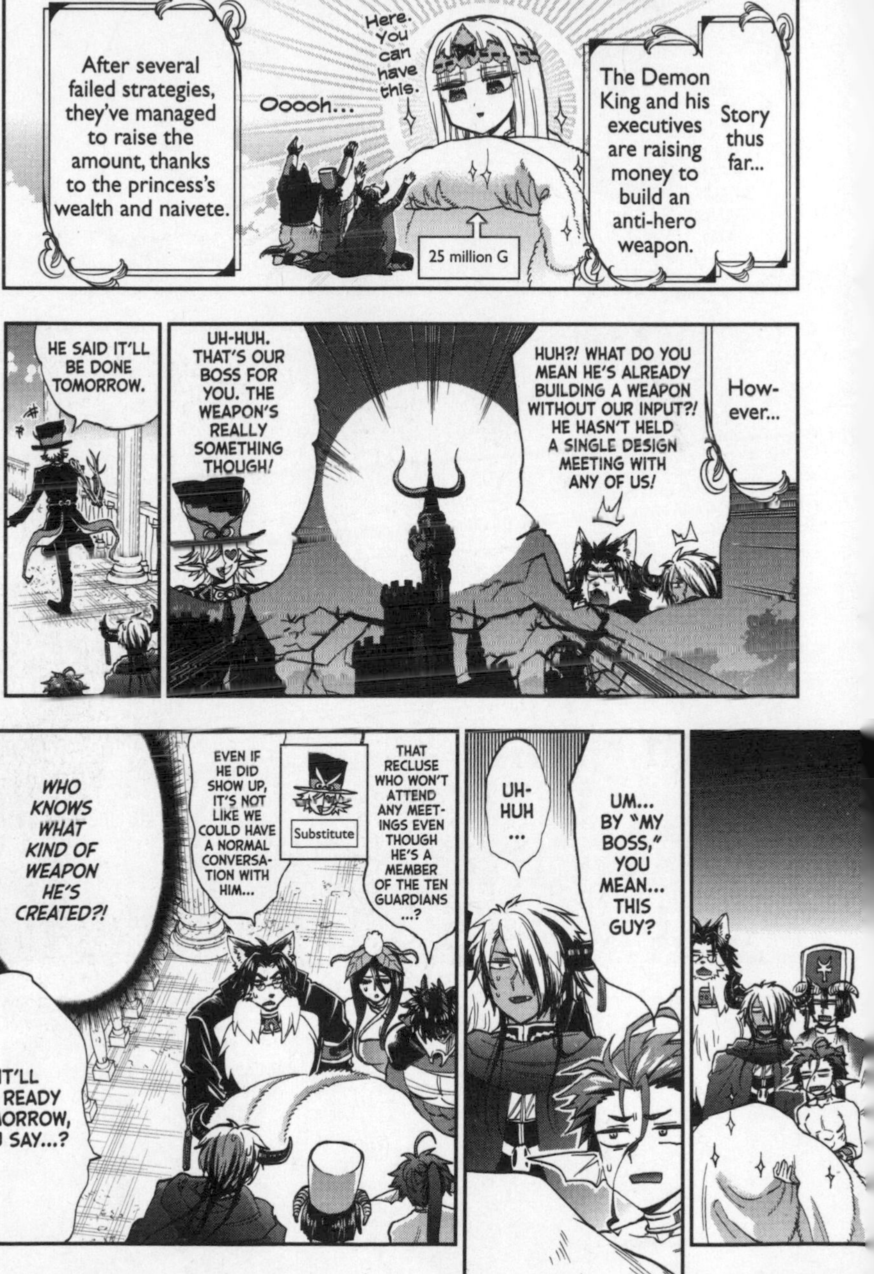
Story thus far...
The Demon King and his executives are raising money to build an anti-hero weapon.
Here. You can have this.
Ooooh...
25 million G
After several failed strategies, they've managed to raise the amount, thanks to the princess's wealth and naivete.
However...
HUH?! WHAT DO YOU MEAN HE'S ALREADY BUILDING A WEAPON WITHOUT OUR INPUT?! HE HASN'T HELD A SINGLE DESIGN MEETING WITH ANY OF US!
UH-HUH. THAT'S OUR BOSS FOR YOU. THE WEAPON'S REALLY SOMETHING THOUGH!
HE SAID IT'LL BE DONE TOMORROW.
UM... BY "MY BOSS," YOU MEAN... THIS GUY?
UH-HUH...
THAT RECLUSE WHO WON'T ATTEND ANY MEET-INGS EVEN THOUGH HE'S A MEMBER OF THE TEN GUARDIANS...?
Substitute
EVEN IF HE DID SHOW UP, IT'S NOT LIKE WE COULD HAVE A NORMAL CONVERSA-TION WITH HIM...
WHO KNOWS WHAT KIND OF WEAPON HE'S CREATED?!
IT'LL BE READY TOMORROW, YOU SAY...?

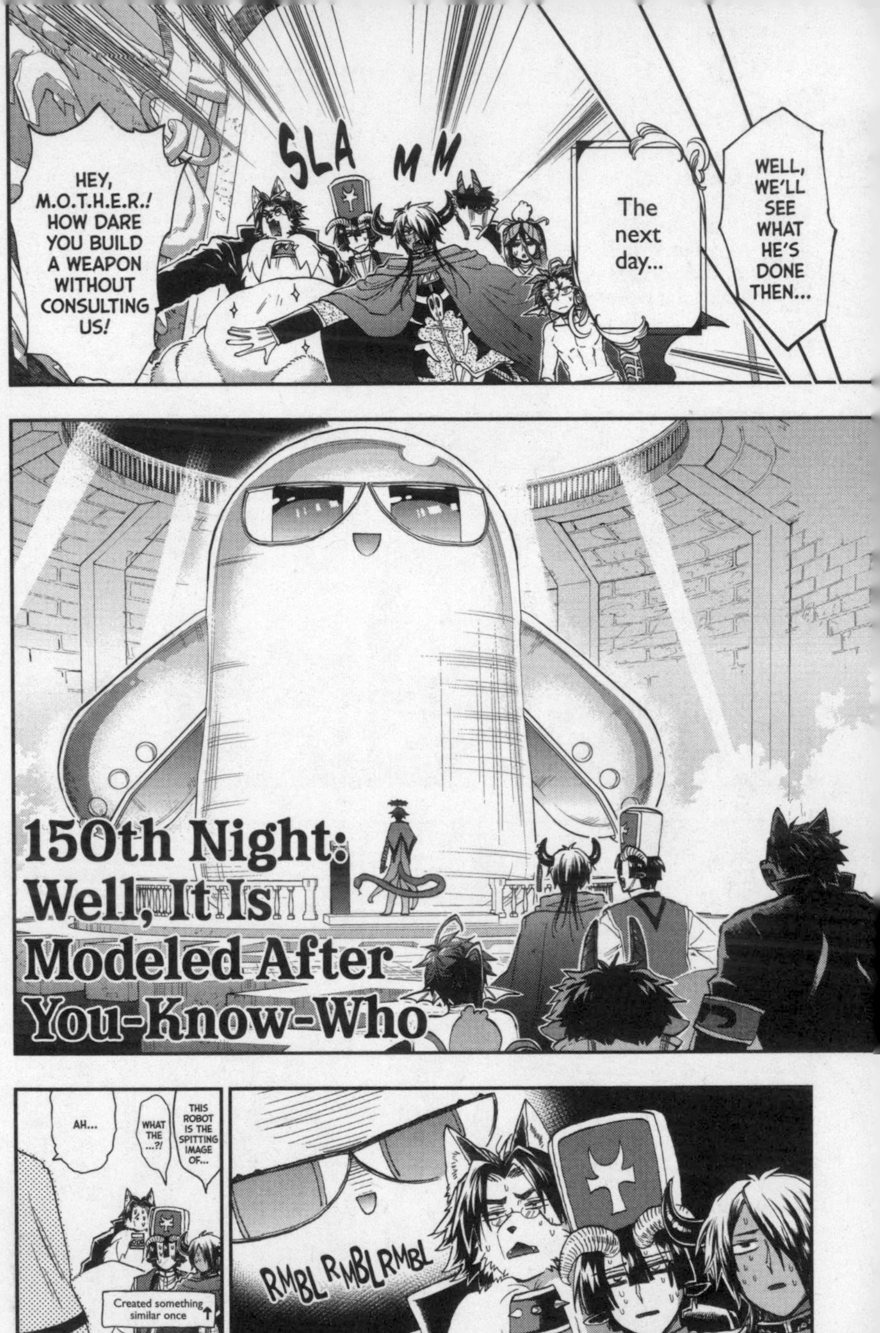
WELL, WE'LL SEE WHAT HE'S DONE THEN...
The next day...
SLAMM
HEY, M.O.T.H.E.R.! HOW DARE YOU BUILD A WEAPON WITHOUT CONSULTING US!
150th Night: Well, It Is Modeled After You-Know-Who
RMBL RMBL RMBL
THIS ROBOT IS THE SPITTING IMAGE OF...
WHAT THE ...?!
AH...
Created something similar once ↑

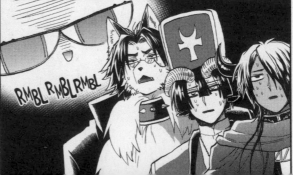

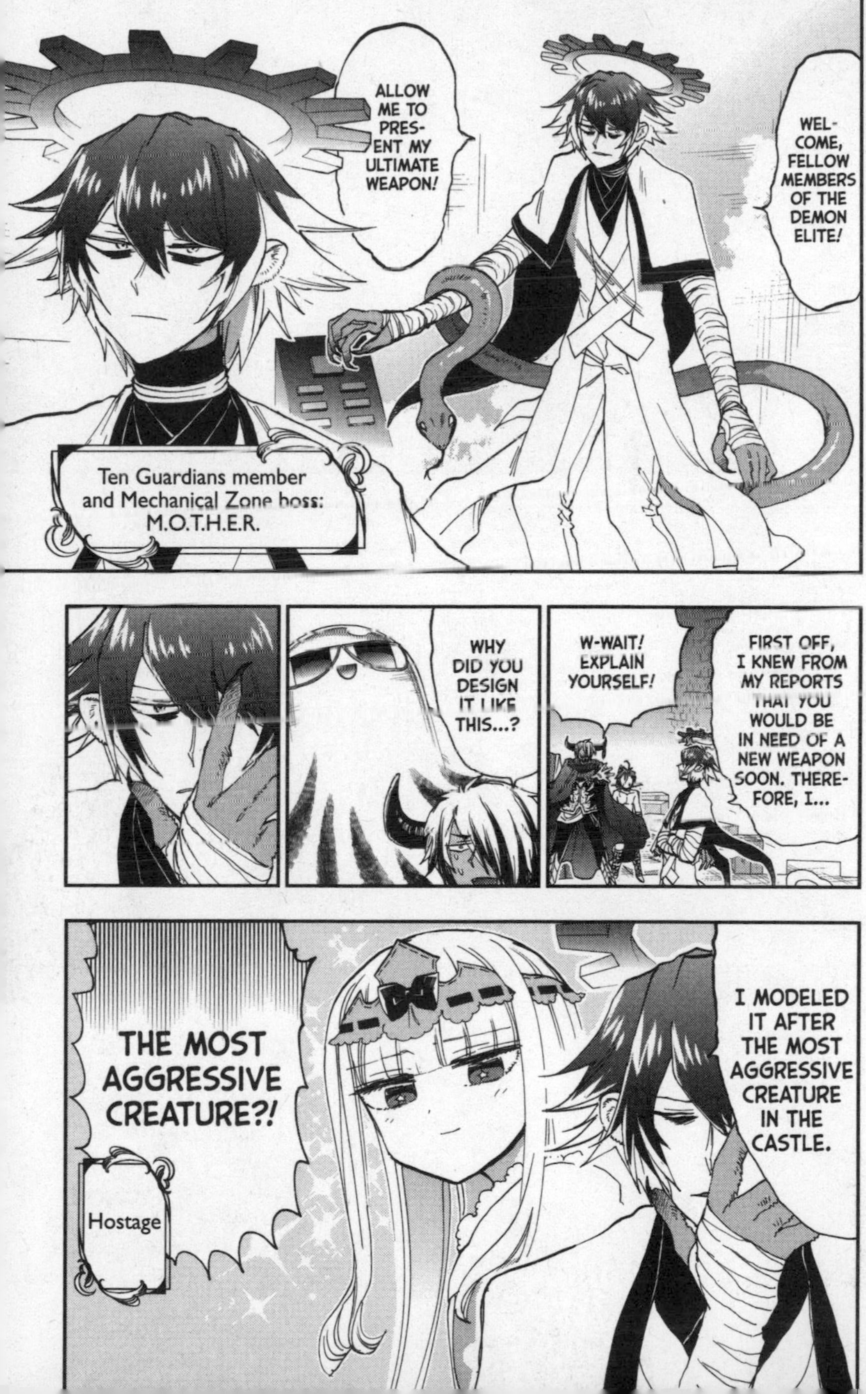
WEL-
COME,
FELLOW
MEMBERS
OF THE
DEMON
ELITE!
ALLOW
ME TO
PRES-
ENT MY
ULTIMATE
WEAPON!
Ten Guardians member
and Mechanical Zone boss:
M.O.T.H.E.R.
FIRST OFF,
I KNEW FROM
MY REPORTS
THAT YOU
WOULD BE
IN NEED OF A
NEW WEAPON
SOON. THERE-
FORE, I...
W-WAIT!
EXPLAIN
YOURSELF!
WHY
DID YOU
DESIGN
IT LIKE
THIS...?
I MODELED
IT AFTER
THE MOST
AGGRESSIVE
CREATURE
IN THE
CASTLE.
THE MOST
AGGRESSIVE
CREATURE?!
Hostage

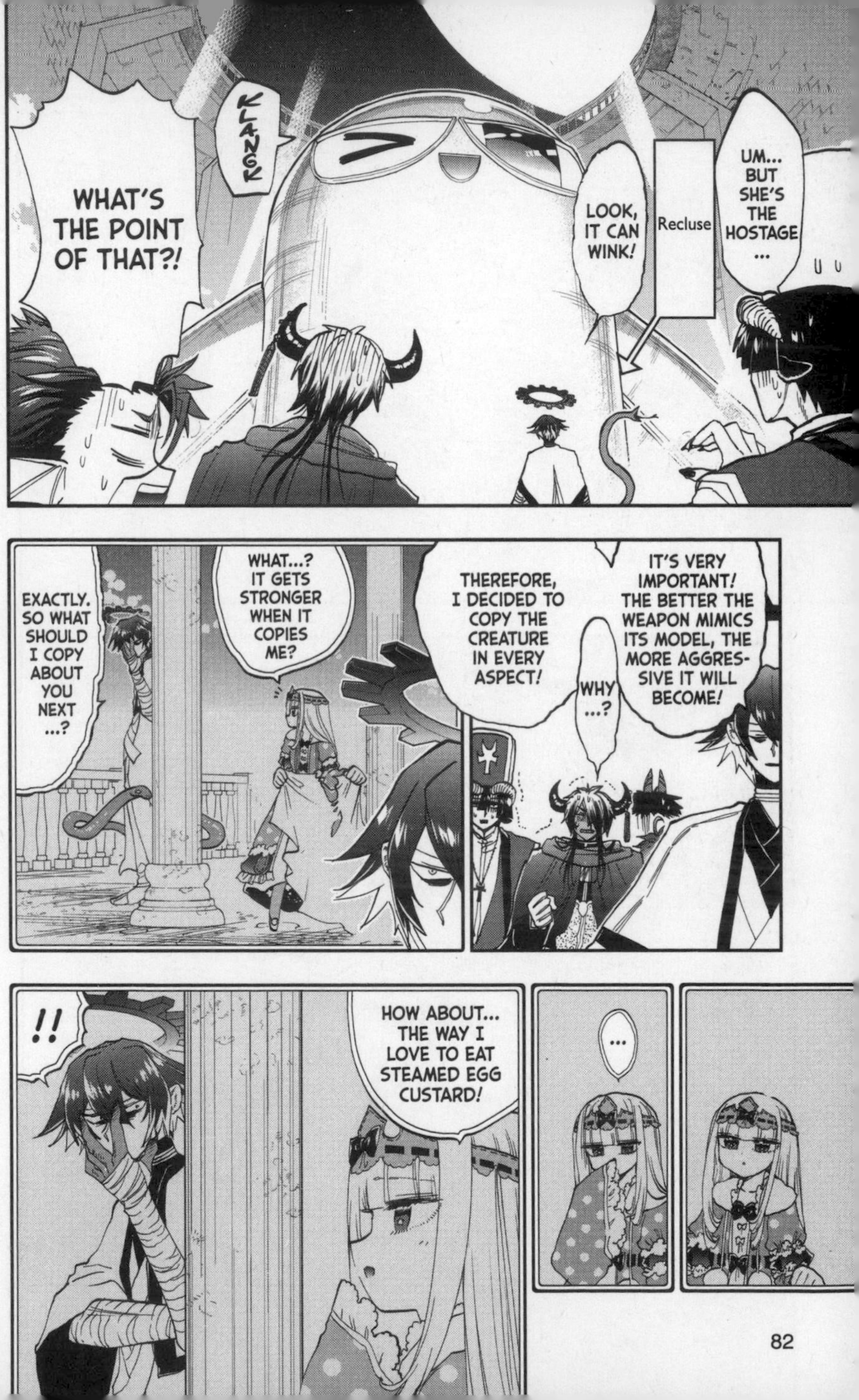
UM... BUT SHE'S THE HOSTAGE ...
Recluse
LOOK, IT CAN WINK!
KLANGK
WHAT'S THE POINT OF THAT?!
IT'S VERY IMPORTANT! THE BETTER THE WEAPON MIMICS ITS MODEL, THE MORE AGGRES-SIVE IT WILL BECOME!
THEREFORE, I DECIDED TO COPY THE CREATURE IN EVERY ASPECT!
WHY ...?
WHAT...? IT GETS STRONGER WHEN IT COPIES ME?
EXACTLY. SO WHAT SHOULD I COPY ABOUT YOU NEXT ...?
...
HOW ABOUT... THE WAY I LOVE TO EAT STEAMED EGG CUSTARD!
!!

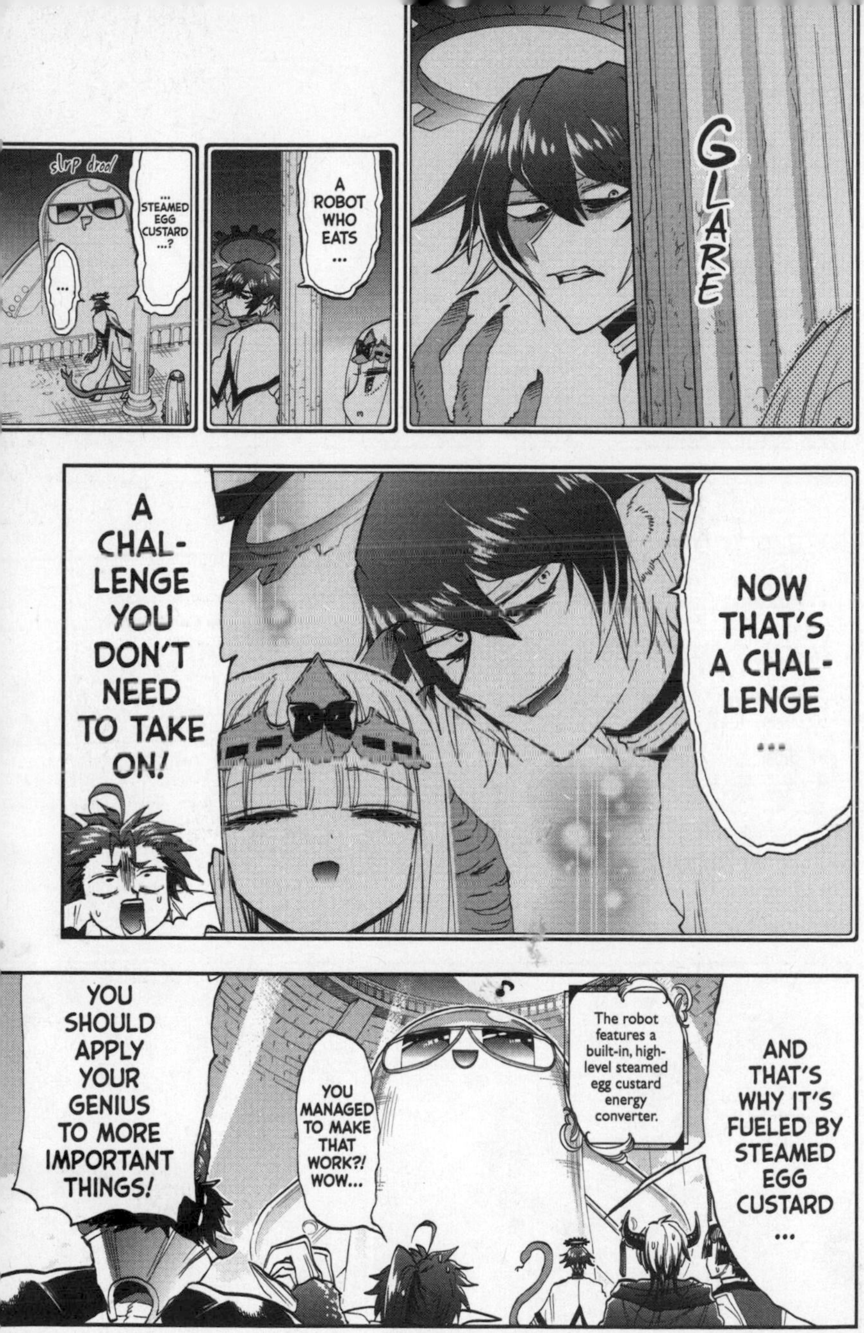
GLARE
A ROBOT WHO EATS ...
... STEAMED EGG CUSTARD ...?
...
slrp drool
NOW THAT'S A CHALLENGE ...
A CHALLENGE YOU DON'T NEED TO TAKE ON!
AND THAT'S WHY IT'S FUELED BY STEAMED EGG CUSTARD ...
The robot features a built-in, high-level steamed egg custard energy converter.
YOU MANAGED TO MAKE THAT WORK?! WOW...
YOU SHOULD APPLY YOUR GENIUS TO MORE IMPORTANT THINGS!

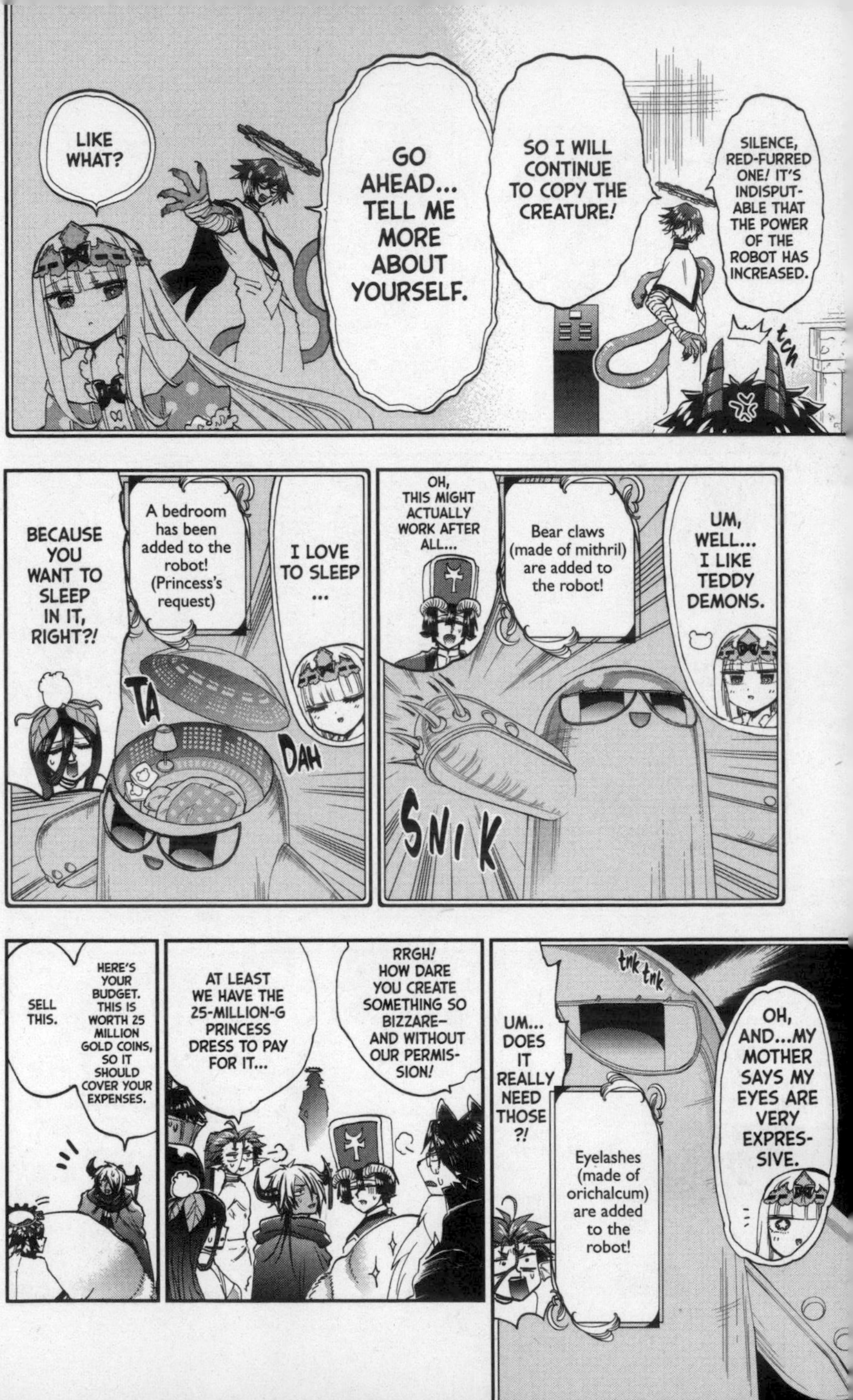
SILENCE, RED-FURRED ONE! IT'S INDISPUTABLE THAT THE POWER OF THE ROBOT HAS INCREASED.
tch
SO I WILL CONTINUE TO COPY THE CREATURE!
GO AHEAD... TELL ME MORE ABOUT YOURSELF.
LIKE WHAT?
UM, WELL... I LIKE TEDDY DEMONS.
Bear claws (made of mithril) are added to the robot!
OH, THIS MIGHT ACTUALLY WORK AFTER ALL...
SNIK
I LOVE TO SLEEP ...
A bedroom has been added to the robot! (Princess's request)
BECAUSE YOU WANT TO SLEEP IN IT, RIGHT?!
TA
DAH
tnk tnk
OH, AND...MY MOTHER SAYS MY EYES ARE VERY EXPRES-SIVE.
Eyelashes (made of orichalcum) are added to the robot!
UM... DOES IT REALLY NEED THOSE?!
RRGH! HOW DARE YOU CREATE SOMETHING SO BIZZARE— AND WITHOUT OUR PERMIS-SION!
AT LEAST WE HAVE THE 25-MILLION-G PRINCESS DRESS TO PAY FOR IT...
HERE'S YOUR BUDGET. THIS IS WORTH 25 MILLION GOLD COINS, SO IT SHOULD COVER YOUR EXPENSES.
SELL THIS.

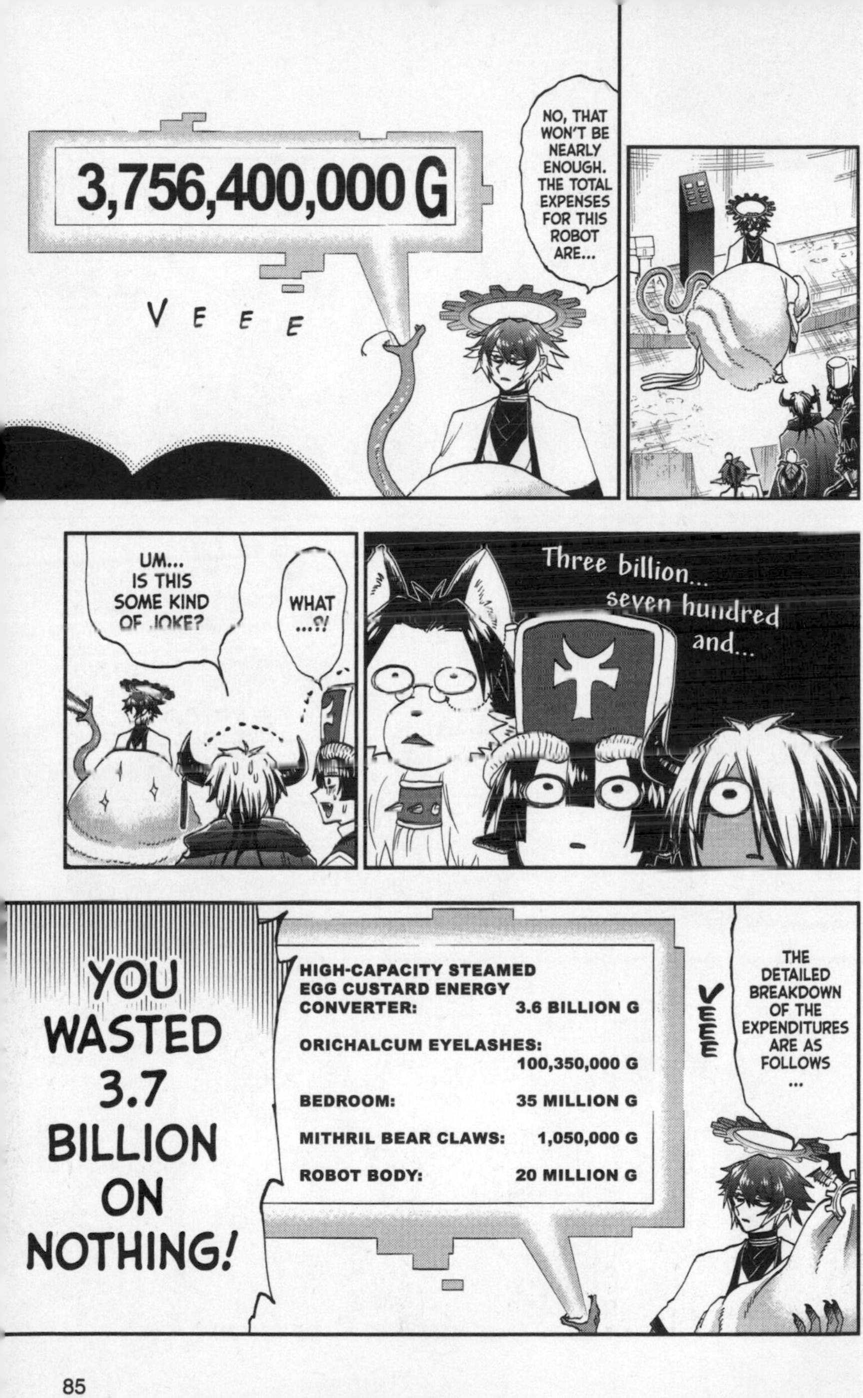
NO, THAT WON'T BE NEARLY ENOUGH. THE TOTAL EXPENSES FOR THIS ROBOT ARE...
3,756,400,000 G
VEEE
Three billion... seven hundred and...
WHAT ...?!
UM... IS THIS SOME KIND OF JOKE?
THE DETAILED BREAKDOWN OF THE EXPENDITURES ARE AS FOLLOWS ...
VEEE
HIGH-CAPACITY STEAMED EGG CUSTARD ENERGY CONVERTER: 3.6 BILLION G
ORICHALCUM EYELASHES: 100,350,000 G
BEDROOM: 35 MILLION G
MITHRIL BEAR CLAWS: 1,050,000 G
ROBOT BODY: 20 MILLION G
YOU WASTED 3.7 BILLION ON NOTHING!

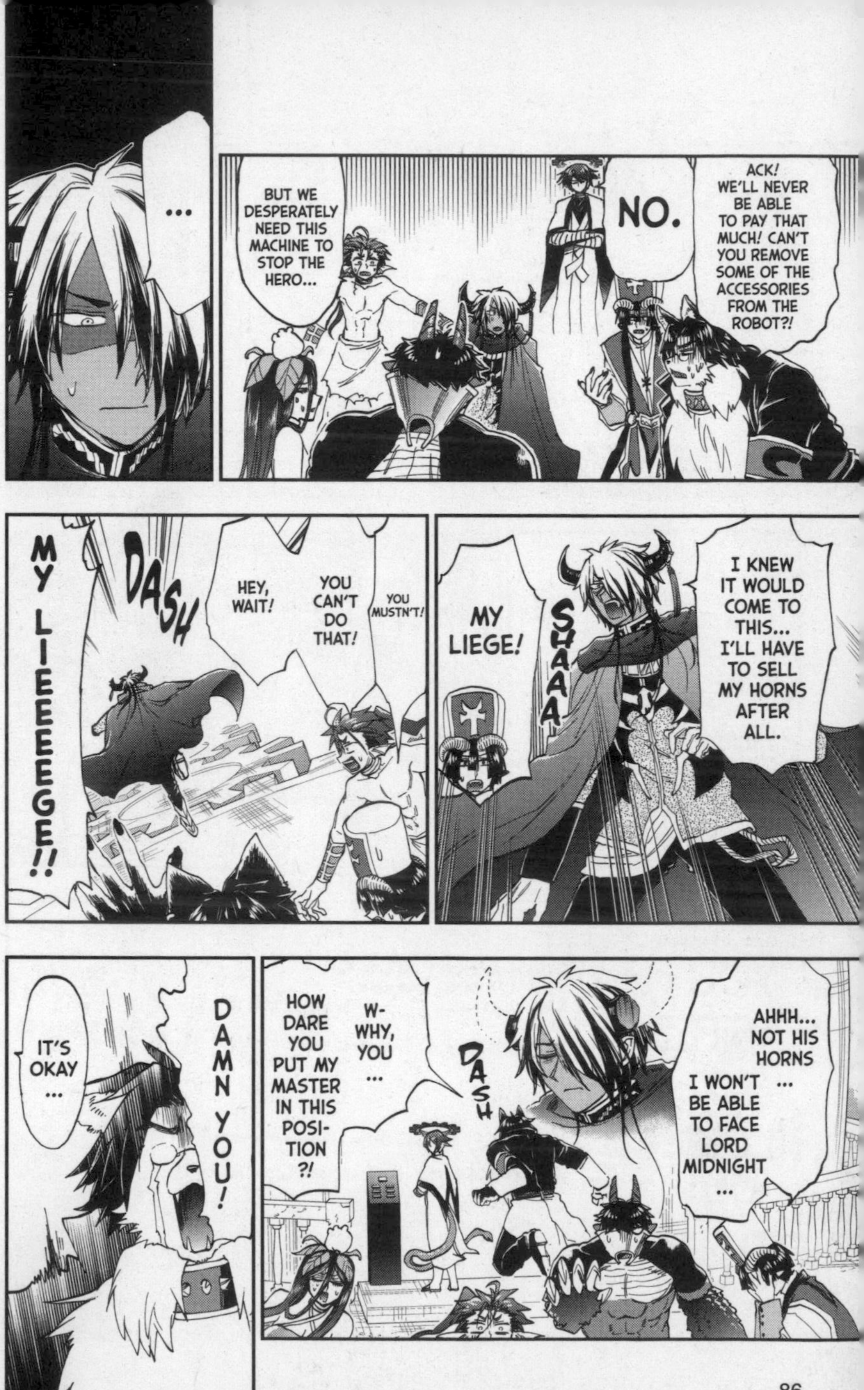
ACK! WE'LL NEVER BE ABLE TO PAY THAT MUCH! CAN'T YOU REMOVE SOME OF THE ACCESSORIES FROM THE ROBOT?!
NO.
BUT WE DESPERATELY NEED THIS MACHINE TO STOP THE HERO...
...
I KNEW IT WOULD COME TO THIS... I'LL HAVE TO SELL MY HORNS AFTER ALL.
SHAAAA
MY LIEGE!
YOU MUSTN'T!
YOU CAN'T DO THAT!
HEY, WAIT!
DASH
MY LIEEEEEGE!!
AHHH... NOT HIS HORNS ...
I WON'T BE ABLE TO FACE LORD MIDNIGHT ...
DASH
W-WHY, YOU ...
HOW DARE YOU PUT MY MASTER IN THIS POSITION?!
DAMN YOU!
IT'S OKAY ...

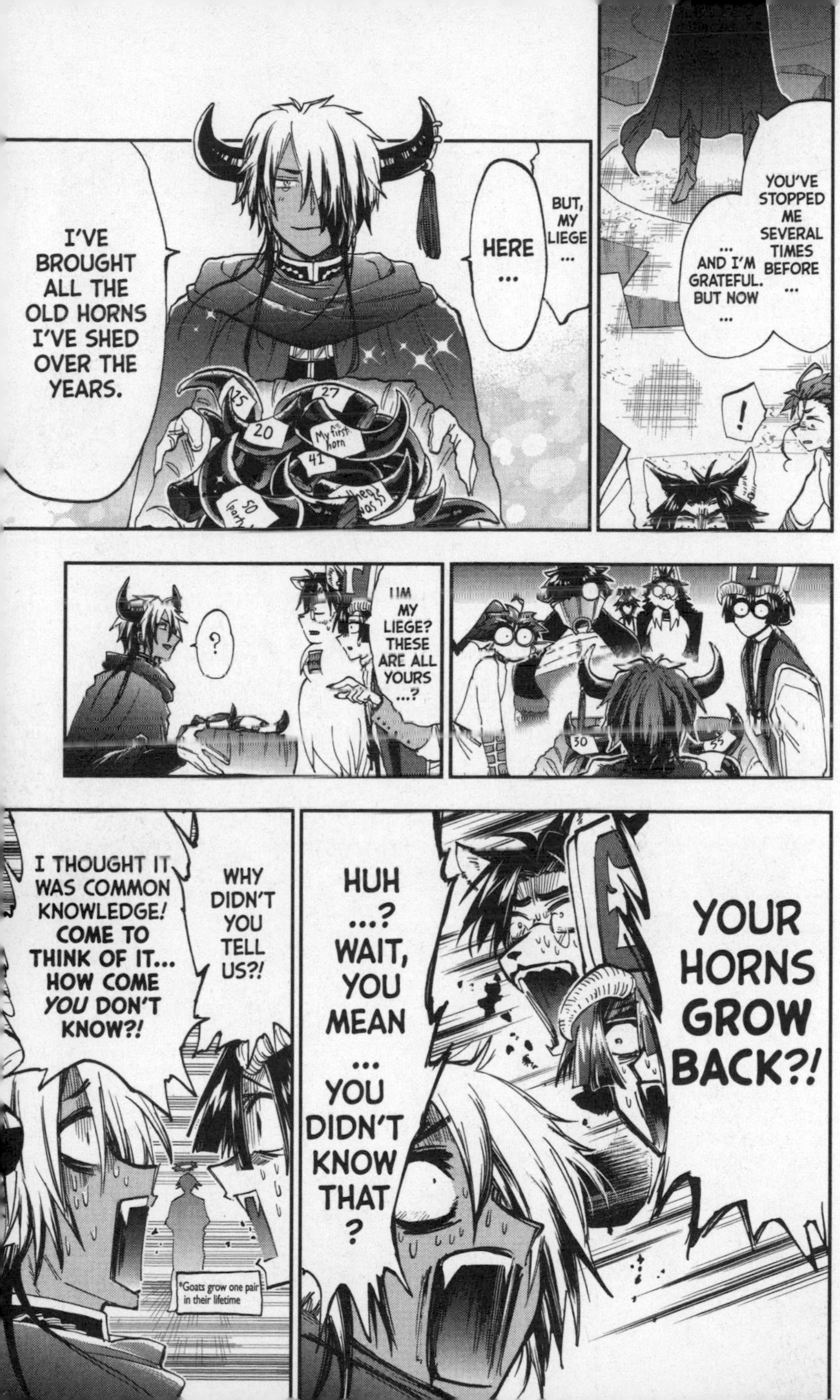
YOU'VE STOPPED ME SEVERAL TIMES BEFORE ...
... AND I'M GRATEFUL. BUT NOW ...
!
BUT, MY LIEGE ...
HERE ...
I'VE BROUGHT ALL THE OLD HORNS I'VE SHED OVER THE YEARS.
27
15
20
My first horn
41
50 (part)
30
55
UM MY LIEGE? THESE ARE ALL YOURS ...?
?
YOUR HORNS GROW BACK?!
HUH ...? WAIT, YOU MEAN ... YOU DIDN'T KNOW THAT ?
WHY DIDN'T YOU TELL US?!
I THOUGHT IT WAS COMMON KNOWLEDGE! COME TO THINK OF IT... HOW COME *YOU* DON'T KNOW?!
*Goats grow one pair in their lifetime

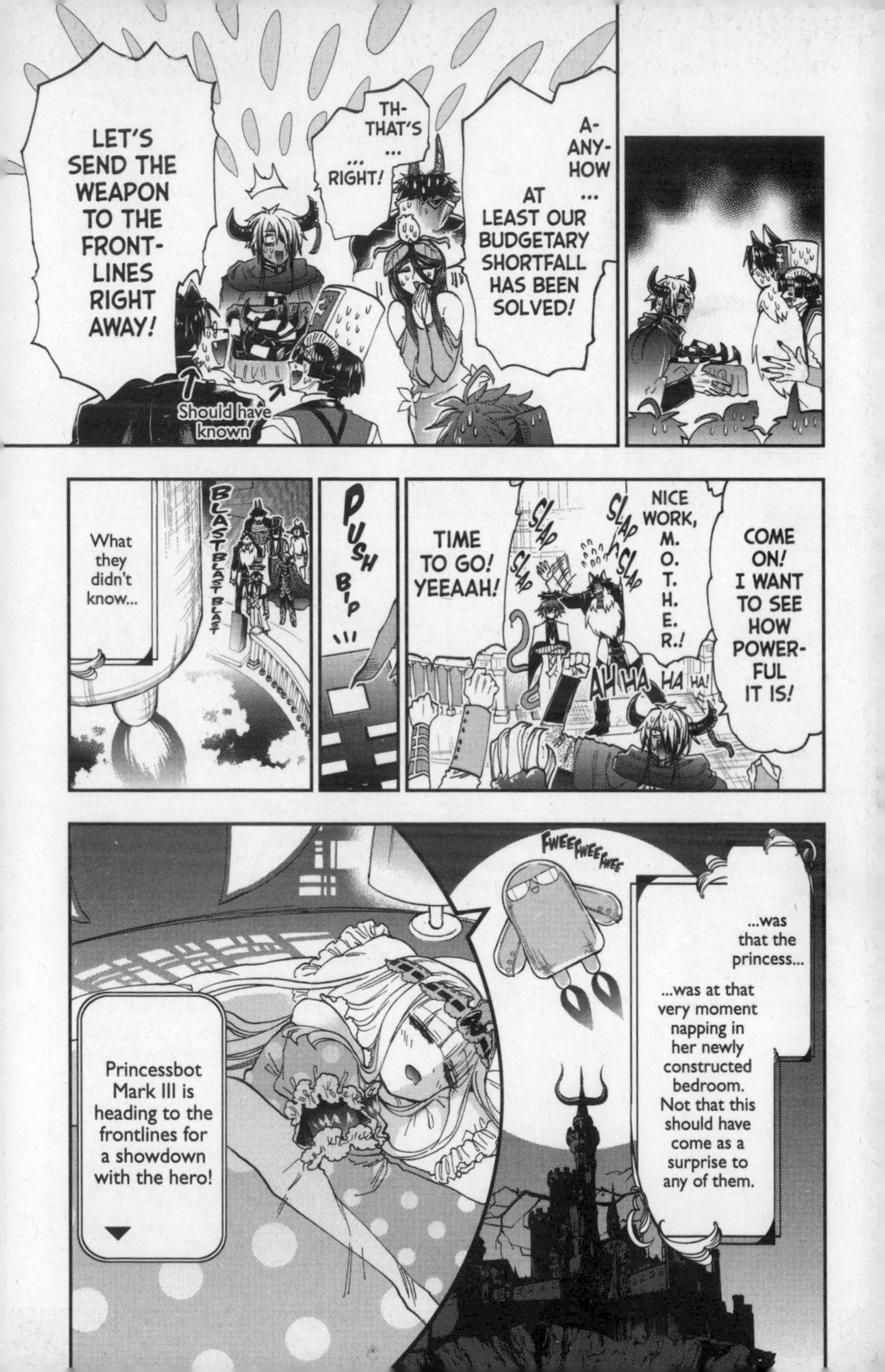
A- ANY- HOW ... AT LEAST OUR BUDGETARY SHORTFALL HAS BEEN SOLVED!
TH- THAT'S ... ... RIGHT!
LET'S SEND THE WEAPON TO THE FRONT-LINES RIGHT AWAY!
Should have known
COME ON! I WANT TO SEE HOW POWER-FUL IT IS!
NICE WORK, M.O.T.H.E.R.!
SLAP SLAP SLAP SLAP
AH HA HA HA!
TIME TO GO! YEEAAH!
PUSH
BIP
BLAST BLAST BLAST
What they didn't know...
...was that the princess...
...was at that very moment napping in her newly constructed bedroom. Not that this should have come as a surprise to any of them.
FWEEFWEEFWEE
Princessbot Mark III is heading to the frontlines for a showdown with the hero!

Princessbot Mark III

Klangk

Power: ☆☆☆☆☆☆☆☆
Price Tag: ☆☆☆☆☆☆☆☆☆☆☆☆☆

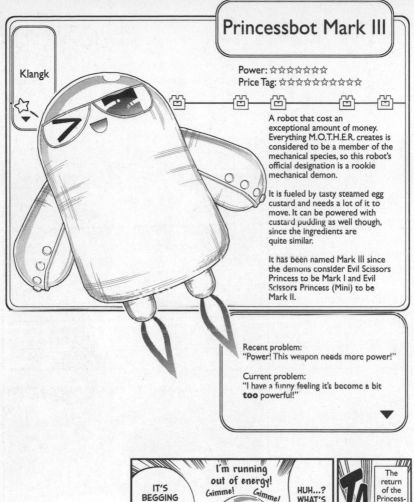

A robot that cost an exceptional amount of money. Everything M.O.T.H.E.R. creates is considered to be a member of the mechanical species, so this robot's official designation is a rookie mechanical demon.

It is fueled by tasty steamed egg custard and needs a lot of it to move. It can be powered with custard pudding as well though, since the ingredients are quite similar.

It has been named Mark III since the demons consider Evil Scissors Princess to be Mark I and Evil Scissors Princess (Mini) to be Mark II.

Recent problem:
"Power! This weapon needs more power!"

Current problem:
"I have a funny feeling it's become a bit **too** powerful!"

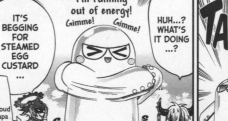

The return of the Princess-bot!
TA DAH
HUH...? WHAT'S IT DOING ...?
I'm running out of energy!
Gimme! Gimme!
IT'S BEGGING FOR STEAMED EGG CUSTARD ...
Proud papa
STOMP
STOMP

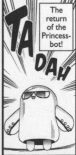

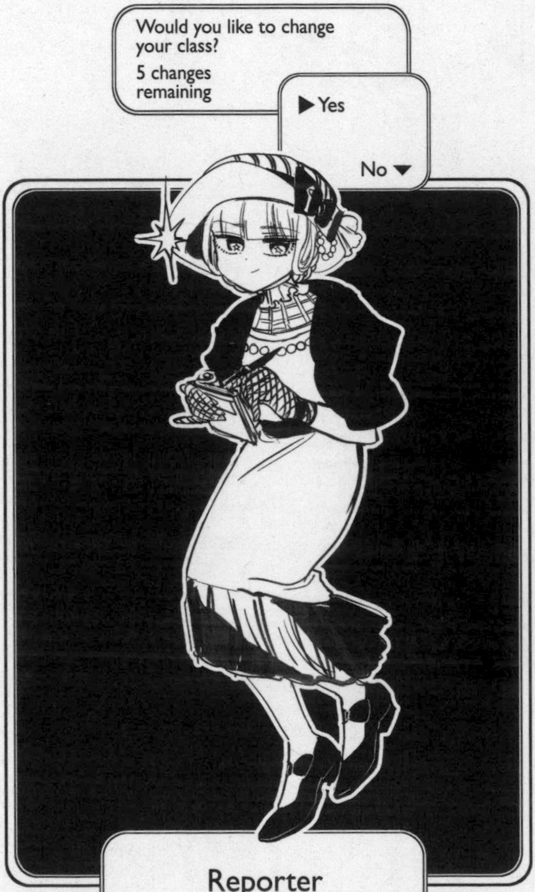
Would you like to change your class?
5 changes remaining
▶Yes
No
Reporter
"I've got a scoop!"

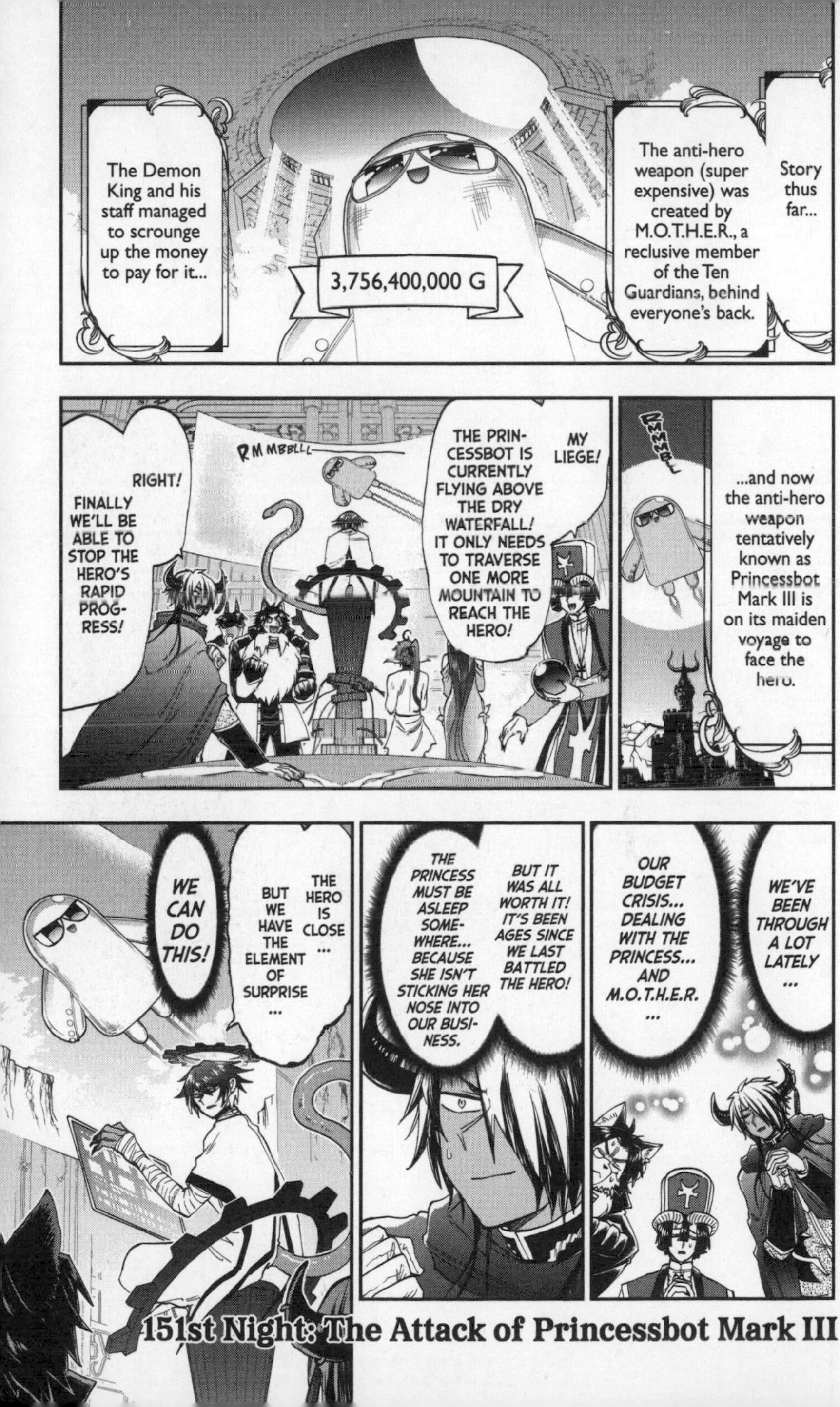
Story thus far...
The anti-hero weapon (super expensive) was created by M.O.T.H.E.R., a reclusive member of the Ten Guardians, behind everyone's back.
3,756,400,000 G
The Demon King and his staff managed to scrounge up the money to pay for it...
RMMMBLL
...and now the anti-hero weapon tentatively known as Princessbot Mark III is on its maiden voyage to face the hero.
MY LIEGE!
THE PRINCESSBOT IS CURRENTLY FLYING ABOVE THE DRY WATERFALL! IT ONLY NEEDS TO TRAVERSE ONE MORE MOUNTAIN TO REACH THE HERO!
RMMBBLLL
RIGHT! FINALLY WE'LL BE ABLE TO STOP THE HERO'S RAPID PROGRESS!
WE'VE BEEN THROUGH A LOT LATELY...
OUR BUDGET CRISIS... DEALING WITH THE PRINCESS... AND M.O.T.H.E.R. ...
BUT IT WAS ALL WORTH IT! IT'S BEEN AGES SINCE WE LAST BATTLED THE HERO!
THE PRINCESS MUST BE ASLEEP SOMEWHERE... BECAUSE SHE ISN'T STICKING HER NOSE INTO OUR BUSINESS.
THE HERO IS CLOSE...
BUT WE HAVE THE ELEMENT OF SURPRISE...
WE CAN DO THIS!
151st Night: The Attack of Princessbot Mark III

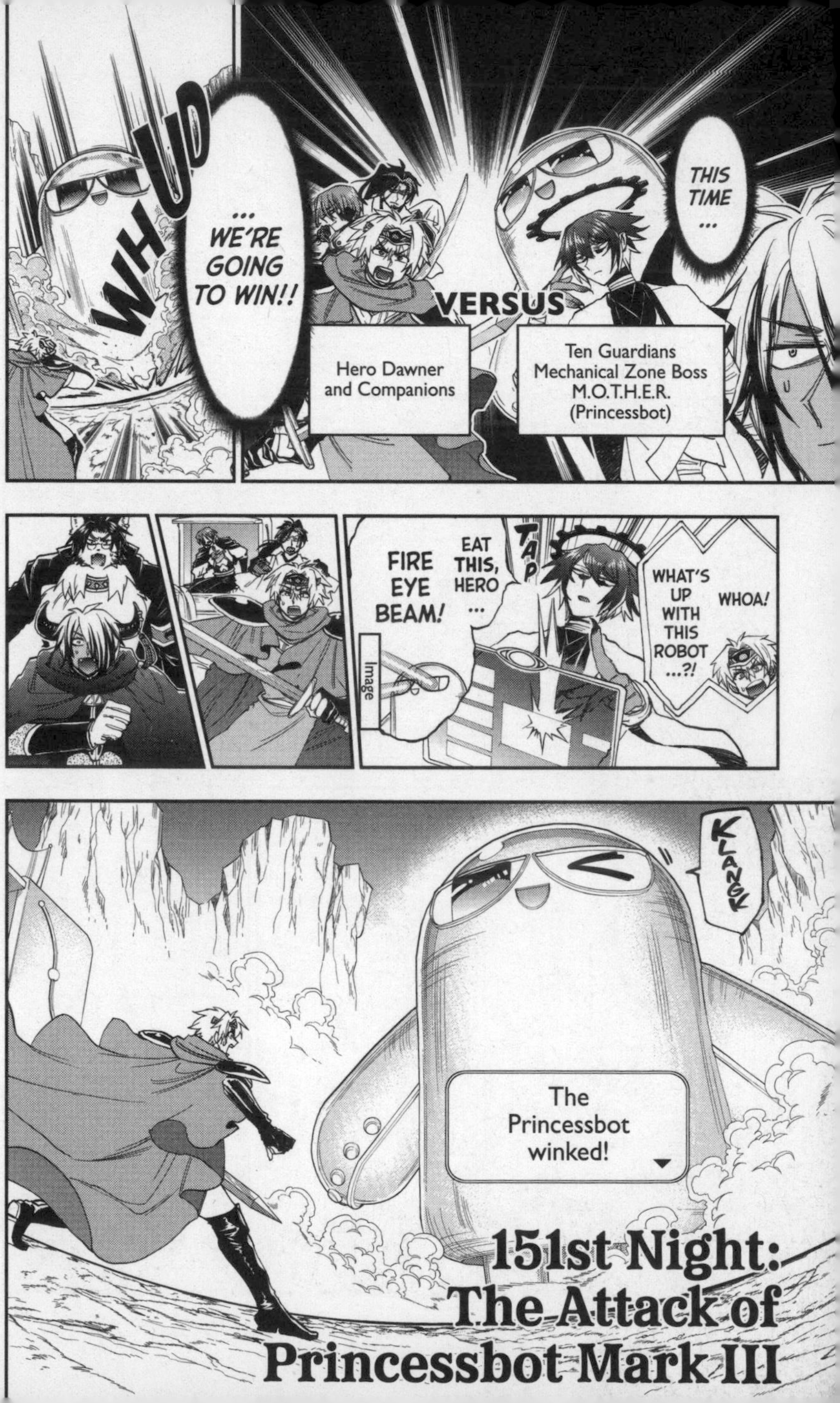
THIS TIME ...
VERSUS
Ten Guardians Mechanical Zone Boss M.O.T.H.E.R. (Princessbot)
Hero Dawner and Companions
WHUD
... WE'RE GOING TO WIN!!
WHOA!
WHAT'S UP WITH THIS ROBOT ...?!
TAP
EAT THIS, HERO ...
FIRE EYE BEAM!
Image
KLANGK
The Princessbot winked!
151st Night: The Attack of Princessbot Mark III

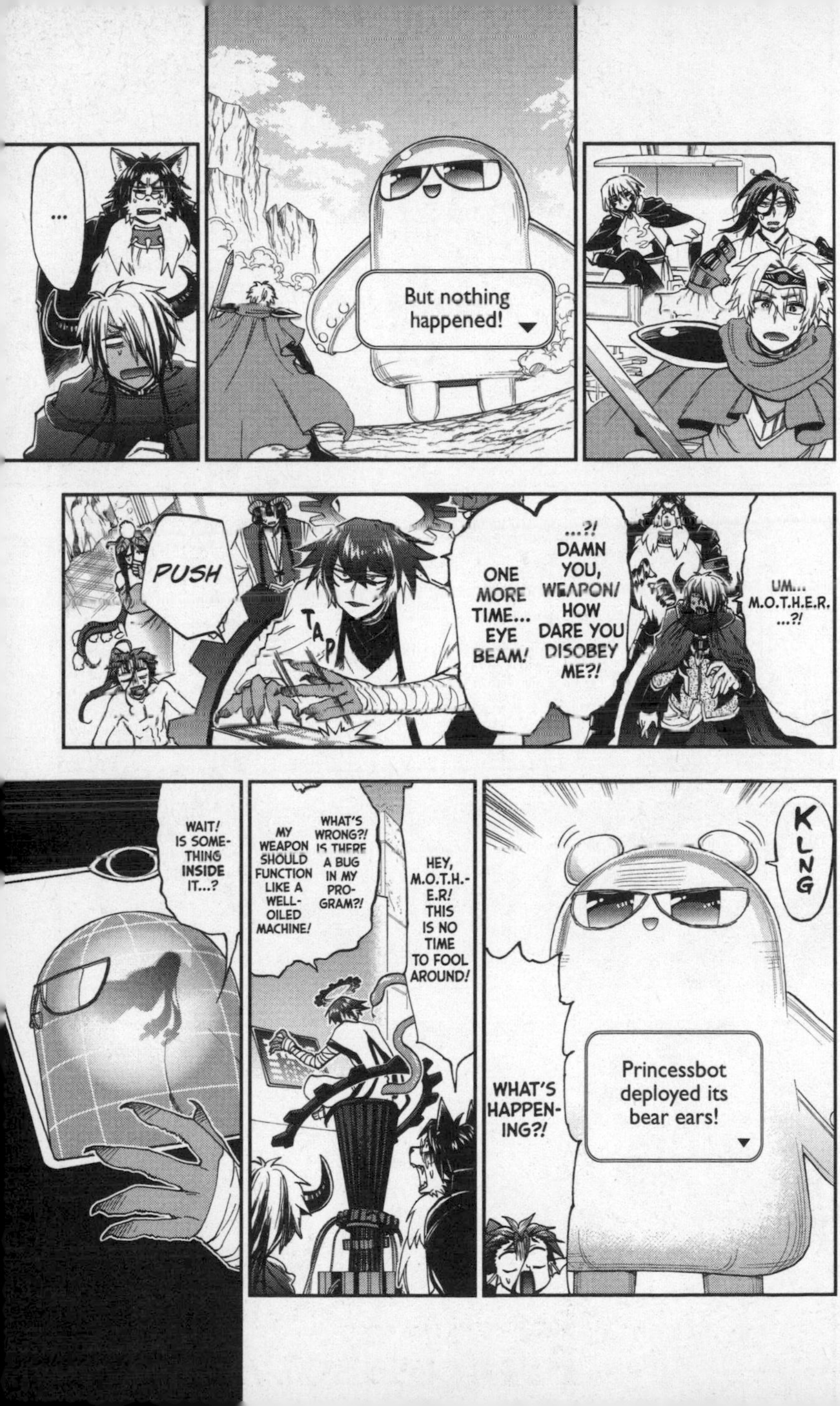
But nothing happened!
...
UM... M.O.T.H.E.R. ...?!
...?! DAMN YOU, WEAPON! HOW DARE YOU DISOBEY ME?!
ONE MORE TIME... EYE BEAM!
TAP
PUSH
KLNG
Princessbot deployed its bear ears!
WHAT'S HAPPENING?!
HEY, M.O.T.H.E.R! THIS IS NO TIME TO FOOL AROUND!
WHAT'S WRONG?! IS THERE A BUG IN MY PROGRAM?!
MY WEAPON SHOULD FUNCTION LIKE A WELL-OILED MACHINE!
WAIT! IS SOMETHING INSIDE IT...?

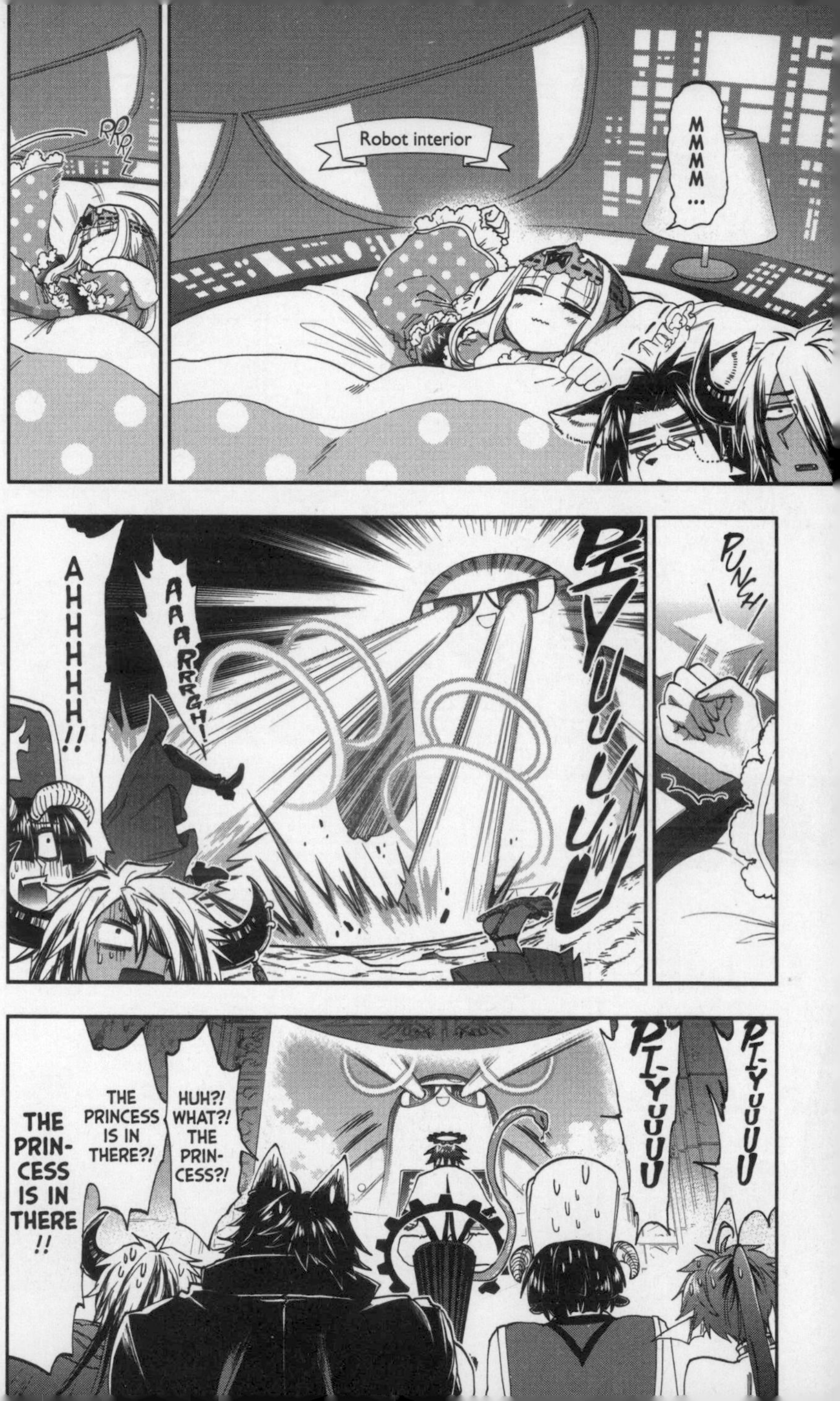
MMMM...
Robot interior
RRRL
PUNCH
PEYUUUUUUU
AAAARRRGH!
AHHHHHH!!
PI-YUUUUUU
PI-YUUUUU
HUH?! WHAT?! THE PRINCESS?!
THE PRINCESS IS IN THERE?!
THE PRINCESS IS IN THERE!!

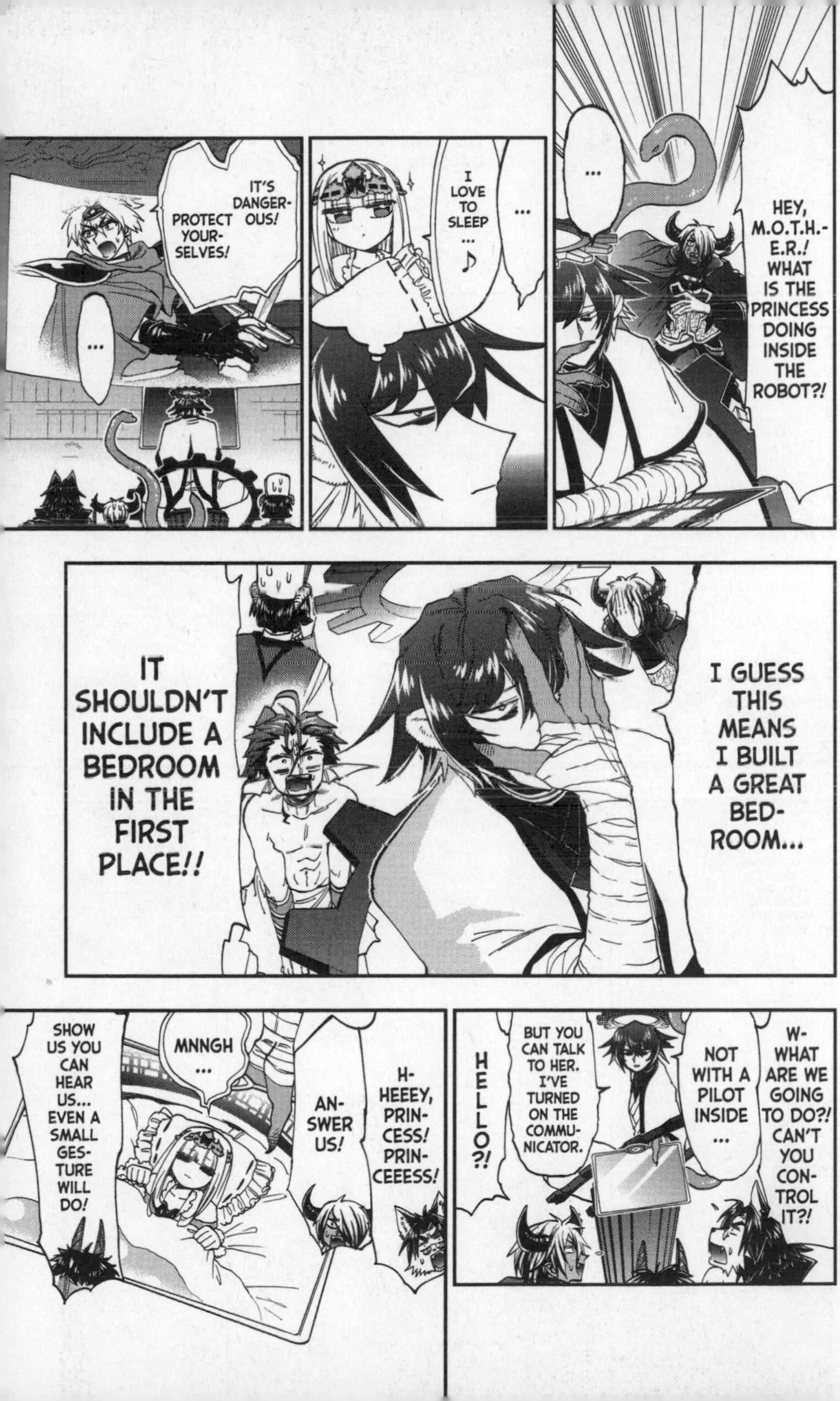
HEY, M.O.T.H.E.R.! WHAT IS THE PRINCESS DOING INSIDE THE ROBOT?!
...
...
I LOVE TO SLEEP ... ♪
IT'S DANGEROUS! PROTECT YOURSELVES!
...
I GUESS THIS MEANS I BUILT A GREAT BEDROOM...
IT SHOULDN'T INCLUDE A BEDROOM IN THE FIRST PLACE!!
W-WHAT ARE WE GOING TO DO?! CAN'T YOU CONTROL IT?!
NOT WITH A PILOT INSIDE ...
BUT YOU CAN TALK TO HER. I'VE TURNED ON THE COMMUNICATOR.
HELLO?!
H-HEEEY, PRINCESS! PRINCEEESS!
ANSWER US!
MNNGH ...
SHOW US YOU CAN HEAR US... EVEN A SMALL GESTURE WILL DO!

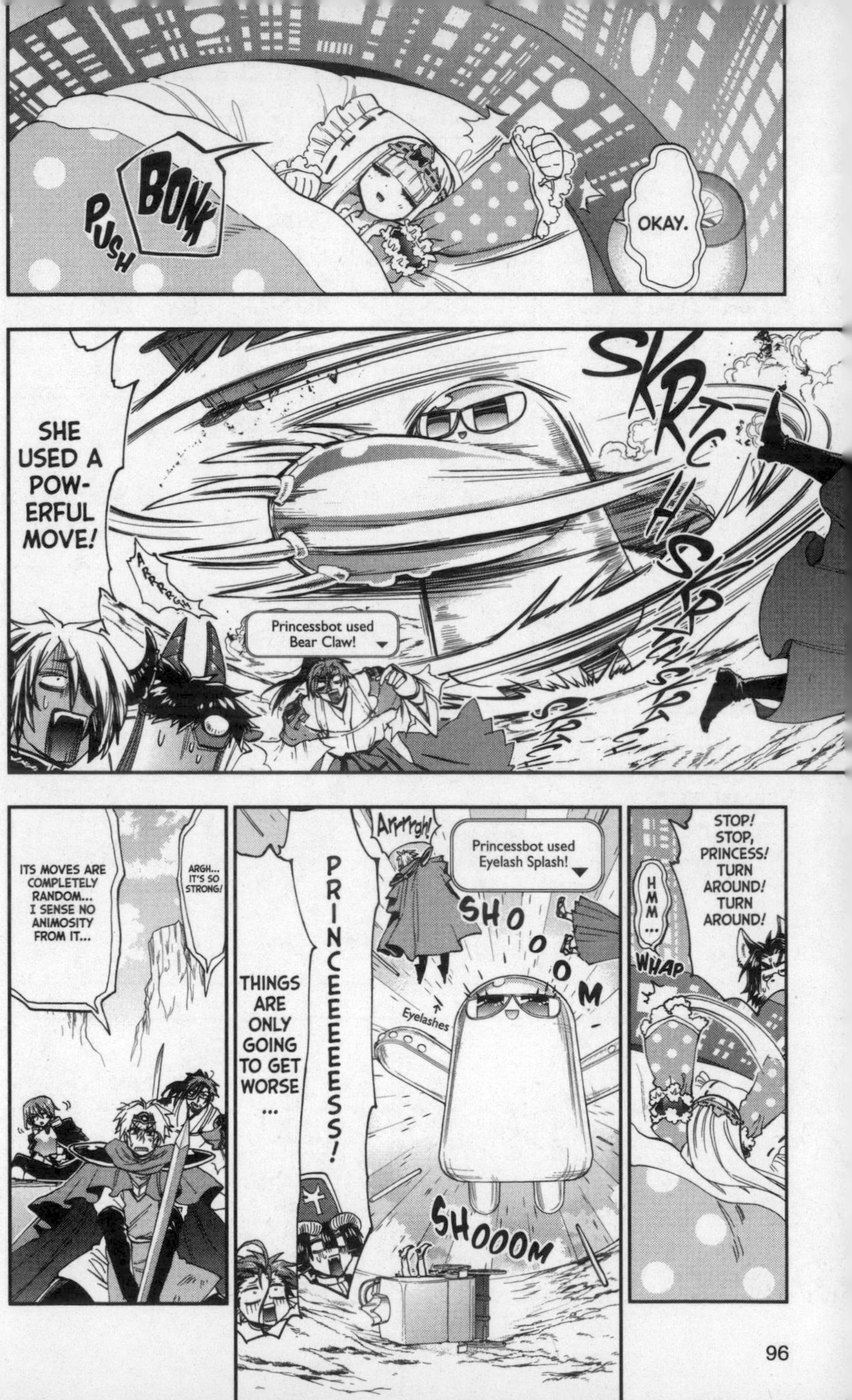

OKAY.
BONK
PUSH
SKRTCH
SHE USED A POW-ERFUL MOVE!
Princessbot used Bear Claw!
STOP! STOP, PRINCESS! TURN AROUND! TURN AROUND!
HMM...
WHAP
Princessbot used Eyelash Splash!
Arrrrgh!
SHOOOOM
Eyelashes
PRINCEEEEESS!
THINGS ARE ONLY GOING TO GET WORSE...
SHOOOM
ARGH... IT'S SO STRONG!
ITS MOVES ARE COMPLETELY RANDOM... I SENSE NO ANIMOSITY FROM IT...

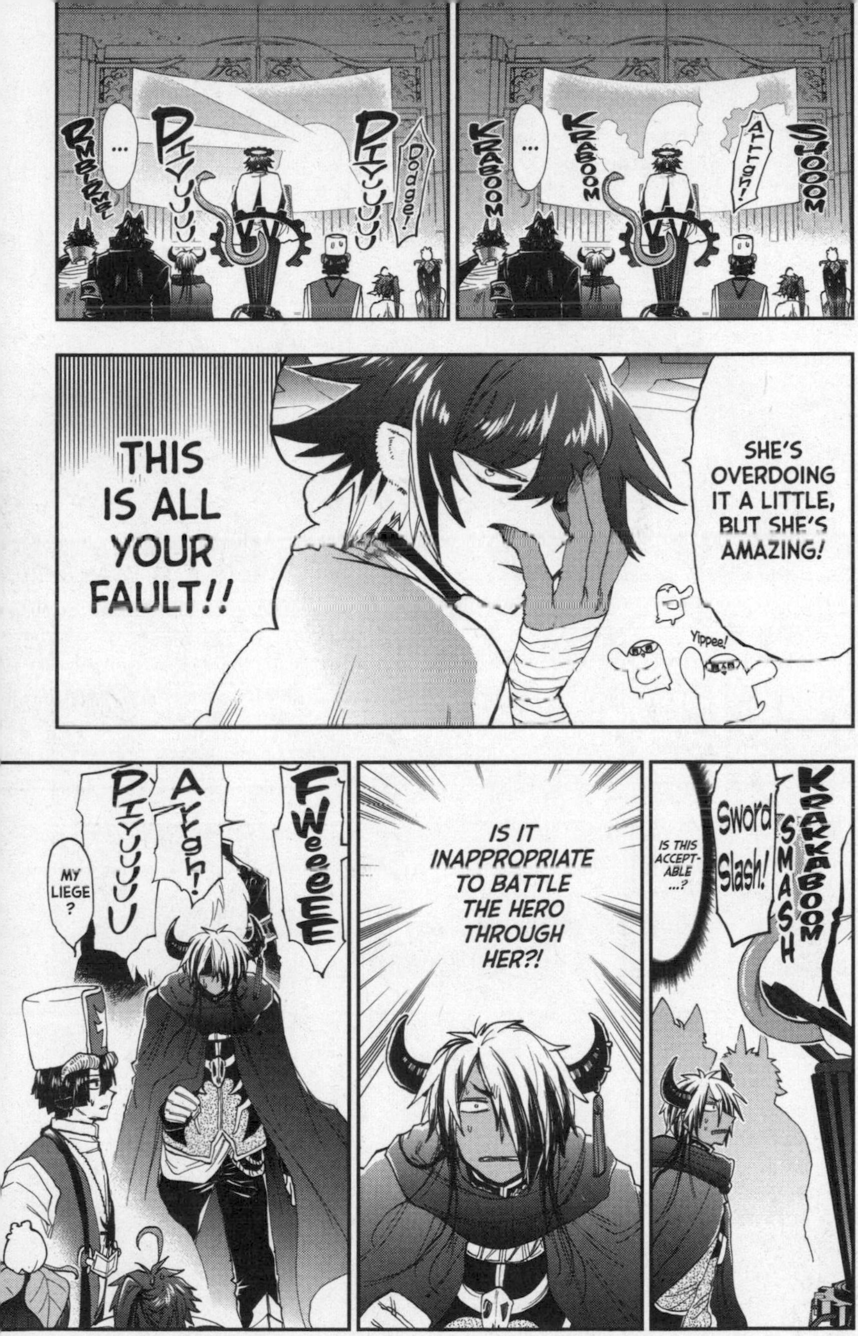
SHOOOOM
Arrgh!
KRABOOM
...
KRABOOM
Dodge!
PIYUUUUU
PIYUUUUU
...
RMBLRMBL
SHE'S OVERDOING IT A LITTLE, BUT SHE'S AMAZING!
Yippee!
THIS IS ALL YOUR FAULT!!
KRAKKABOOM
SMASH
Sword Slash!
IS THIS ACCEPTABLE ...?
IS IT INAPPROPRIATE TO BATTLE THE HERO THROUGH HER?!
FWeeeEEE
Arrgh!
PIYUUUUU
MY LIEGE?

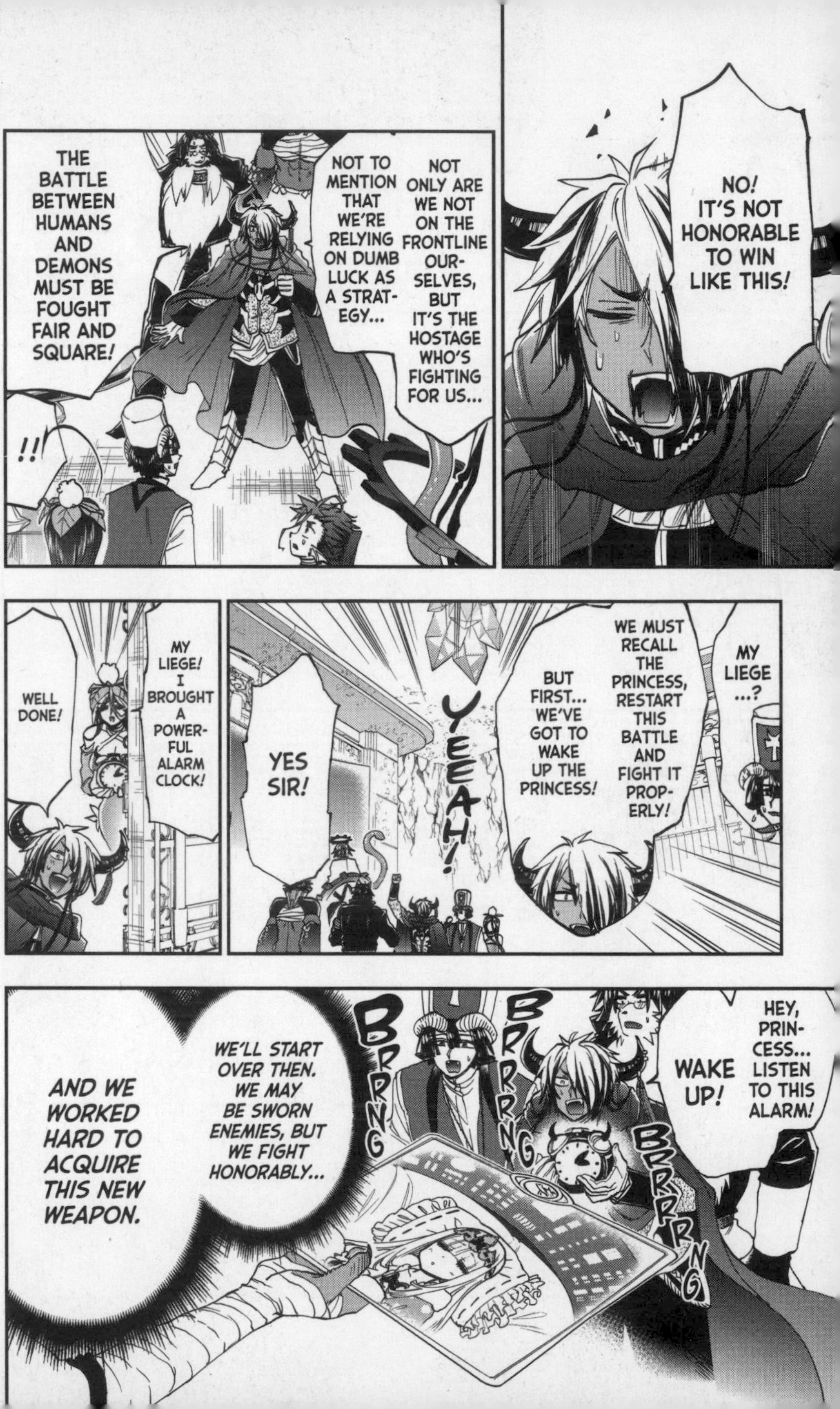
NO! IT'S NOT HONORABLE TO WIN LIKE THIS!
NOT ONLY ARE WE NOT ON THE FRONTLINE OURSELVES, BUT IT'S THE HOSTAGE WHO'S FIGHTING FOR US...
NOT TO MENTION THAT WE'RE RELYING ON DUMB LUCK AS A STRATEGY...
THE BATTLE BETWEEN HUMANS AND DEMONS MUST BE FOUGHT FAIR AND SQUARE!
!!
MY LIEGE...?
WE MUST RECALL THE PRINCESS, RESTART THIS BATTLE AND FIGHT IT PROPERLY!
BUT FIRST... WE'VE GOT TO WAKE UP THE PRINCESS!
YEEAAH!
YES SIR!
MY LIEGE! I BROUGHT A POWERFUL ALARM CLOCK!
WELL DONE!
HEY, PRINCESS... LISTEN TO THIS ALARM!
WAKE UP!
BRRRRRNG
BRRRRNG
BRRRNG
WE'LL START OVER THEN. WE MAY BE SWORN ENEMIES, BUT WE FIGHT HONORABLY...
AND WE WORKED HARD TO ACQUIRE THIS NEW WEAPON.

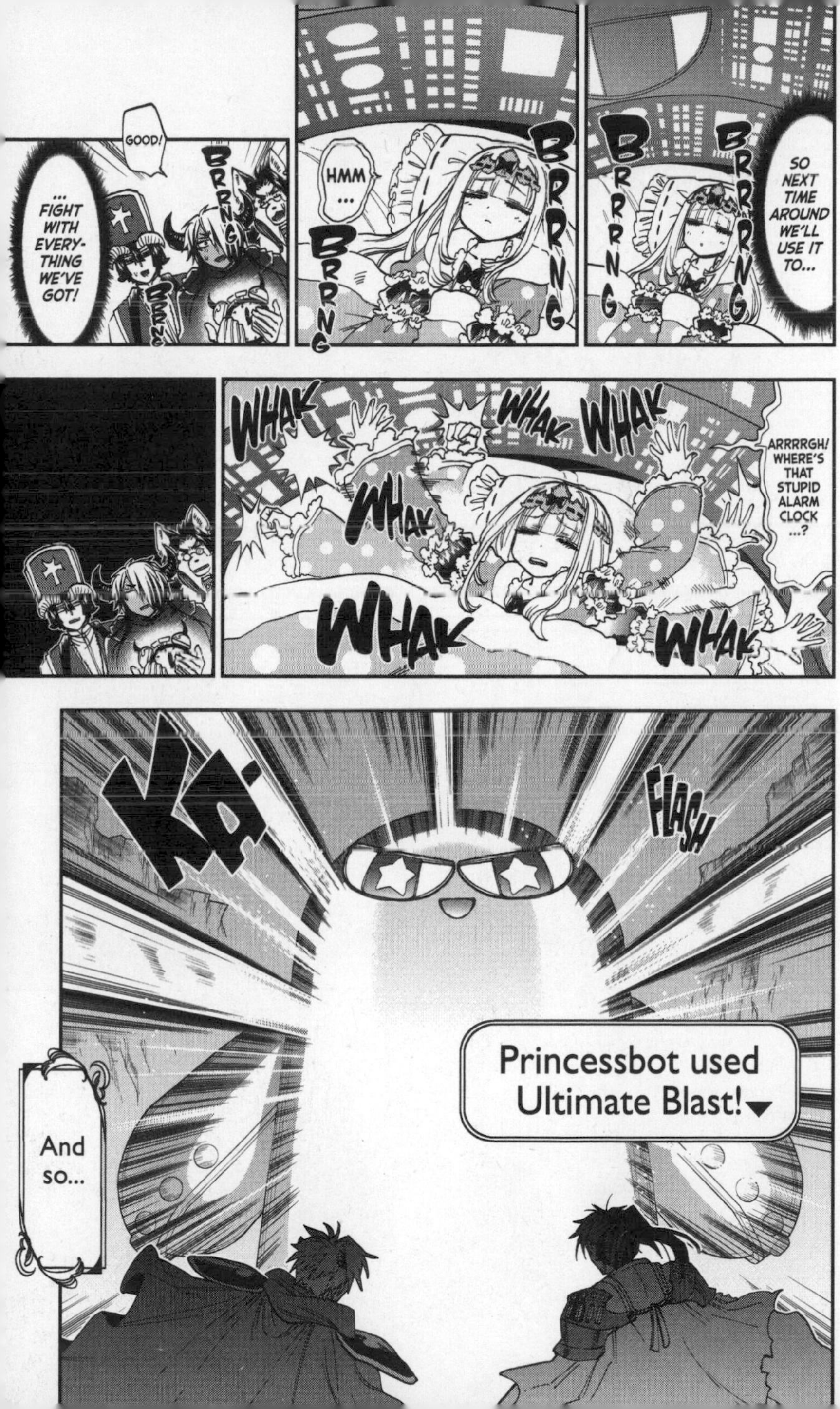
SO NEXT TIME AROUND WE'LL USE IT TO...
BRRRNG
BRRRNG
HMM...
BRRRNG
BRRNG
GOOD!
...FIGHT WITH EVERYTHING WE'VE GOT!
BRRRNG!
ARRRRGH! WHERE'S THAT STUPID ALARM CLOCK...?
WHAK
WHAK
WHAK
WHAK
WHAK
WHAK
KA!
FLASH
Princessbot used Ultimate Blast!
And so...

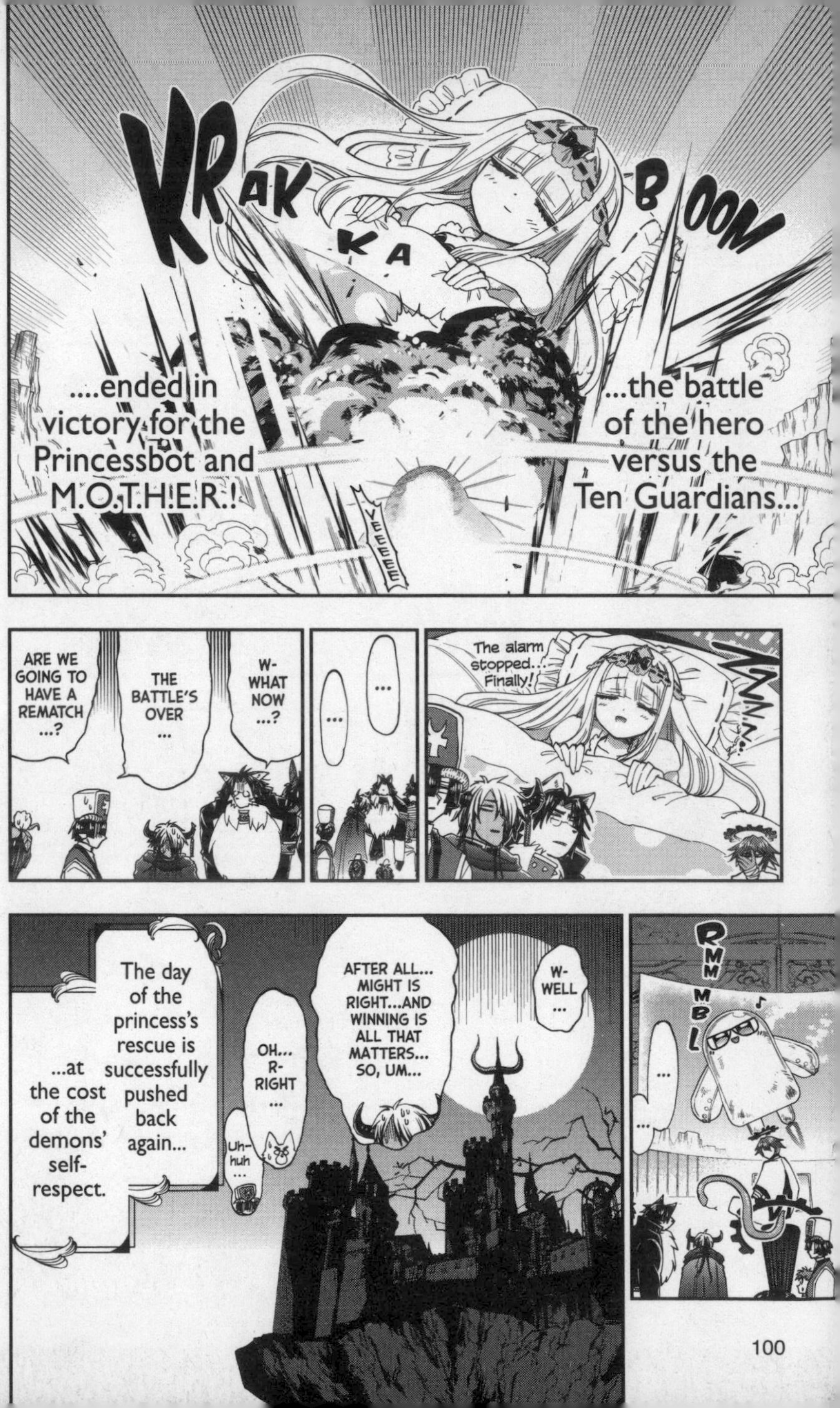

...the battle of the hero versus the Ten Guardians...
KRAK KA BOOM
....ended in victory for the Princessbot and M.O.T.H.E.R.!
VEEEEE
The alarm stopped... Finally!
ZZZZZ
...
...
W-WHAT NOW ...?
THE BATTLE'S OVER ...
ARE WE GOING TO HAVE A REMATCH ...?
RMMMBL
...
...
W-WELL ...
AFTER ALL... MIGHT IS RIGHT...AND WINNING IS ALL THAT MATTERS... SO, UM...
OH... R-RIGHT ...
Uh-huh ...
The day of the princess's rescue is successfully pushed back again...
...at the cost of the demons' self-respect.

M.O.T.H.E.R.

Secretive: ☆☆☆☆☆☆☆☆☆☆
Worrywart: ☆☆☆☆☆☆☆☆☆

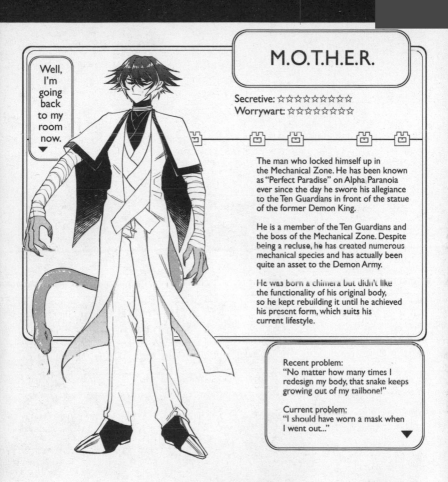

Well, I'm going back to my room now.

The man who locked himself up in the Mechanical Zone. He has been known as "Perfect Paradise" on Alpha Paranoia ever since the day he swore his allegiance to the Ten Guardians in front of the statue of the former Demon King.

He is a member of the Ten Guardians and the boss of the Mechanical Zone. Despite being a recluse, he has created numerous mechanical species and has actually been quite an asset to the Demon Army.

He was born a chimera but didn't like the functionality of his original body, so he kept rebuilding it until he achieved his present form, which suits his current lifestyle.

Recent problem:
"No matter how many times I redesign my body, that snake keeps growing out of my tailbone!"

Current problem:
"I should have worn a mask when I went out..."

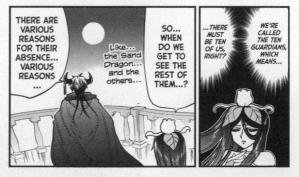

WE'RE CALLED THE TEN GUARDIANS, WHICH MEANS...
...THERE MUST BE TEN OF US, RIGHT?
SO... WHEN DO WE GET TO SEE THE REST OF THEM...?
THERE ARE VARIOUS REASONS FOR THEIR ABSENCE... VARIOUS REASONS ...
Like... the Sand Dragon... and the others...

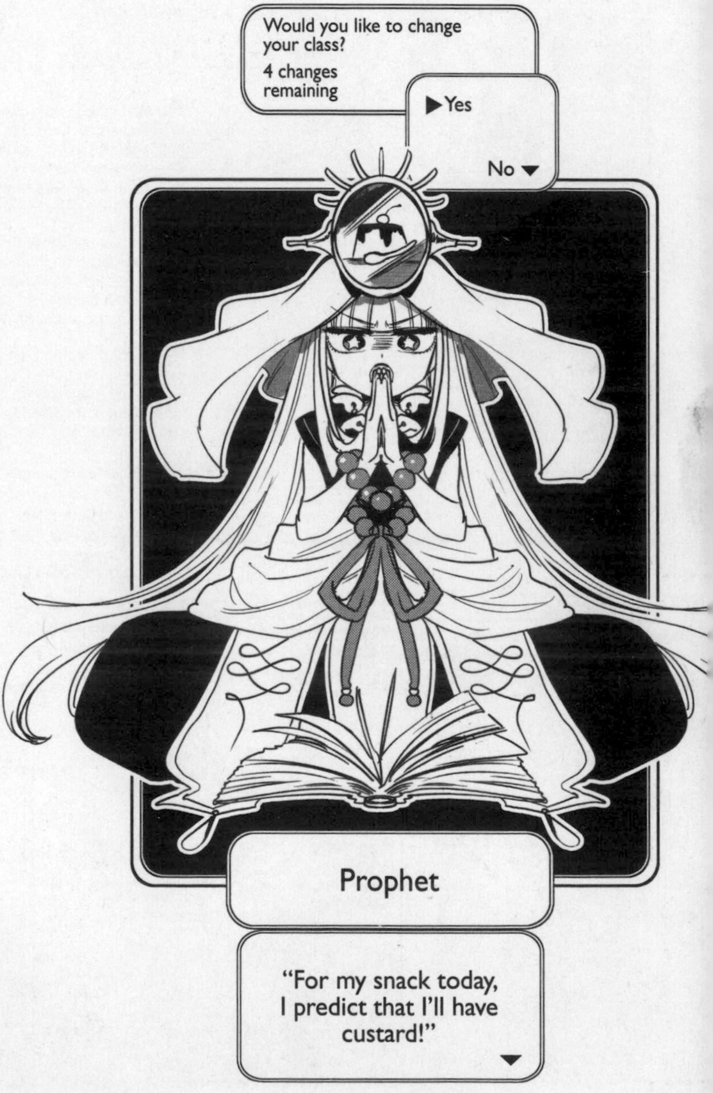
Would you like to change your class?
4 changes remaining
▶Yes
No ▼
Prophet
"For my snack today, I predict that I'll have custard!"

152nd Night: Little Demon King and His Horns

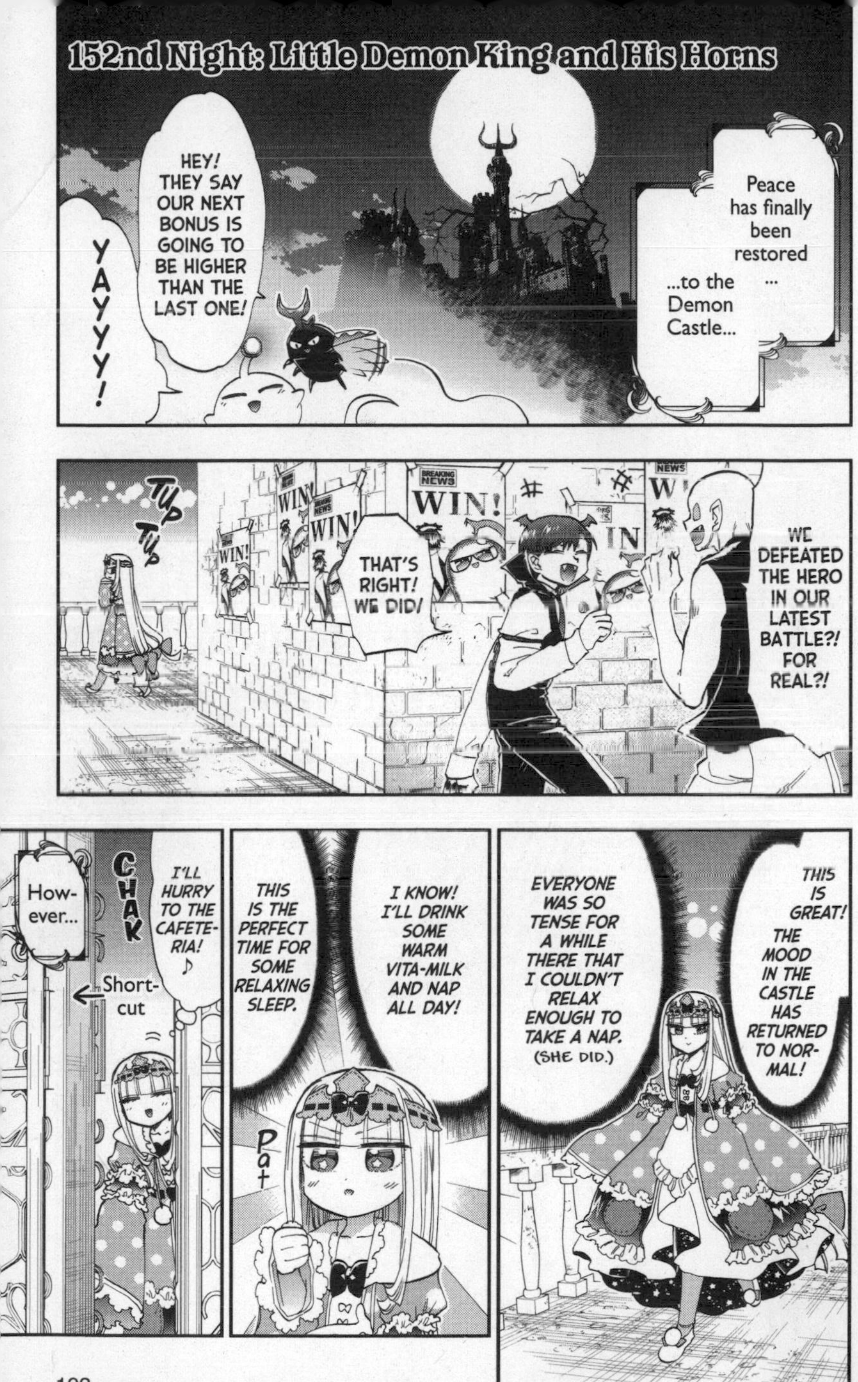

Peace has finally been restored...
...to the Demon Castle...
HEY! THEY SAY OUR NEXT BONUS IS GOING TO BE HIGHER THAN THE LAST ONE!
YAYYYY!
WE DEFEATED THE HERO IN OUR LATEST BATTLE?! FOR REAL?!
THAT'S RIGHT! WE DID!
WIN!
BREAKING NEWS
TUP TUP
THIS IS GREAT! THE MOOD IN THE CASTLE HAS RETURNED TO NORMAL!
EVERYONE WAS SO TENSE FOR A WHILE THERE THAT I COULDN'T RELAX ENOUGH TO TAKE A NAP.
(SHE DID.)
I KNOW! I'LL DRINK SOME WARM VITA-MILK AND NAP ALL DAY!
THIS IS THE PERFECT TIME FOR SOME RELAXING SLEEP.
Pat
I'LL HURRY TO THE CAFETERIA! ♪
CHAK
However...
← Shortcut

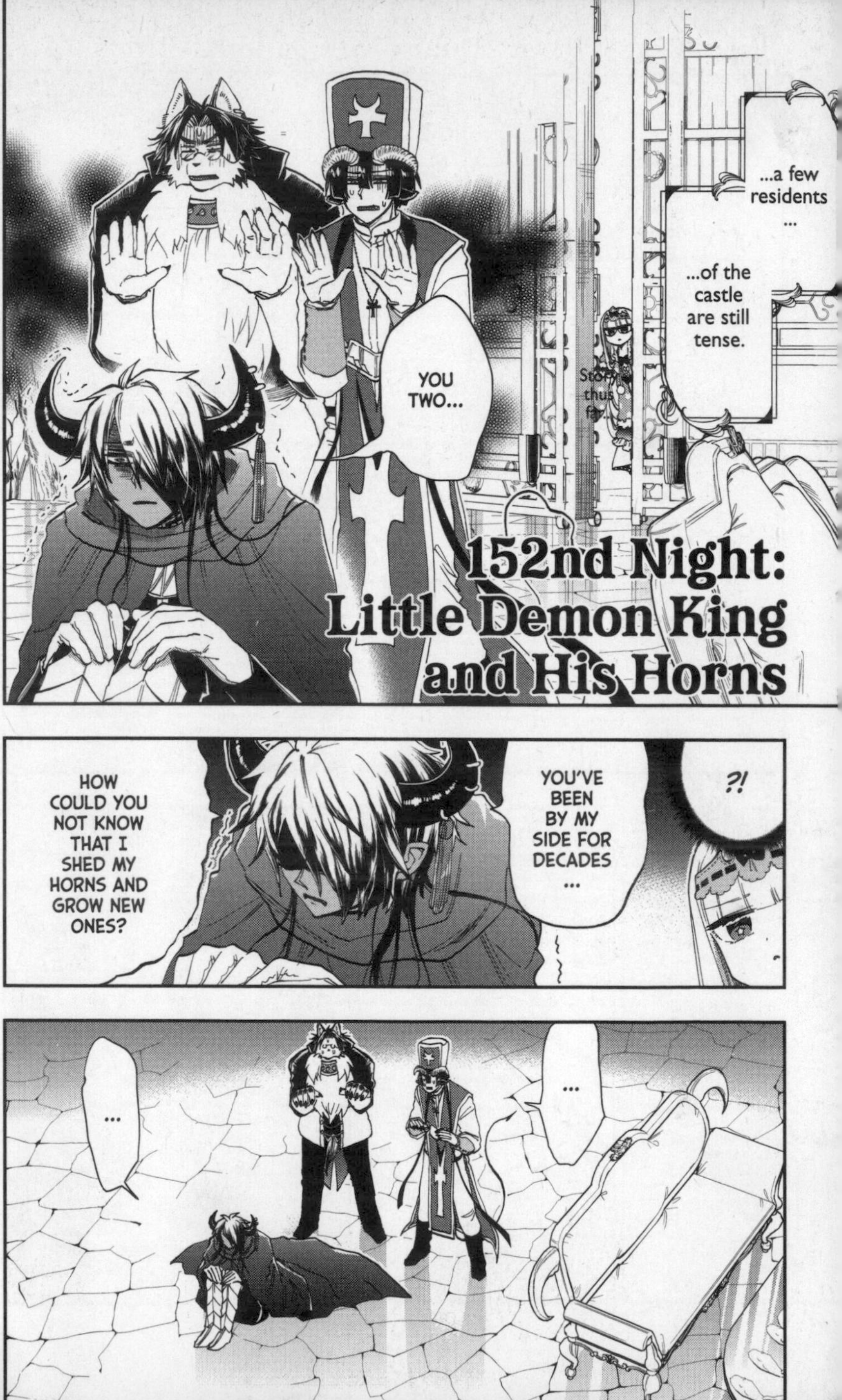
...a few residents ...
...of the castle are still tense.
Story thus far...
YOU TWO...
152nd Night: Little Demon King and His Horns
?!
YOU'VE BEEN BY MY SIDE FOR DECADES ...
HOW COULD YOU NOT KNOW THAT I SHED MY HORNS AND GROW NEW ONES?
...
...

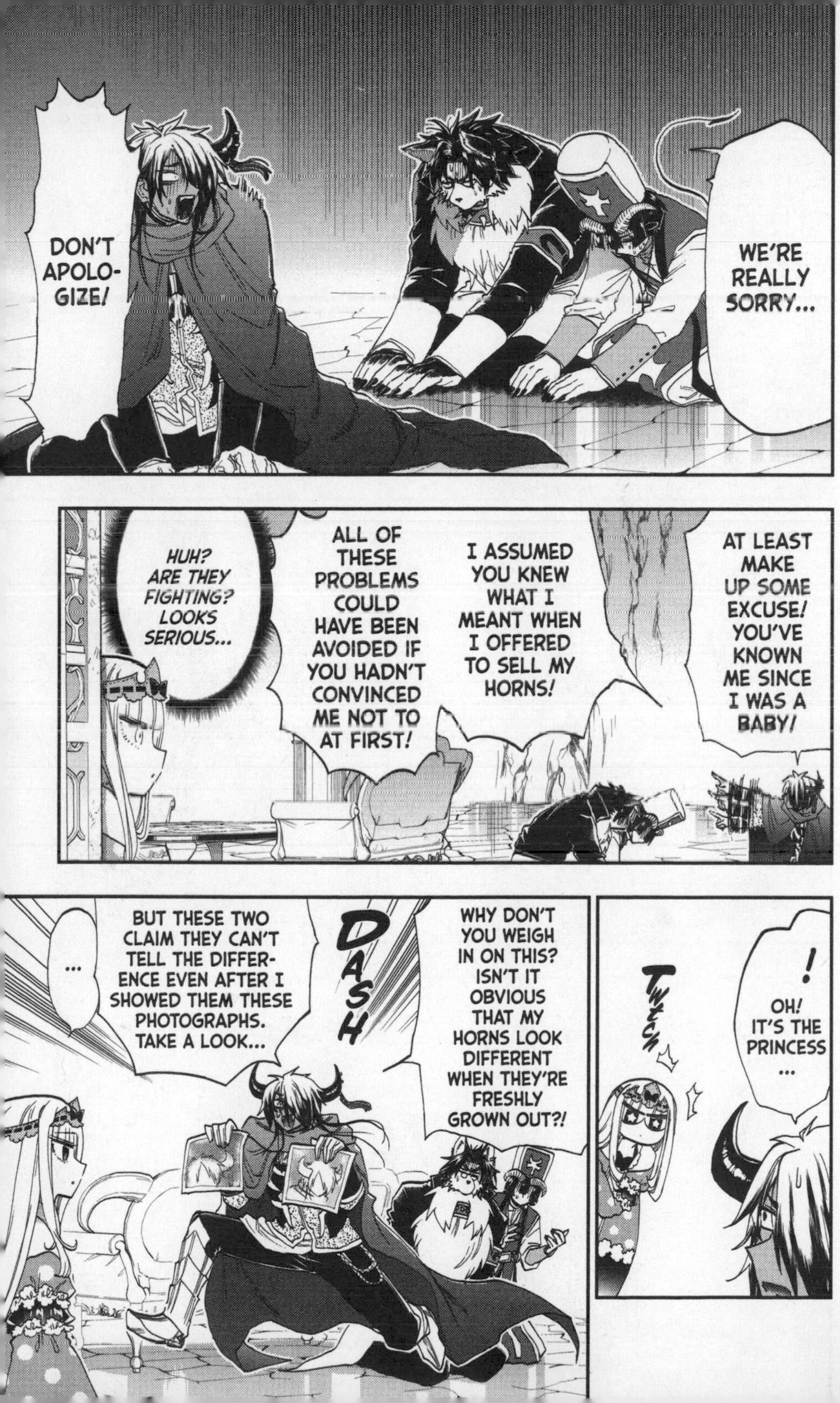
WE'RE REALLY SORRY...
DON'T APOLO-GIZE!
AT LEAST MAKE UP SOME EXCUSE! YOU'VE KNOWN ME SINCE I WAS A BABY!
I ASSUMED YOU KNEW WHAT I MEANT WHEN I OFFERED TO SELL MY HORNS!
ALL OF THESE PROBLEMS COULD HAVE BEEN AVOIDED IF YOU HADN'T CONVINCED ME NOT TO AT FIRST!
HUH? ARE THEY FIGHTING? LOOKS SERIOUS...
!
OH! IT'S THE PRINCESS...
TWITCH
WHY DON'T YOU WEIGH IN ON THIS? ISN'T IT OBVIOUS THAT MY HORNS LOOK DIFFERENT WHEN THEY'RE FRESHLY GROWN OUT?!
DASH
BUT THESE TWO CLAIM THEY CAN'T TELL THE DIFFER-ENCE EVEN AFTER I SHOWED THEM THESE PHOTOGRAPHS. TAKE A LOOK...
...

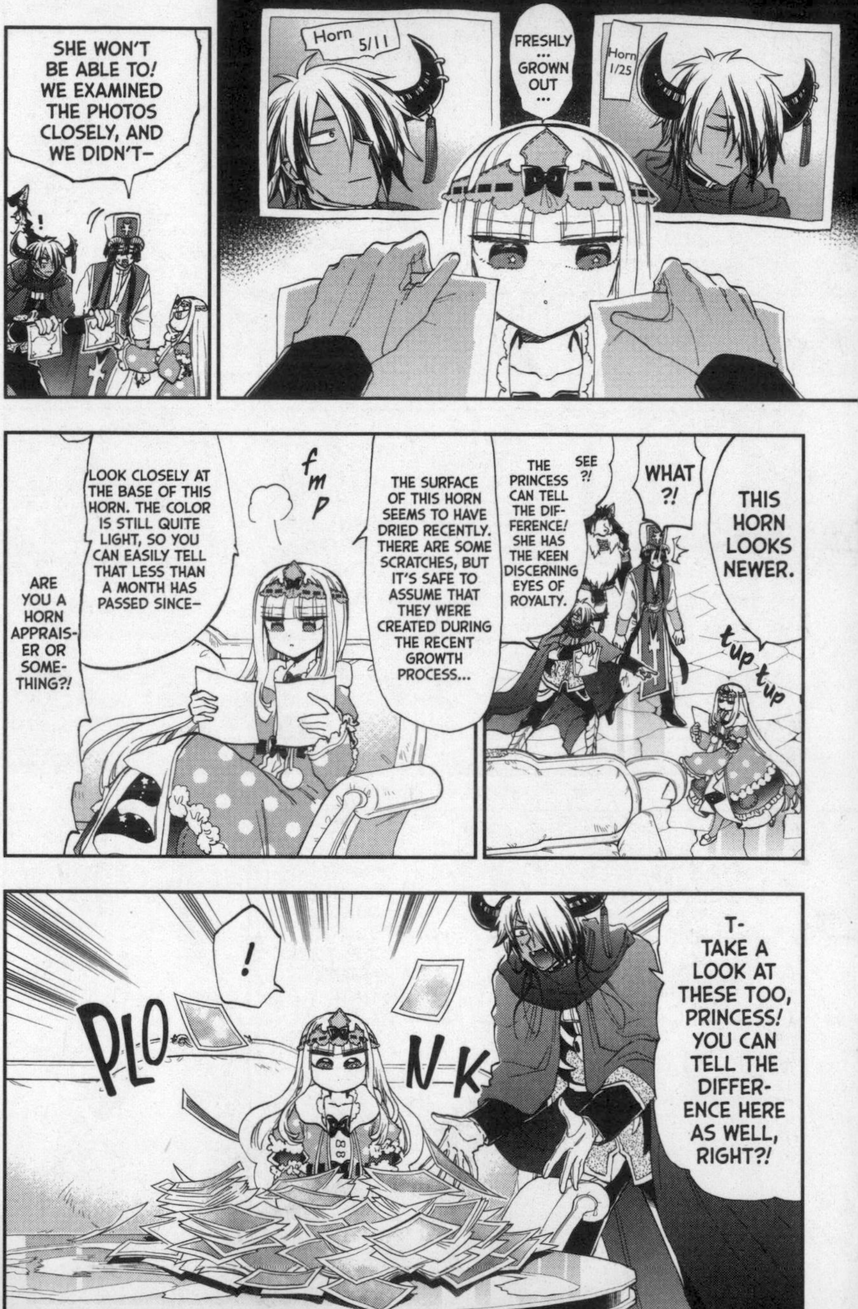
Horn 1/25
FRESHLY ... GROWN OUT ...
Horn 5/11
SHE WON'T BE ABLE TO! WE EXAMINED THE PHOTOS CLOSELY, AND WE DIDN'T–
!
THIS HORN LOOKS NEWER.
WHAT?!
tup tup
SEE?!
THE PRINCESS CAN TELL THE DIFFERENCE! SHE HAS THE KEEN DISCERNING EYES OF ROYALTY.
THE SURFACE OF THIS HORN SEEMS TO HAVE DRIED RECENTLY. THERE ARE SOME SCRATCHES, BUT IT'S SAFE TO ASSUME THAT THEY WERE CREATED DURING THE RECENT GROWTH PROCESS...
fmp
LOOK CLOSELY AT THE BASE OF THIS HORN. THE COLOR IS STILL QUITE LIGHT, SO YOU CAN EASILY TELL THAT LESS THAN A MONTH HAS PASSED SINCE–
ARE YOU A HORN APPRAISER OR SOMETHING?!
T- TAKE A LOOK AT THESE TOO, PRINCESS! YOU CAN TELL THE DIFFERENCE HERE AS WELL, RIGHT?!
!
PLONK

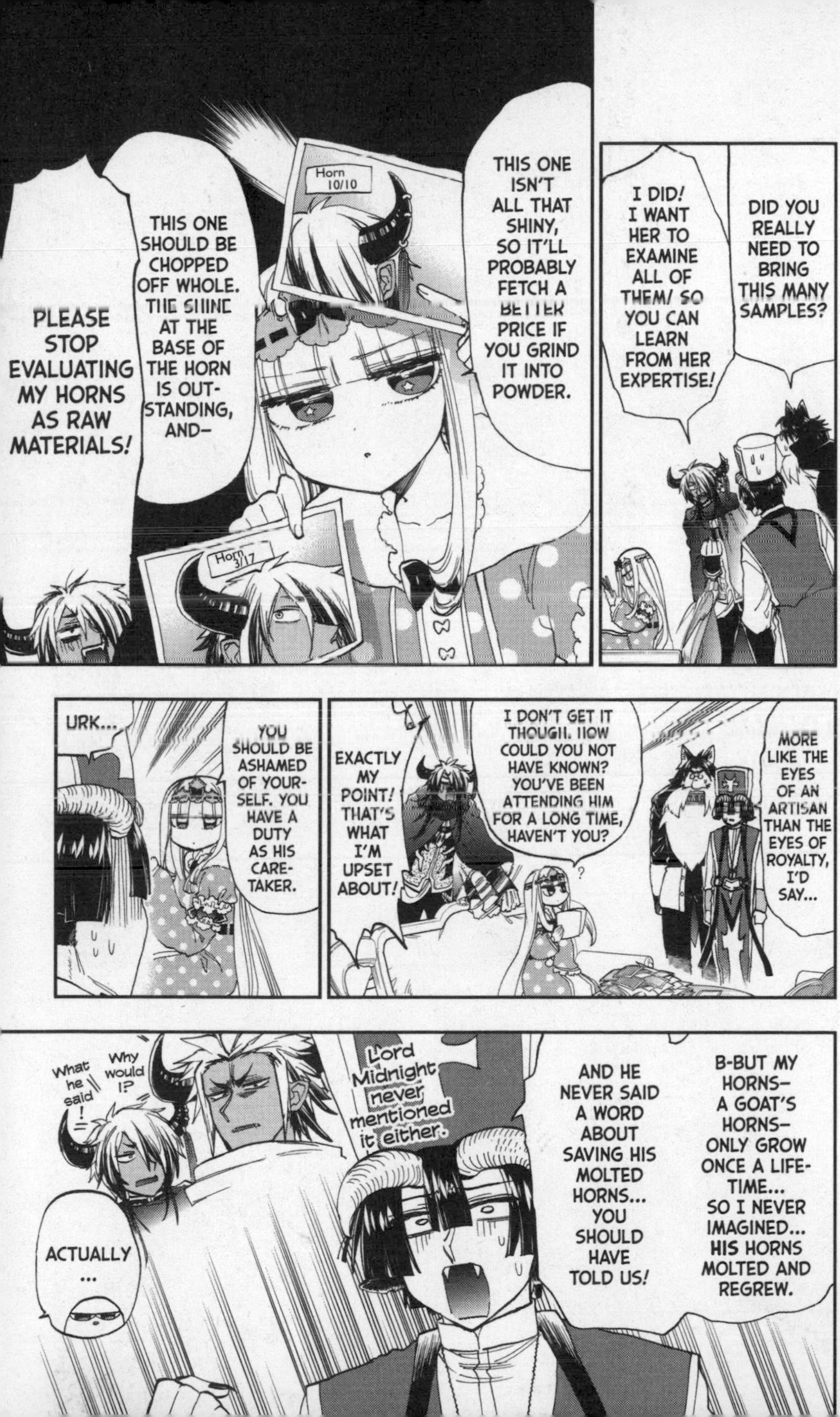
DID YOU REALLY NEED TO BRING THIS MANY SAMPLES?
I DID! I WANT HER TO EXAMINE ALL OF THEM! SO YOU CAN LEARN FROM HER EXPERTISE!
THIS ONE ISN'T ALL THAT SHINY, SO IT'LL PROBABLY FETCH A BETTER PRICE IF YOU GRIND IT INTO POWDER.
Horn 10/10
THIS ONE SHOULD BE CHOPPED OFF WHOLE. THE SHINE AT THE BASE OF THE HORN IS OUT-STANDING, AND–
Horn 3/17
PLEASE STOP EVALUATING MY HORNS AS RAW MATERIALS!
MORE LIKE THE EYES OF AN ARTISAN THAN THE EYES OF ROYALTY, I'D SAY...
I DON'T GET IT THOUGH. HOW COULD YOU NOT HAVE KNOWN? YOU'VE BEEN ATTENDING HIM FOR A LONG TIME, HAVEN'T YOU?
?
EXACTLY MY POINT! THAT'S WHAT I'M UPSET ABOUT!
YOU SHOULD BE ASHAMED OF YOUR-SELF. YOU HAVE A DUTY AS HIS CARE-TAKER.
URK...
B-BUT MY HORNS– A GOAT'S HORNS– ONLY GROW ONCE A LIFE-TIME... SO I NEVER IMAGINED... HIS HORNS MOLTED AND REGREW.
AND HE NEVER SAID A WORD ABOUT SAVING HIS MOLTED HORNS... YOU SHOULD HAVE TOLD US!
Lord Midnight never mentioned it either.
Why would I!?
What he said!
ACTUALLY ...

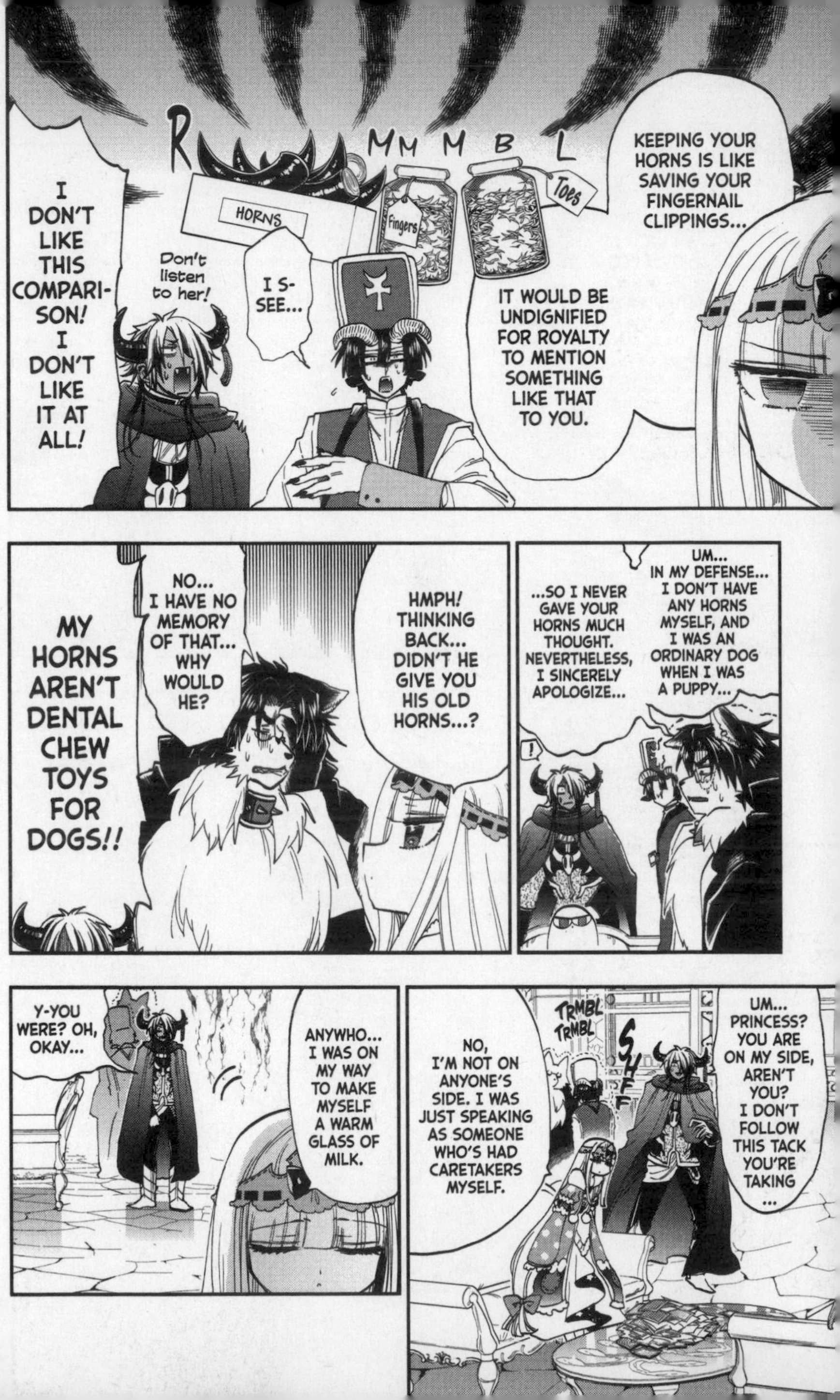
KEEPING YOUR HORNS IS LIKE SAVING YOUR FINGERNAIL CLIPPINGS...
IT WOULD BE UNDIGNIFIED FOR ROYALTY TO MENTION SOMETHING LIKE THAT TO YOU.
RMMMBL
Toes
Fingers
HORNS
I S-SEE...
Don't listen to her!
I DON'T LIKE THIS COMPARI-SON! I DON'T LIKE IT AT ALL!
UM... IN MY DEFENSE... I DON'T HAVE ANY HORNS MYSELF, AND I WAS AN ORDINARY DOG WHEN I WAS A PUPPY...
...SO I NEVER GAVE YOUR HORNS MUCH THOUGHT. NEVERTHELESS, I SINCERELY APOLOGIZE...
!
HMPH! THINKING BACK... DIDN'T HE GIVE YOU HIS OLD HORNS...?
NO... I HAVE NO MEMORY OF THAT... WHY WOULD HE?
MY HORNS AREN'T DENTAL CHEW TOYS FOR DOGS!!
UM... PRINCESS? YOU ARE ON MY SIDE, AREN'T YOU? I DON'T FOLLOW THIS TACK YOU'RE TAKING...
SHFF
TRMBL TRMBL
NO, I'M NOT ON ANYONE'S SIDE. I WAS JUST SPEAKING AS SOMEONE WHO'S HAD CARETAKERS MYSELF.
ANYWHO... I WAS ON MY WAY TO MAKE MYSELF A WARM GLASS OF MILK.
Y-YOU WERE? OH, OKAY...

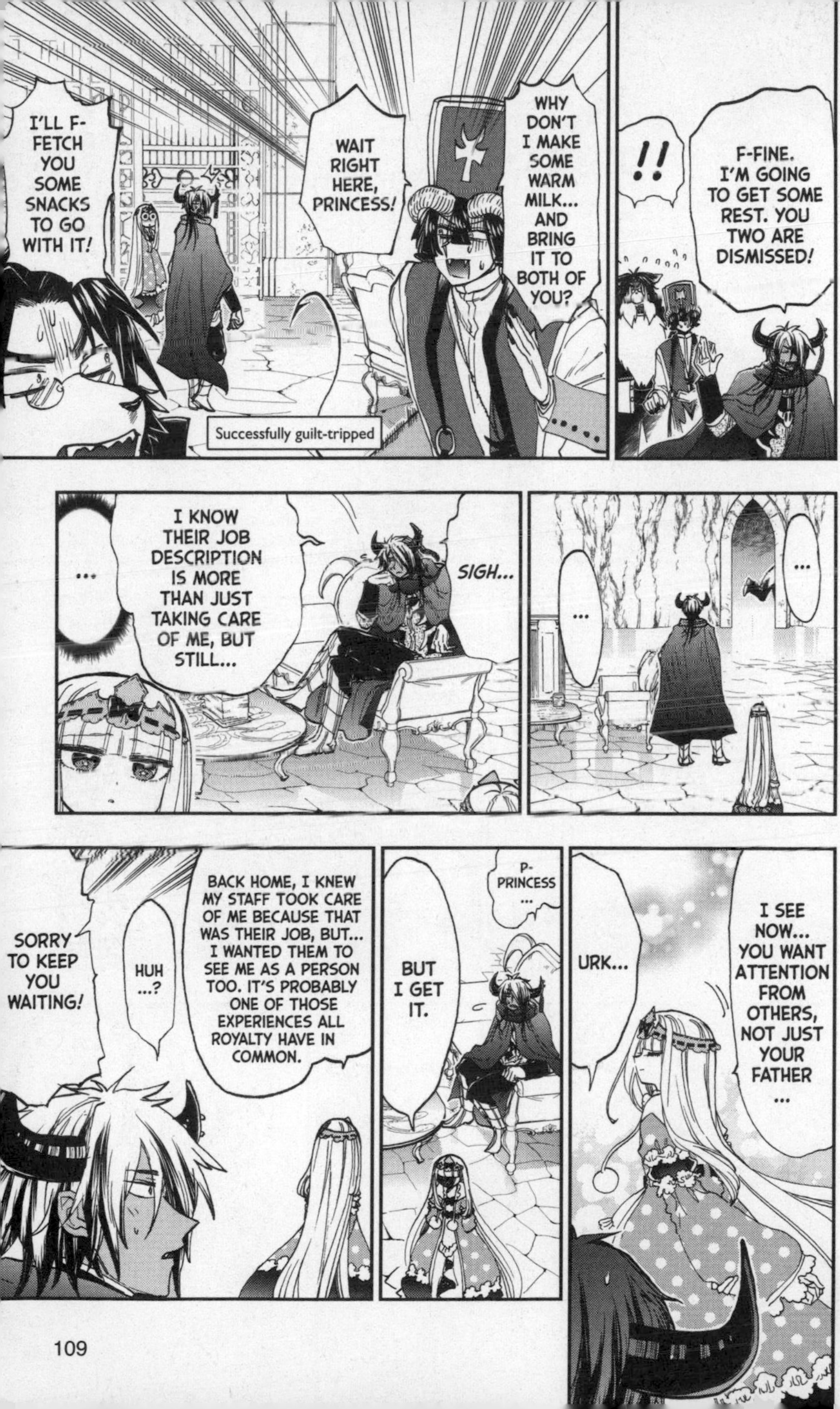
F-FINE. I'M GOING TO GET SOME REST. YOU TWO ARE DISMISSED!
!!
WHY DON'T I MAKE SOME WARM MILK... AND BRING IT TO BOTH OF YOU?
WAIT RIGHT HERE, PRINCESS!
I'LL F-FETCH YOU SOME SNACKS TO GO WITH IT!
Successfully guilt-tripped
...
...
SIGH...
I KNOW THEIR JOB DESCRIPTION IS MORE THAN JUST TAKING CARE OF ME, BUT STILL...
...
I SEE NOW... YOU WANT ATTENTION FROM OTHERS, NOT JUST YOUR FATHER...
URK...
P-PRINCESS...
BUT I GET IT.
BACK HOME, I KNEW MY STAFF TOOK CARE OF ME BECAUSE THAT WAS THEIR JOB, BUT... I WANTED THEM TO SEE ME AS A PERSON TOO. IT'S PROBABLY ONE OF THOSE EXPERIENCES ALL ROYALTY HAVE IN COMMON.
HUH...?
SORRY TO KEEP YOU WAITING!

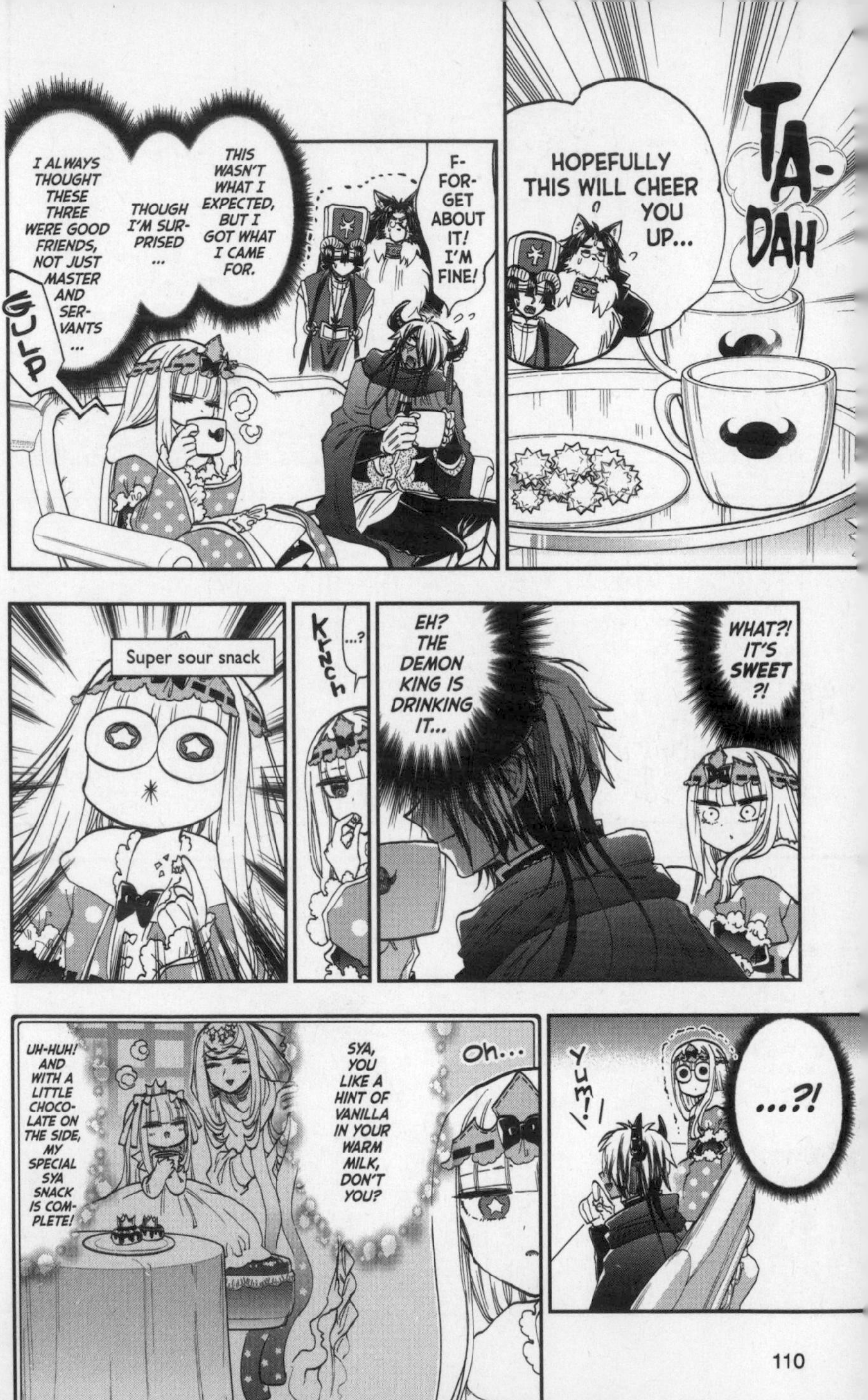
TA-DAH
HOPEFULLY THIS WILL CHEER YOU UP...
F-FORGET ABOUT IT! I'M FINE!
THIS WASN'T WHAT I EXPECTED, BUT I GOT WHAT I CAME FOR.
THOUGH I'M SURPRISED...
I ALWAYS THOUGHT THESE THREE WERE GOOD FRIENDS, NOT JUST MASTER AND SERVANTS...
GULP
WHAT?! IT'S SWEET?!
EH? THE DEMON KING IS DRINKING IT...
...?
Krnch
Super sour snack
...?!
Yum!
Oh...
SYA, YOU LIKE A HINT OF VANILLA IN YOUR WARM MILK, DON'T YOU?
UH-HUH! AND WITH A LITTLE CHOCOLATE ON THE SIDE, MY SPECIAL SYA SNACK IS COMPLETE!

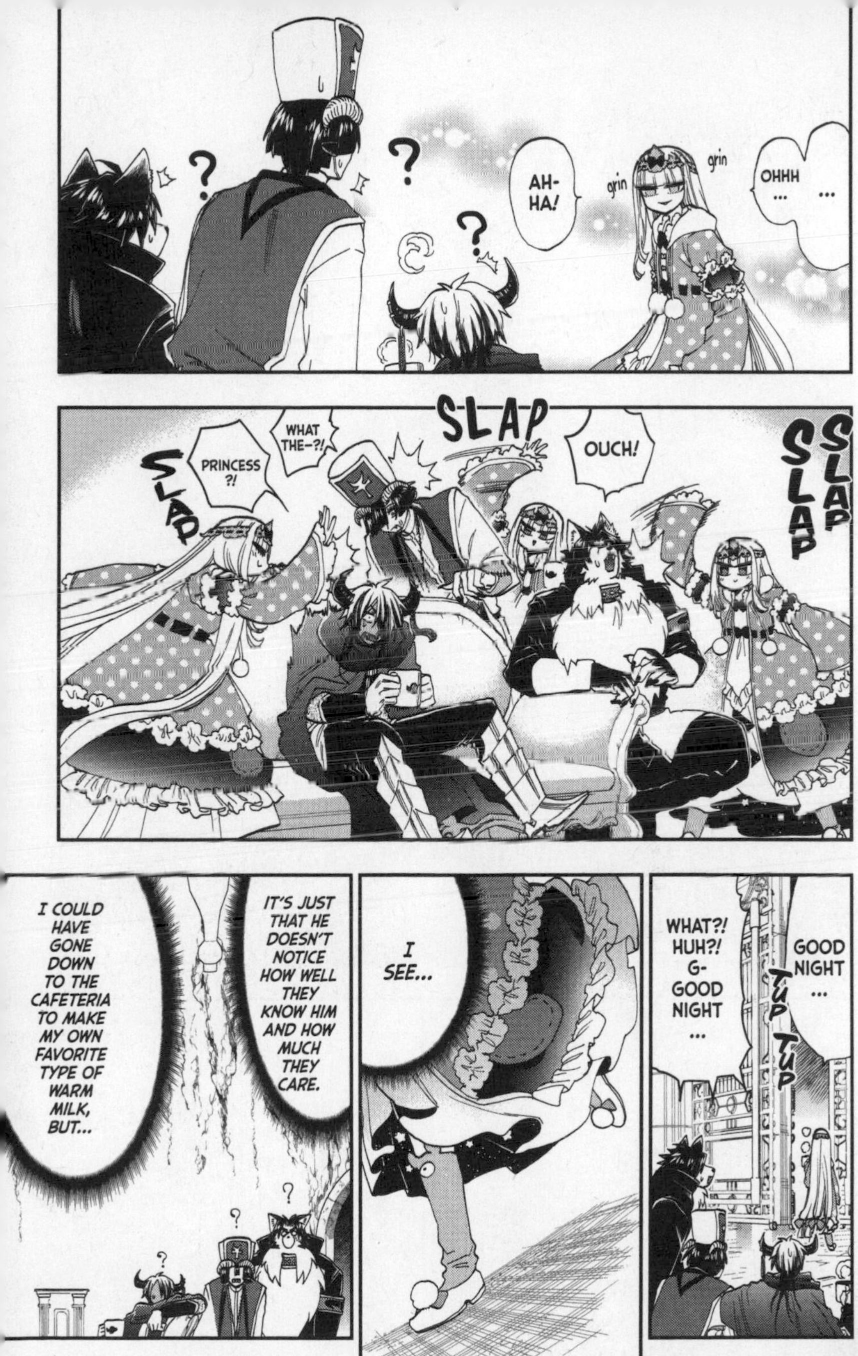
OHHH ... ...
grin
grin
AH-HA!
SLAP SLAP
SLAP
OUCH!
SLAP
WHAT THE-?!
PRINCESS ?!
SLAP
GOOD NIGHT ...
TUP TUP
WHAT?! HUH?! G-GOOD NIGHT ...
I SEE...
IT'S JUST THAT HE DOESN'T NOTICE HOW WELL THEY KNOW HIM AND HOW MUCH THEY CARE.
I COULD HAVE GONE DOWN TO THE CAFETERIA TO MAKE MY OWN FAVORITE TYPE OF WARM MILK, BUT...

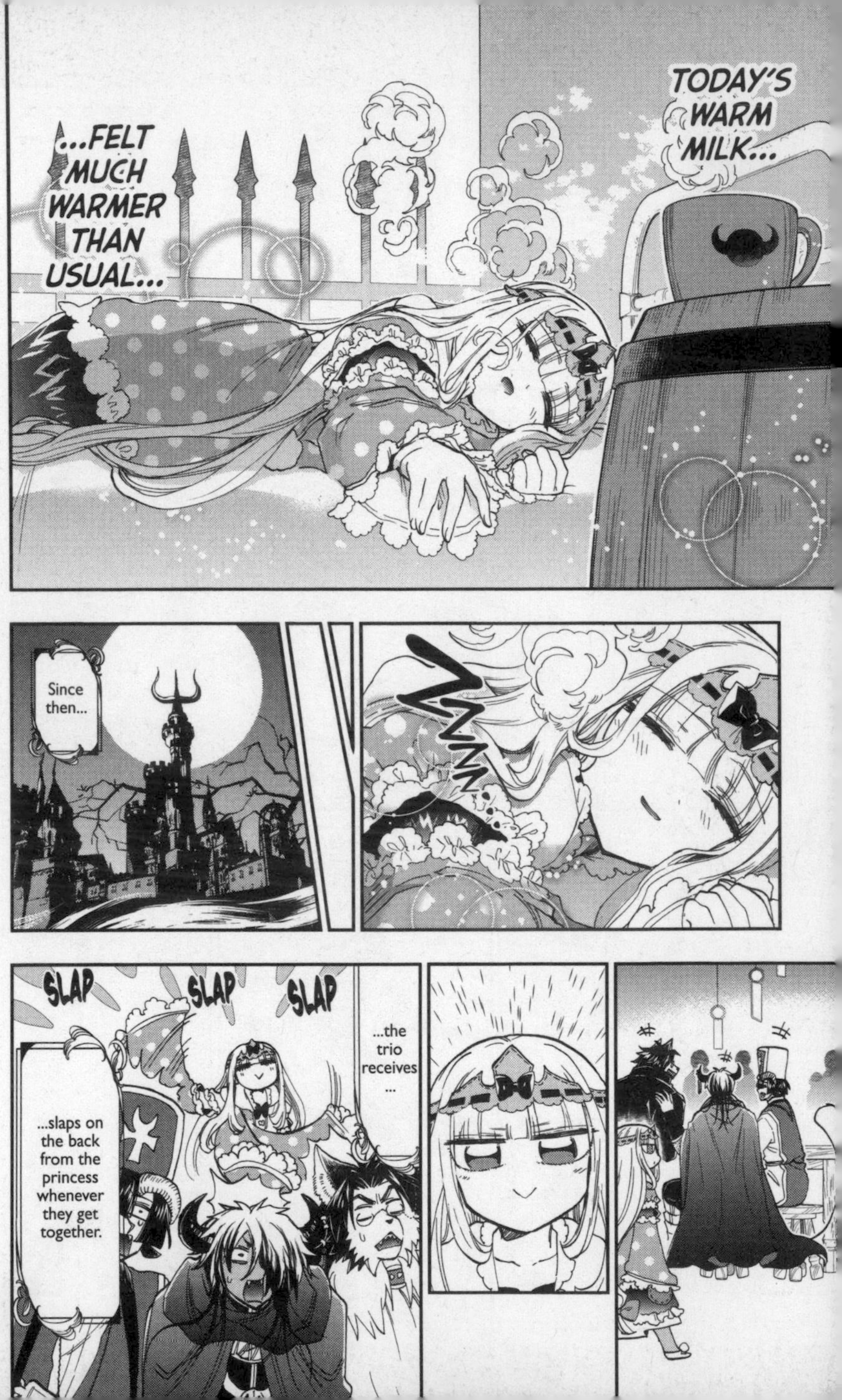
TODAY'S WARM MILK...
...FELT MUCH WARMER THAN USUAL...
ZZZ
Since then...
...the trio receives ...
SLAP
SLAP
SLAP
...slaps on the back from the princess whenever they get together.

HEIGHT CHART 1

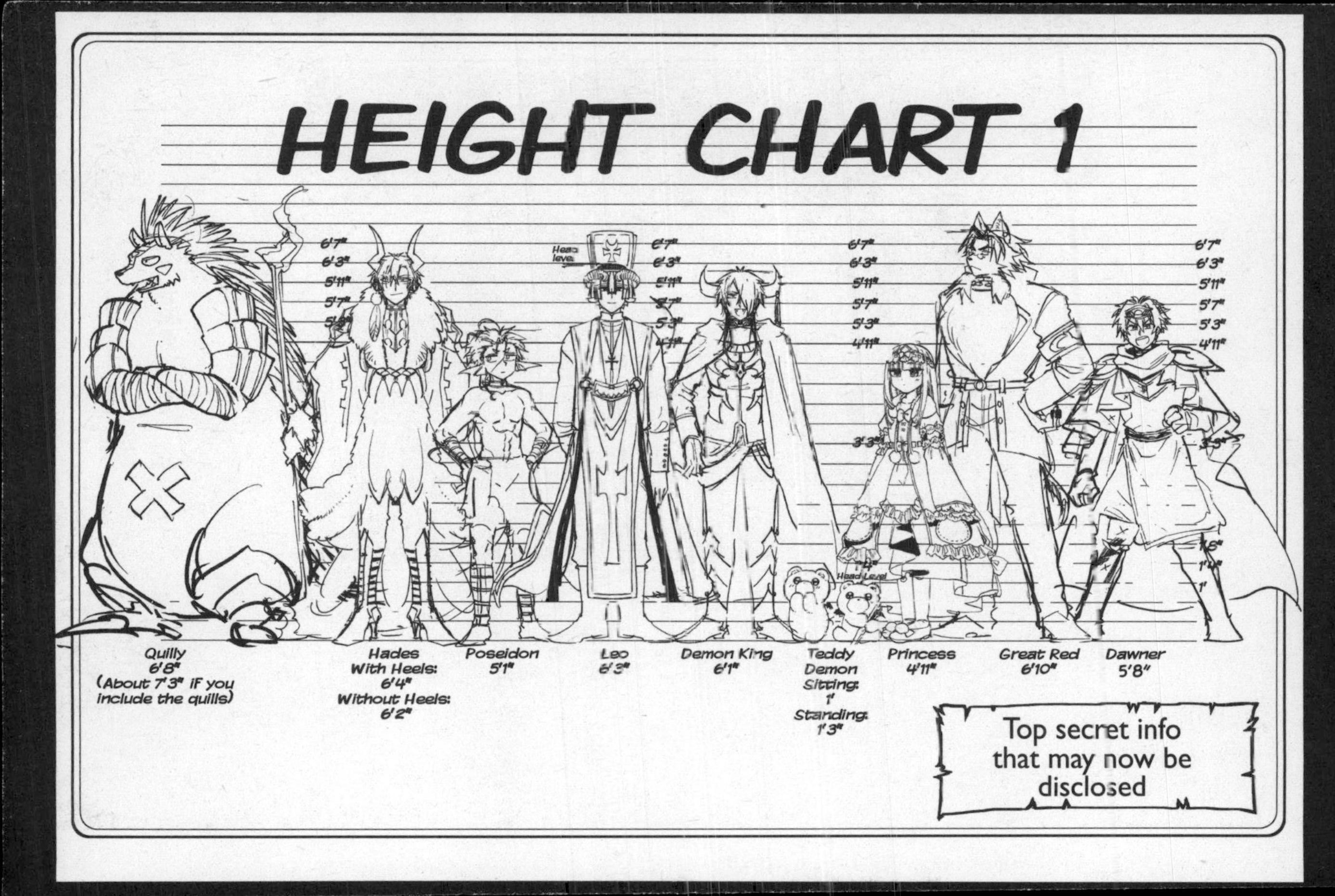

6'7"
6'3"
5'11"
5'7"
5'3"
4'11"
3'3"
1'8"
1'4"
1'
Head level
Quilly
6'8"
(About 7'3" if you include the quills)
Hades
With Heels:
6'4"
Without Heels:
6'2"
Poseidon
5'1"
Leo
6'3"
Demon King
6'1"
Teddy Demon
Sitting:
1'
Standing:
1'3"
Princess
4'11"
Great Red
6'10"
Dawner
5'8"

Top secret info that may now be disclosed

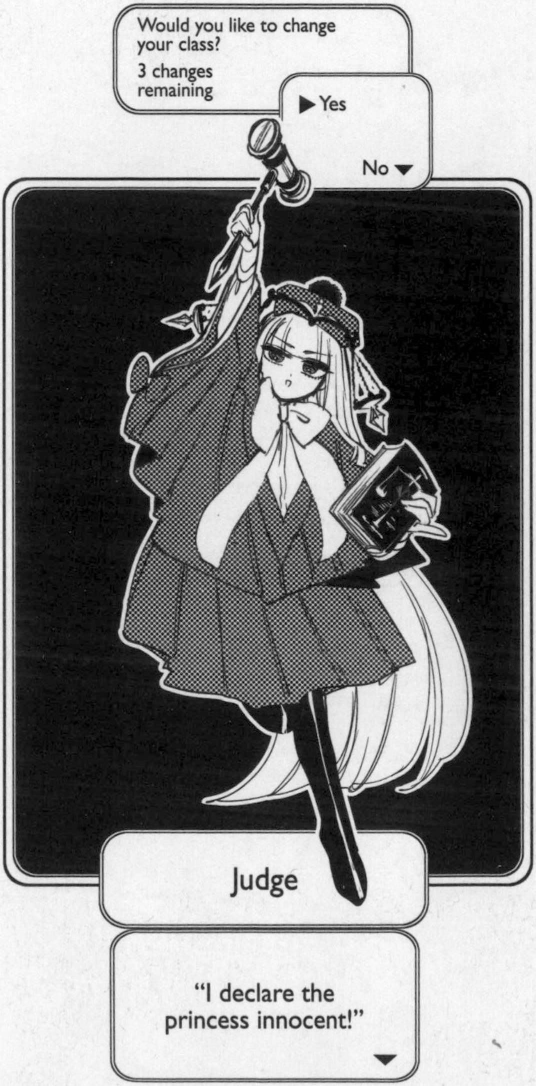
Would you like to change your class?
3 changes remaining
▶Yes
No
Judge
"I declare the princess innocent!"

153rd Night: Zero-Defense Princess vs. Full-Defense Man

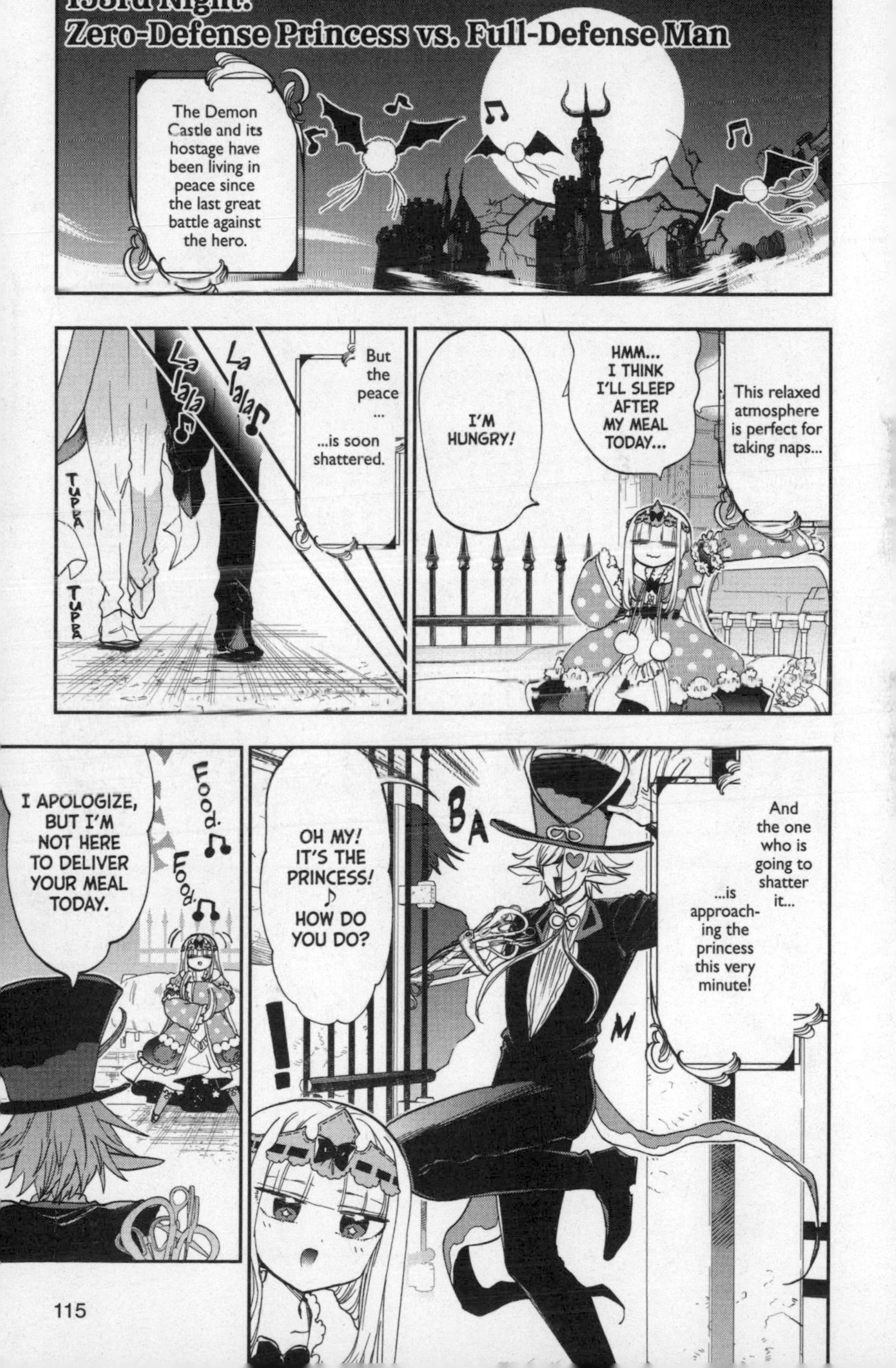

The Demon Castle and its hostage have been living in peace since the last great battle against the hero.
This relaxed atmosphere is perfect for taking naps...
HMM... I THINK I'LL SLEEP AFTER MY MEAL TODAY...
I'M HUNGRY!
But the peace ...
...is soon shattered.
La lalala
La lalala
TUPPA
TUPPA
And the one who is going to shatter it...
...is approaching the princess this very minute!
BA
M
OH MY! IT'S THE PRINCESS! ♪ HOW DO YOU DO?
!
Food.
Food.
I APOLOGIZE, BUT I'M NOT HERE TO DELIVER YOUR MEAL TODAY.

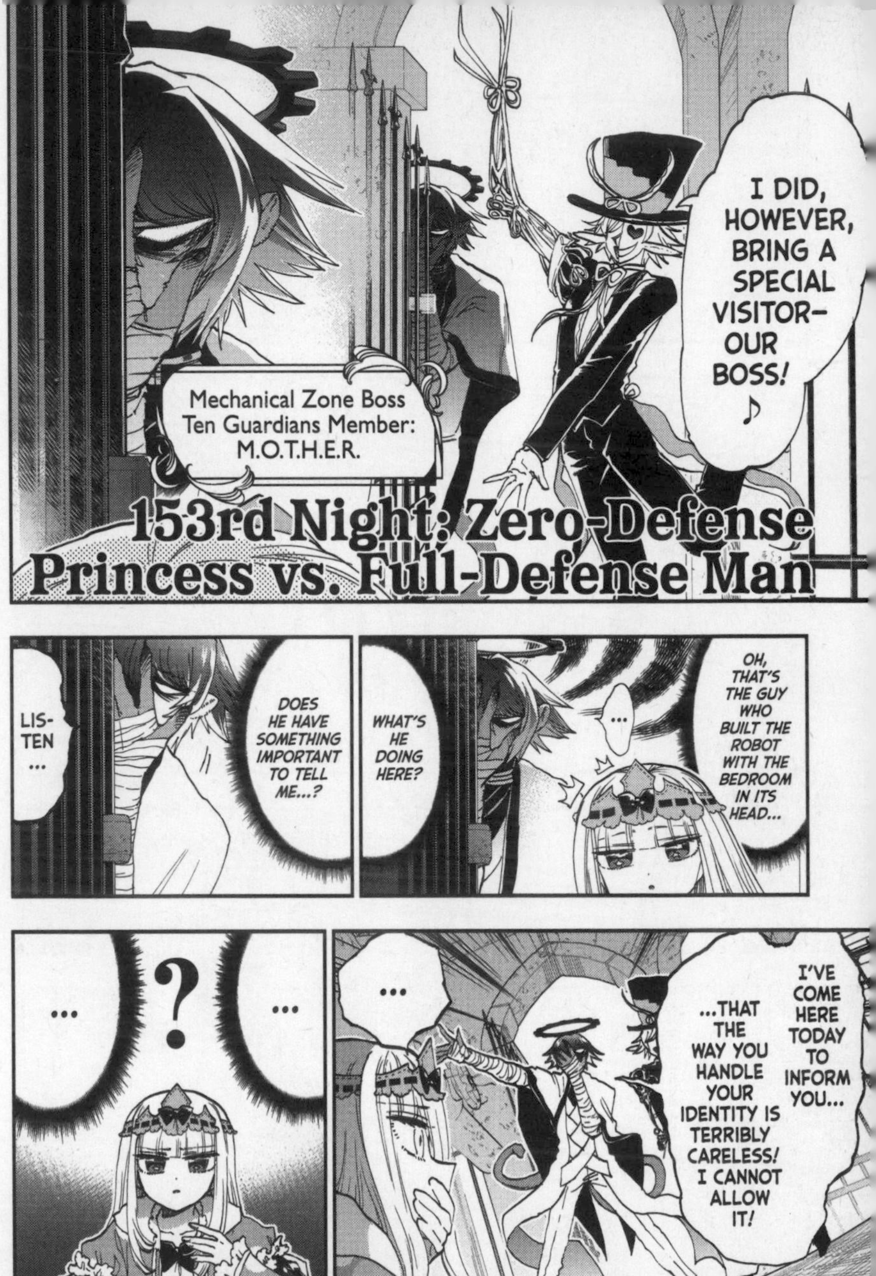
I DID, HOWEVER, BRING A SPECIAL VISITOR— OUR BOSS! ♪
Mechanical Zone Boss Ten Guardians Member: M.O.T.H.E.R.
153rd Night: Zero-Defense Princess vs. Full-Defense Man
OH, THAT'S THE GUY WHO BUILT THE ROBOT WITH THE BEDROOM IN ITS HEAD...
...
WHAT'S HE DOING HERE?
DOES HE HAVE SOMETHING IMPORTANT TO TELL ME...?
LIS- TEN ...
I'VE COME HERE TODAY TO INFORM YOU...
...THAT THE WAY YOU HANDLE YOUR IDENTITY IS TERRIBLY CARELESS! I CANNOT ALLOW IT!
...
...
?
...

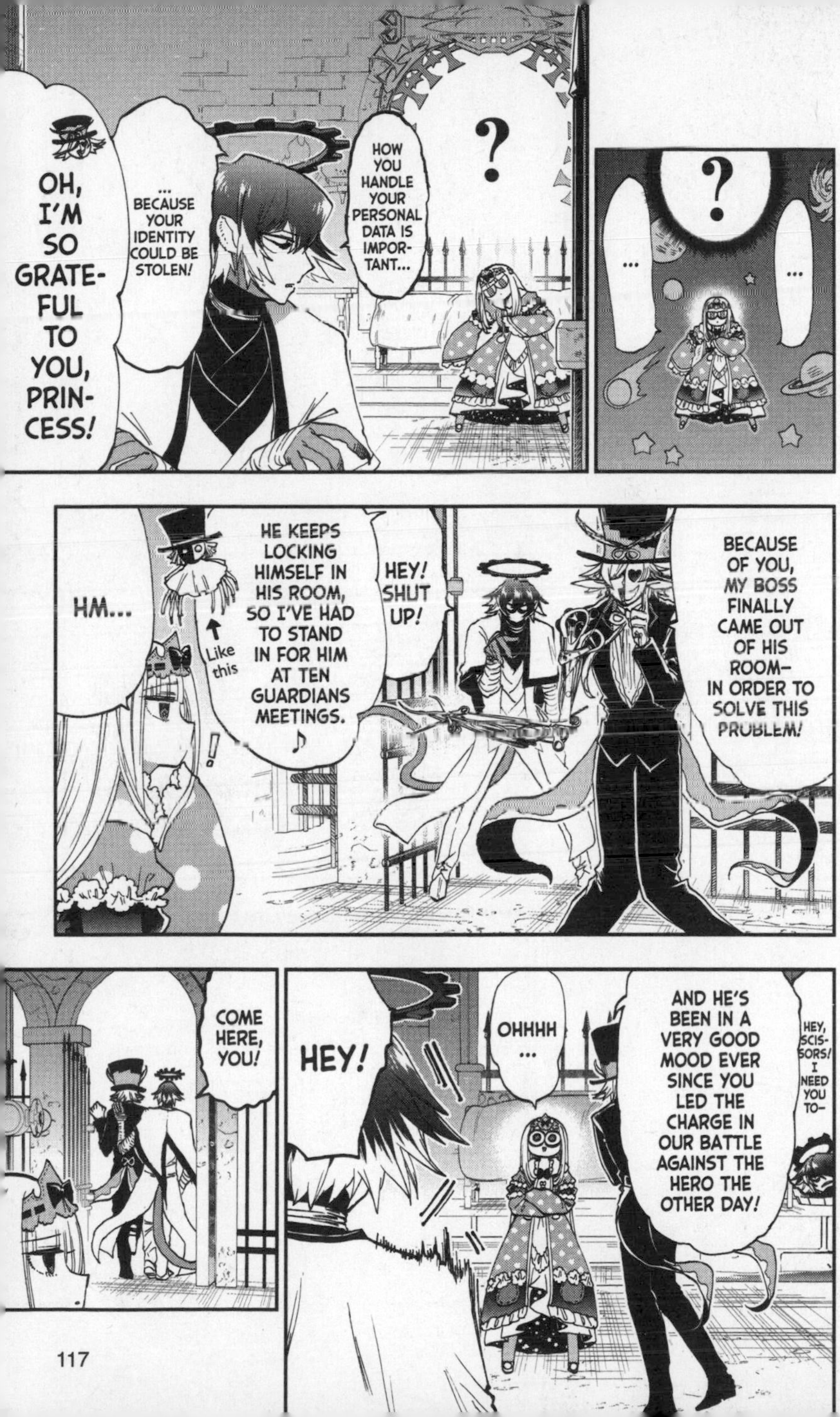
?
...
...
?
HOW YOU HANDLE YOUR PERSONAL DATA IS IMPOR-TANT...
... BECAUSE YOUR IDENTITY COULD BE STOLEN!
OH, I'M SO GRATE-FUL TO YOU, PRIN-CESS!
BECAUSE OF YOU, MY BOSS FINALLY CAME OUT OF HIS ROOM— IN ORDER TO SOLVE THIS PROBLEM!
HEY! SHUT UP!
HE KEEPS LOCKING HIMSELF IN HIS ROOM, SO I'VE HAD TO STAND IN FOR HIM AT TEN GUARDIANS MEETINGS. ♪
Like this
!
HM...
HEY, SCIS-SORS! I NEED YOU TO—
AND HE'S BEEN IN A VERY GOOD MOOD EVER SINCE YOU LED THE CHARGE IN OUR BATTLE AGAINST THE HERO THE OTHER DAY!
OHHHH ...
HEY!
COME HERE, YOU!

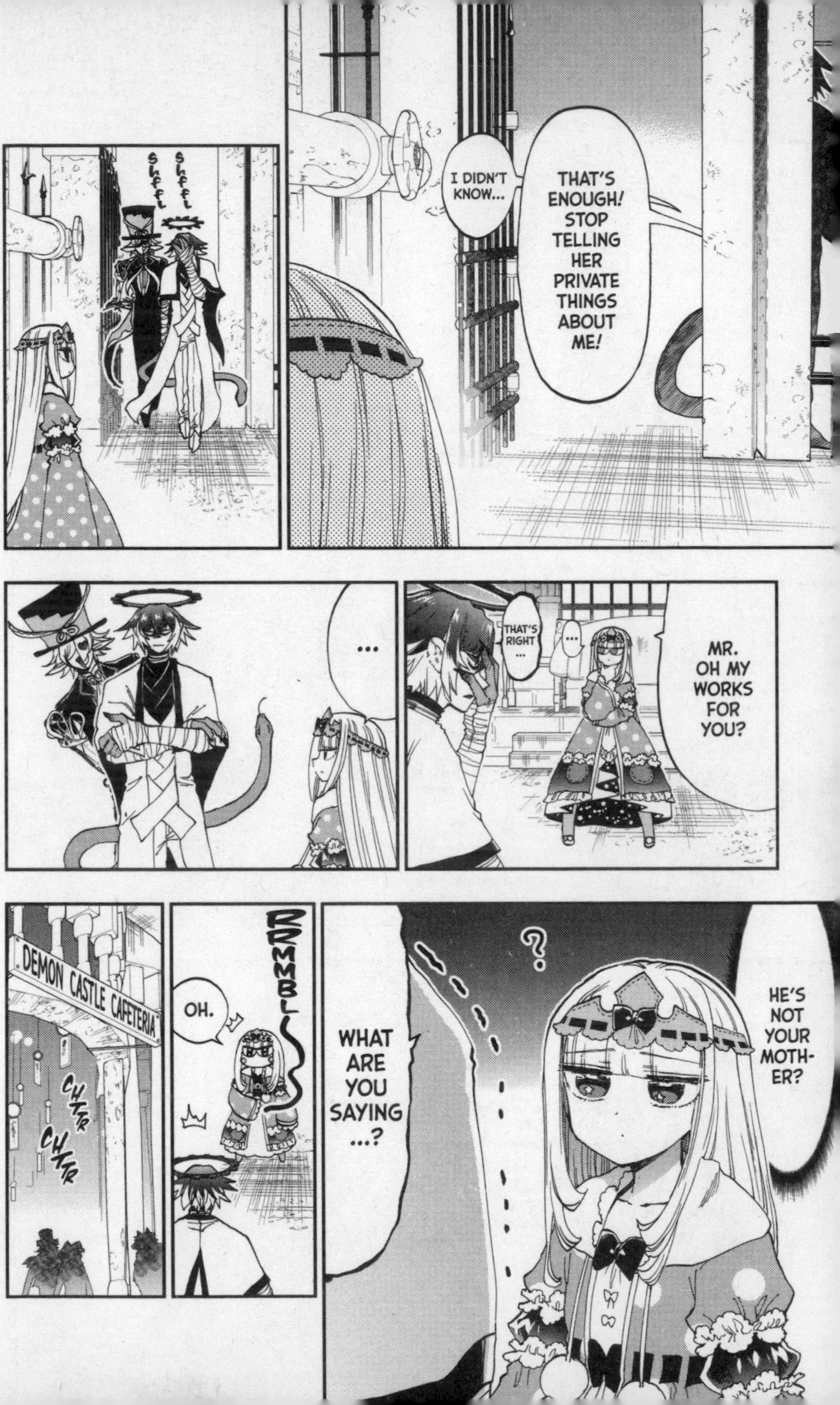
THAT'S ENOUGH! STOP TELLING HER PRIVATE THINGS ABOUT ME!
I DIDN'T KNOW...
shffl
shffl
MR. OH MY WORKS FOR YOU?
THAT'S RIGHT ...
...
...
HE'S NOT YOUR MOTH-ER?
?
WHAT ARE YOU SAYING ...?
RRMMBL
OH.
DEMON CASTLE CAFETERIA
CHTTR
CHTTR

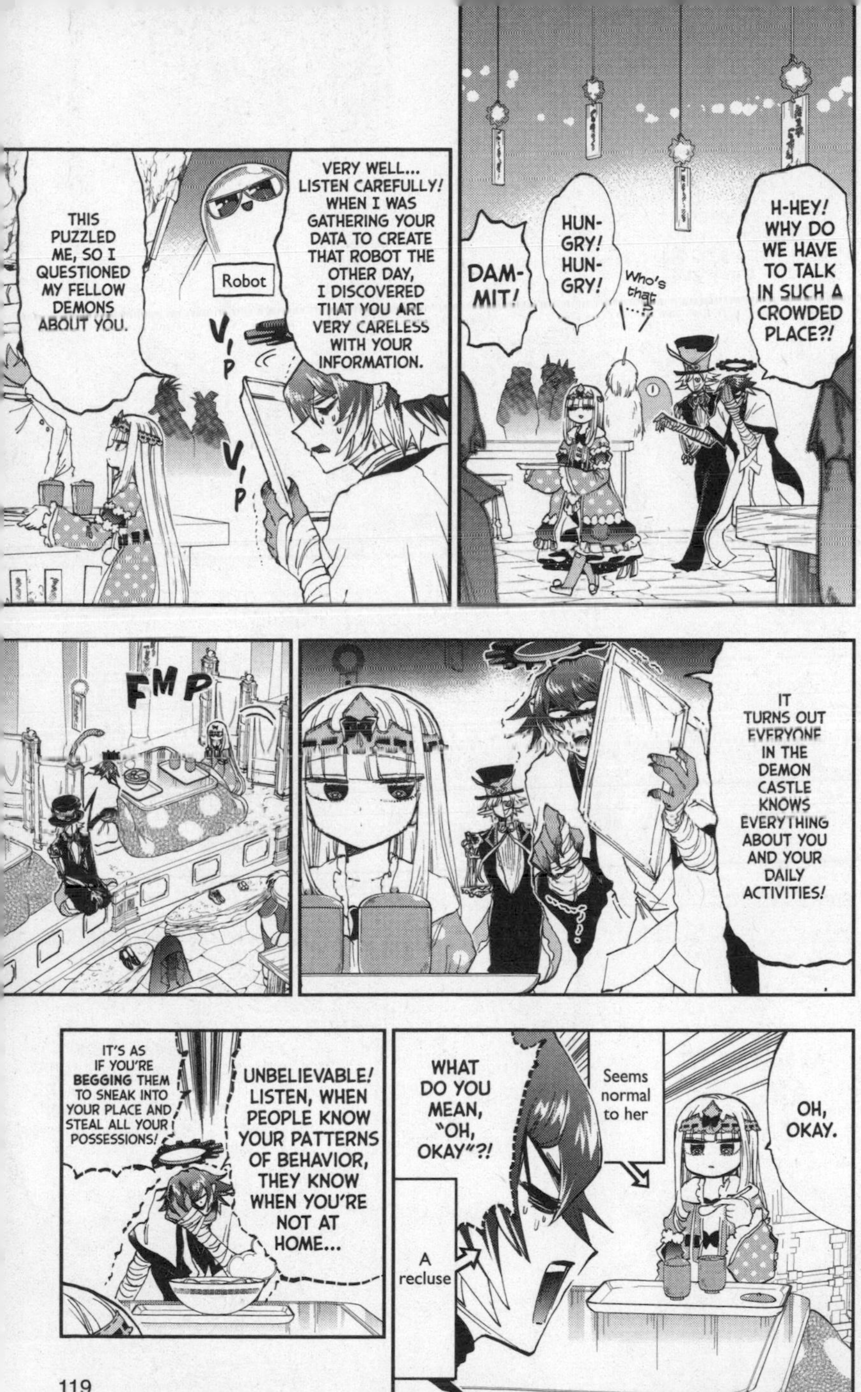

H-HEY! WHY DO WE HAVE TO TALK IN SUCH A CROWDED PLACE?!
HUN-GRY! HUN-GRY!
Who's that...?
DAM-MIT!
VERY WELL... LISTEN CAREFULLY! WHEN I WAS GATHERING YOUR DATA TO CREATE THAT ROBOT THE OTHER DAY, I DISCOVERED THAT YOU ARE VERY CARELESS WITH YOUR INFORMATION.
Robot
THIS PUZZLED ME, SO I QUESTIONED MY FELLOW DEMONS ABOUT YOU.
VIP
VIP
IT TURNS OUT EVERYONE IN THE DEMON CASTLE KNOWS EVERYTHING ABOUT YOU AND YOUR DAILY ACTIVITIES!
FMP
OH, OKAY.
Seems normal to her
WHAT DO YOU MEAN, "OH, OKAY"?!
A recluse
UNBELIEVABLE! LISTEN, WHEN PEOPLE KNOW YOUR PATTERNS OF BEHAVIOR, THEY KNOW WHEN YOU'RE NOT AT HOME...
IT'S AS IF YOU'RE BEGGING THEM TO SNEAK INTO YOUR PLACE AND STEAL ALL YOUR POSSESSIONS!

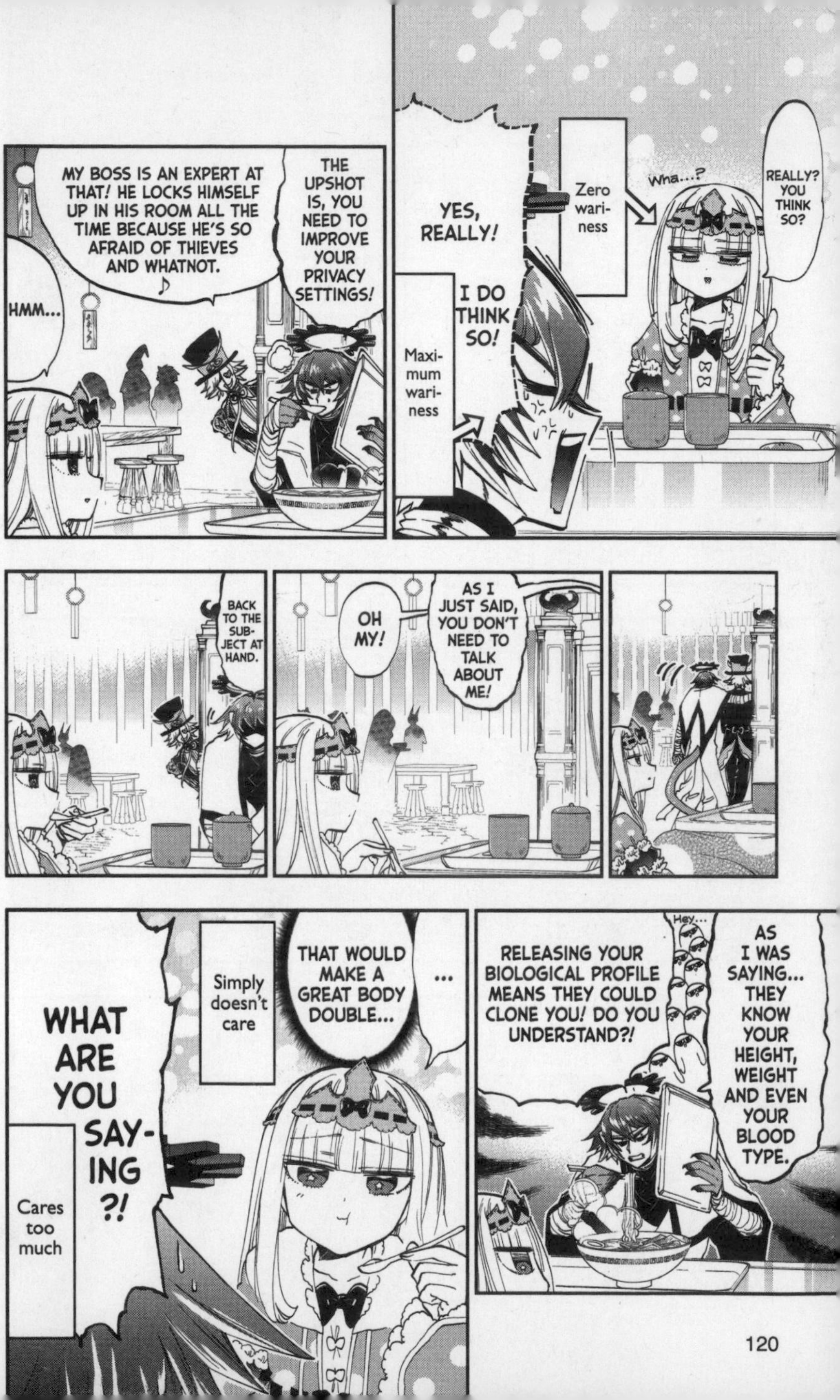
REALLY? YOU THINK SO?
Wha...?
Zero wariness
YES, REALLY!
I DO THINK SO!
Maximum wariness
THE UPSHOT IS, YOU NEED TO IMPROVE YOUR PRIVACY SETTINGS!
MY BOSS IS AN EXPERT AT THAT! HE LOCKS HIMSELF UP IN HIS ROOM ALL THE TIME BECAUSE HE'S SO AFRAID OF THIEVES AND WHATNOT. ♪
HMM...
AS I JUST SAID, YOU DON'T NEED TO TALK ABOUT ME!
OH MY!
BACK TO THE SUBJECT AT HAND.
AS I WAS SAYING... THEY KNOW YOUR HEIGHT, WEIGHT AND EVEN YOUR BLOOD TYPE.
Hey...
RELEASING YOUR BIOLOGICAL PROFILE MEANS THEY COULD CLONE YOU! DO YOU UNDERSTAND?!
...
THAT WOULD MAKE A GREAT BODY DOUBLE...
Simply doesn't care
WHAT ARE YOU SAYING?!
Cares too much

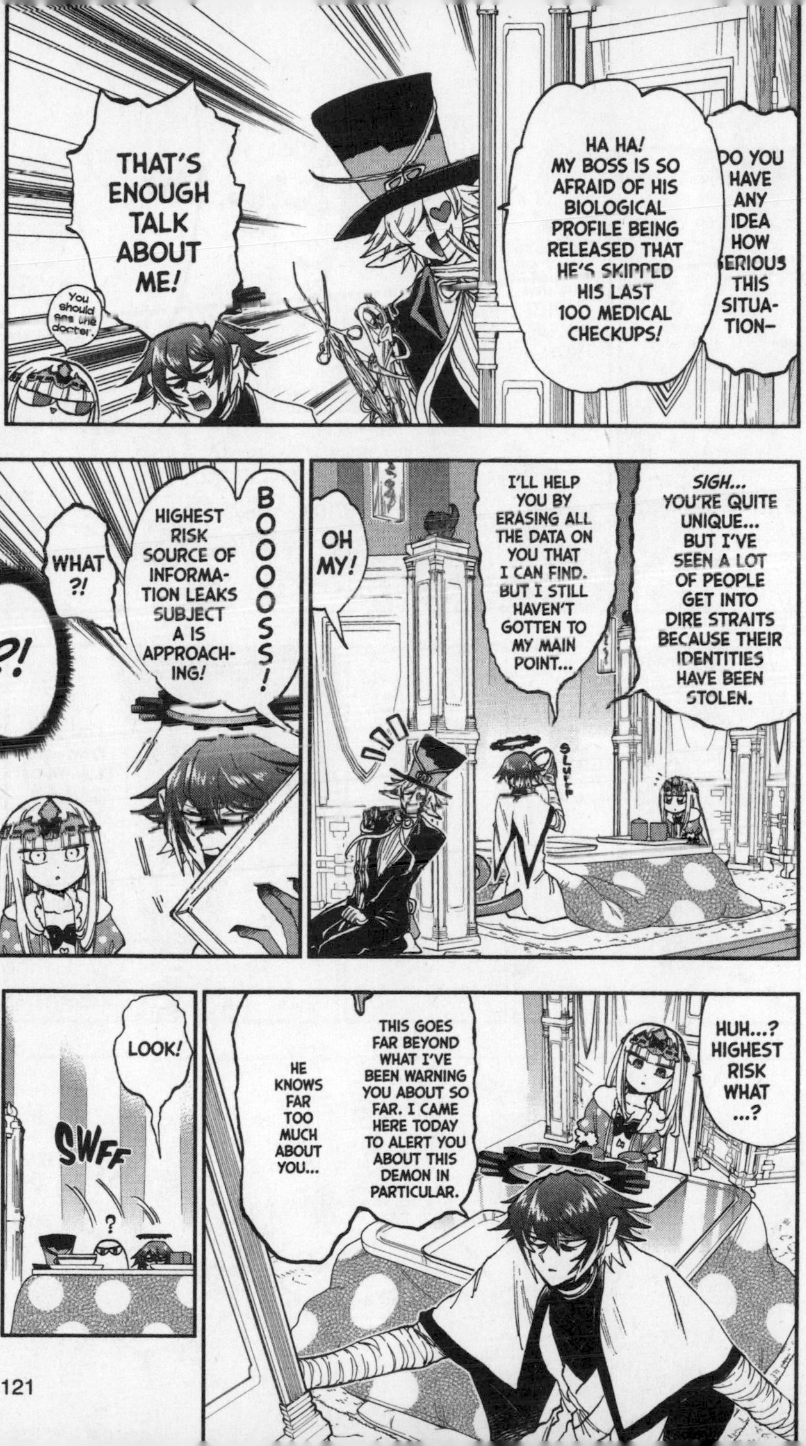
DO YOU HAVE ANY IDEA HOW SERIOUS THIS SITUATION–
HA HA! MY BOSS IS SO AFRAID OF HIS BIOLOGICAL PROFILE BEING RELEASED THAT HE'S SKIPPED HIS LAST 100 MEDICAL CHECKUPS!
THAT'S ENOUGH TALK ABOUT ME!
You should see the doctor.
SIGH... YOU'RE QUITE UNIQUE... BUT I'VE SEEN A LOT OF PEOPLE GET INTO DIRE STRAITS BECAUSE THEIR IDENTITIES HAVE BEEN STOLEN.
I'LL HELP YOU BY ERASING ALL THE DATA ON YOU THAT I CAN FIND. BUT I STILL HAVEN'T GOTTEN TO MY MAIN POINT...
OH MY!
SLURP
BOOOOOSS!
HIGHEST RISK SOURCE OF INFORMATION LEAKS SUBJECT A IS APPROACHING!
WHAT?!
?!
HUH...? HIGHEST RISK WHAT...?
THIS GOES FAR BEYOND WHAT I'VE BEEN WARNING YOU ABOUT SO FAR. I CAME HERE TODAY TO ALERT YOU ABOUT THIS DEMON IN PARTICULAR.
HE KNOWS FAR TOO MUCH ABOUT YOU...
LOOK!
SWFF
?

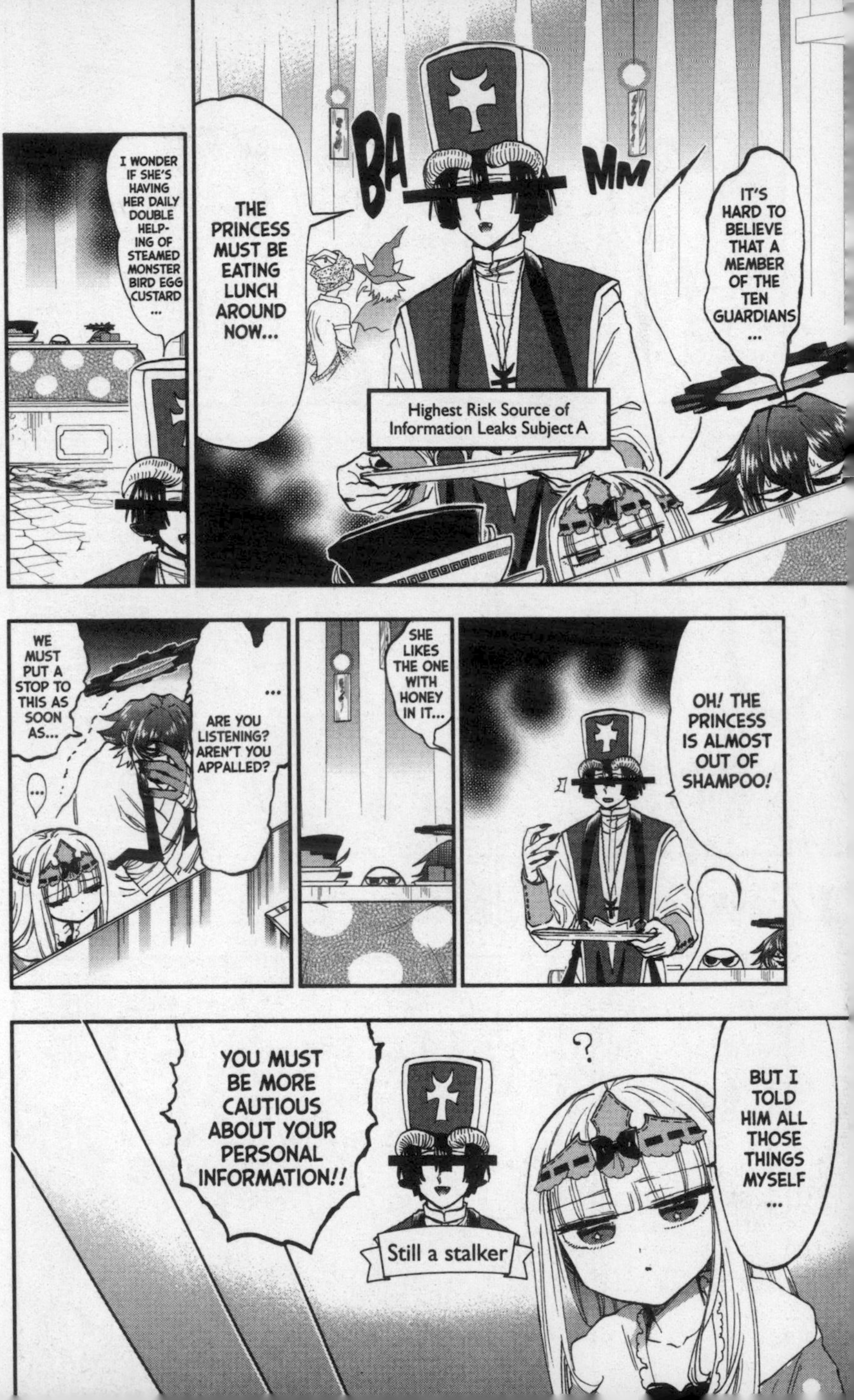
IT'S HARD TO BELIEVE THAT A MEMBER OF THE TEN GUARDIANS ...
BAMM
THE PRINCESS MUST BE EATING LUNCH AROUND NOW...
Highest Risk Source of Information Leaks Subject A
I WONDER IF SHE'S HAVING HER DAILY DOUBLE HELP-ING OF STEAMED MONSTER BIRD EGG CUSTARD ...
OH! THE PRINCESS IS ALMOST OUT OF SHAMPOO!
SHE LIKES THE ONE WITH HONEY IN IT...
WE MUST PUT A STOP TO THIS AS SOON AS...
... ARE YOU LISTENING? AREN'T YOU APPALLED?
...
BUT I TOLD HIM ALL THOSE THINGS MYSELF ...
?
YOU MUST BE MORE CAUTIOUS ABOUT YOUR PERSONAL INFORMATION!!
Still a stalker

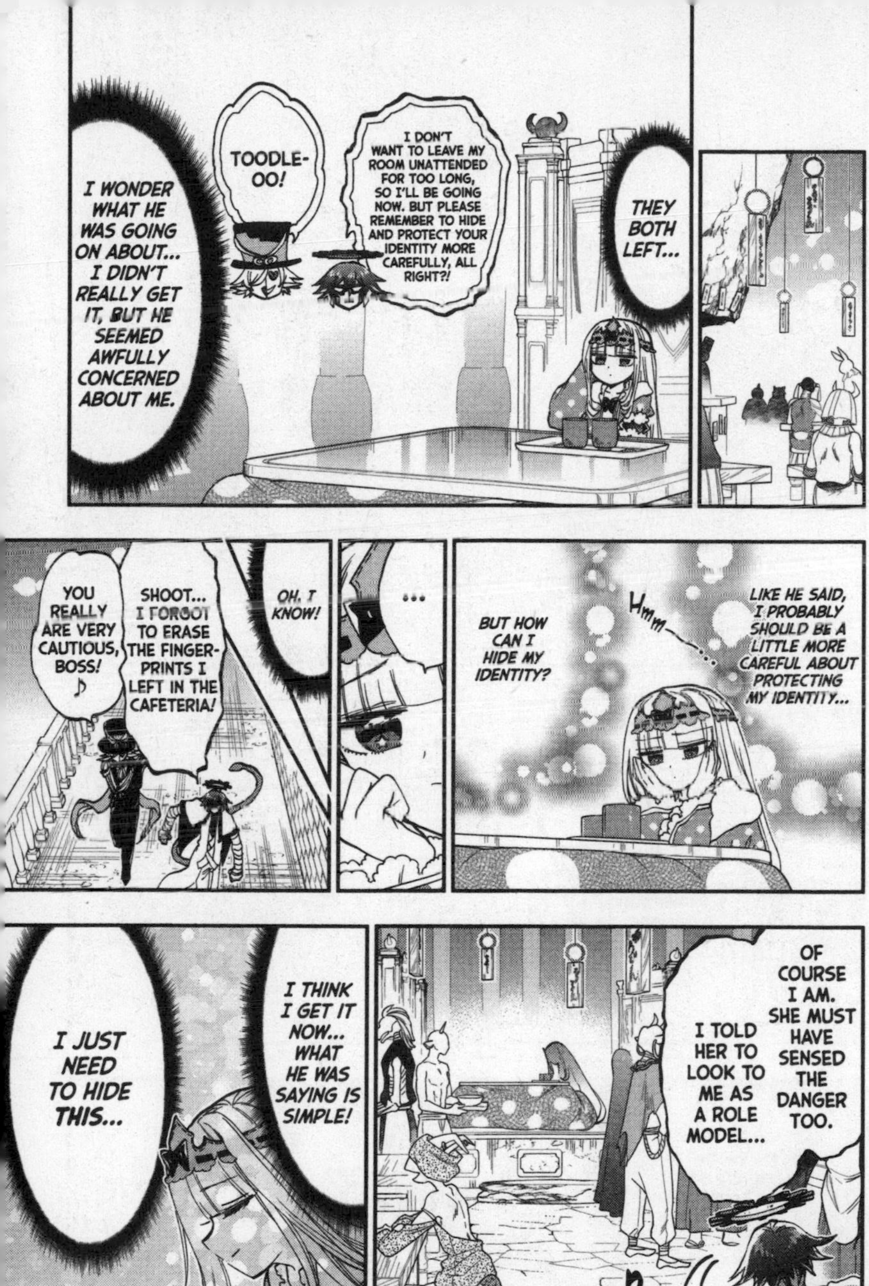
THEY BOTH LEFT...
I DON'T WANT TO LEAVE MY ROOM UNATTENDED FOR TOO LONG, SO I'LL BE GOING NOW. BUT PLEASE REMEMBER TO HIDE AND PROTECT YOUR IDENTITY MORE CAREFULLY, ALL RIGHT?!
TOODLE-OO!
I WONDER WHAT HE WAS GOING ON ABOUT... I DIDN'T REALLY GET IT, BUT HE SEEMED AWFULLY CONCERNED ABOUT ME.
LIKE HE SAID, I PROBABLY SHOULD BE A LITTLE MORE CAREFUL ABOUT PROTECTING MY IDENTITY...
Hmm~...
BUT HOW CAN I HIDE MY IDENTITY?
...
OH, I KNOW!
SHOOT... I FORGOT TO ERASE THE FINGER-PRINTS I LEFT IN THE CAFETERIA!
YOU REALLY ARE VERY CAUTIOUS, BOSS! ♪
OF COURSE I AM. SHE MUST HAVE SENSED THE DANGER TOO.
I TOLD HER TO LOOK TO ME AS A ROLE MODEL...
Peek
I THINK I GET IT NOW... WHAT HE WAS SAYING IS SIMPLE!
I JUST NEED TO HIDE THIS...

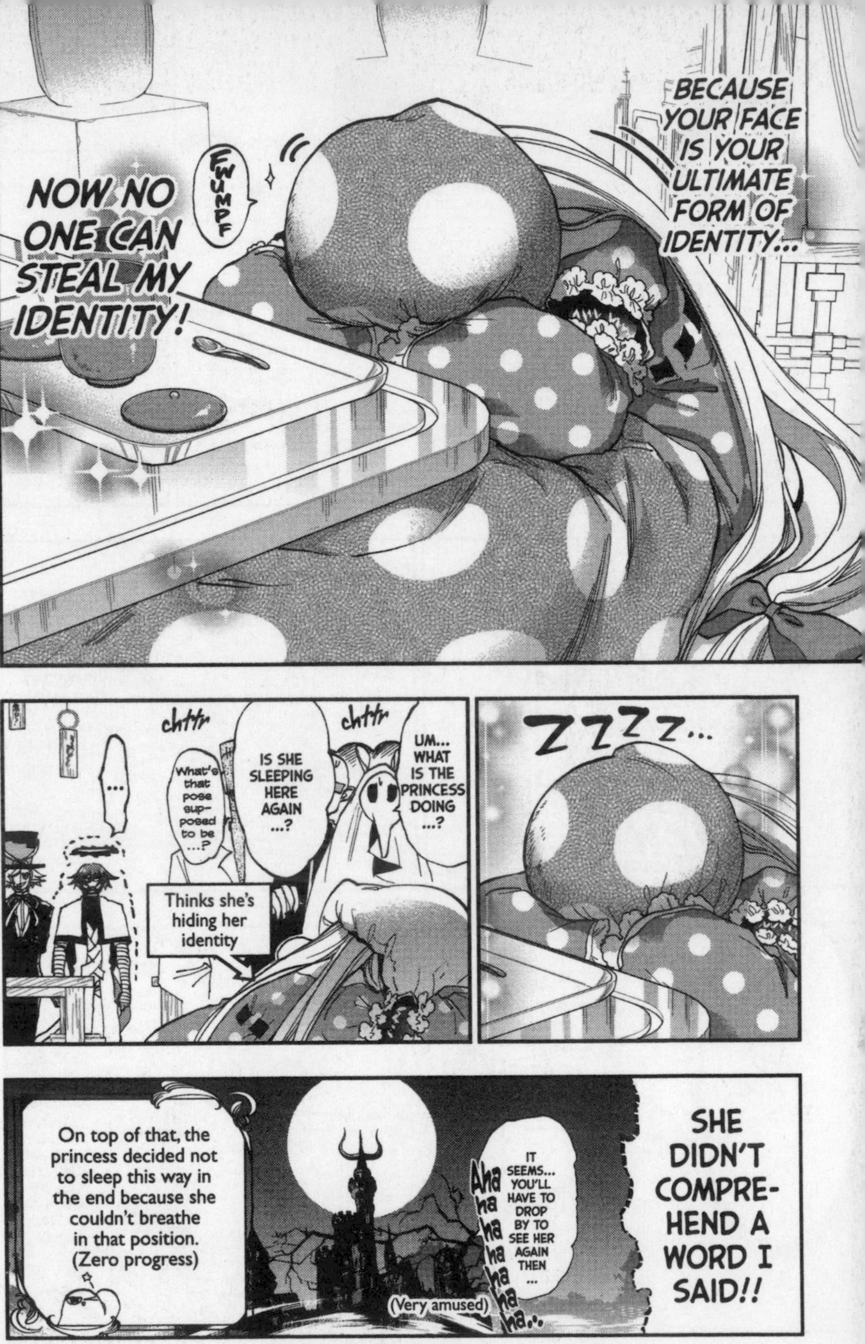
BECAUSE YOUR FACE IS YOUR ULTIMATE FORM OF IDENTITY...
FWUMPF
NOW NO ONE CAN STEAL MY IDENTITY!
ZZZz...
UM... WHAT IS THE PRINCESS DOING...?
chttr
IS SHE SLEEPING HERE AGAIN...?
What's that pose sup-posed to be...?
chttr
...
Thinks she's hiding her identity
SHE DIDN'T COMPRE-HEND A WORD I SAID!!
IT SEEMS... YOU'LL HAVE TO DROP BY TO SEE HER AGAIN THEN...
Ahahahahaha...
(Very amused)
On top of that, the princess decided not to sleep this way in the end because she couldn't breathe in that position. (Zero progress)

Scissors Sorcerer Uncensored

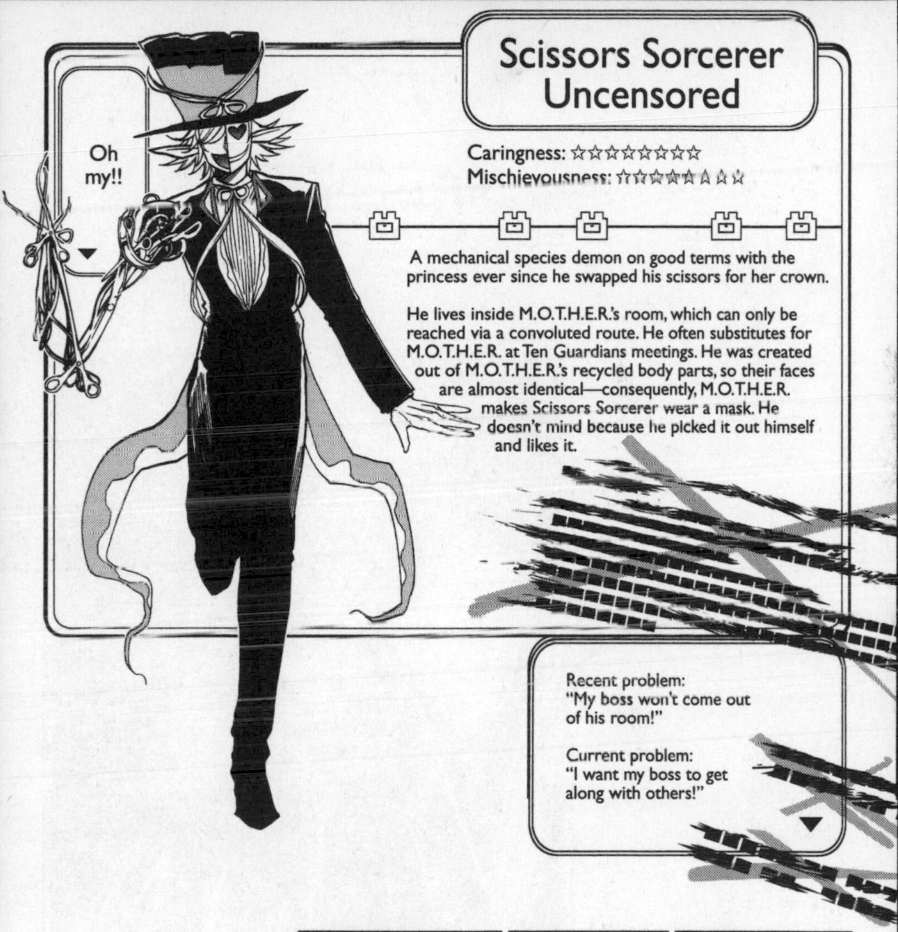
Oh my!!

Caringness: ☆☆☆☆☆☆☆☆
Mischievousness: ☆☆☆☆☆☆☆☆

A mechanical species demon on good terms with the princess ever since he swapped his scissors for her crown.

He lives inside M.O.T.H.E.R.'s room, which can only be reached via a convoluted route. He often substitutes for M.O.T.H.E.R. at Ten Guardians meetings. He was created out of M.O.T.H.E.R.'s recycled body parts, so their faces are almost identical—consequently, M.O.T.H.E.R. makes Scissors Sorcerer wear a mask. He doesn't mind because he picked it out himself and likes it.

Recent problem:
"My boss won't come out of his room!"

Current problem:
"I want my boss to get along with others!"

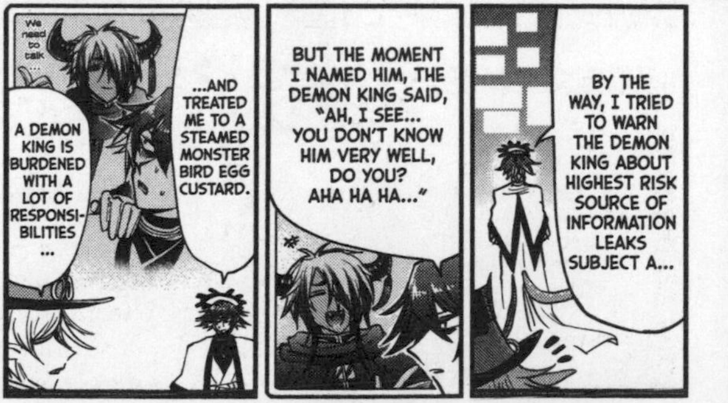
BY THE WAY, I TRIED TO WARN THE DEMON KING ABOUT HIGHEST RISK SOURCE OF INFORMATION LEAKS SUBJECT A...
BUT THE MOMENT I NAMED HIM, THE DEMON KING SAID, "AH, I SEE... YOU DON'T KNOW HIM VERY WELL, DO YOU? AHA HA HA..."
...AND TREATED ME TO A STEAMED MONSTER BIRD EGG CUSTARD.
We need to talk...
A DEMON KING IS BURDENED WITH A LOT OF RESPONSIBILITIES...

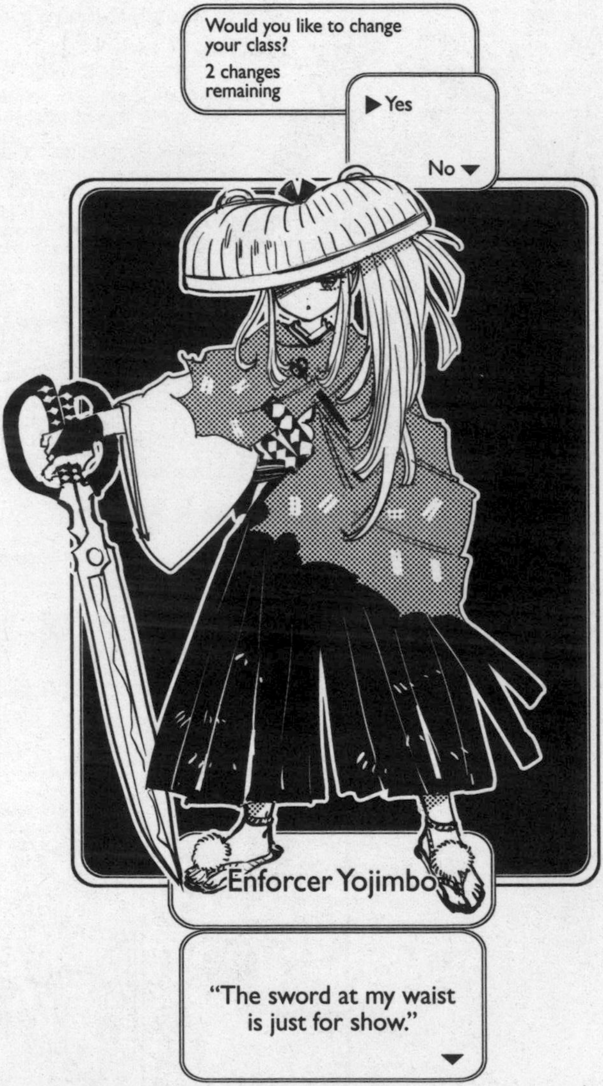
Would you like to change your class?
2 changes remaining
▶Yes
No
Enforcer Yojimbo
"The sword at my waist is just for show."

154th Night: It's Rude to Just Point

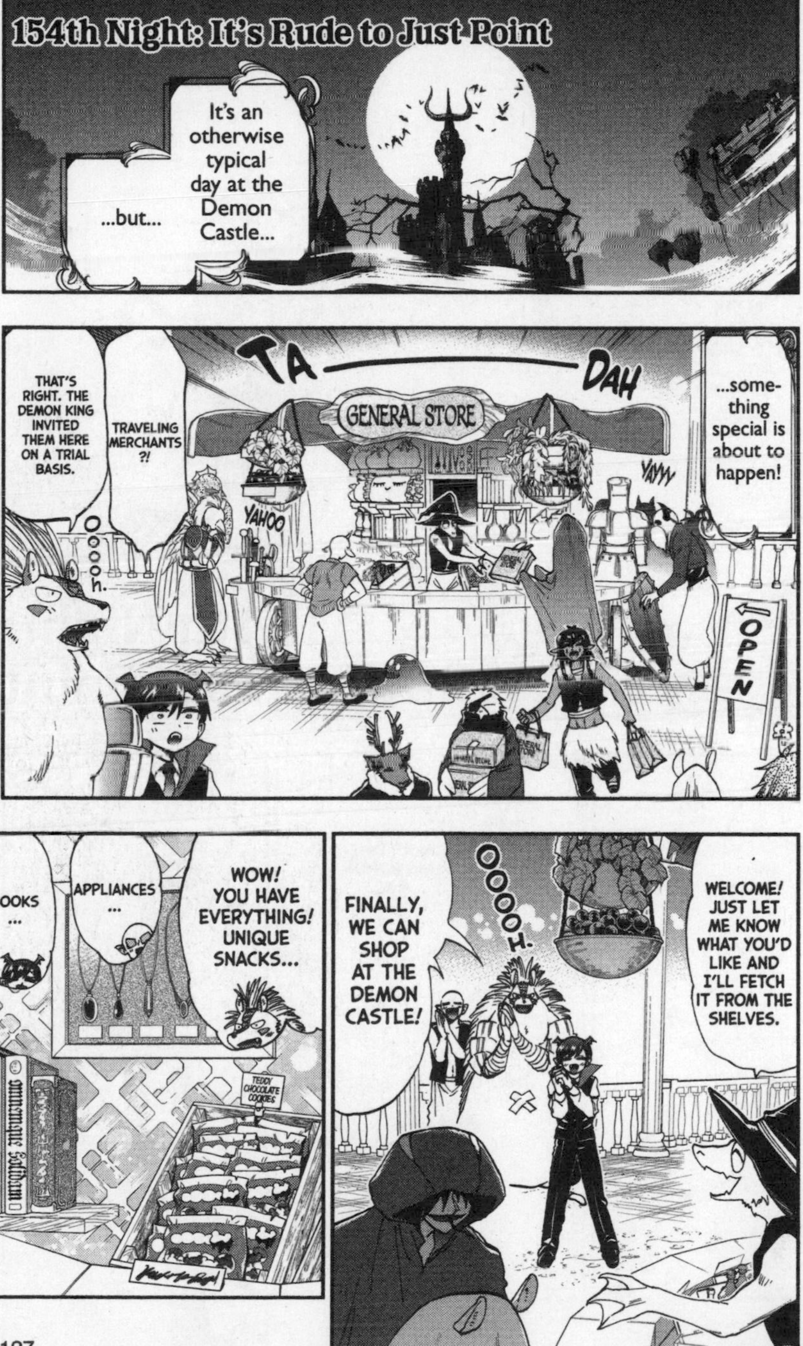
It's an otherwise typical day at the Demon Castle...
...but...
...some-thing special is about to happen!
TA——DAH
GENERAL STORE
YAYYY
TRAVELING MERCHANTS?!
THAT'S RIGHT. THE DEMON KING INVITED THEM HERE ON A TRIAL BASIS.
YAHOO
Ooooh.
OPEN
WELCOME! JUST LET ME KNOW WHAT YOU'D LIKE AND I'LL FETCH IT FROM THE SHELVES.
OOOOOH.
FINALLY, WE CAN SHOP AT THE DEMON CASTLE!
WOW! YOU HAVE EVERYTHING! UNIQUE SNACKS...
APPLIANCES...
BOOKS...
TEDDY CHOCOLATE COOKIES

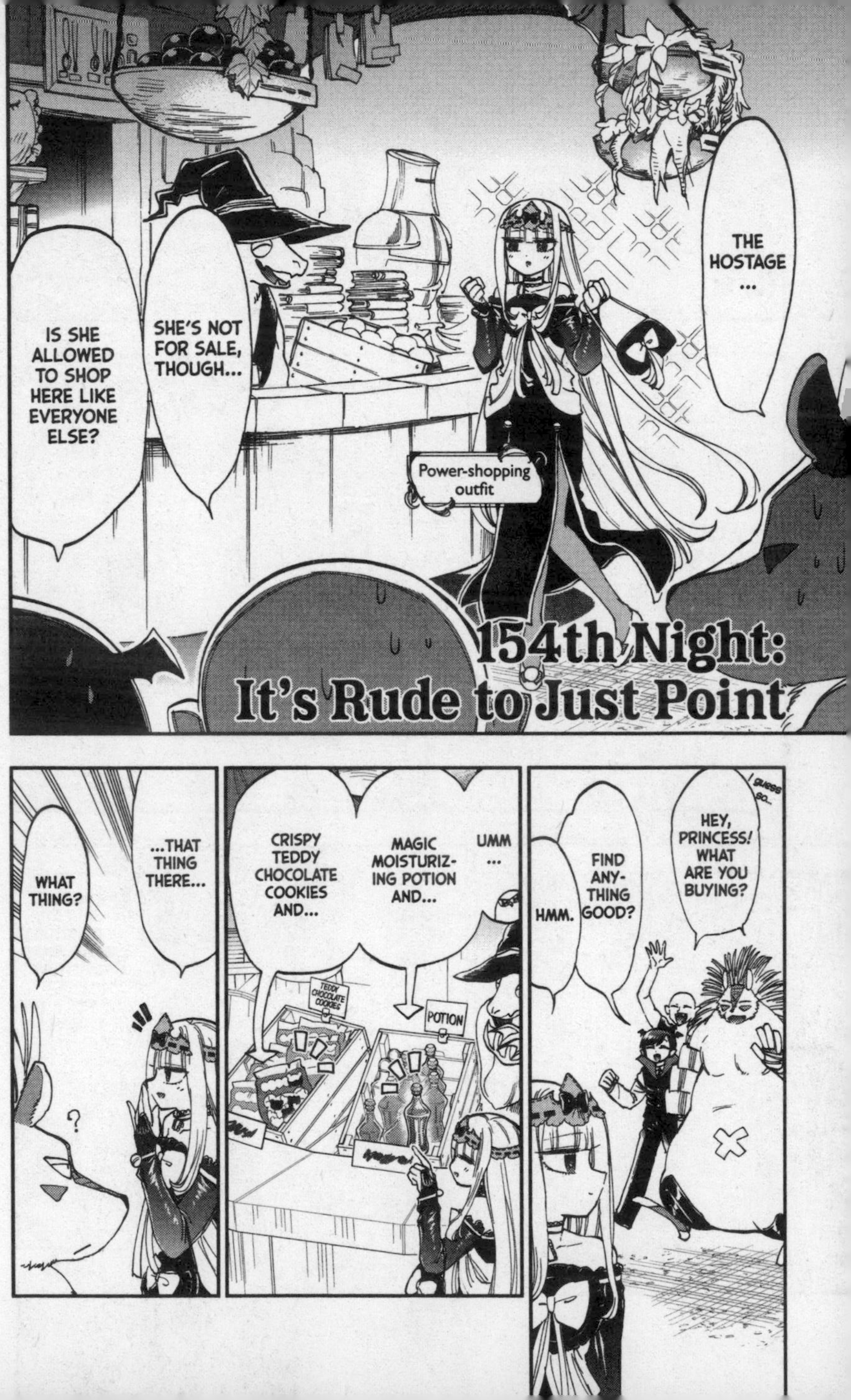
THE HOSTAGE ...
SHE'S NOT FOR SALE, THOUGH...
IS SHE ALLOWED TO SHOP HERE LIKE EVERYONE ELSE?
Power-shopping outfit
154th Night: It's Rude to Just Point
I guess so...
HEY, PRINCESS! WHAT ARE YOU BUYING?
FIND ANYTHING GOOD?
HMM.
UMM ...
MAGIC MOISTURIZING POTION AND...
CRISPY TEDDY CHOCOLATE COOKIES AND...
TEDDY CHOCOLATE COOKIES
POTION
...THAT THING THERE...
WHAT THING?

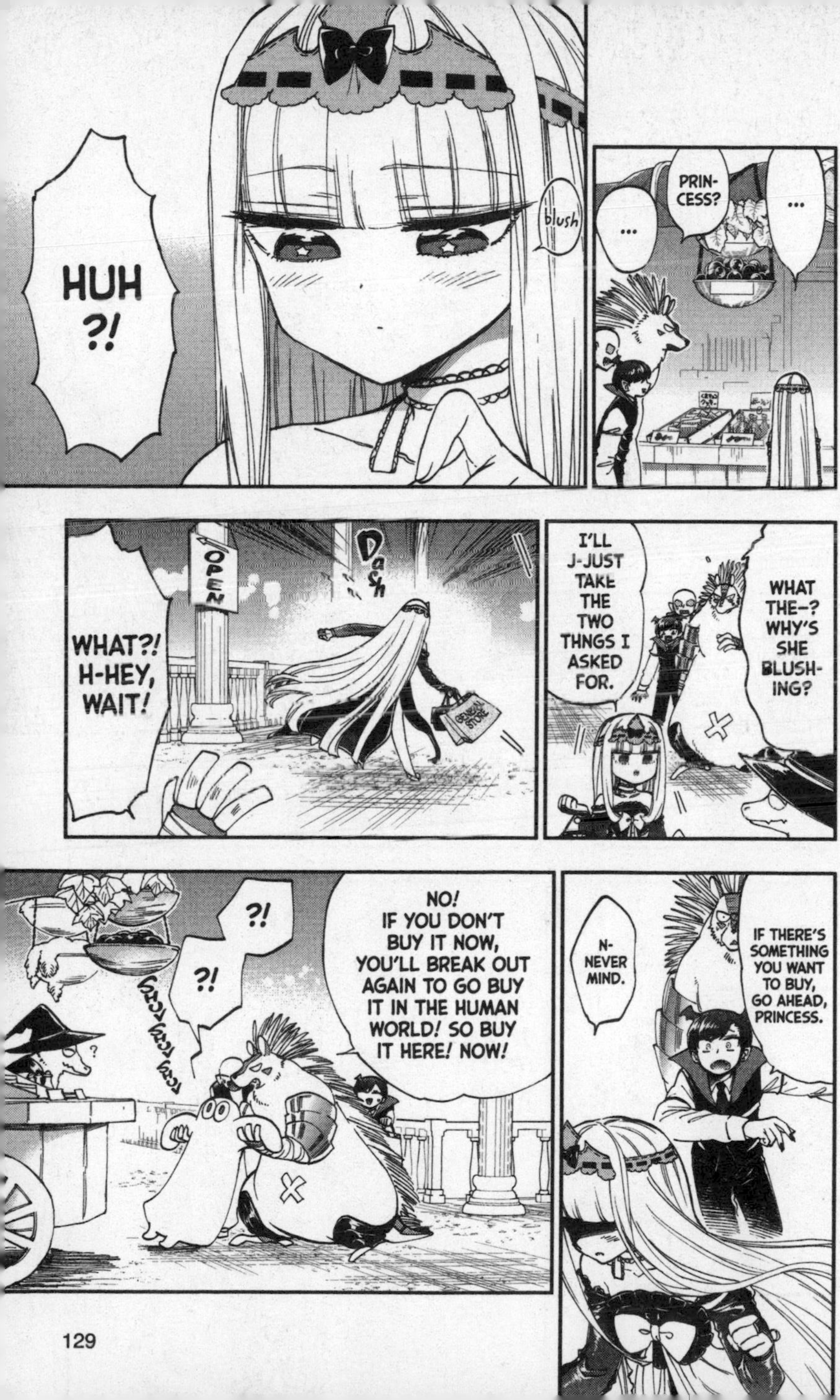

PRIN-CESS?
...
...
blush
HUH ?!
I'LL J-JUST TAKE THE TWO THNGS I ASKED FOR.
WHAT THE—? WHY'S SHE BLUSH-ING?
OPEN
Dash
GENERAL STORE
WHAT?! H-HEY, WAIT!
IF THERE'S SOMETHING YOU WANT TO BUY, GO AHEAD, PRINCESS.
N-NEVER MIND.
NO! IF YOU DON'T BUY IT NOW, YOU'LL BREAK OUT AGAIN TO GO BUY IT IN THE HUMAN WORLD! SO BUY IT HERE! NOW!
?!
?!

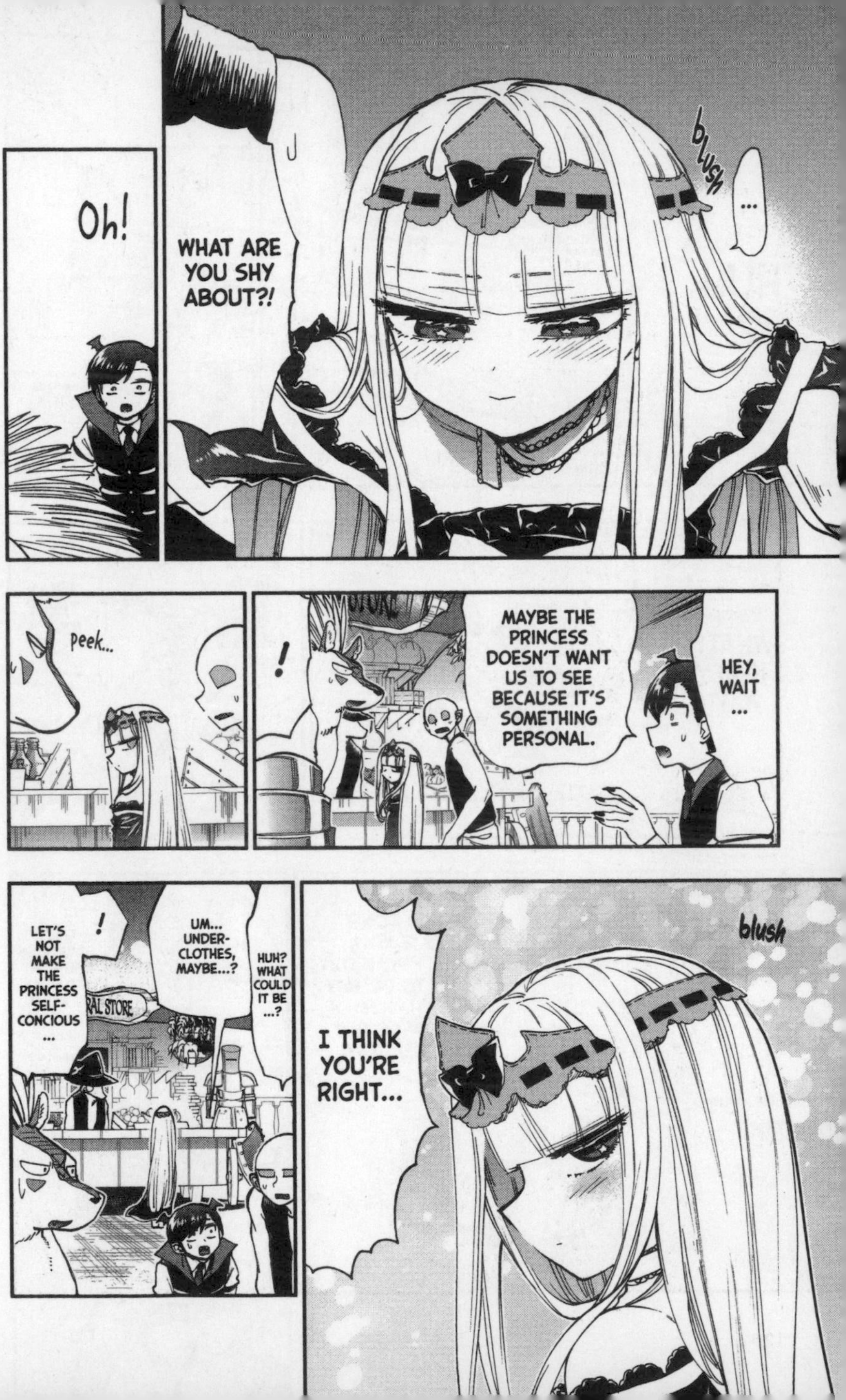
blush
...
WHAT ARE YOU SHY ABOUT?!
Oh!
HEY, WAIT ...
MAYBE THE PRINCESS DOESN'T WANT US TO SEE BECAUSE IT'S SOMETHING PERSONAL.
!
peek...
blush
I THINK YOU'RE RIGHT...
HUH? WHAT COULD IT BE ...?
UM... UNDER-CLOTHES, MAYBE...?
!
LET'S NOT MAKE THE PRINCESS SELF-CONCIOUS ...
...

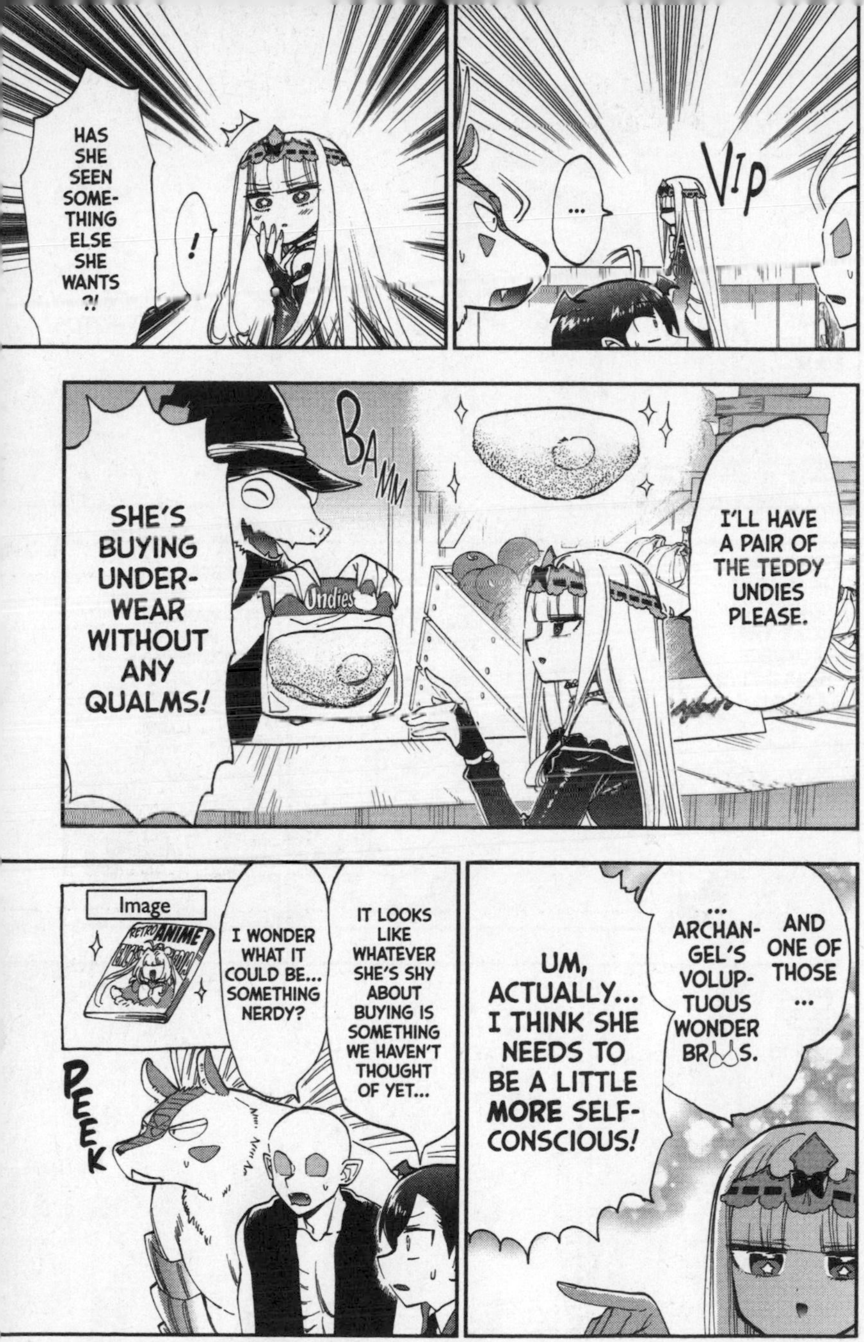
VIP
...
!
HAS SHE SEEN SOME-THING ELSE SHE WANTS ?!
I'LL HAVE A PAIR OF THE TEDDY UNDIES PLEASE.
BAMM
Undies
SHE'S BUYING UNDER-WEAR WITHOUT ANY QUALMS!
AND ONE OF THOSE ...
... ARCHAN-GEL'S VOLUP-TUOUS WONDER BRAS.
UM, ACTUALLY... I THINK SHE NEEDS TO BE A LITTLE MORE SELF-CONSCIOUS!
IT LOOKS LIKE WHATEVER SHE'S SHY ABOUT BUYING IS SOMETHING WE HAVEN'T THOUGHT OF YET...
I WONDER WHAT IT COULD BE... SOMETHING NERDY?
Image
RETRO ANIME
PEEK

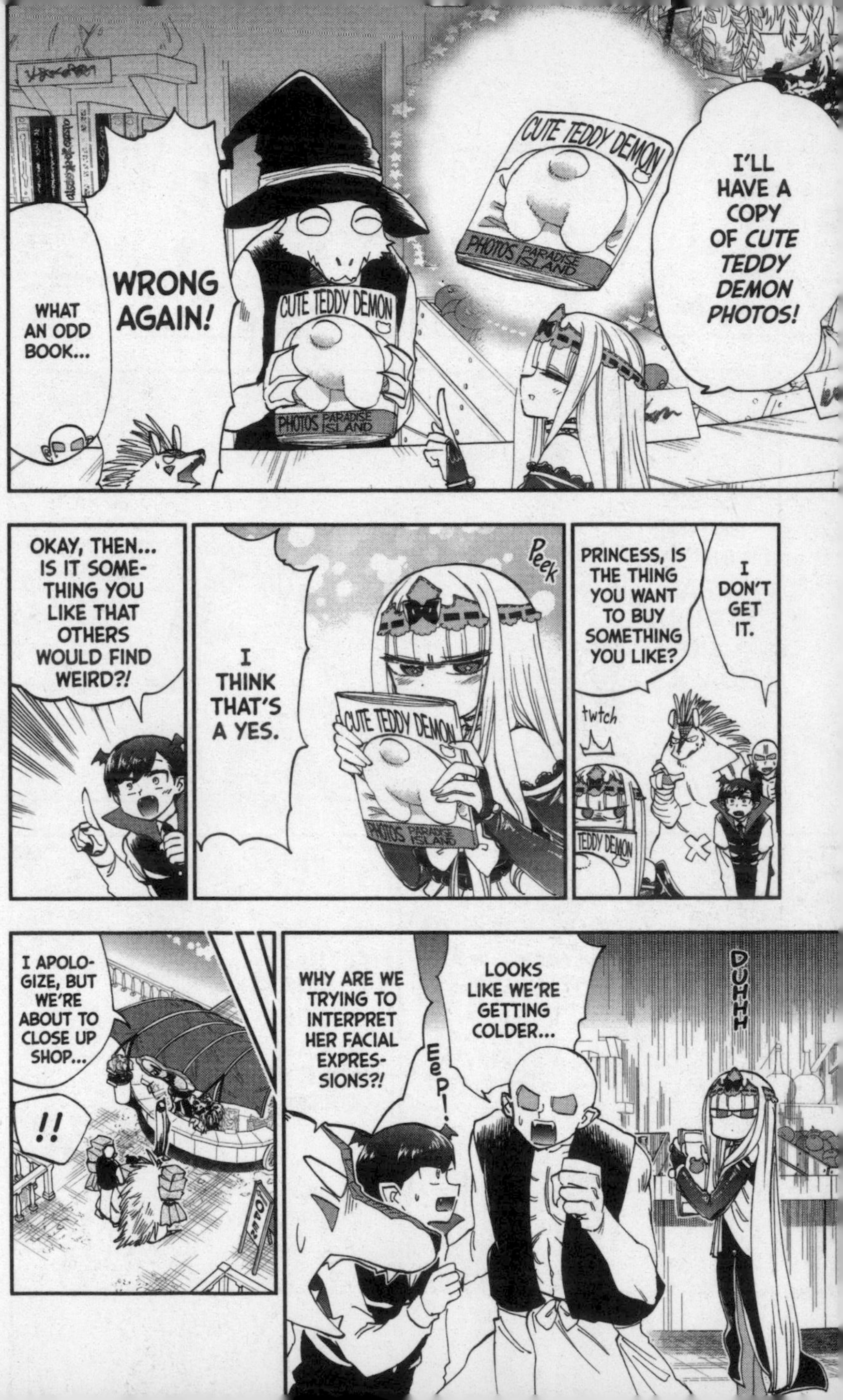
I'LL HAVE A COPY OF CUTE TEDDY DEMON PHOTOS!
CUTE TEDDY DEMON
PHOTOS PARADISE ISLAND
WRONG AGAIN!
CUTE TEDDY DEMON
PHOTOS PARADISE ISLAND
WHAT AN ODD BOOK...
I DON'T GET IT.
PRINCESS, IS THE THING YOU WANT TO BUY SOMETHING YOU LIKE?
twtch
TEDDY DEMON
Peek
I THINK THAT'S A YES.
CUTE TEDDY DEMON
PHOTOS PARADISE ISLAND
OKAY, THEN... IS IT SOMETHING YOU LIKE THAT OTHERS WOULD FIND WEIRD?!
DUHHH
LOOKS LIKE WE'RE GETTING COLDER...
WHY ARE WE TRYING TO INTERPRET HER FACIAL EXPRESSIONS?!
EeP!
I APOLOGIZE, BUT WE'RE ABOUT TO CLOSE UP SHOP...
!!

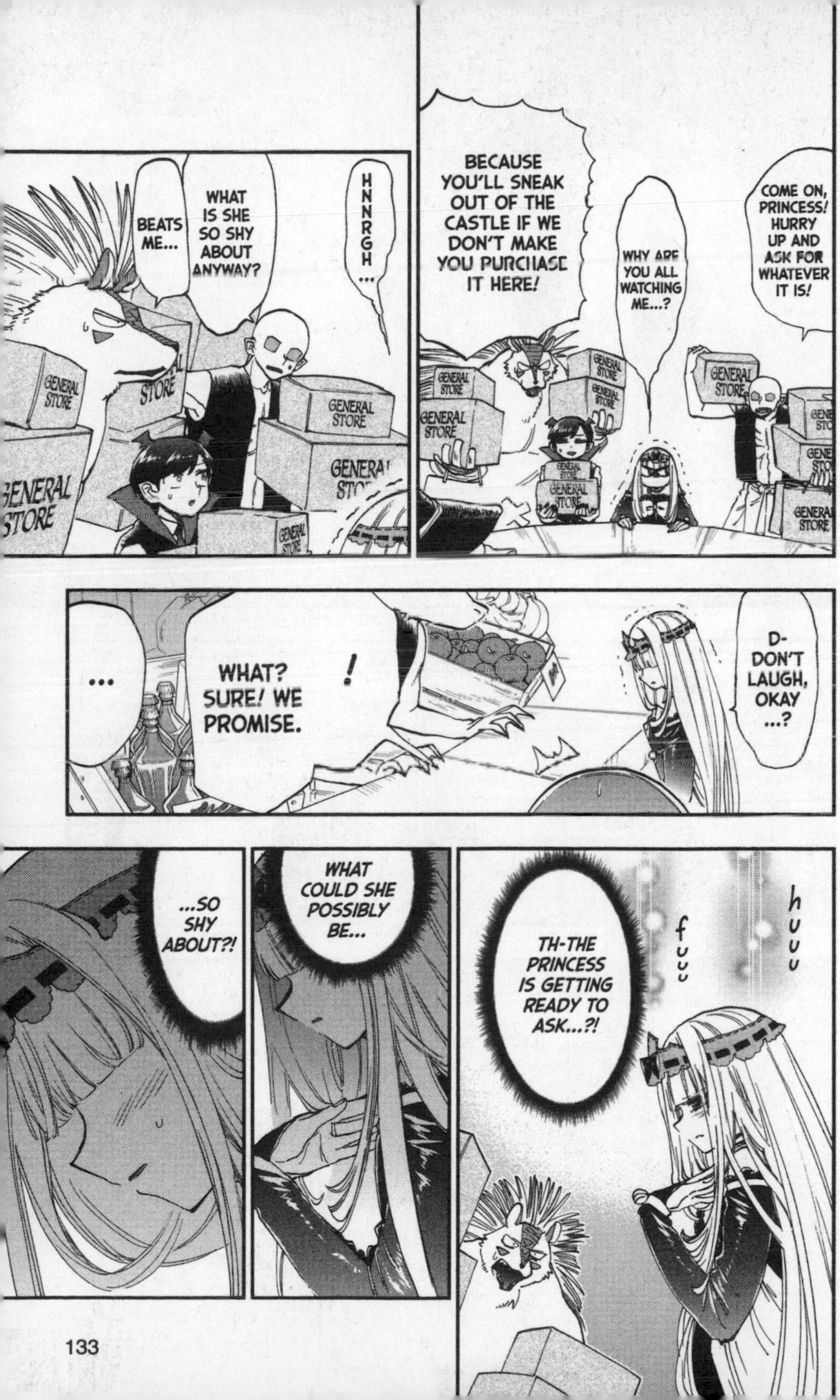
COME ON, PRINCESS! HURRY UP AND ASK FOR WHATEVER IT IS!
WHY ARE YOU ALL WATCHING ME...?
BECAUSE YOU'LL SNEAK OUT OF THE CASTLE IF WE DON'T MAKE YOU PURCHASE IT HERE!
GENERAL STORE
HNNRGH...
WHAT IS SHE SO SHY ABOUT ANYWAY?
BEATS ME...
D-DON'T LAUGH, OKAY...?
!
WHAT? SURE! WE PROMISE.
...
huuu
fuuu
TH-THE PRINCESS IS GETTING READY TO ASK...?!
WHAT COULD SHE POSSIBLY BE...
...SO SHY ABOUT?!

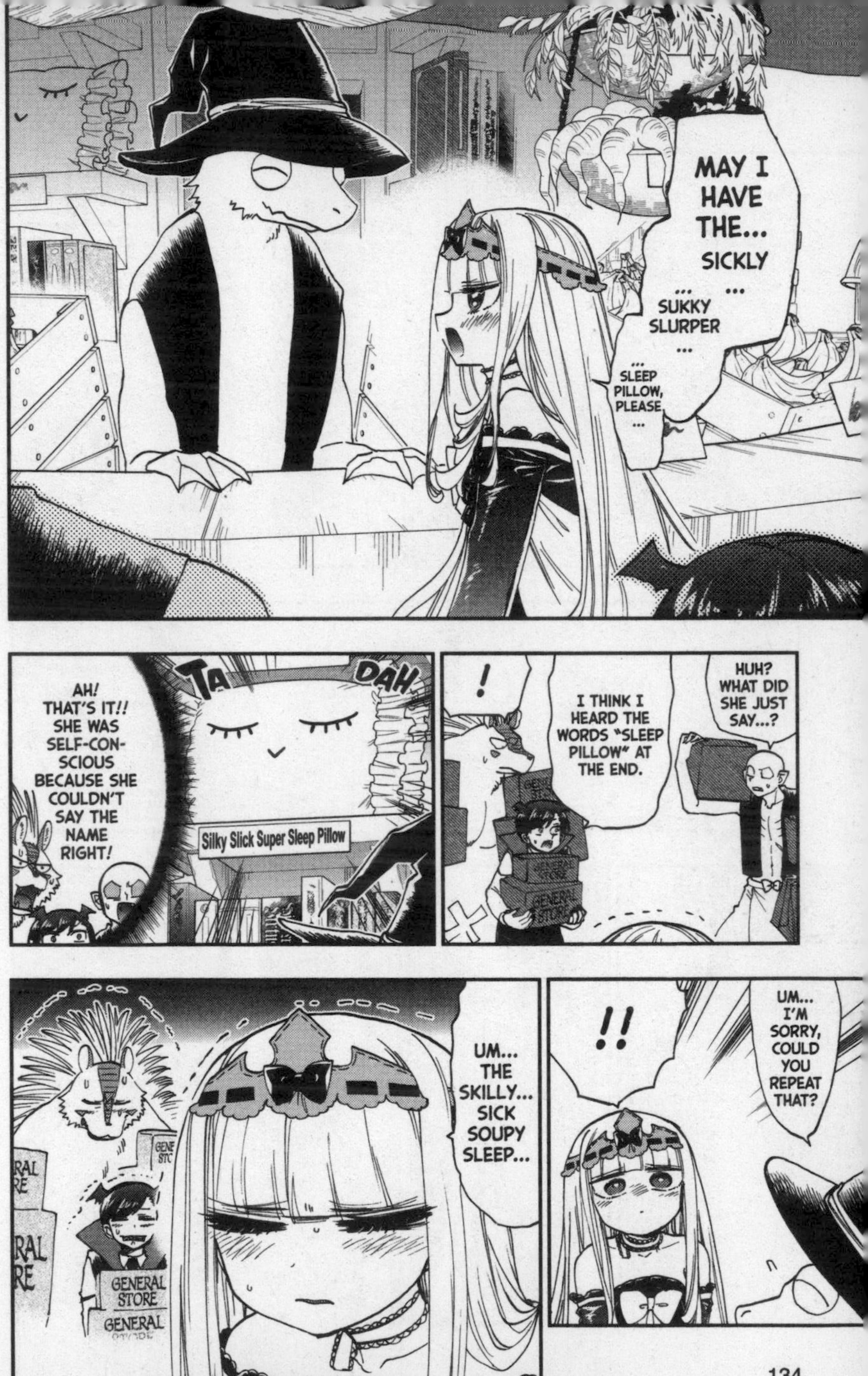
MAY I HAVE THE... SICKLY ...
... SUKKY SLURPER ...
... SLEEP PILLOW, PLEASE ...
HUH? WHAT DID SHE JUST SAY...?
I THINK I HEARD THE WORDS "SLEEP PILLOW" AT THE END.
!
TA DAH
AH! THAT'S IT!! SHE WAS SELF-CONSCIOUS BECAUSE SHE COULDN'T SAY THE NAME RIGHT!
Silky Slick Super Sleep Pillow
UM... I'M SORRY, COULD YOU REPEAT THAT?
!!
UM... THE SKILLY... SICK SOUPY SLEEP...

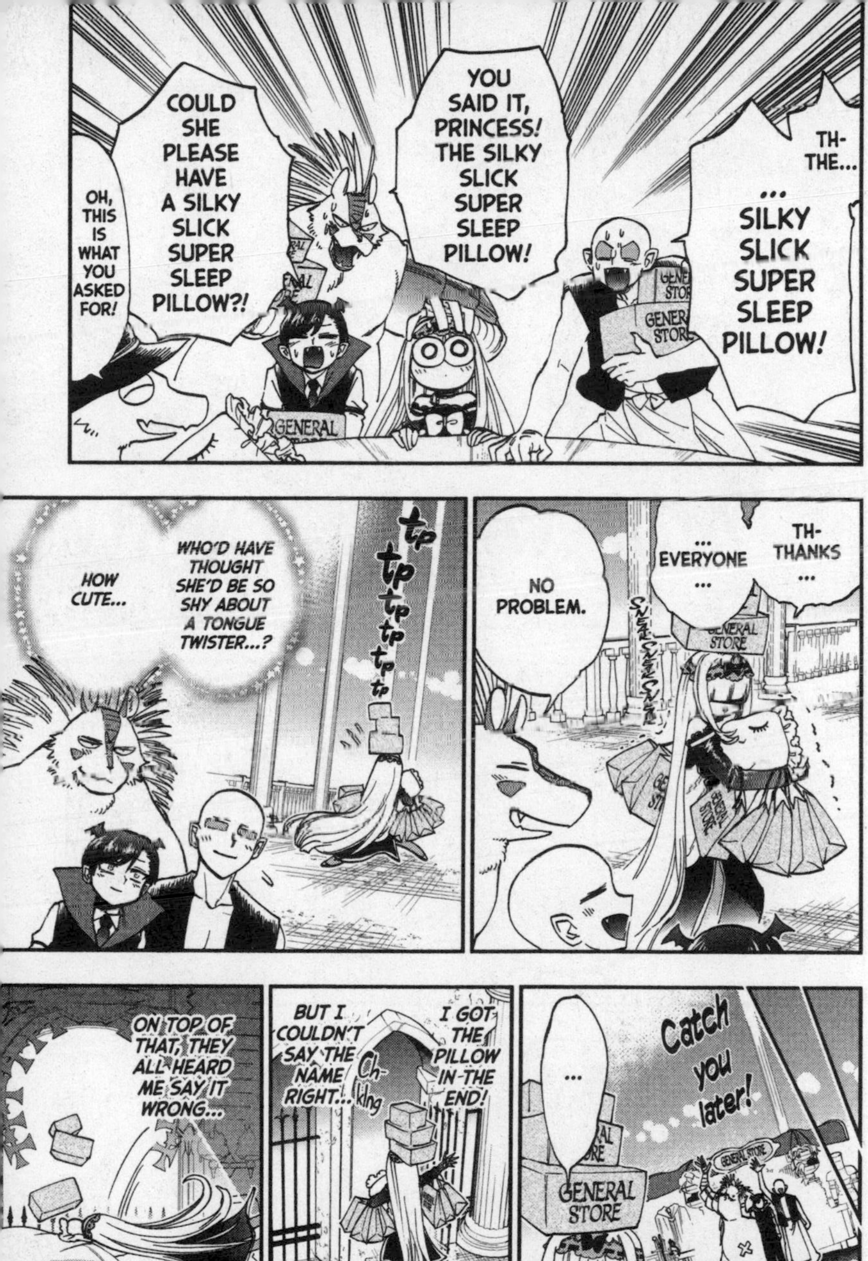

TH- THE...
...SILKY SLICK SUPER SLEEP PILLOW!
YOU SAID IT, PRINCESS! THE SILKY SLICK SUPER SLEEP PILLOW!
COULD SHE PLEASE HAVE A SILKY SLICK SUPER SLEEP PILLOW?!
OH, THIS IS WHAT YOU ASKED FOR!
GENERAL STORE
TH- THANKS...
...EVERYONE...
NO PROBLEM.
GENERAL STORE
tp tp tp tp tp tp
WHO'D HAVE THOUGHT SHE'D BE SO SHY ABOUT A TONGUE TWISTER...?
HOW CUTE...
Catch you later!
...
GENERAL STORE
I GOT THE PILLOW IN THE END!
Ch-kling
BUT I COULDN'T SAY THE NAME RIGHT...
ON TOP OF THAT, THEY ALL HEARD ME SAY IT WRONG...

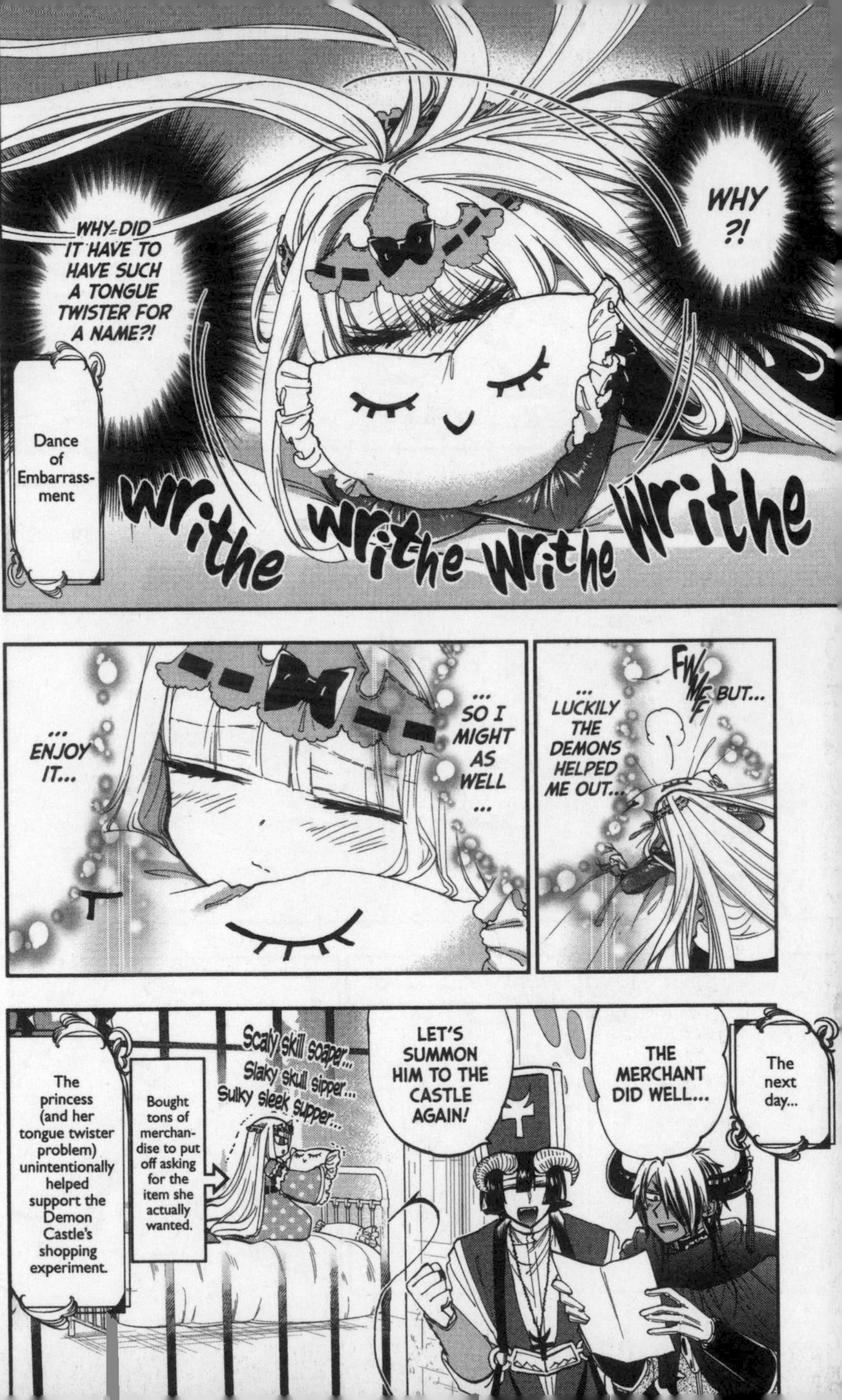
WHY ?!
WHY DID IT HAVE TO HAVE SUCH A TONGUE TWISTER FOR A NAME?!
Dance of Embarrass-ment
writhe writhe writhe writhe
FWMF
BUT...
... LUCKILY THE DEMONS HELPED ME OUT...
... SO I MIGHT AS WELL ...
... ENJOY IT...
The next day...
THE MERCHANT DID WELL...
LET'S SUMMON HIM TO THE CASTLE AGAIN!
Scaly skill soaper... Slaky skull sipper... Sulky sleek supper...
Bought tons of merchan-dise to put off asking for the item she actually wanted.
The princess (and her tongue twister problem) unintentionally helped support the Demon Castle's shopping experiment.

HEIGHT CHART 2

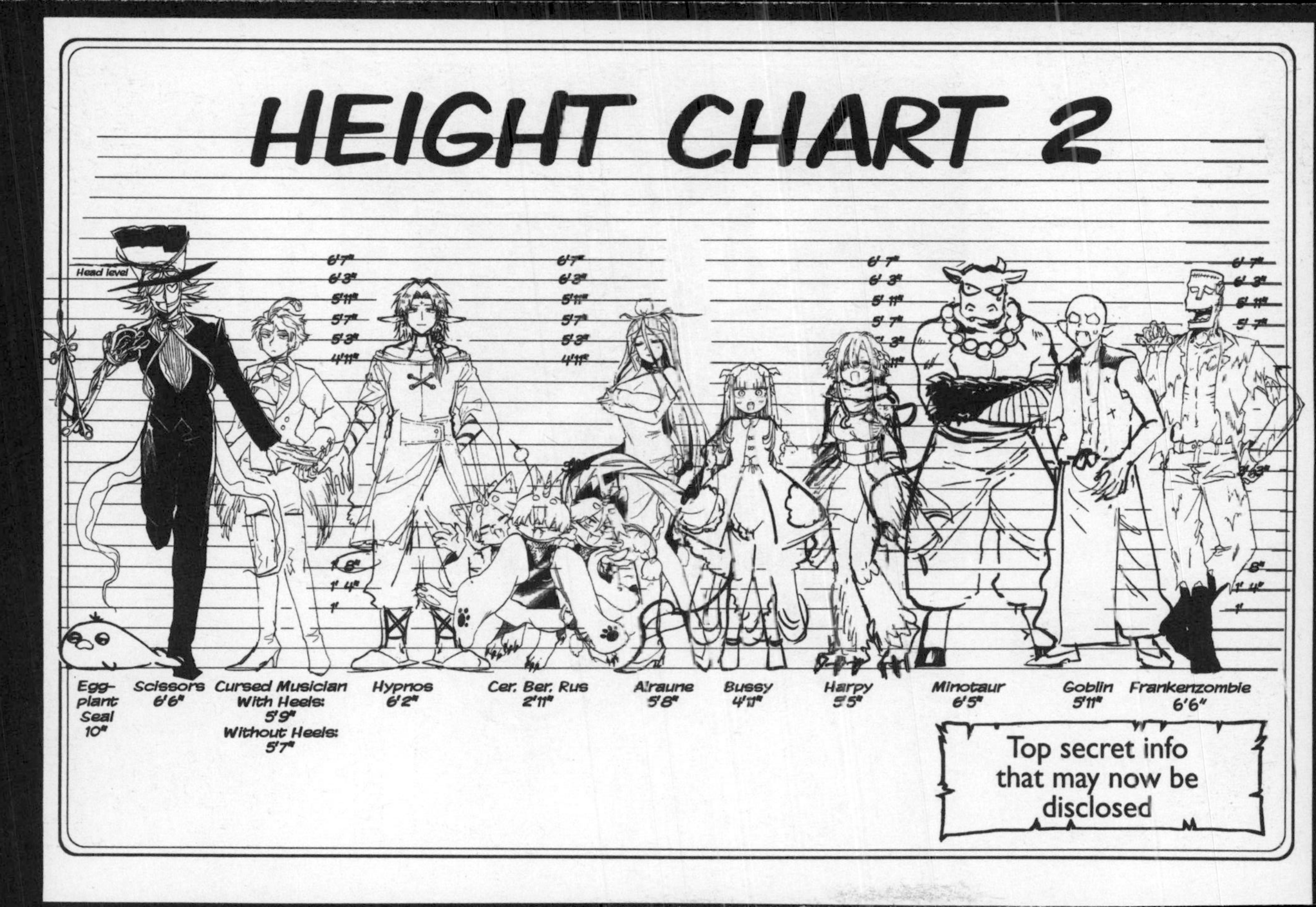
Head level
6'7"
6'3"
5'11"
5'7"
5'3"
4'11"
1' 8"
1' 4"
1'
Egg-plant Seal 10"
Scissors 6'6"
Cursed Musician With Heels: 5'9" Without Heels: 5'7"
Hypnos 6'2"
Cer. Ber. Rus 2'11"
Alraune 5'8"
Bussy 4'11"
Harpy 5'5"
Minotaur 6'5"
Goblin 5'11"
Frankenzombie 6'6"

Top secret info that may now be disclosed

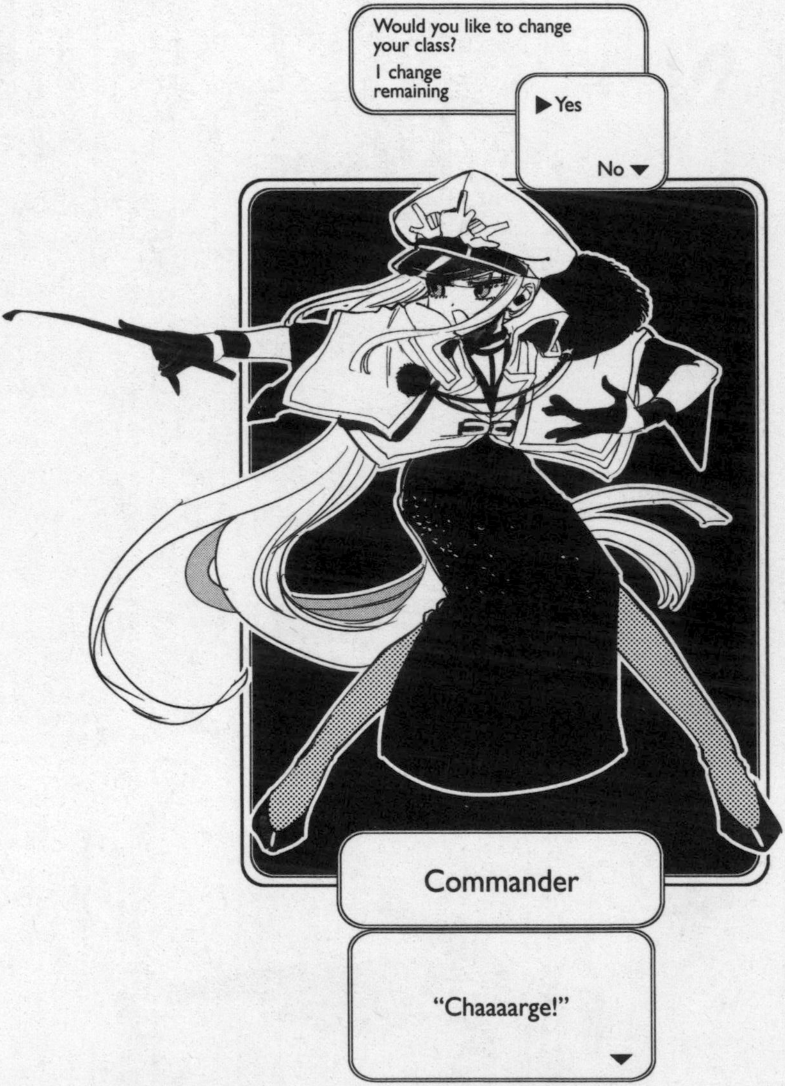
Would you like to change your class?
I change remaining
▶Yes
No ▼
Commander
"Chaaaarge!"

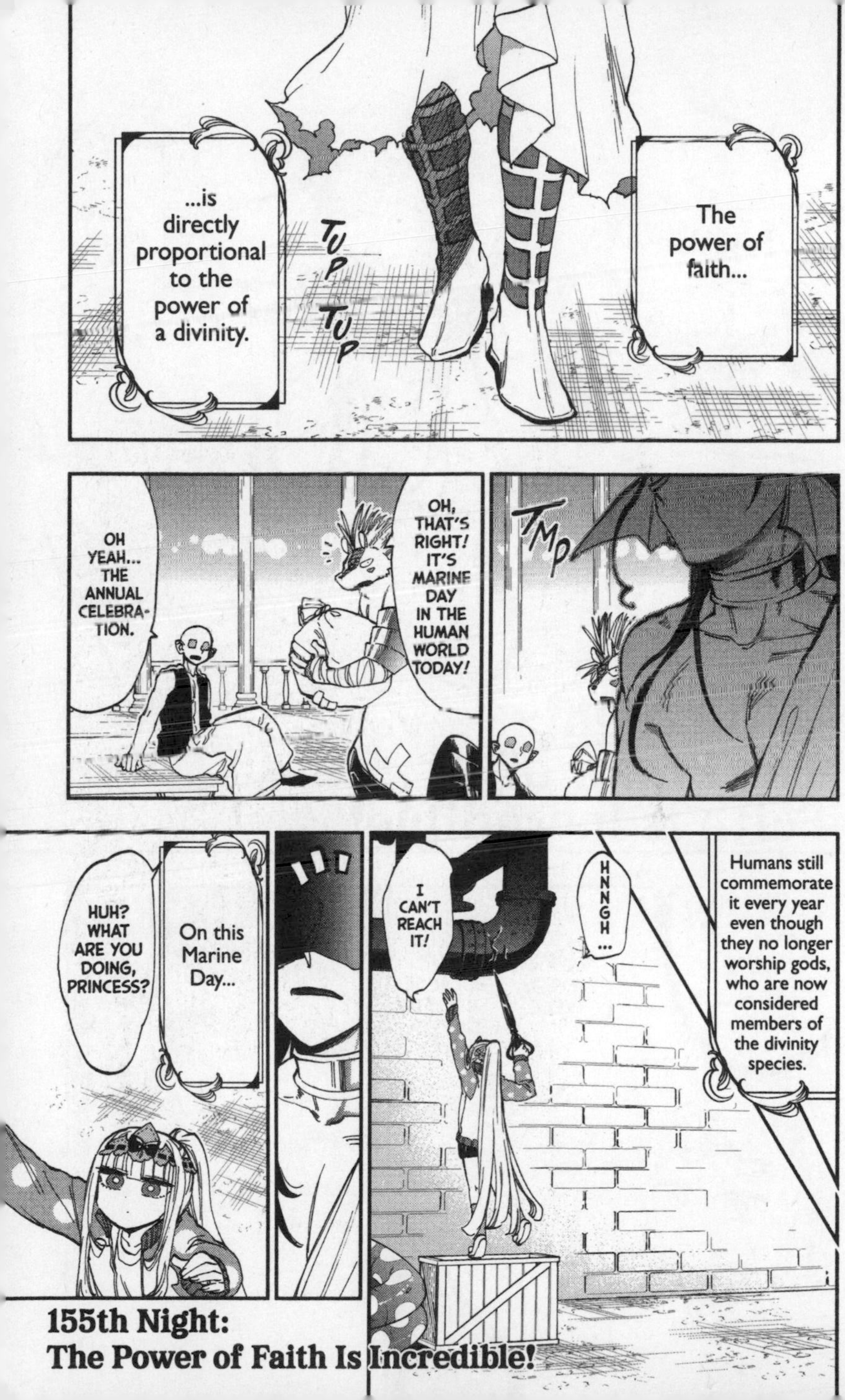
The power of faith...
TUP TUP
...is directly proportional to the power of a divinity.
TMP
OH, THAT'S RIGHT! IT'S MARINE DAY IN THE HUMAN WORLD TODAY!
OH YEAH... THE ANNUAL CELEBRATION.
Humans still commemorate it every year even though they no longer worship gods, who are now considered members of the divinity species.
HNNGH...
I CAN'T REACH IT!
On this Marine Day...
HUH? WHAT ARE YOU DOING, PRINCESS?

155th Night: The Power of Faith Is Incredible!

155th Night: The Power of Faith Is Incredible!

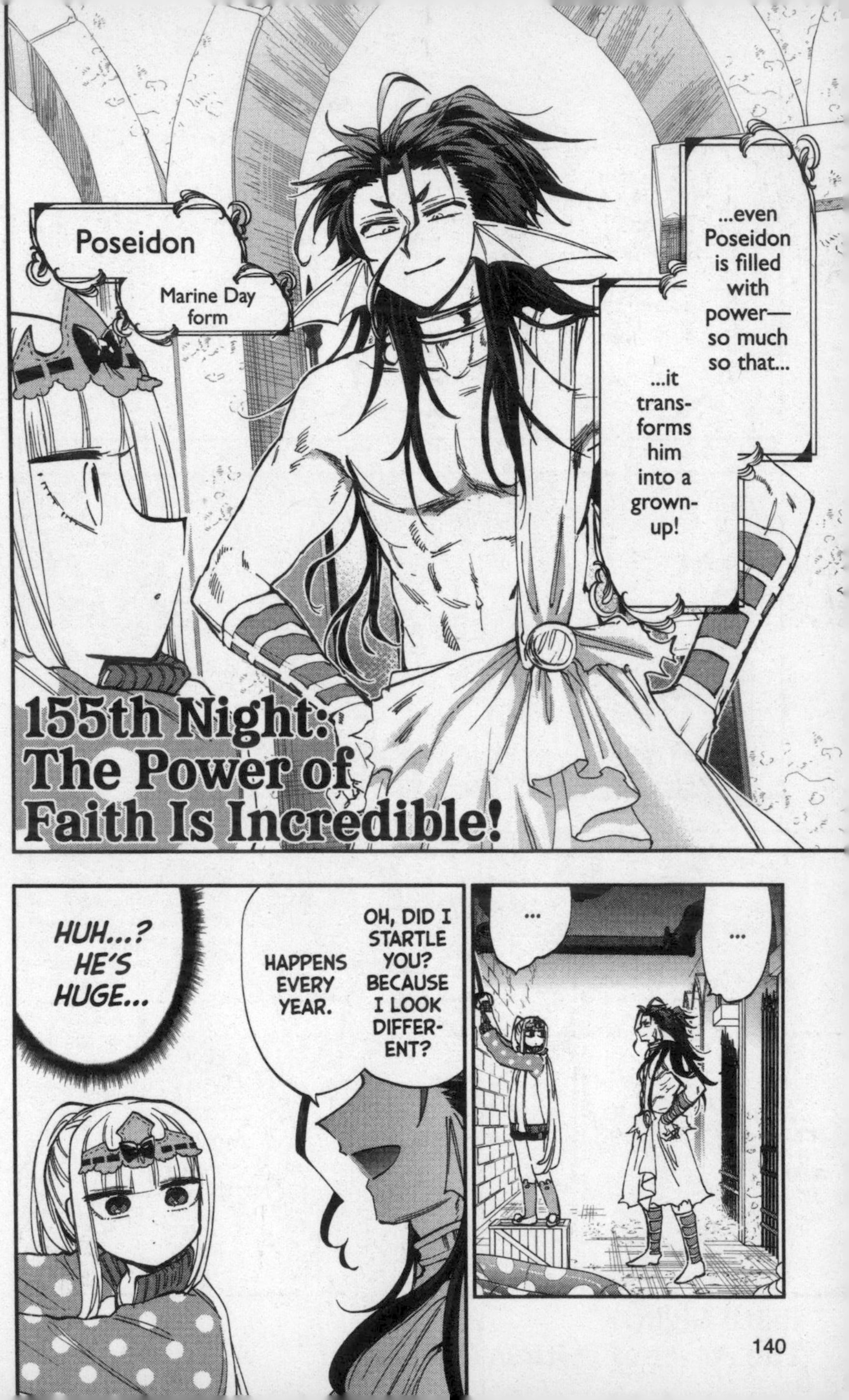
...even Poseidon is filled with power— so much so that...
...it trans-forms him into a grown-up!
Poseidon
Marine Day form
...
...
OH, DID I STARTLE YOU? BECAUSE I LOOK DIFFER-ENT?
HAPPENS EVERY YEAR.
HUH...? HE'S HUGE...

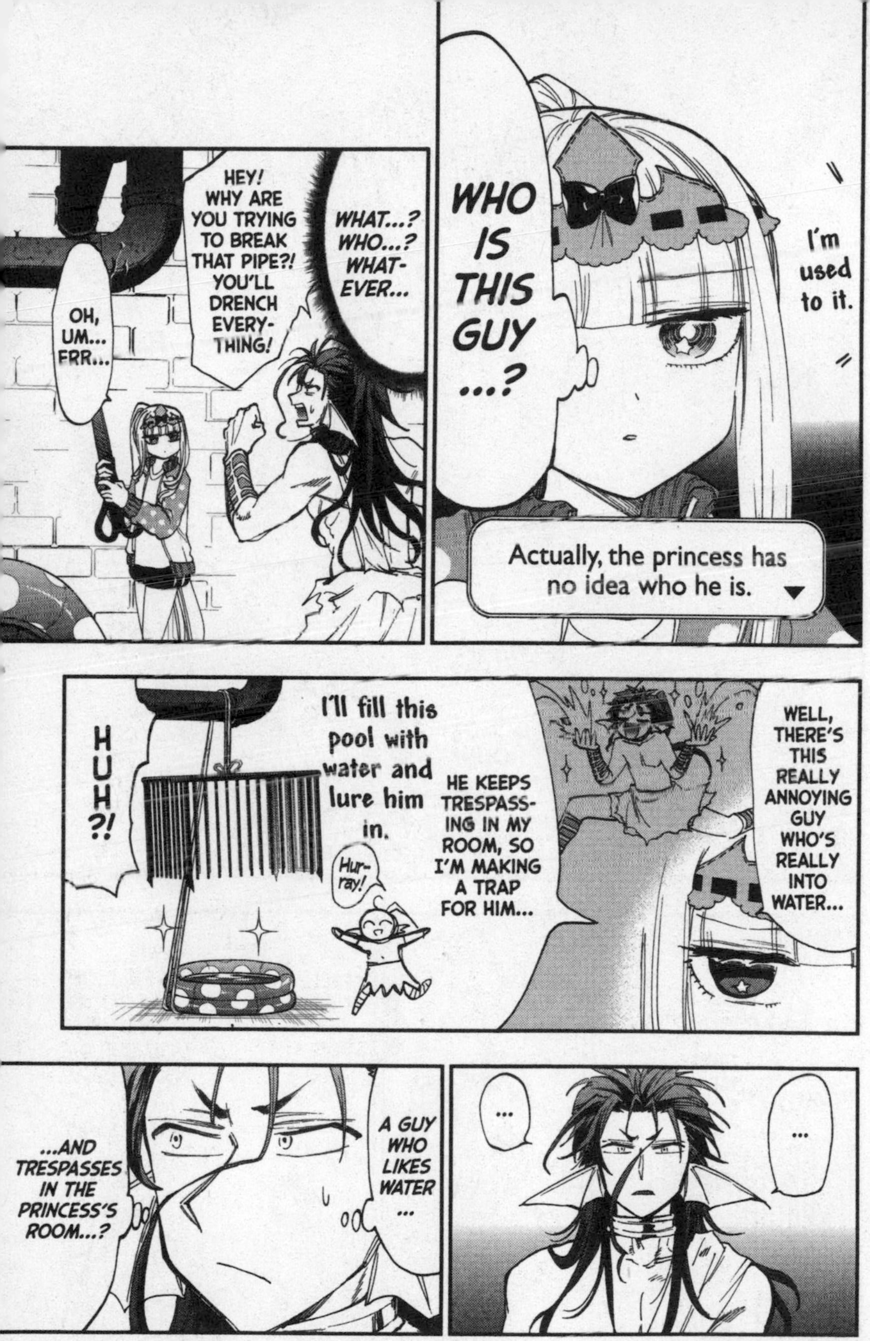

WHO IS THIS GUY ...?
I'm used to it.
Actually, the princess has no idea who he is.
WHAT...? WHO...? WHAT-EVER...
HEY! WHY ARE YOU TRYING TO BREAK THAT PIPE?! YOU'LL DRENCH EVERY-THING!
OH, UM... ERR...
WELL, THERE'S THIS REALLY ANNOYING GUY WHO'S REALLY INTO WATER...
HE KEEPS TRESPASS-ING IN MY ROOM, SO I'M MAKING A TRAP FOR HIM...
I'll fill this pool with water and lure him in.
Hur-ray!
HUH?!
...
...
A GUY WHO LIKES WATER ...
...AND TRESPASSES IN THE PRINCESS'S ROOM...?

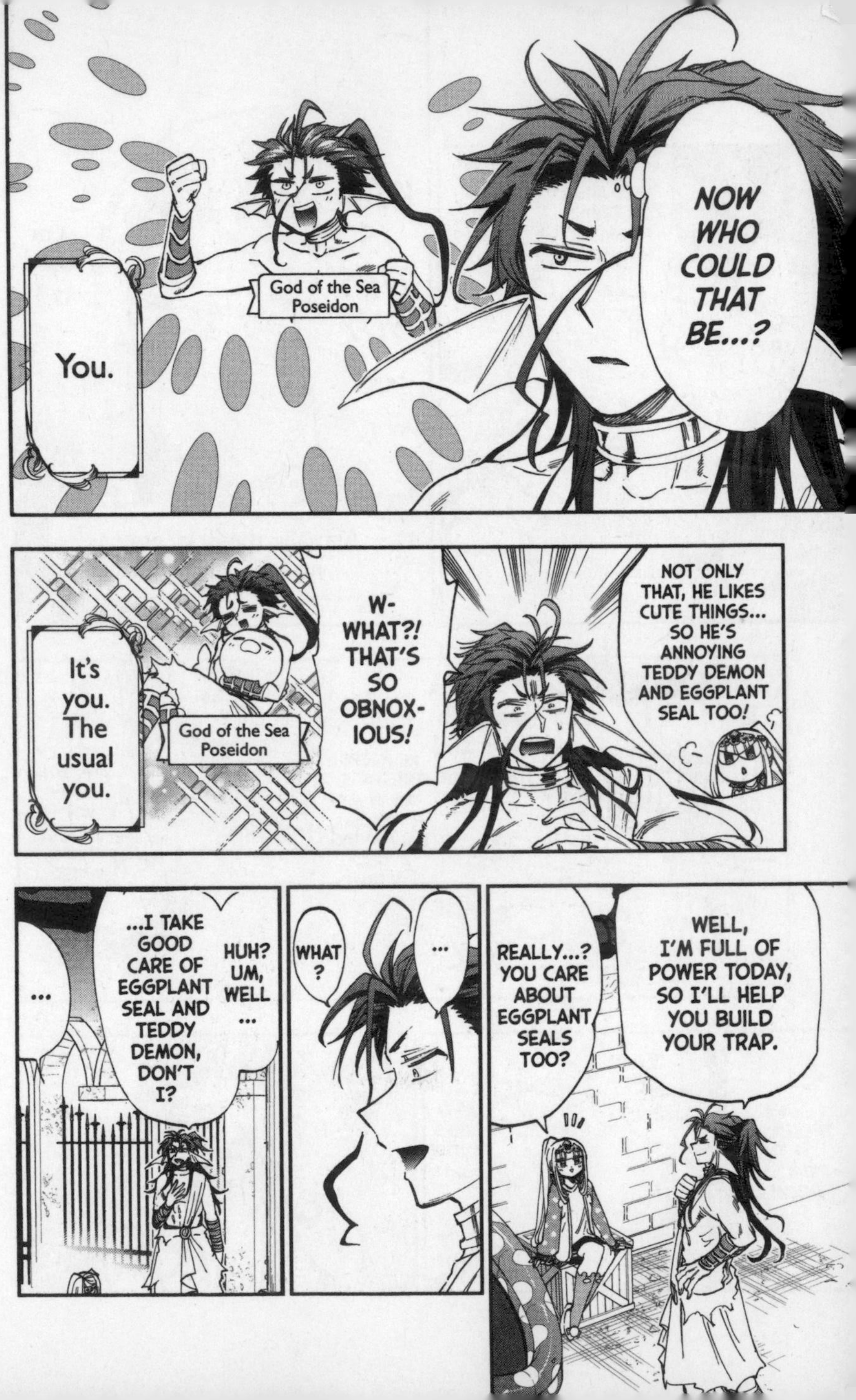
NOW WHO COULD THAT BE...?
God of the Sea Poseidon
You.
NOT ONLY THAT, HE LIKES CUTE THINGS... SO HE'S ANNOYING TEDDY DEMON AND EGGPLANT SEAL TOO!
W-WHAT?! THAT'S SO OBNOX-IOUS!
God of the Sea Poseidon
It's you. The usual you.
WELL, I'M FULL OF POWER TODAY, SO I'LL HELP YOU BUILD YOUR TRAP.
REALLY...? YOU CARE ABOUT EGGPLANT SEALS TOO?
...
WHAT?
HUH? UM, WELL ...
...I TAKE GOOD CARE OF EGGPLANT SEAL AND TEDDY DEMON, DON'T I?
...

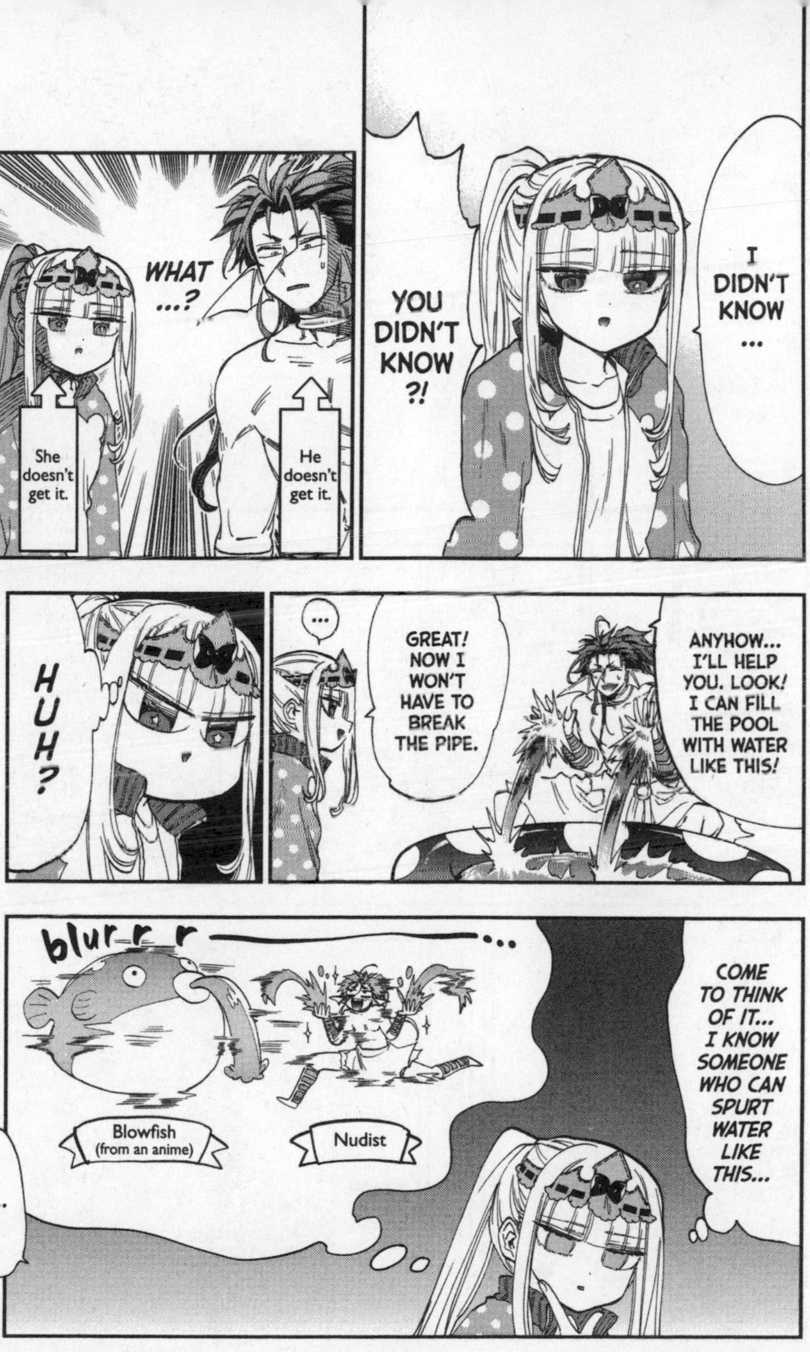
I DIDN'T KNOW ...
YOU DIDN'T KNOW ?!
WHAT ...?
He doesn't get it.
She doesn't get it.
ANYHOW... I'LL HELP YOU. LOOK! I CAN FILL THE POOL WITH WATER LIKE THIS!
GREAT! NOW I WON'T HAVE TO BREAK THE PIPE.
...
HUH?
COME TO THINK OF IT... I KNOW SOMEONE WHO CAN SPURT WATER LIKE THIS...
blurr r r ——...
Nudist
Blowfish (from an anime)
...

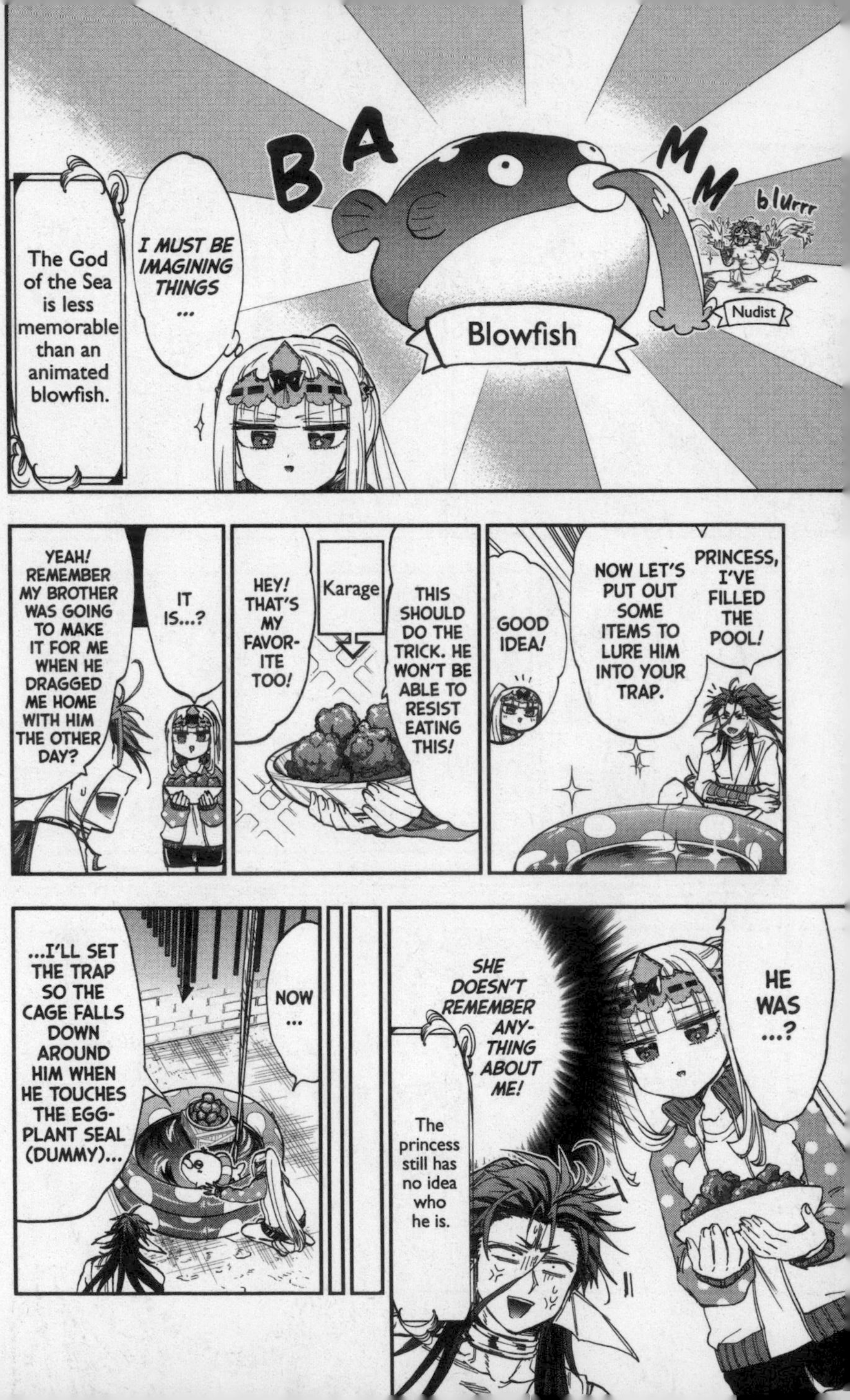
BAMM
blurrr
Nudist
Blowfish
I MUST BE IMAGINING THINGS ...
The God of the Sea is less memorable than an animated blowfish.
PRINCESS, I'VE FILLED THE POOL!
NOW LET'S PUT OUT SOME ITEMS TO LURE HIM INTO YOUR TRAP.
GOOD IDEA!
THIS SHOULD DO THE TRICK. HE WON'T BE ABLE TO RESIST EATING THIS!
Karage
HEY! THAT'S MY FAVOR-ITE TOO!
IT IS...?
YEAH! REMEMBER MY BROTHER WAS GOING TO MAKE IT FOR ME WHEN HE DRAGGED ME HOME WITH HIM THE OTHER DAY?
HE WAS ...?
SHE DOESN'T REMEMBER ANY-THING ABOUT ME!
The princess still has no idea who he is.
NOW ...
...I'LL SET THE TRAP SO THE CAGE FALLS DOWN AROUND HIM WHEN HE TOUCHES THE EGG-PLANT SEAL (DUMMY)...

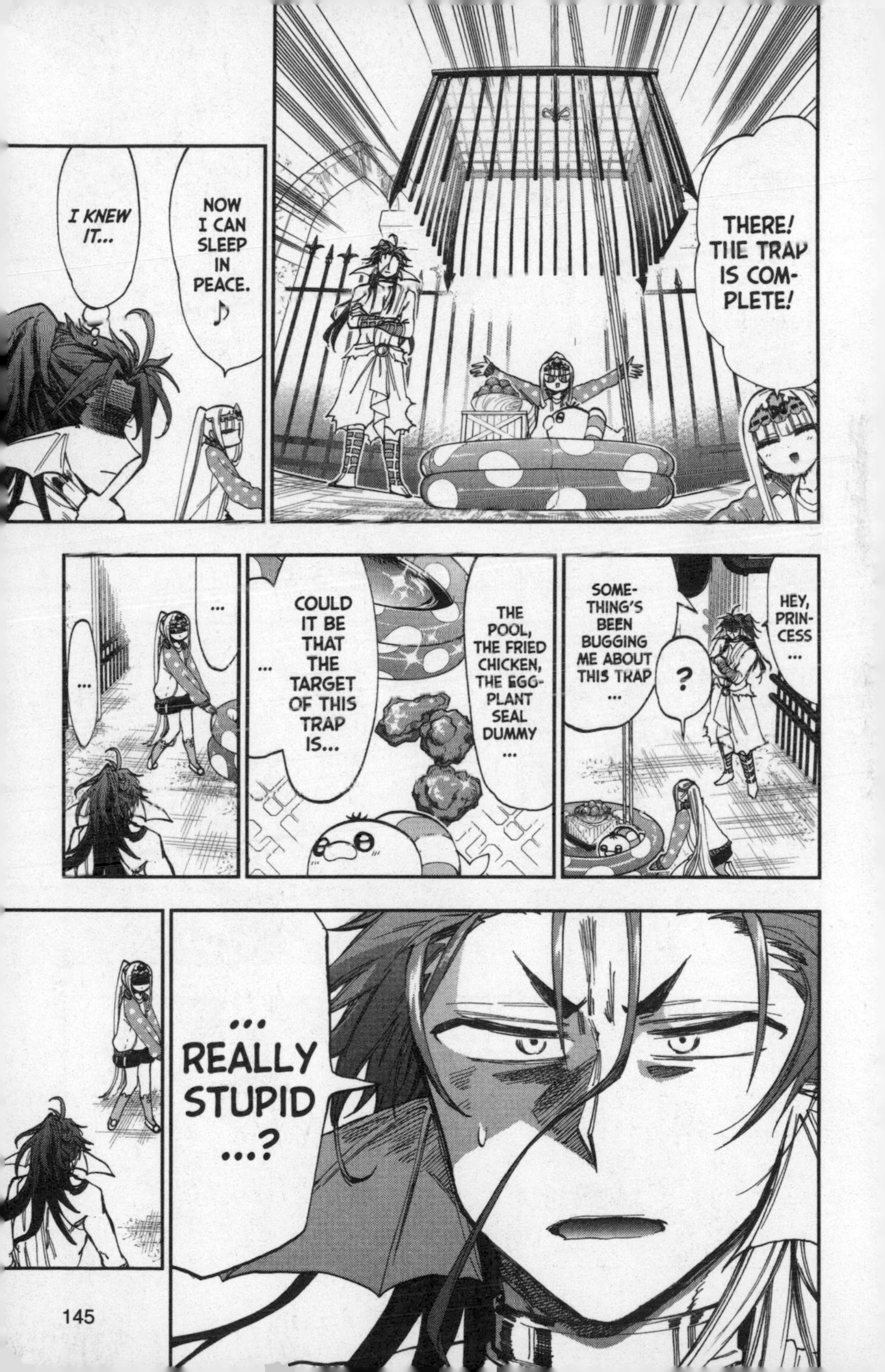
THERE! THE TRAP IS COMPLETE!
NOW I CAN SLEEP IN PEACE. ♪
I KNEW IT...
HEY, PRINCESS...
SOMETHING'S BEEN BUGGING ME ABOUT THIS TRAP...
?
THE POOL, THE FRIED CHICKEN, THE EGGPLANT SEAL DUMMY...
COULD IT BE THAT THE TARGET OF THIS TRAP IS...
...
...
...
...REALLY STUPID...?

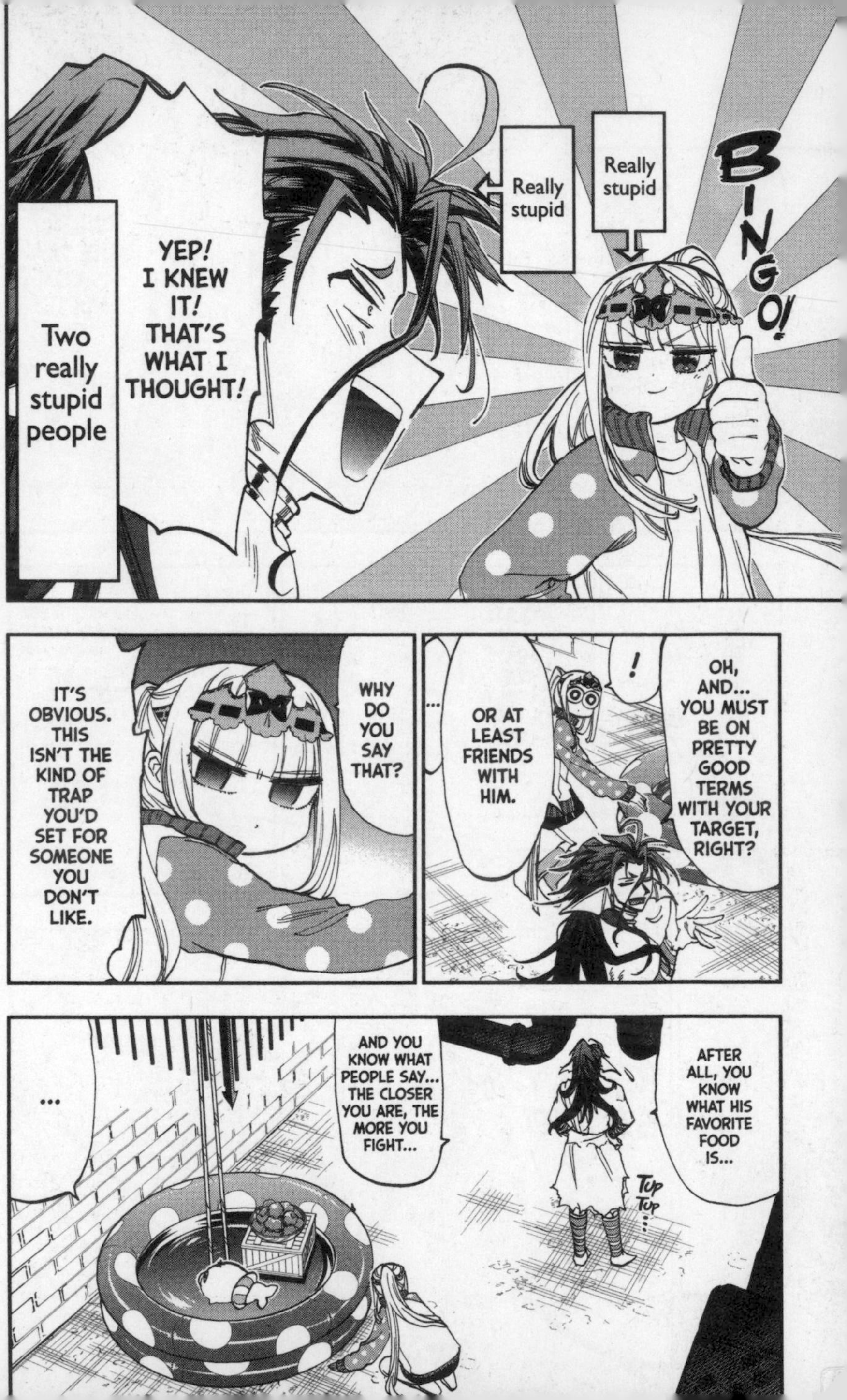
BINGO!
Really stupid
Really stupid
YEP! I KNEW IT! THAT'S WHAT I THOUGHT!
Two really stupid people
OH, AND... YOU MUST BE ON PRETTY GOOD TERMS WITH YOUR TARGET, RIGHT?
!
OR AT LEAST FRIENDS WITH HIM.
...
WHY DO YOU SAY THAT?
IT'S OBVIOUS. THIS ISN'T THE KIND OF TRAP YOU'D SET FOR SOMEONE YOU DON'T LIKE.
AFTER ALL, YOU KNOW WHAT HIS FAVORITE FOOD IS...
TUP TUP...
AND YOU KNOW WHAT PEOPLE SAY... THE CLOSER YOU ARE, THE MORE YOU FIGHT...
...

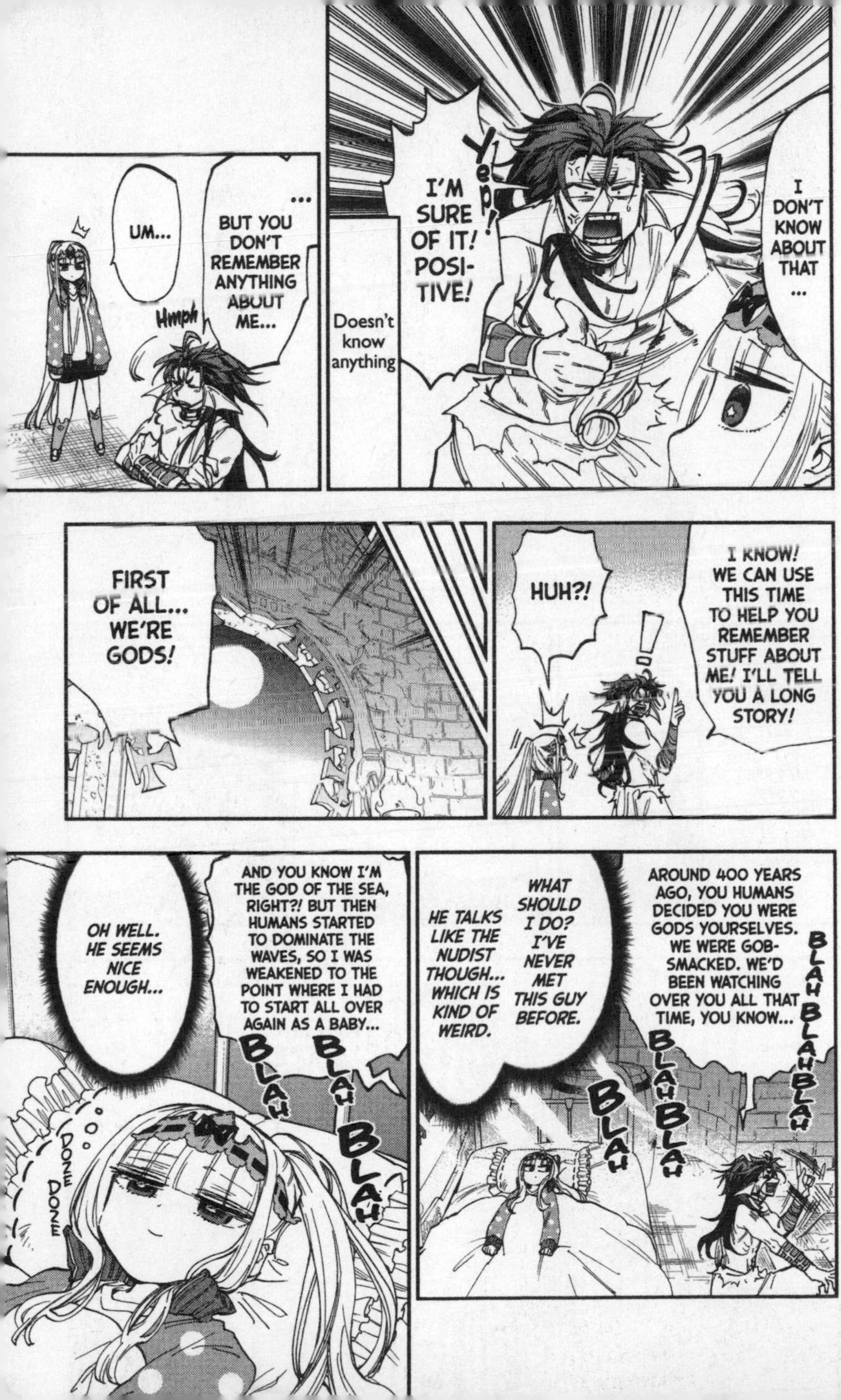
I DON'T KNOW ABOUT THAT...
Yep!
I'M SURE OF IT! POSITIVE!
Doesn't know anything
...BUT YOU DON'T REMEMBER ANYTHING ABOUT ME...
UM...
Hmph
I KNOW! WE CAN USE THIS TIME TO HELP YOU REMEMBER STUFF ABOUT ME! I'LL TELL YOU A LONG STORY!
HUH?!
!
FIRST OF ALL... WE'RE GODS!
AROUND 400 YEARS AGO, YOU HUMANS DECIDED YOU WERE GODS YOURSELVES. WE WERE GOB-SMACKED. WE'D BEEN WATCHING OVER YOU ALL THAT TIME, YOU KNOW...
BLAH BLAH BLAH BLAH
BLAH BLAH BLAH
WHAT SHOULD I DO? I'VE NEVER MET THIS GUY BEFORE.
HE TALKS LIKE THE NUDIST THOUGH... WHICH IS KIND OF WEIRD.
AND YOU KNOW I'M THE GOD OF THE SEA, RIGHT?! BUT THEN HUMANS STARTED TO DOMINATE THE WAVES, SO I WAS WEAKENED TO THE POINT WHERE I HAD TO START ALL OVER AGAIN AS A BABY...
BLAH BLAH BLAH
OH WELL. HE SEEMS NICE ENOUGH...
DOZE DOZE

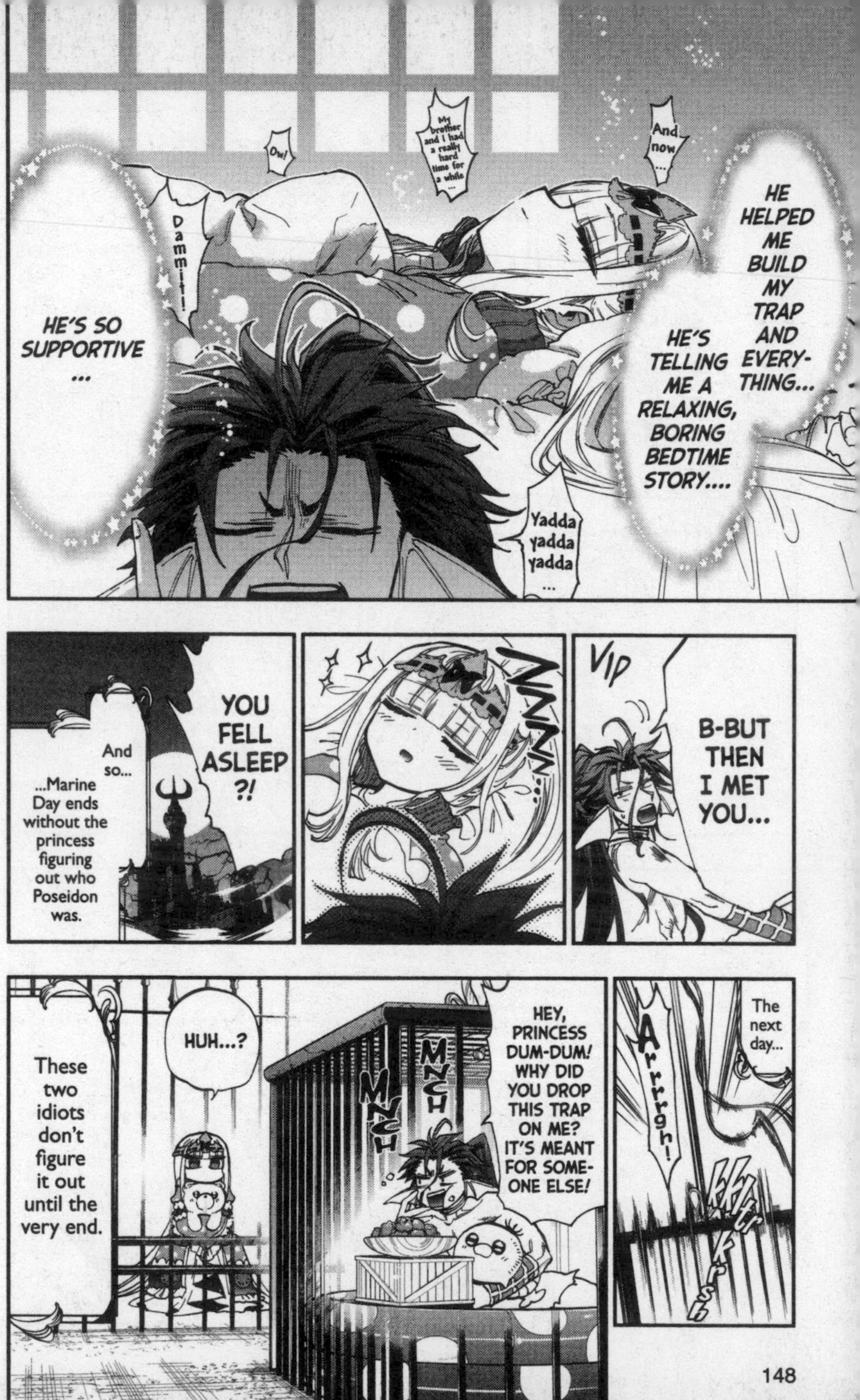

HE HELPED ME BUILD MY TRAP AND EVERY-THING...
And now...
HE'S TELLING ME A RELAXING, BORING BEDTIME STORY....
Yadda yadda yadda...
My brother and I had a really hard time for a while...
Ow!
Dammit!
HE'S SO SUPPORTIVE...
B-BUT THEN I MET YOU...
YOU FELL ASLEEP?!
And so... ...Marine Day ends without the princess figuring out who Poseidon was.
The next day...
Arrrgh!
HEY, PRINCESS DUM-DUM! WHY DID YOU DROP THIS TRAP ON ME? IT'S MEANT FOR SOME-ONE ELSE!
MNCH
MNCH
HUH...?
These two idiots don't figure it out until the very end.

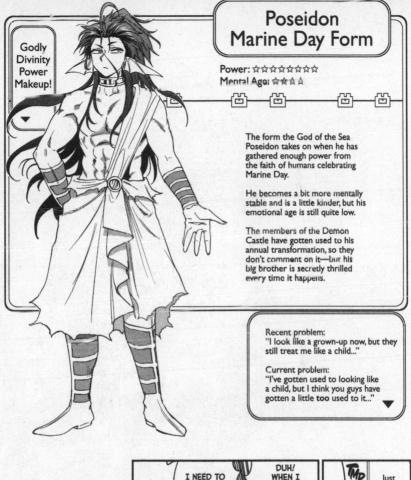

Poseidon Marine Day Form

Godly Divinity Power Makeup!

Power: ☆☆☆☆☆☆☆☆☆
Mental Age: ☆☆☆☆

The form the God of the Sea Poseidon takes on when he has gathered enough power from the faith of humans celebrating Marine Day.

He becomes a bit more mentally stable and is a little kinder, but his emotional age is still quite low.

The members of the Demon Castle have gotten used to his annual transformation, so they don't comment on it—but his big brother is secretly thrilled every time it happens.

Recent problem:
"I look like a grown-up now, but they still treat me like a child..."

Current problem:
"I've gotten used to looking like a child, but I think you guys have gotten a little too used to it..."

Just before Marine Day ends...
WHAT'S THE RUSH?
TMP TMP TMP TMP
DUH! WHEN I TRANSFORM BACK, MY CLOTHES WILL BE TOO BIG AND FALL OFF!
I NEED TO AT LEAST PUT ON SOME UNDERWEAR BEFORE THAT HAPPENS!
WHY AREN'T YOU WEARING UNDER-WEAR NOW?!
TMP
TMP TMP
TMP

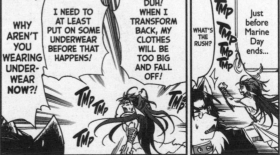

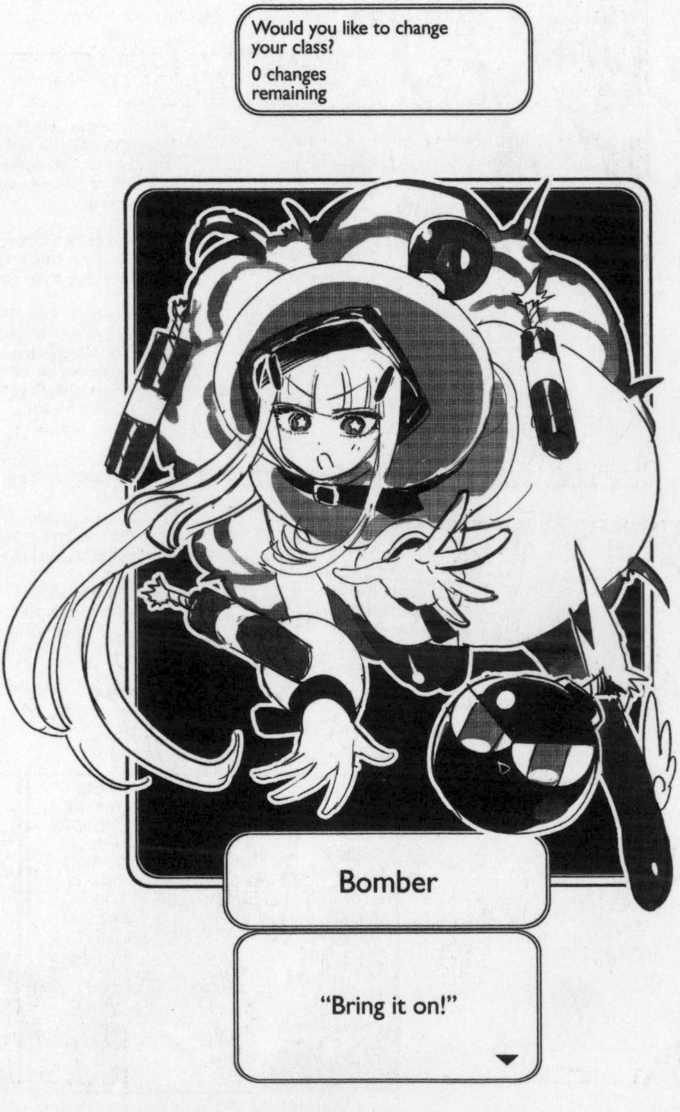
Would you like to change your class?
0 changes remaining
Bomber
"Bring it on!"

156th Night: Demon Castle Mint Farm

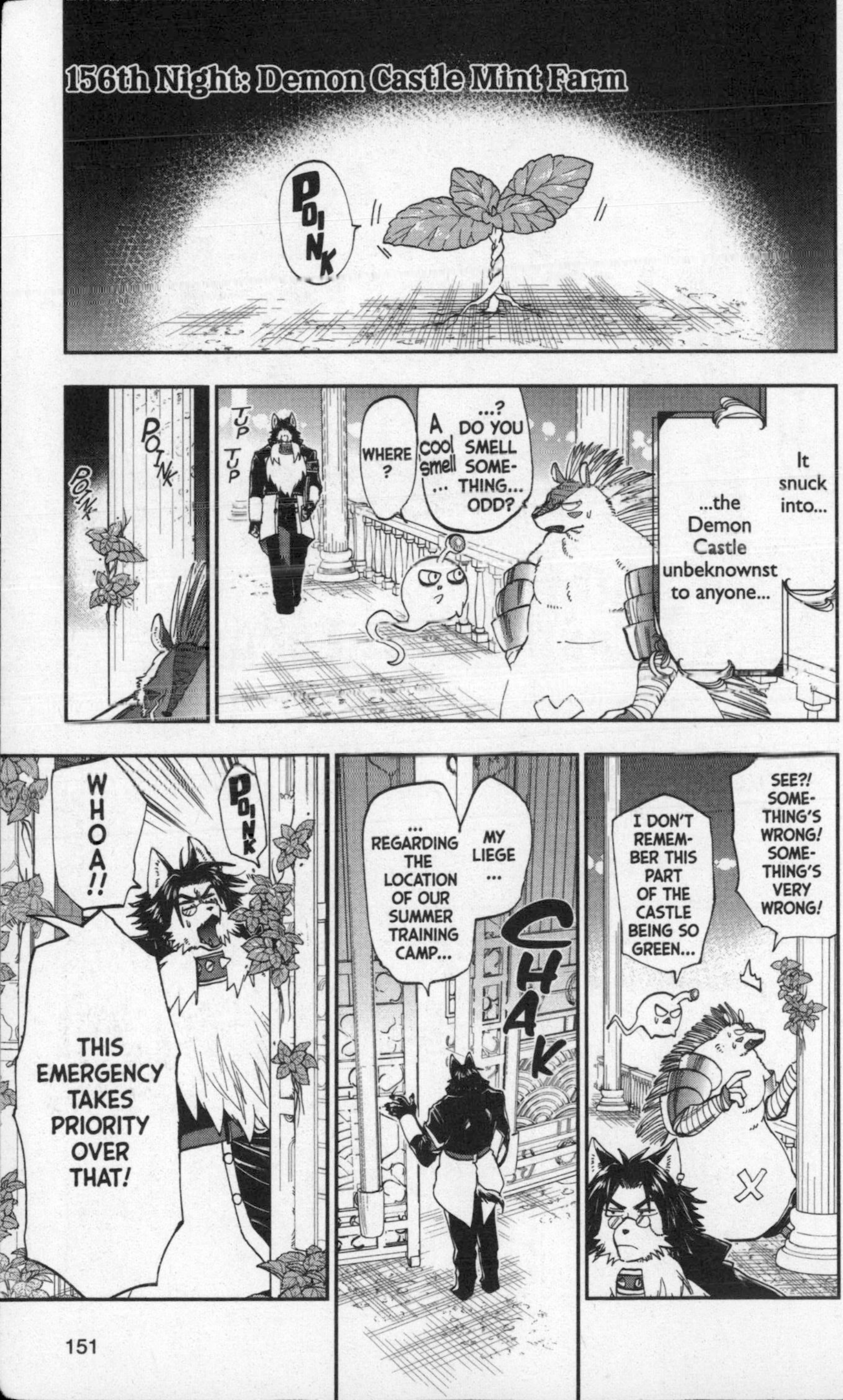
POINK
It snuck into...
...the Demon Castle unbeknownst to anyone...
...? DO YOU SMELL SOME-THING... ODD?
A cool smell...
WHERE?
TUP TUP
POINK
POINK
SEE?! SOME-THING'S WRONG! SOME-THING'S VERY WRONG!
I DON'T REMEM-BER THIS PART OF THE CASTLE BEING SO GREEN...
MY LIEGE...
...REGARDING THE LOCATION OF OUR SUMMER TRAINING CAMP...
CHAK
POINK
WHOA!!
THIS EMERGENCY TAKES PRIORITY OVER THAT!

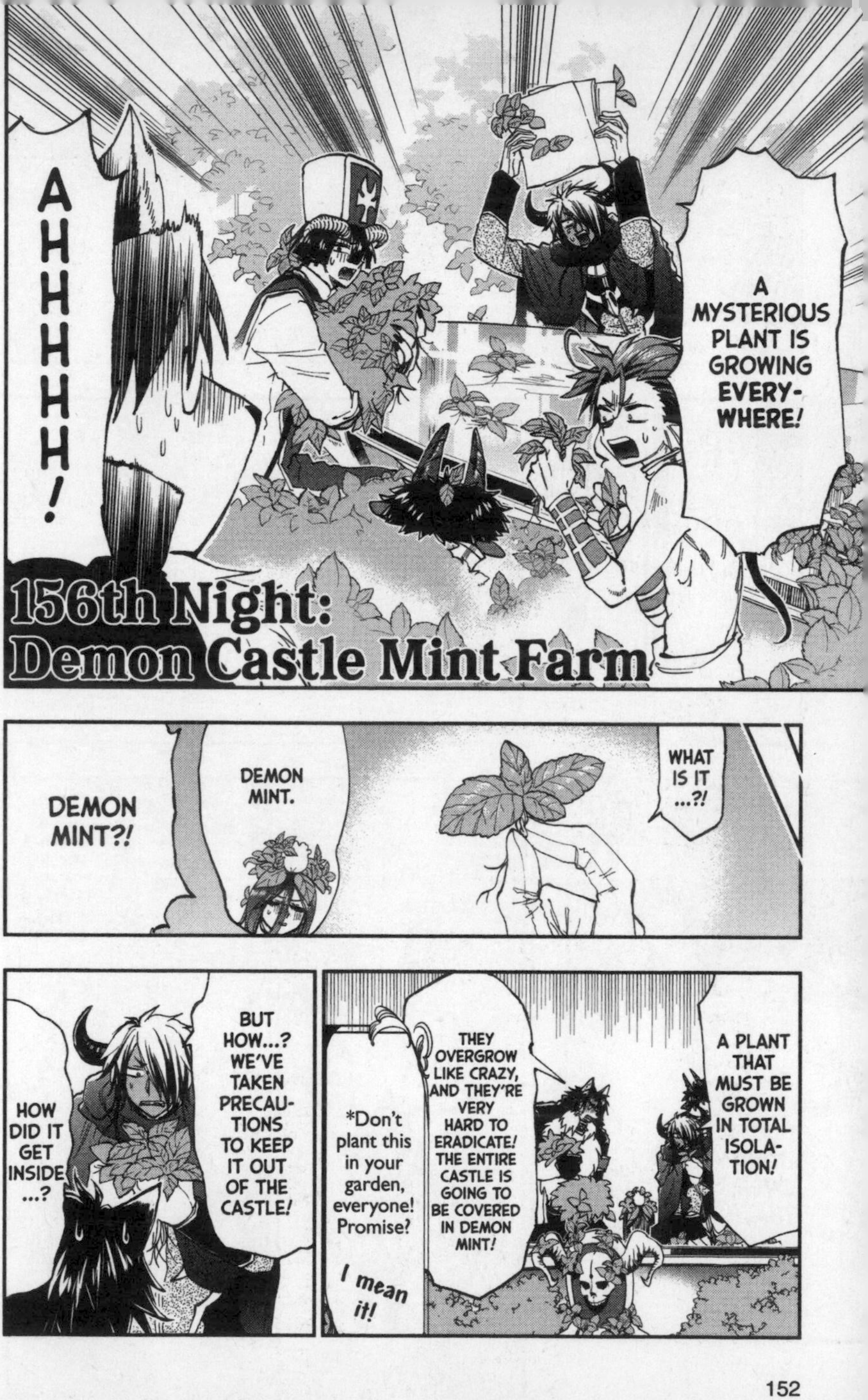
A MYSTERIOUS PLANT IS GROWING EVERY-WHERE!
AHHHHH!
156th Night: Demon Castle Mint Farm
WHAT IS IT ...?!
DEMON MINT.
DEMON MINT?!
A PLANT THAT MUST BE GROWN IN TOTAL ISOLA-TION!
THEY OVERGROW LIKE CRAZY, AND THEY'RE VERY HARD TO ERADICATE! THE ENTIRE CASTLE IS GOING TO BE COVERED IN DEMON MINT!
*Don't plant this in your garden, everyone! Promise?
I mean it!
BUT HOW...? WE'VE TAKEN PRECAU-TIONS TO KEEP IT OUT OF THE CASTLE!
HOW DID IT GET INSIDE ...?

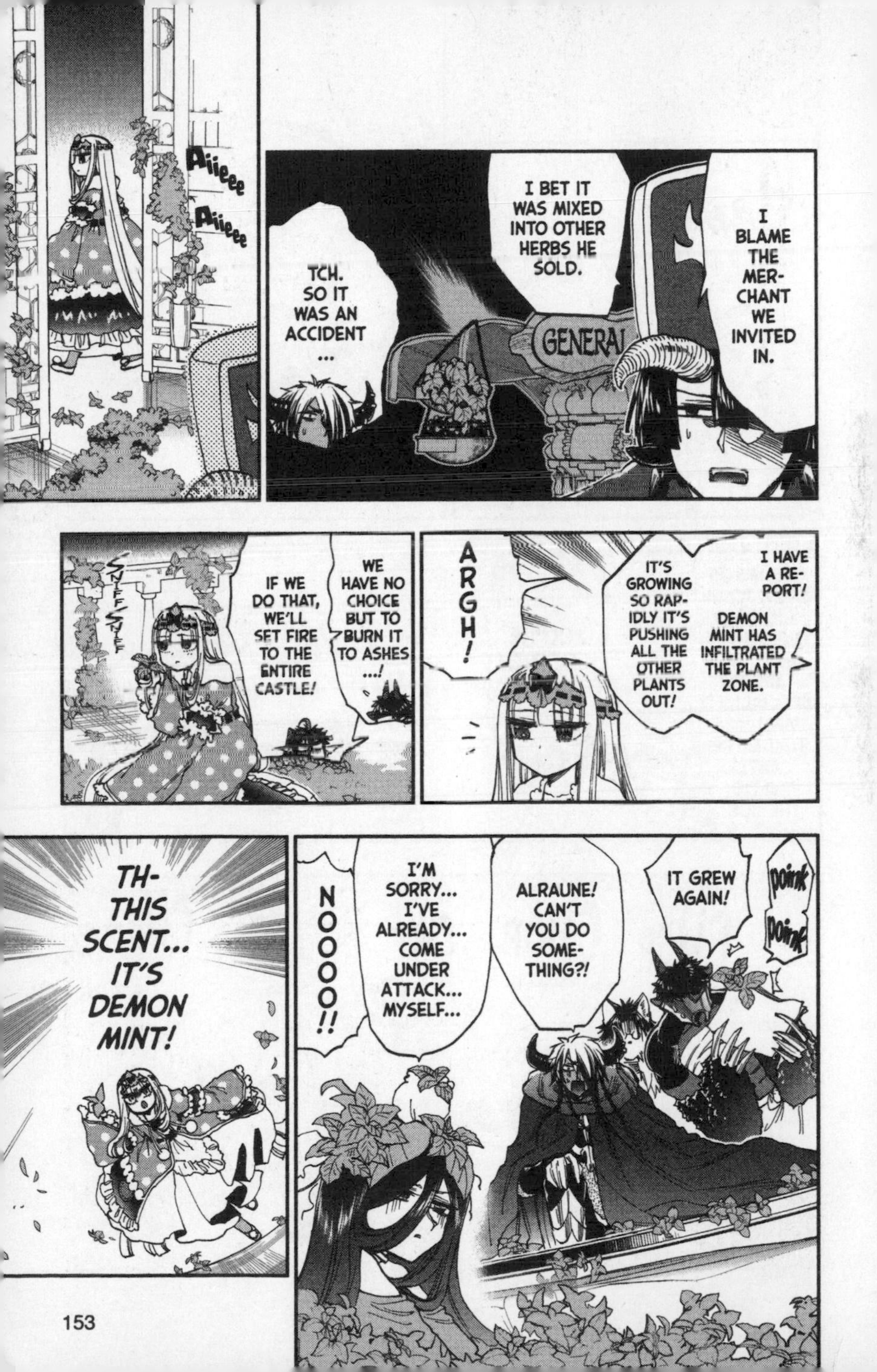
I BLAME THE MER-CHANT WE INVITED IN.
I BET IT WAS MIXED INTO OTHER HERBS HE SOLD.
TCH. SO IT WAS AN ACCIDENT ...
GENERAL
Aiieee
Aiieee
I HAVE A RE-PORT!
DEMON MINT HAS INFILTRATED THE PLANT ZONE.
IT'S GROWING SO RAP-IDLY IT'S PUSHING ALL THE OTHER PLANTS OUT!
ARGH!
WE HAVE NO CHOICE BUT TO BURN IT TO ASHES ...!
IF WE DO THAT, WE'LL SET FIRE TO THE ENTIRE CASTLE!
SNIFF SNIFF
poink
poink
IT GREW AGAIN!
ALRAUNE! CAN'T YOU DO SOME-THING?!
I'M SORRY... I'VE ALREADY... COME UNDER ATTACK... MYSELF...
NOOOOO!!
TH-THIS SCENT... IT'S DEMON MINT!

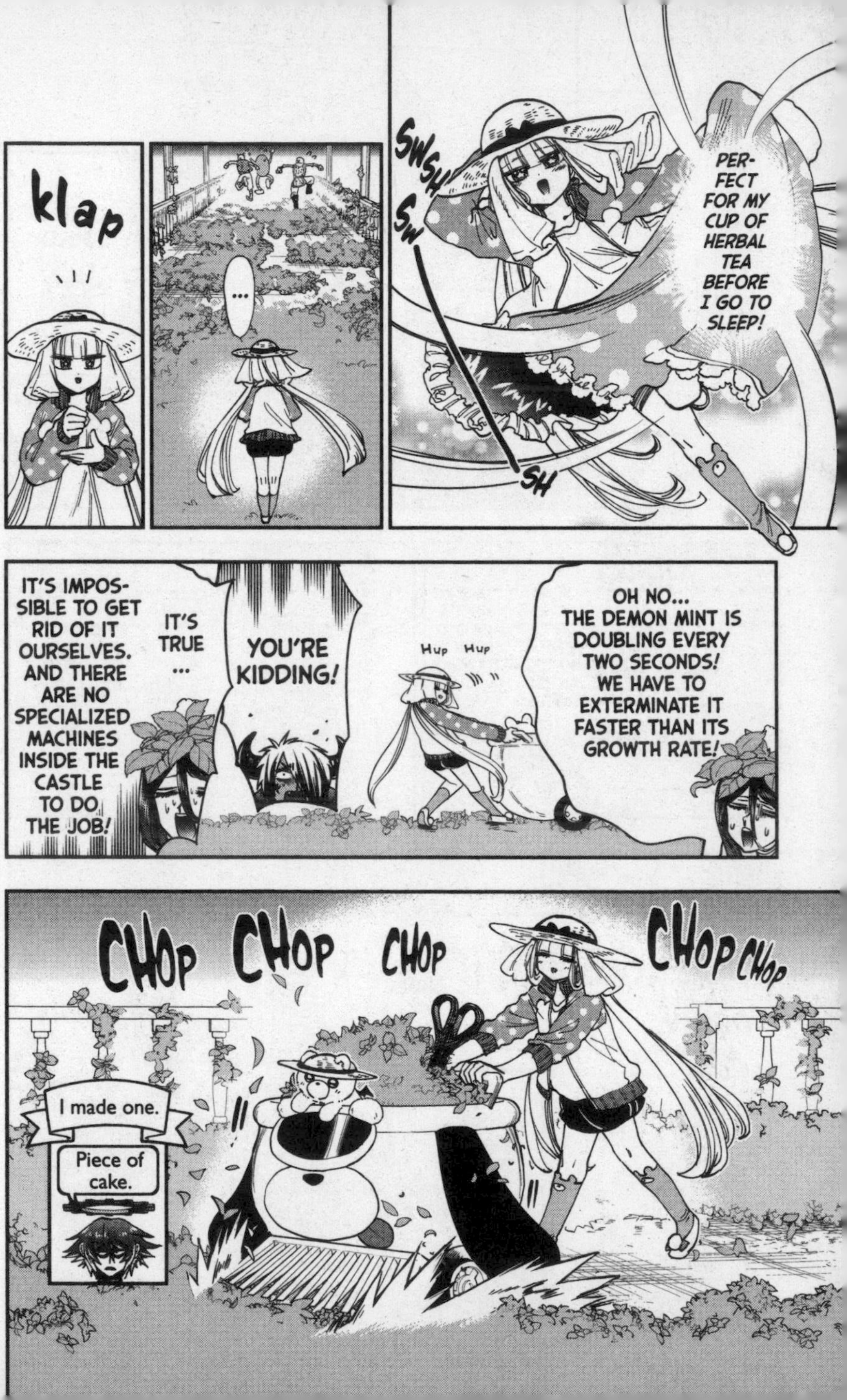
SWSH
SW
SH
PER-FECT FOR MY CUP OF HERBAL TEA BEFORE I GO TO SLEEP!
....
klap
OH NO... THE DEMON MINT IS DOUBLING EVERY TWO SECONDS! WE HAVE TO EXTERMINATE IT FASTER THAN ITS GROWTH RATE!
Hup Hup
YOU'RE KIDDING!
IT'S TRUE ...
IT'S IMPOS-SIBLE TO GET RID OF IT OURSELVES. AND THERE ARE NO SPECIALIZED MACHINES INSIDE THE CASTLE TO DO THE JOB!
CHOP CHOP
CHOP
CHOP
CHOP
I made one.
Piece of cake.

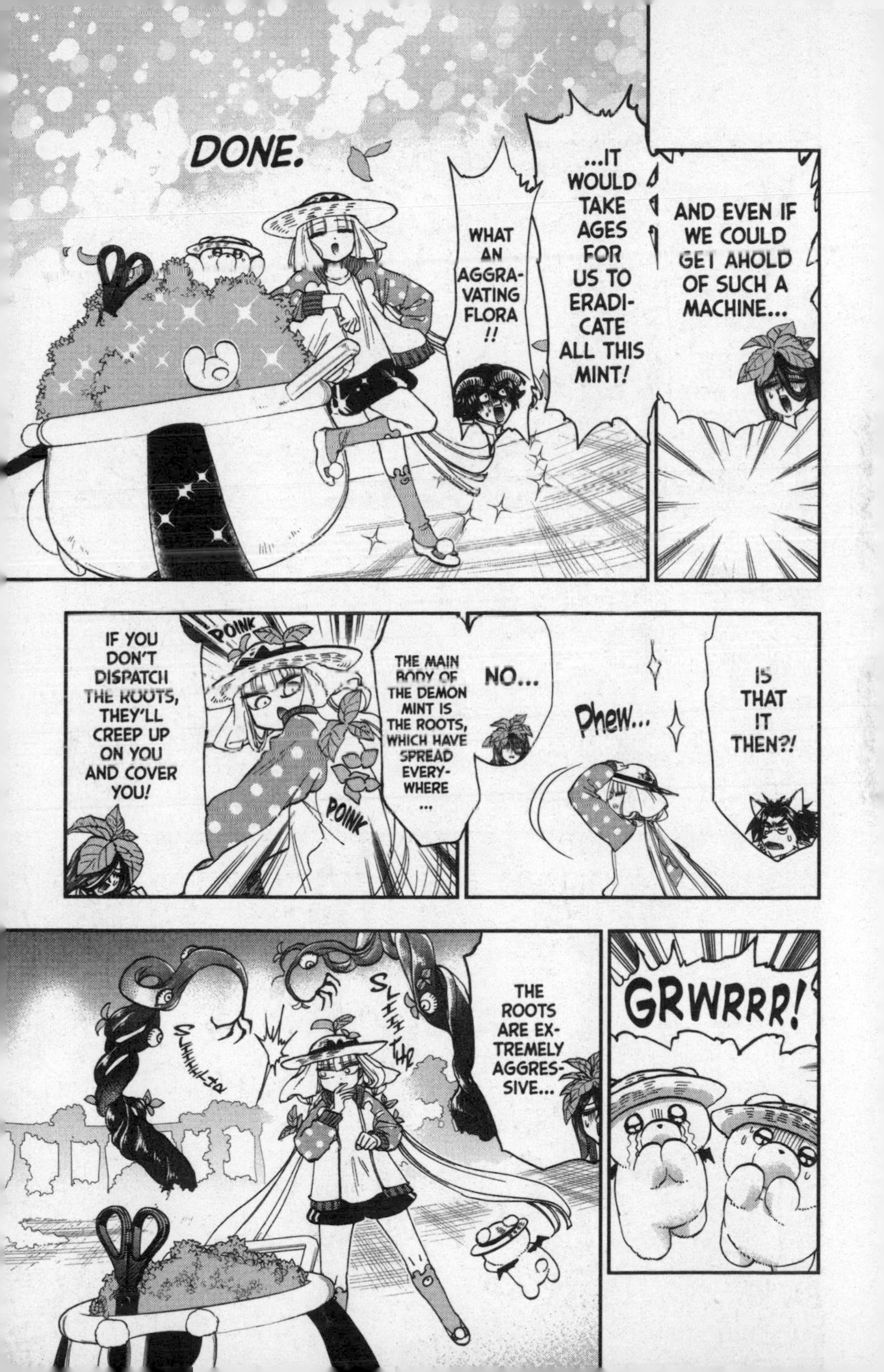
AND EVEN IF WE COULD GET AHOLD OF SUCH A MACHINE...
...IT WOULD TAKE AGES FOR US TO ERADICATE ALL THIS MINT!
WHAT AN AGGRAVATING FLORA!!
DONE.
IS THAT IT THEN?!
Phew...
NO...
THE MAIN BODY OF THE DEMON MINT IS THE ROOTS, WHICH HAVE SPREAD EVERYWHERE...
POINK
IF YOU DON'T DISPATCH THE ROOTS, THEY'LL CREEP UP ON YOU AND COVER YOU!
POINK
GRWRRR!
THE ROOTS ARE EXTREMELY AGGRESSIVE...

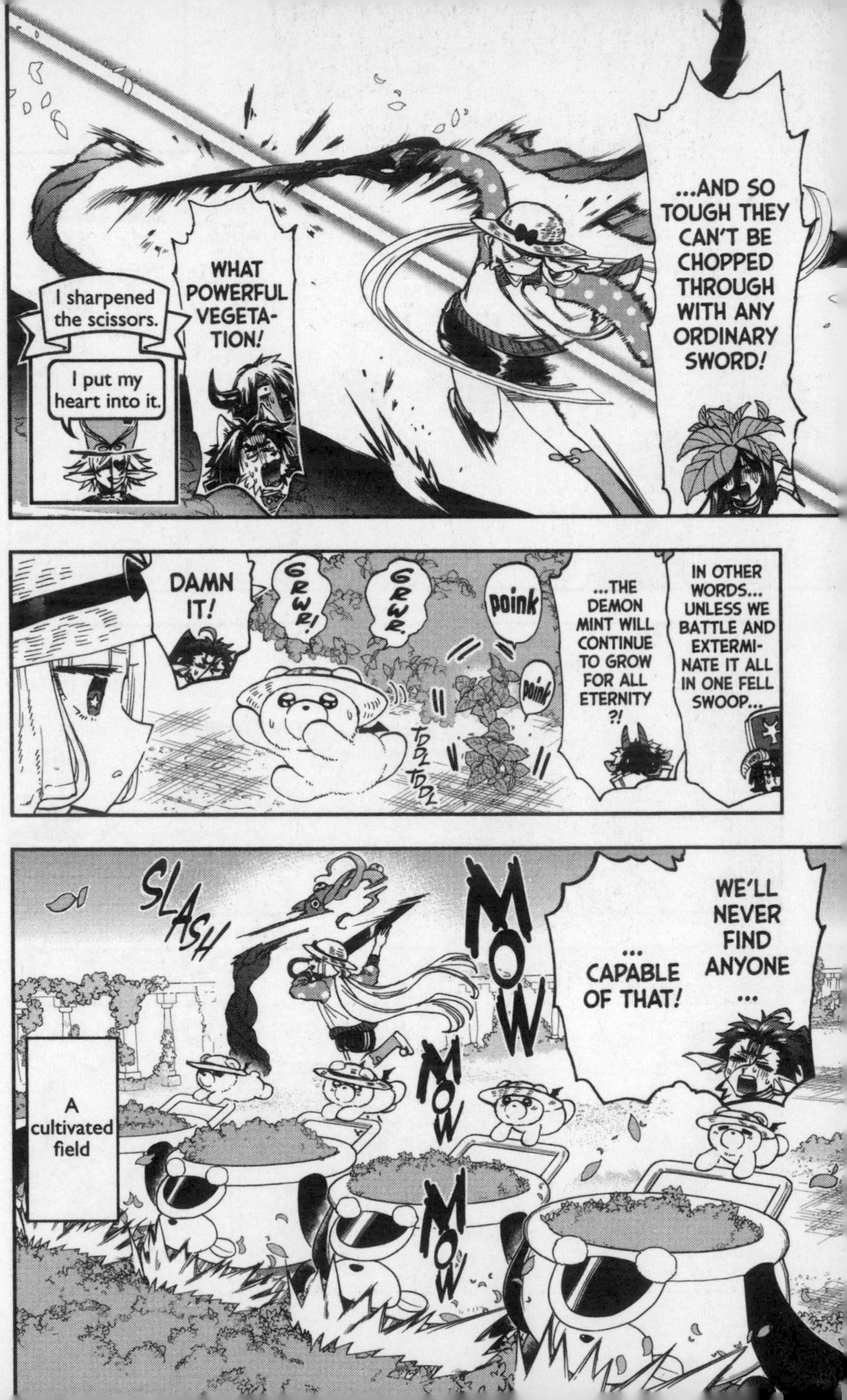
...AND SO TOUGH THEY CAN'T BE CHOPPED THROUGH WITH ANY ORDINARY SWORD!
WHAT POWERFUL VEGETATION!
I sharpened the scissors.
I put my heart into it.
IN OTHER WORDS... UNLESS WE BATTLE AND EXTERMINATE IT ALL IN ONE FELL SWOOP...
...THE DEMON MINT WILL CONTINUE TO GROW FOR ALL ETERNITY ?!
poink
poink
GRWR.
GRWR!
DAMN IT!
TDDL TDDL
WE'LL NEVER FIND ANYONE ...
... CAPABLE OF THAT!
MOW
MOW
MOW
SLASH
A cultivated field

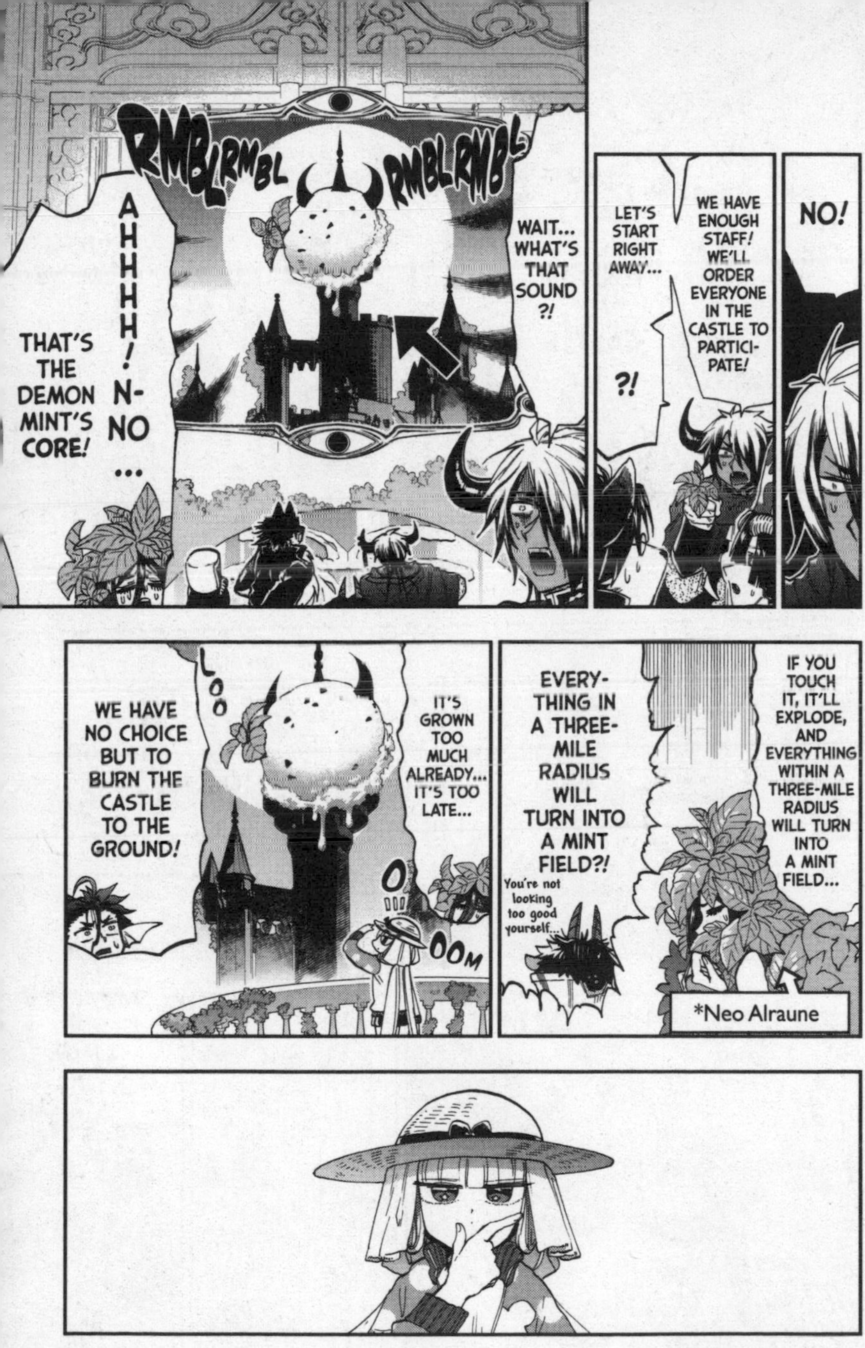
NO!
WE HAVE ENOUGH STAFF! WE'LL ORDER EVERYONE IN THE CASTLE TO PARTICIPATE!
LET'S START RIGHT AWAY...
?!
WAIT... WHAT'S THAT SOUND?!
RMBLRMBL
RMBLRMBL
AHHHH! N-NO...
THAT'S THE DEMON MINT'S CORE!
IF YOU TOUCH IT, IT'LL EXPLODE, AND EVERYTHING WITHIN A THREE-MILE RADIUS WILL TURN INTO A MINT FIELD...
EVERYTHING IN A THREE-MILE RADIUS WILL TURN INTO A MINT FIELD?!
You're not looking too good yourself...
*Neo Alraune
IT'S GROWN TOO MUCH ALREADY... IT'S TOO LATE...
LOO
OOM
WE HAVE NO CHOICE BUT TO BURN THE CASTLE TO THE GROUND!

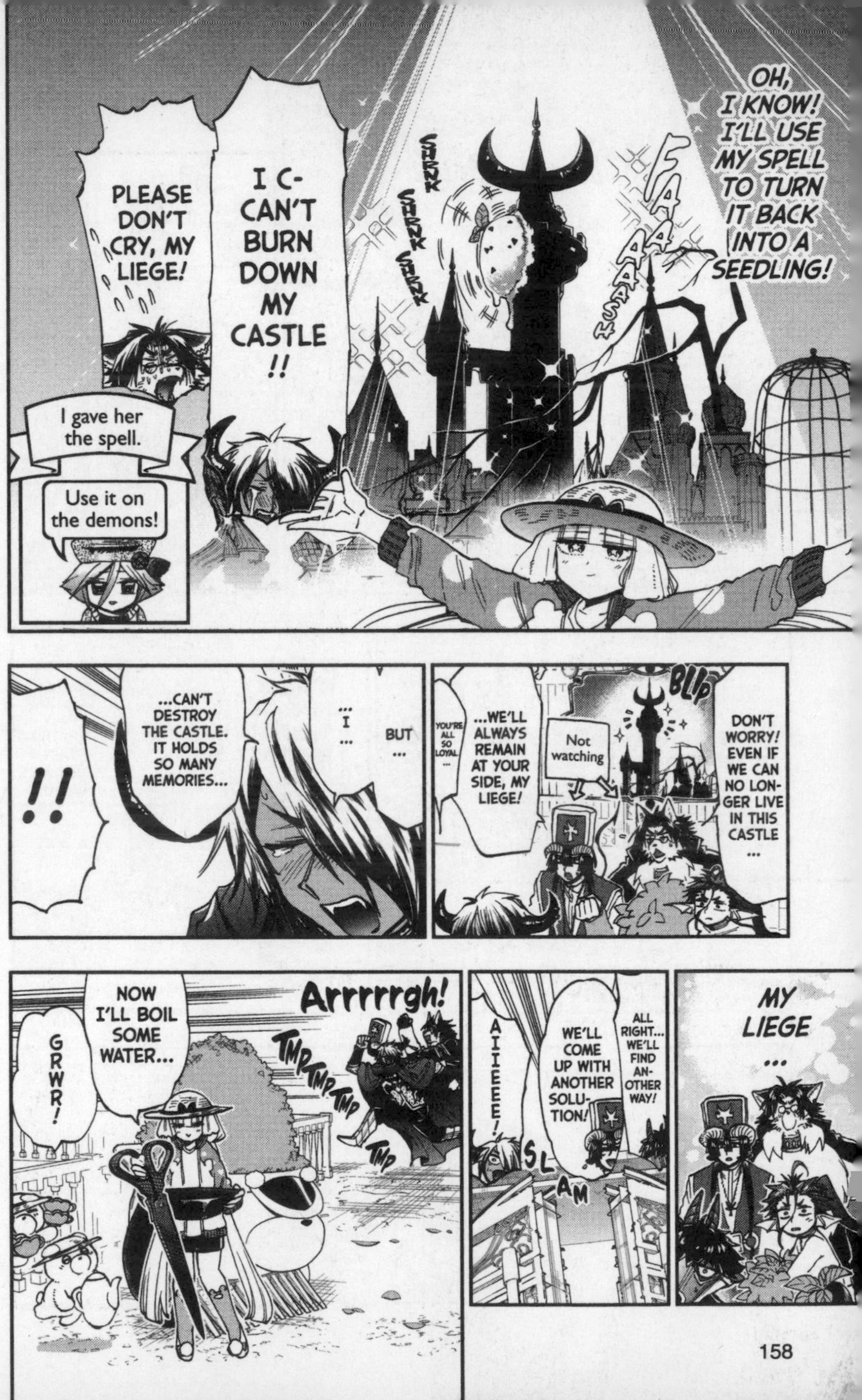
OH, I KNOW! I'LL USE MY SPELL TO TURN IT BACK INTO A SEEDLING!
FAAAASH
SHRNK SHRNK SHRNK
I C-CAN'T BURN DOWN MY CASTLE !!
PLEASE DON'T CRY, MY LIEGE!
I gave her the spell.
Use it on the demons!
BLIP
DON'T WORRY! EVEN IF WE CAN NO LONGER LIVE IN THIS CASTLE...
...WE'LL ALWAYS REMAIN AT YOUR SIDE, MY LIEGE!
YOU'RE ALL SO LOYAL...
Not watching
BUT...
...I...
...CAN'T DESTROY THE CASTLE. IT HOLDS SO MANY MEMORIES...
!!
MY LIEGE...
ALL RIGHT... WE'LL FIND ANOTHER WAY!
WE'LL COME UP WITH ANOTHER SOLUTION!
AIIEEEE!
SLAM
Arrrrrgh!
TMP TMP TMP TMP TMP
NOW I'LL BOIL SOME WATER...
GRWR!

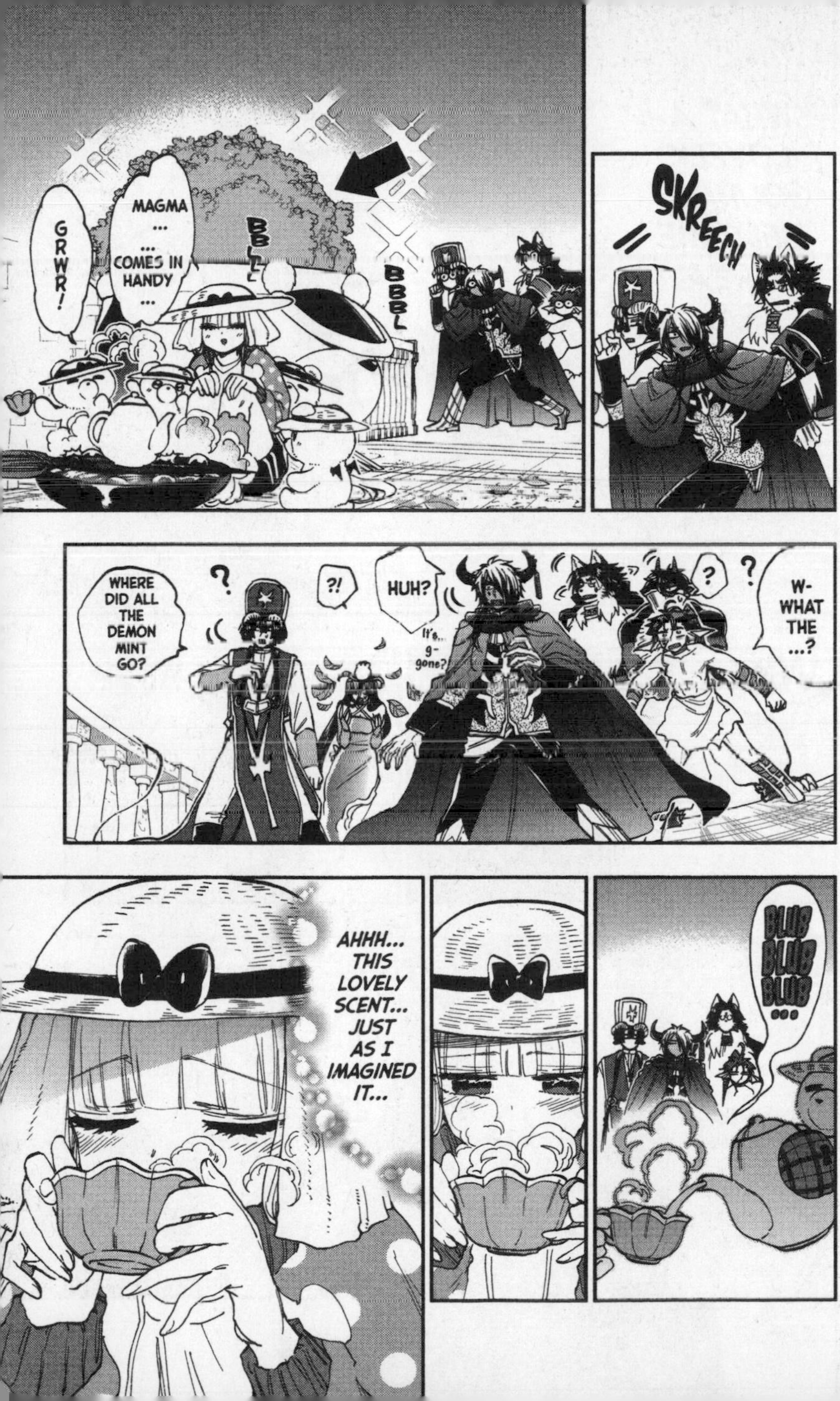
SKREECH
BBBL
BBL
MAGMA ... ... COMES IN HANDY ...
GRWR!
W-WHAT THE ...?
?
?
It's.. g-gone?
HUH?
?!
?
WHERE DID ALL THE DEMON MINT GO?
BLUB BLUB BLUB ...
AHHH... THIS LOVELY SCENT... JUST AS I IMAGINED IT...

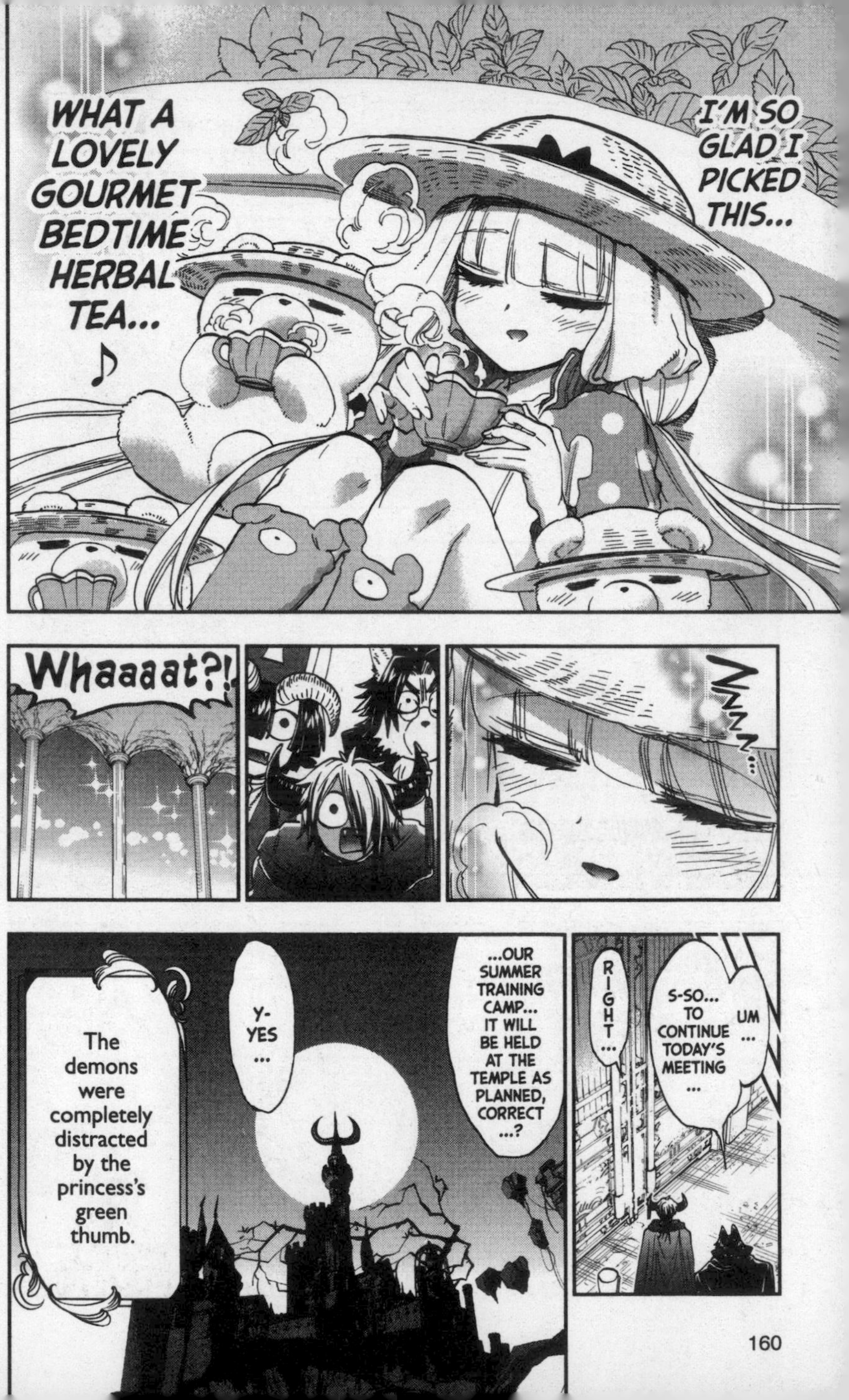

I'M SO GLAD I PICKED THIS...
WHAT A LOVELY GOURMET BEDTIME HERBAL TEA... ♪
ZZZZ...
Whaaaat?!
S-SO... TO CONTINUE TODAY'S MEETING...
UM...
RIGHT...
...OUR SUMMER TRAINING CAMP... IT WILL BE HELD AT THE TEMPLE AS PLANNED, CORRECT...?
Y-YES...
The demons were completely distracted by the princess's green thumb.

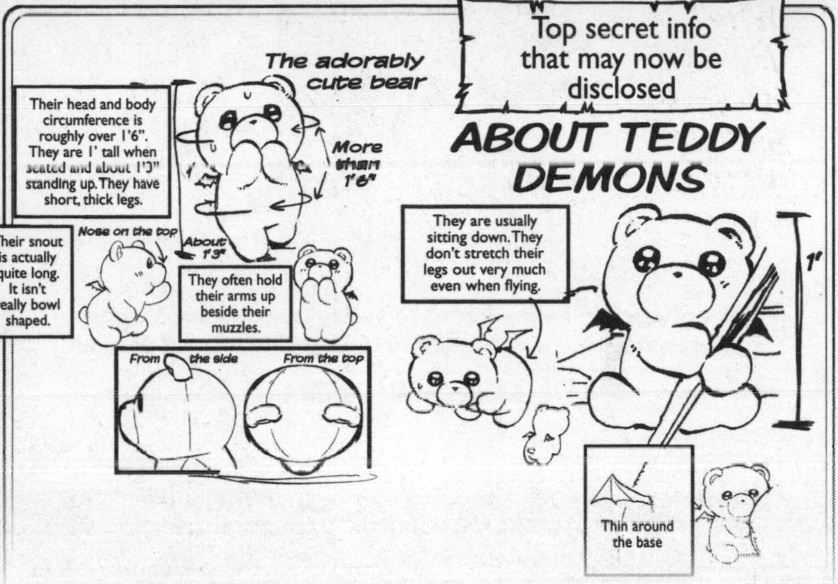
Top secret info that may now be disclosed
ABOUT TEDDY DEMONS
They are usually sitting down. They don't stretch their legs out very much even when flying.
1'
Thin around the base
The adorably cute bear
Their head and body circumference is roughly over 1'6". They are 1' tall when seated and about 1'3" standing up. They have short, thick legs.
More than 1'6"
About 1'3"
Nose on the top
Their snout is actually quite long. It isn't really bowl shaped.
They often hold their arms up beside their muzzles.
From the side
From the top

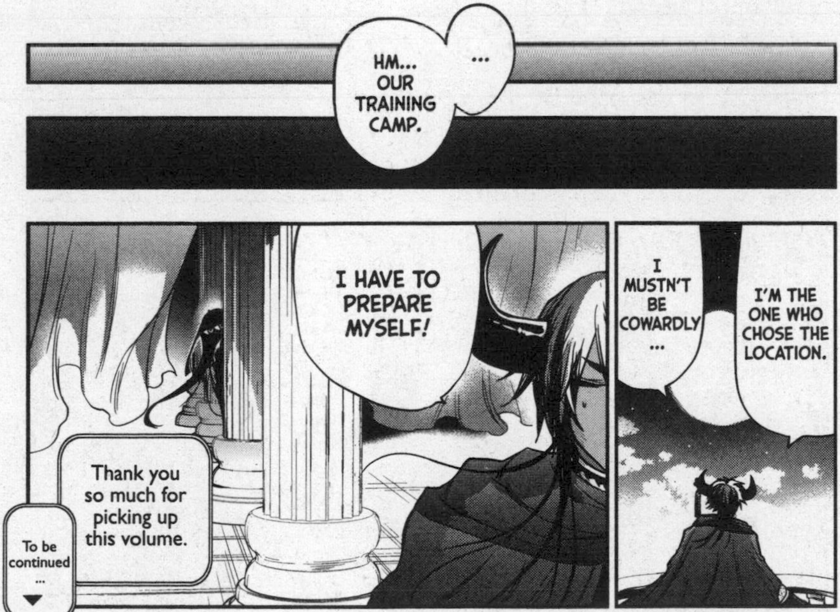
...
HM... OUR TRAINING CAMP.
I'M THE ONE WHO CHOSE THE LOCATION.
I MUSTN'T BE COWARDLY ...
I HAVE TO PREPARE MYSELF!
Thank you so much for picking up this volume.
To be continued ...

I'm ecstatically happy because Teddy Demon merchandise has been released and *Sleepy Princess* is getting an anime!*

– KAGIJI KUMANOMATA

*In Japan

Princessbot Mark III
MATERIALS
Orichalcum
Legendary Crystal Glass
Steamed Monster Bird
Egg Custard

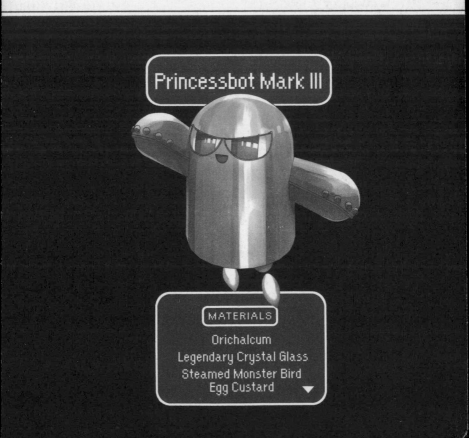

Those who lurk beneath the cover...

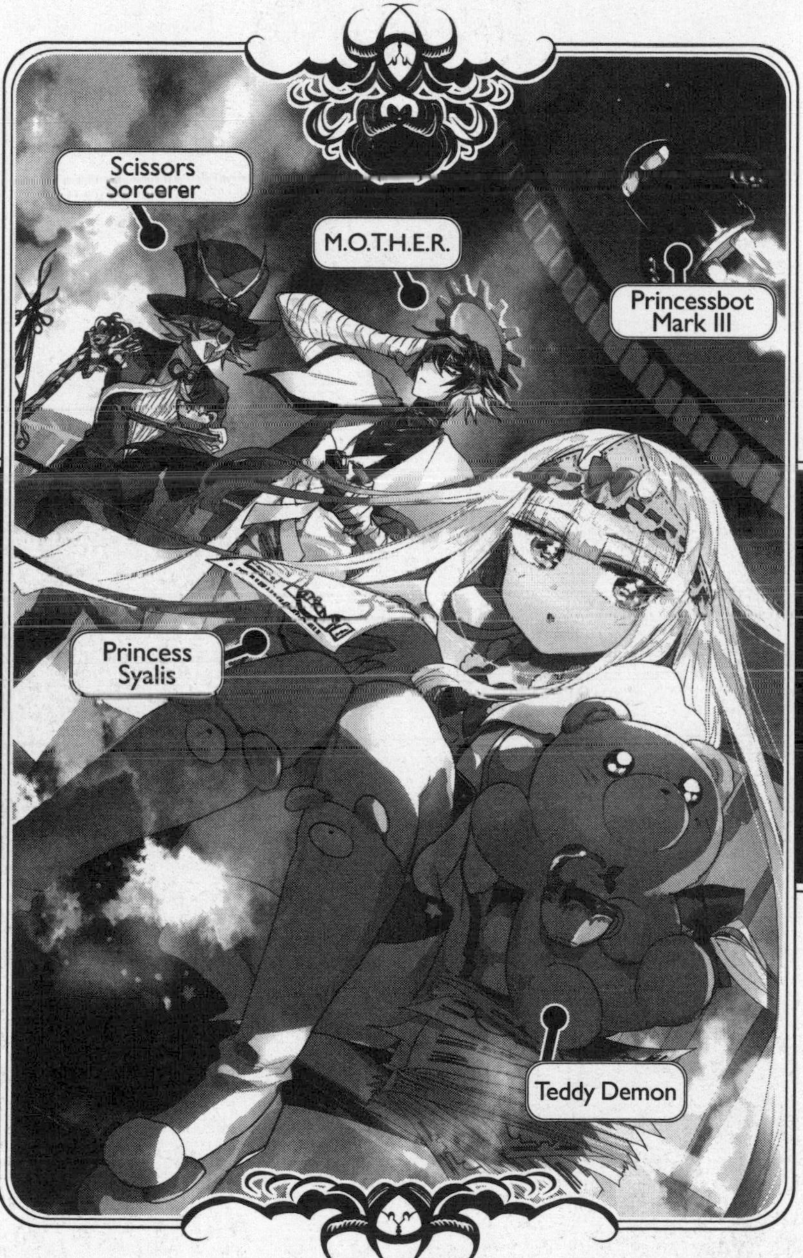
Scissors Sorcerer
M.O.T.H.E.R.
Princessbot Mark III
Princess Syalis
Teddy Demon

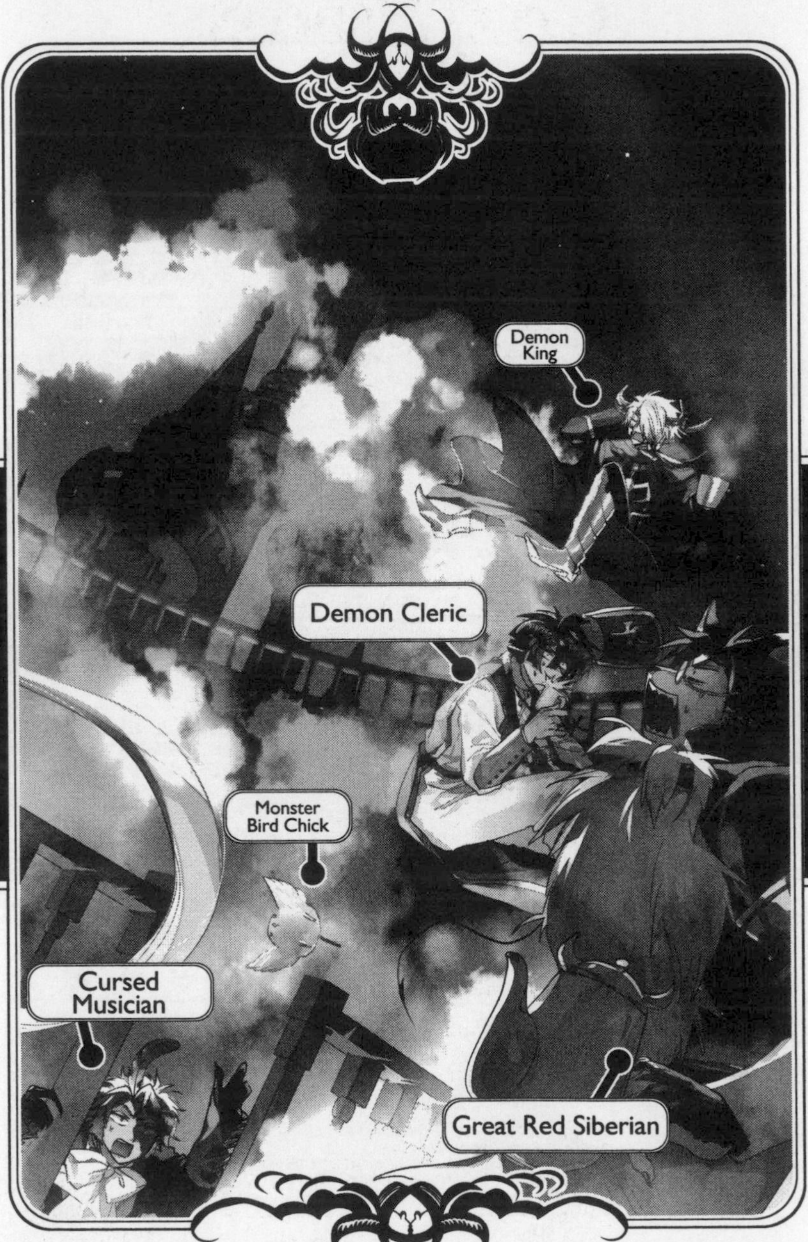
Demon King
Demon Cleric
Monster Bird Chick
Great Red Siberian
Cursed Musician

SLEEPY PRINCESS IN THE DEMON CASTLE

12

Shonen Sunday Edition

STORY AND ART BY

KAGIJI KUMANOMATA

MAOUJO DE OYASUMI Vol. 12
by Kagiji KUMANOMATA
© 2016 Kagiji KUMANOMATA
All rights reserved.
Original Japanese edition published by SHOGAKUKAN.
English translation rights in the United States of America, Canada,
the United Kingdom, Ireland, Australia and New Zealand arranged
with SHOGAKUKAN.

TRANSLATION **TETSUICHIRO MIYAKI**

ENGLISH ADAPTATION **ANNETTE ROMAN**

TOUCH-UP ART & LETTERING **JAMES GAUBATZ**

COVER & INTERIOR DESIGN **ALICE LEWIS**

EDITOR **ANNETTE ROMAN**

Printed in the U.S.A.

Published by VIZ Media, LLC
P.O. Box 77010
San Francisco, CA 94107

10 9 8 7 6 5 4 3 2 1
First printing, June 2020

VIZ MEDIA

viz.com

shonensunday.com

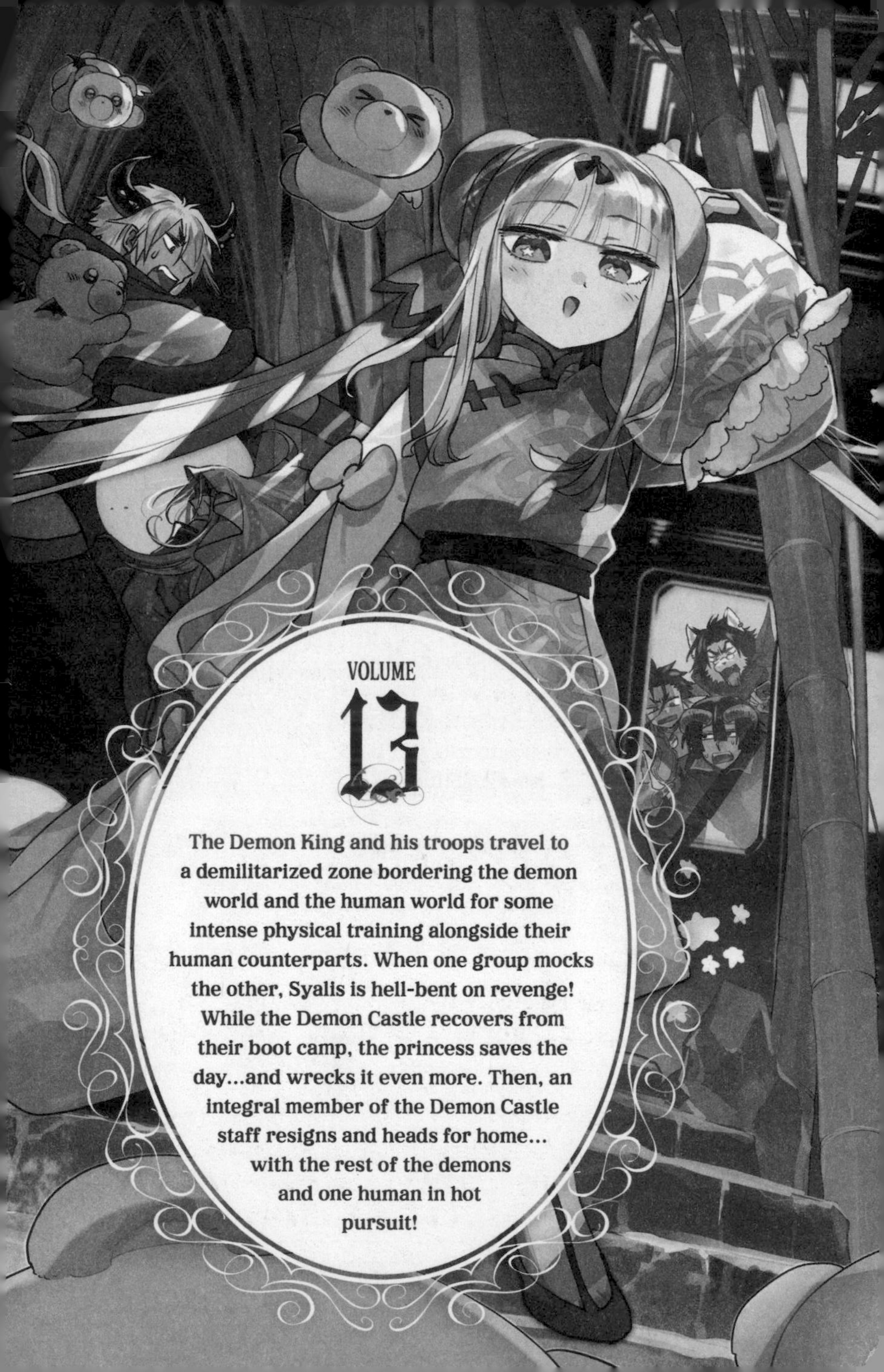
VOLUME
13
The Demon King and his troops travel to a demilitarized zone bordering the demon world and the human world for some intense physical training alongside their human counterparts. When one group mocks the other, Syalis is hell-bent on revenge! While the Demon Castle recovers from their boot camp, the princess saves the day...and wrecks it even more. Then, an integral member of the Demon Castle staff resigns and heads for home... with the rest of the demons and one human in hot pursuit!

Komi Can't Communicate

Story & Art by Tomohito Oda

The journey to a hundred friends begins with a single conversation.

Socially anxious high school student Shoko Komi's greatest dream is to make some friends, but everyone at school mistakes her crippling social anxiety for cool reserve. With the whole student body keeping its distance and Komi unable to utter a single word, friendship might be forever beyond her reach.

VIZ

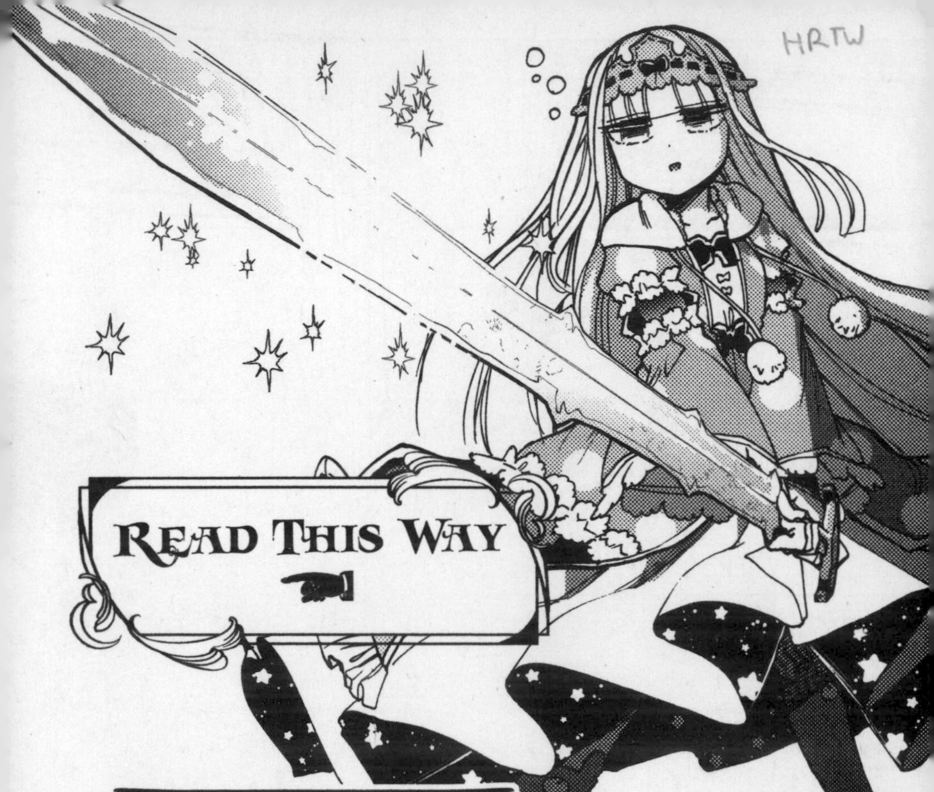
READ THIS WAY

STOP!

You may be reading the wrong way!

In keeping with the original Japanese comic format, this book reads from right to left—so action, sound effects and word balloons are completely reversed to preserve the orientation of the original artwork.

Check out the diagram shown here to get the hang of things, and then turn to the other side of the book to get started!

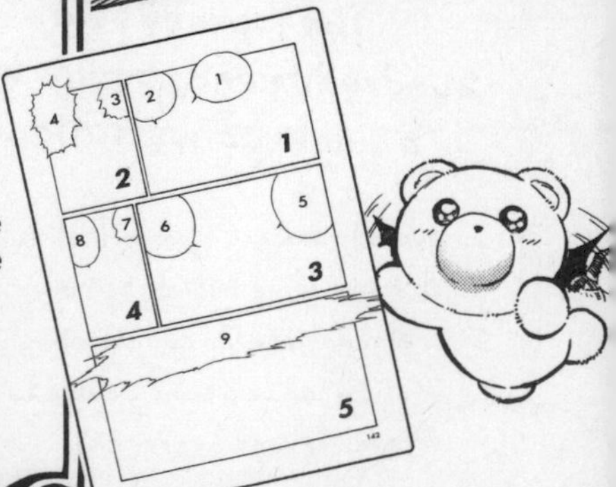
1
1
2
3
2
4
5
3
5
6
7
4
8
9
5